Readers' comments received by the author of

Bed and Breakfast in the Northeast

Best of genre. Thoroughly researched and accurate.
—Haven Guest House, Vineyard Haven, Massachusetts

You made our host homes come alive.
—Bed and Breakfast Associates Bay Colony

We have seen some of our guests spend two or three hours just reading about people and their places. —Helen and Donald Gould, Williamsburg, Massachusetts

We learned a lot about our hosts from your book.
—Berkshire Bed and Breakfast Connection

Gives all the answers to questions people ask when they call for reservations — even whether anyone in residence smokes.
—Jeanne Lewis, Fairfield-by-the-Sea, Westerly, Rhode Island

After we discovered your book, we tried our first B&B in New York. Our hosts and their wonderful hospitality were just as you described.
—P.J. Fetterman, Cambridge, Pennsylvania

. . . delightful, accurate, interesting, helpful . . . a pleasure to read and poke through.
—Jane Hence, Essex, Connecticut

A really needed B&B book! The way you did it tells people exactly what they like to know. And it's a good book to read for entertainment.
—Martha Dorais, New Hampshire

The little anecdotes you've selected to clarify and describe accommodations and hosts do much to show how comfortable and relaxing staying in a B&B home can be.
—Elaine Borowick, West Hyannisport, Massachusetts

Splendid.
—Helen Ellison, Shore Inne, Groton Long Point, Connecticut

A winner.
—Kit Shane, Bloomington, Indiana

Because of BED AND BREAKFAST IN THE NORTHEAST we now hear from all parts of the country.
—Boston Bed and Breakfast

The book makes B&B contagious.
—Rae Eastman, West Cornwall, Connecticut

Books by Bernice Chesler

Editor and Coordinator
The ZOOM Catalog
Do a ZOOMdo
People You'd Like to Know

Co-author
The Family Guide to Cape Cod

Author
In and Out of Boston with (or without) Children
Mainstreaming through the Media
Bed and Breakfast in the Northeast

BED AND BREAKFAST IN THE NORTHEAST

FROM MAINE TO WASHINGTON, D.C., 300 SELECTED B&Bs

*Plus a guide to thousands more
throughout the United States and eastern Canada*

by Bernice Chesler

The Globe Pequot Press

Chester, Connecticut 06412

Library of Congress Catalogue Card Number: 83-48194

ISBN: 0-87106-917-2

Manufactured in the United States of America
Third Printing

Cover painting of The Phoenix in Narragansett, Rhode Island.
Cover painting by David Schulz
Text illustrations by Ragna Tischler Goddard
Cover and book design by Barbara Marks

To David

CONTENTS

(continued)

INTRODUCTION

Some say it came from England, Ireland, and the continent. Some say it's a rejuvenated form of the tourist home with the addition of breakfast. Many say its time has come in the United States. Welcome bed and breakfast!

Enthusiasm can be contagious. Every day while writing this book I have had reason to agree with the host who said, "Aren't people wonderful? And after you read the morning paper, doesn't it make you feel good to be able to say that?" As a researcher for articles, books, and documentary films I have had the opportunity to meet many caring and sharing people throughout the country, but it is hard to recall another project that involves individuals who *all* love what they are doing.

B&B really is a people-to-people idea. Even though facilities and settings make a difference, what guests frequently remember is a particular conversation or situation. The color schemes of almost all the B&Bs we have stayed in — both here in the Northeast and abroad — escape me, but there is something about every host and ambiance that has made a lasting impression. During our stays we have learned about local customs, history, and architecture. Occasionally we have returned and followed family doings. Our immersion in a region has always been fleeting but genuine, thanks to the people we have met.

Now that the concept has finally caught on (been accepted) on this side of the ocean, we found the need for an informative source that would help with preplanning (particularly for the height of the season); with last-minute decisions (particularly for out-of-season); or with some place that just might even be in what seems to be the middle of nowhere. The result is *Bed and Breakfast in the Northeast*, the first B&B book to focus on this region and the first, I believe, to help the reader/traveler to "know thy host." ·

I began research on this book with the notion that all places described would be reasonably priced and would serve a full breakfast. And I had strong opinions about the number of guest rooms (just how many people can a host relate to at once?) and about host family involvement.

I mellowed to some extent but there are guidelines that have held.

In order for a host to be considered by *Bed and Breakfast in the Northeast*, breakfast must be served or available in the house. Having the morning repast at a coffee shop next door or a block away just isn't the same. Continental breakfast is the norm in many areas. Full breakfast — with or without exotic dishes — is routinely served in others. Although breakfast is often the time when good conversation provides the personal contact that B&B is basically set up for, city B&Bs — particularly on weekdays — may be an exception. There, hosts themselves are more likely to be in a hurry to leave in the morning.

Some B&Bs located in out-of-the-way places or near ski areas serve dinner. Although some inns pleaded a very good case of hospitality, those that regularly serve dinners to overnight guests or to the public, or that have a bar on the premises, are not herein considered bed-and-breakfast places. Every place described has a host in residence. I shied away from managed B&Bs with absentee owners. And unhosted facilities, cottages, or units with kitchenettes also seemed tangential to the focus of this book.

Because B&B is, in my interpretation, essentially in a home setting, details include information about smoking, pets, children, foreign languages, facilities available for parking, the kitchen or laundry, farm tours offered — and more. Indeed, B&Bs vary. In the European tradition of bed and breakfast, you are expected to leave after breakfast. Although that is the arrangement at many American homes, some hosts in this country have embellished the system; guests may be allowed to stay through the day or be invited to use the grounds.

There has been a steady stream of heartwarming letters from hosts and guests. Some have been typewritten, some done in calligraphy. Others were scribbled on notebook paper. "I forgot to tell you . . ." appeared on the backs of envelopes. Enclosed animal pictures of "important members of the B&B family" would make a terrific gallery exhibit. Excerpts from the correspondence, from interviews, and from conversations enjoyed during overnight stays are sprinkled throughout this book.

Now, as press time nears, I am hearing about still more hosts. When someone says that the whole world of real estate seems to be going condo, my reaction is that it is really all going B&B. In the compact and diversified Northeast it is possible to go from B&B to B&B by public transportation, by car, by canoe, by bicycle, or on foot along the Appalachian Trail. You can sleep in brass or canopied beds, in fourposters or in bunk beds. B&B hosts live in apartments and town houses, in beach houses and ranch houses, in homes listed on the National Register of Historic Places, in gracious Georgians and Victorians. There are solar homes, farmhouses, and restored colonials. And some are magnificently maintained estates.

Why are these people hosting? Many of the descriptions will satisfy your curiosity. Few in private homes host to make a living. Some do it to rationalize keeping the old place. Some do it to be able to buy the old place. Other hosts use the income to defray expenses. A few contribute the money to their favorite charity. It's amazing to think of the number of people who dream about being innkeepers; for many, B&B hosting — either publicly or through a reservation service — seems to be a happy compromise or at least a good test. Whatever the reason, B&B will never be a get-rich-quick project, even though it may look that way upcountry during foliage season.

All hosts say they like people. Experienced hosts usually add that that's not enough. Dozens have reiterated that it helps to have high energy and that you have to be on all the time. They also suggest that you have to be "the type," just as most guests are. Full-time innkeepers will tell you that it is not all glamor, but they are a pretty happy lot — despite the occasional guests who make hosts feel like self-trained psychologists. One Massachusetts host couple felt very important (and they were) when they were the home base for relatives of a hospitalized patient. And in Maine there's the woman who, after her first year of hosting, asked how she could possibly charge her wonderful new friends when they returned next year.

On the following pages you will hear from guests who felt hesitant or even daring or brave to try B&B, only to report that they now are hooked. "Do you believe that she even greeted me with a glass of wine (or cup of lemonade)?" was written many times. Dozens of "treated like family" comments arrived. Two people wrote of being introduced to marriage partners by hosts.

At times I have had to resist the temptation to add more guidebook information for a particular area. For the most part, the hints offered are those attractions and activities that the hosts find appealing to B&B guests.

Information is as up-to-date as possible. Successful hosts have been known to add a room; change the bed size; change the menu, the decor, and yes, the rates too.

The contribution of European B&B hosts should be acknowledged. They have provided inspiration for many American travelers who now are delighted to be hosts or to be able to enjoy the more personalized style of travel right here.

Four people offered strong support during the preparation of *Bed and Breakfast in the Northeast.* First on board, just when zillions of pieces of paper were coming and going, was Jo Madden. She kept them coming and going, — systematically and — in true B&B style — with a human touch. Lillian Stern typed the detailed manuscript with great accuracy and speed — and in good humor. Editor Jay Howland instantly caught the spirit of B&B and a feeling for the minutiae. She had a good ear as well as eye — and was a joy to work with. Throughout, David, my husband, listened to the extraordinary-letter-of-the-day, chauffeured and cycled copy to the typist, offered judgment when I solicited objectivity, and carried out just about all of my usual household tasks.

Thanks go too to the hundreds of guests who have submitted testimonials about the warmth and hospitality that they have experienced. The exuberant letters underscore the friendships that have been formed through B&B.

Bernice Chesler

All further suggestions about people and places are welcome and will be considered for the next edition. There is no association to join. No one can pay or is paid to be in the book. All selections are made by the author. Please address correspondence to Bernice Chesler, The Globe Pequot Press, Box Q, Old Chester Road, Chester, CT 06412.

ANSWERS
TO FREQUENTLY ASKED QUESTIONS

What is bed and breakfast?

It is a package arrangement that includes overnight accommodations and breakfast. The B&Bs described in this book are hosted by individuals, couples, maybe three friends in business together, or families — in private homes or in small inns. Every place is different and reflects the host(s).

Breakfast is usually the only meal served to guests. It may be continental (juice or bakery and beverage) or full.

The bath could be a private or shared arrangement. Of course if you are the only guest, a designated shared guest bath becomes private.

How much do they cost?

Rates start at $10 per person a night. Many are $30–$40 for two people. Rural regions tend to be less expensive. Some B&Bs in high-demand areas are in the $65–$75 range. A few are a little more. Private baths may cost more than shared. Location and season can affect the rate. Hosts who have lived in the B&B for years sometimes charge less than newcomers, sometimes because they haven't had to buy at today's real estate prices and/or because they believe that the traveler should be able to find reasonably priced accommodations. Because of all these variables the rate may or may not be indicative of facilities, amenities, or the size or elaborateness of breakfast. A B&B is almost always much less expensive than a hotel in the same area; and for just economic comparison, breakfast should be taken into account.

Other money thoughts: Unless credit cards are in the B&B description, please do not expect hosts to accept them. Ask if personal checks are acceptable. Most small places prefer cash or travelers' checks. And it's a good idea to check on deposit requirements; return policies differ.

Required local or state taxes vary from place to place and are not included in the listed rates.

Is B&B like a hotel?

Not at all! It's not intended to be. Perhaps one Connecticut host put it best: "We seem to live in an era when the human touch is becoming a lost pleasure. We will never threaten Hilton, Marriott, or Holiday Inns. How many times have you written a thank-you note to them?"

Depending on the size and layout of the B&B, it may not provide the privacy (or the loneliness) of a hotel. Television is not an important feature. Neither is a phone in the room. There's no elevator service and rarely is there an ice machine down the hall.

B&Bs range from simple to elegant. As at home, nothing is standardized. Every room is different. Many are freshly and imaginatively decorated. You have reason to expect comfortable accommodations. Most are not just clean — they are immaculate.

Who are the hosts?

Some young families (fewer, seemingly, than in Europe). Young couples. Many parents of grown children. Grandparents (28 grandchildren is the top number in this book). Graduate students. Retirees. Singles. Natives and transplants. People who know how to help and when to leave you alone. People who are sensitive to the wishes of nonsmokers. Sharers all. They represent hundreds of occupations. A sociologist or an architect could probably make quite a study with the variety of people and their backgrounds and settings.

Where are they?

Not everywhere — yet. But B&B is a flourishing movement in metropolitan cities, in university towns, in tourist and resort regions, and in many rural areas. Some communities have organizations responsible for soliciting hosts so that visitors will be attracted to an area that currently has few accommodations. In other locations neighbors and/or town fathers express concern that one room (or maybe three or four) available to paying overnight guests will mean a change of character in the neighborhood. Currently bed and breakfast doesn't fit into any category on the books of most lawmakers; zoning can be an issue.

What is a reservation service?

In the B&B world, it is primarily an American phenomenon. For hosts, it's a private way of going public because the host remains anonymous until the service matches host and guest. No signs are on the house or building. Essentially, only the reservation service knows. The system also allows hosts in private homes to have an irregular hosting schedule.

More information about this blossoming cottage industry is at the beginning of the reservation service chapter in this book.

Who goes to B&Bs?

The endless list includes travelers who are alone or in small groups; travelers who are with or without children, with or without pets; travelers on business or in the area for professional reasons. Vacationers. College shoppers. Parents of college students. Parents of summer campers. International visitors. Conventiongoers. Honeymooners. Relatives of hospitalized patients. Transferees. House hunters. Most are people who are looking for a touch of home. Some want to be pampered. Wherever, there's something for everyone — with the guest book replacing the registration desk.

B&B HOSTS SAY. . .

It's like having your friends come to visit. And you get paid too!

*

It's the best thing I have ever done for myself. You meet people whom you would never meet. Fascinating! Let me tell you about them. . . .

*

People from England, Scotland — all of Europe — just seem to fit right in to the B&B routine. Many American guests are surprised by the way we open our home to them.

*

Those big city folks arrive with a burst of energy and then come down to breakfast completely unwound. What fun to see that repeated all through the season.

*

I am appalled at the number of people who get up and clear the table just as they would do in their own home. I love it!

*

I meet many interesting personalities. Some talk of families, jobs, location, ambition — each person is like a chapter of a book.

*

The enthusiasm guests bring with them is very contagious and we vicariously enjoy their vacation experiences.

*

I delight in giving guests a sightseeing trip around our town.

One couple took a liking to our grandfather clock. It turned out that the husband, disturbed that it didn't work, had fixed his own at one time. With little encouragement, he and my husband had it apart, leveled, cleaned, and working.

*

If a shy or aloof person arrives, it is a challenge to us to get that person to open up — much like their arriving as a bud and nurturing them so that they leave as a flower.

*

At times when I've taken on a complicated breakfast menu, the stoves need tending, the table has to be set, and I have to pick up the milk at the farm nearby, I feel as if I'll collapse. And then a guest will suddenly appear and offer to flip the pancakes or grind the coffee, and somehow it all falls into place!

*

My kids love the assortment of cereals we now have in the house.

*

I have no structured time with guests. In fact I find if I join them in a social fashion, I become the center of attention and dominate their conversation by answering their questions. I answer the same questions so often that there have been times I have gotten half way through "my story" and been gripped by the fear that I have told this same story to these people before — hence my eagerness to be included in Bed and Breakfast in the Northeast. (Oh Lord, let this be the last time I have to tell it!)

*

We work ALL the time! And we do everything ourselves. It's just the change we were looking for when we decided we didn't need all that money and the lifestyle that went with it.

*

Since we are casual and relaxed, our guests tend to be so. We are easily accessible but do not suffocate our guests by hovering.

One of the fascinating aspects of running a B&B involves the reaction of friends and neighbors when they first heard we were doing it. I now tell them, "When you have lost a husband or a wife (this is the second marriage for both of us), you realize things don't matter a lot and in most cases, they can be replaced. People do matter and they cannot be." We have met only wonderful people. We have heard from almost everyone who has been here. . . . Another acquaintance had a very surprising reaction. "I never could be comfortable having strangers in my house." My response to her, "You know, when I first met (my new husband) he was a total stranger to me."

*

A perfect career for someone with grown children. A challenging and social and creative endeavor. The world comes to your doorstep. Guests take YOU away with them by sharing, by advertising, by inviting you to THEIR homes.

*

To do this kind of job you really have to like what you are doing. It's very demanding but also very rewarding. When people stay around for a few days and you start to really get to know them, it's like losing part of your family when they have to go back. When they write or call to say they are coming again, you are already friends and you start off at a completely different point the second time.

*

It is amazing how close one can become with some total strangers in such a short time. I find many of them want to tell me a lot about their families and their situations. By the time they leave we all look forward to their return.

*

We have many repeat guests who become for us very much like an extended family. B&B is a great way to enrich the human connection in one's life.

*

We started doing B&B because we needed the money, but I don't think we'll stop when times get better.

RESERVATION SERVICES AND INFORMATION SOURCES

throughout the United States and eastern Canada

Reservation Services
what they are and how to use them

A reservation service is a business that is organized to match host and guest. It is part of a growing cottage industry that, depending on location, can be seasonal. In a few places it is a full-time job for an individual, a couple, partners, or a small group.

Write for printed information or maybe, better yet, call. The printed information is usually a brochure together with application form that asks about your needs, preferences, purpose of trip, and perhaps special interests. It may also ask about your driver's license and/or place of employment.

A few services publish a directory of homes without addresses and phone numbers but with descriptions. The directory, usually sold (prices are included in the following pages of this book), tells a little about all the homes that the service offers; but you can use a service and its judgment without obtaining the directory.

A call can save a tremendous amount of time even if you reach an answering service or machine. (Return long-distance calls are usually made collect.) When you speak to the service, you can get a sense of the kind of personalized service offered while conveying your thoughts about price range, location, amenities, ambiance, and just how much hospitality you would like. Before placing the call think about bed and bath arrangements, parking, smoking, pets, children, air conditioning — whatever is important to you. And if you tell the service a little about yourself, it could help toward making a more appropriate match.

All commissions are included in the listed rates.

Deposits are usually required. Refund policies differ; inquire.

Although advance notice may be requested by the service, if you can provide enough information and references, and if a host is available that very night or "tomorrow," some services will flex and accommodate you on the spot.

Guests receive name and address of host only after being booked. Only a handful of services distribute printed lists of hosts' names, addresses, and telephone numbers to allow you to book your own B&B.

Generally, reservation service hosts are screened and homes are inspected. Most services are concerned with quality and high standards. Prospective guests' questions about screening procedures should be welcomed. And if a service requests an evaluation from you as guest, give it! (Even if they don't ask you, think about giving one.) Guests' comments can be helpful to everyone. The (predominantly) complimentary ones are often treasured by hosts.

Although most services are set up to list hosts who do not accept guests except through one or more reservation services, there are variations and embellishments. Some services list "public" bed-and-breakfast homes and small inns. And some have houses, apartments, or condominiums that are unhosted so that you have the entire place to yourself. Beyond that, some agencies have expanded to offer all kinds of services — travel packages, car rentals, theater tickets, and B&B-to-B&B tours.

A reservation service acts as a clearinghouse and frequently provides an opportunity to stay at a B&B that would not be available any other way.

THE NATIONAL SCENE

The American Bed & Breakfast Association

Box 23486, Washington, D.C. 20024
Phone: 703/237-9777

For $5 you may purchase *Hostlist,* published in March and September. It is a computerized list of 1300 cities (by state) in the United States and Canada where there are B&Bs. Most are homes; a few are inns. The independent hosts who take direct bookings from guests are listed. Information on private homes affiliated with reservation services includes the city, coded price range, and the name of the service to contact.

The Association has a series of other publications of interest to hosts, guests, and reservation services.

Its network of reservation-service members (anyone may join) is organized nationally, regionally, and in some cases by state.

Bed & Breakfast: The National Network

P.O. Box 4616, Springfield, MA 01101

Presently there are about 20 reservation-service members who have organized to promote cooperation and quality among affiliated agencies. Their free brochure includes a list of those members as well as a guest comment form intended as a public monitoring system, a means of providing direct feedback to this central organization.

The criteria for membership in this group include listing a minimum of 15 B&Bs, being in business for at least a year, and personal and periodic inspections of guest homes. Its logical goals are fulfilled by many (not all!) reservation services. In setting standards the organization has real value. Its exclusivity-of-geographical-area requirement excludes some services that otherwise meet the criteria for membership.

The Bed & Breakfast League Ltd.

3639 Van Ness Street N.W., Washington, DC 20008
Phone: 202/363-7767 Millie Groobey
Open: Year round, Monday–Friday, 9–5.
Listings: A total of 300 hosts located in Washington, D.C., 40 states, the Virgin Islands, Canada, England, France, and Scotland. Homes, apartments, condominiums, and small inns are included. Annual guest membership in the League is required for all but Washington, D.C. bookings (see page 482). Members receive a directory with specific host descriptions and a toll-free number for making reservations. Guest membership fee: $25 for a year starting with enrollment date.
Rates: Singles $28–$42, doubles $30–$50. MasterCard and VISA accepted.

Bed & Breakfast Registry

P.O. Box 80174, St. Paul, MN 55108-0174
Phone: 612/646-4238 Mary Winget, W. Gary Winget, L. Steven Sternberg
Listings: Since starting in February 1982 they have visited and approved for their list B&Bs in 39 states. There are a few in each of the northeastern states, New Jersey excepted. Included are private homes, apartments, condominiums, vacation homes, and small inns. Directory for a specific area is $3.
Rates: Differ according to season and location. Singles $12–$60, doubles $16–$90. No minimum stay requirement, but there is sometimes a small surcharge for a one-night reservation. MasterCard and VISA accepted.

Christian Bed & Breakfast of America

Please see page 40.

Home Suite Homes

Please see page 36.

New Age Travel's "International Spareroom"

Please see page 36.

Special Interest Services

If you would like to meet people who are interested in "building **world peace, goodwill, and understanding,**" you could join SER-VAS — a nonprofit, nongovernmental, interracial, and interfaith organization that has over 4,000 volunteer hosts in 90 countries. (Our family has participated for years and has found it a most rewarding experience.) For host or traveler details, send a self-addressed stamped envelope to U.S. Servas Committee, 11 John Street, Room 406, New York, NY 10038.

As the B&B concept catches on, certain groups are finding that hosting can both be a method of raising funds and offer a degree of assurance that there will be some common interest between host and guest. A few examples:

College and university **alumni organizations** are beginning to establish networks across the country. Check with the alumni office of your institution.

The League of Women Voters chapters in 10 major metropolitan areas have a roster of members who will host other League members. League state offices are the best sources of current information.

Two different directories for **educators** have just released second editions. Educators' Vacation Alternatives, 317 Piedmont Road, Santa Barbara, CA 93105 publishes a directory ($5.50 plus $1 postage) with 21 hosts in California, 17 in other states, 1 in New Zealand, and 2 in Canada. Most are in the $30–$40 range for two. In addition, home exchanges are possible in several states and countries. When ordering, list current or past educational position. . . . Educator's Inn, P.O. Box 603, Lynnfield, MA 01940 lists about 150 hosts in 30 states across the country with California and Massachusetts predominating. Most are in private homes, but inns owned by retired educators or by spouses of educators are described too. Guests make direct bookings. The directory sells for $9.95 and is sold only to — and intended for use only by —

teachers and support personnel, both active and retired. To receive a directory, you must submit an application and proof of employment in the field of education. The average overnight stay is $15 for singles, $20–$30 for doubles.

Another directory is intended for "Unitarian-Universalists, Quakers, Humanists, and Ethical Culturists who are interested in conversations and friendships with others who have **liberal religious leaning.**" About 300 B&B hosts all over the United States and Canada are in *Homecomings* ($8.95). In order to be a guest at any of the B&Bs it is necessary to register your name and affiliation with Homecomings, Inc., P.O. Box 1545, New Milford, CT 06776.

SERVICES LISTED BY HOME STATE

Reservation services are listed alphabetically within each state according to the community in which they are based .

Alabama

Bed & Breakfast Birmingham, Inc.

P.O. Box 31328, Birmingham, AL 35222
Phone: 205/591-6406 Ruth Taylor
Listings: About 30 selected private homes. A few apartments; some are former servants' quarters. All in Birmingham, with contacts in Montgomery.
Rates: $24–$32 for one, $28–$40 for two people. Some students' specials $20–$28. Some exceptional lodgings by special arrangement $50–$90.

Bed & Breakfast Mobile

P.O. Box 66261, Mobile, AL 36606
Phone: 205/473-2939 Anne Wright and Lynn Roberts
Listings: For now, 10. Include an 1847 farmhouse with beautiful grounds on Mobile Bay and homes in a historic district.
Rates: Singles $24–$32, doubles $28–$40. Some exceptional homes $50–$80. Weekly rates are available.

Brunton's Bed & Breakfast

P.O. Box 1066, Scottsboro, AL 35768
Phone: 205/259-1298 Norm and Jerry Brunton
Open: Weekdays (closed weekends).
Listings: Over 200. Include private homes, many off the beaten path but within just a few miles of major arteries; apartments; and condos. Some boats and some dormitories may also be available. Directory $3, refundable with first reservation.
Rates: Singles $19, doubles $20. $5 for extra person in room. $5 fee for same-day service. VISA and MasterCard accepted.

Alaska

Anchorage Bed & Breakfast/Alaska Private Lodgings

P.O. Box 110135, Anchorage, AK 99511
Phone: 907/345-2222 Susie Hansen
Listings: About 20 including private homes and efficiency apartments in private homes. There are log houses, mountainside residences, some in downtown Anchorage, a guest house on an island, a deluxe B&B at Alyeska ski resort, a home with a private airstrip, and homes in the heart of Salmon areas. A few have a two-day minimum stay.
Rates: Singles $25–$75, doubles $33–$75. Winter rates differ.

Stay With A Friend — Alaskan Style

3605 Arctic Boulevard, #173, Anchorage, AK 99503
Phone: 907/274-6445 Irene Pettigrew
Open: June through September.
Listings: About 25 homes, apartments, and condominiums. (Most offer use of laundry facilities and some permit kitchen use.) Located in the Anchorage area near shopping malls, restaurants, churches, bike paths, and parks and near enough to downtown so that you can get to starting point of tours. Winter exchanges with homes in southern regions of the United States.
Note: This program is limited to people 50 years of age or older coming

to Anchorage as tourists or temporary visitors. Early reservation is very important. Also, plan on rental car or alert contact if other transportation necessary. And plan to check in by 6 p.m.
Rates: Singles $25–$35, doubles $35–$45. Apartments for couples: $60 per night. Some weekly rates available.

Fairbanks Bed & Breakfast

Box 74573, Fairbanks, AK 99707
Phone: 907/452-4967 Kent Sturgis and Pat Yockey
Open: Mid-May through mid-September.
Listings: Around 40–50. Private homes include rustic log cabins and good downtown locations. Some private apartments with stocked refrigerators.
Rates: Singles $25, doubles $35. Apartments about $10 more per couple and extra for larger parties.

Alaska Bed & Breakfast Association

526 Seward Street, Juneau, AK 99801
Phone: 907/586-2959
Open: Year round.
Listings: Private homes, apartments, condominiums, cabins, and tents in southeast Alaska. Last-minute reservations may be possible. The service came under new ownership in the spring of 1983 after a year of operation.
Rates: Singles $15–$45, doubles $25–$60. Family and weekly rates available. MasterCard and VISA accepted.

Ketchikan Bed & Breakfast

501 Water Street (P.O. Box 7814) Ketchikan, AK 99901
Phone: 907/225-6044, 247-8444, 225-3498 Dale and Linda Pihlman
Listings: Private homes that have a variety of arrangements — from shared baths to a suite with sitting room, private bath, and Jacuzzi. Tour service also offered.
Rates: Singles $25–$40, doubles $30–$45.

Arizona

Bed and Breakfast in Arizona, Inc.

8433 N. Black Canyon, Suite 160, Phoenix, AZ 85021
Phone: 602/995-2831 Bessie Thompson Lipinski
Open: Monday through Saturday; closed Sundays and holidays.
Listings: Over 200 all over the state. In small towns and cities, in suburban and rural areas. Guest houses, ranches, lodges, cabins, houseboats, apartments, and estates available, in every kind of scenery and climate.
Rates: Not all price ranges are available in all areas. Singles $15–$50, doubles $25–$110, family rates $40–$80. Seventh night is free if in same home. Airport and bus pick-up can be arranged. Minimum stay of two days preferred. VISA and MasterCard accepted.

Mi Casa — Su Casa (Bed and Breakfast)

Box 950, Tempe, AZ 85281
Phone: 602/990-0682 Mrs. Ruth Young
Listings: About 90 located throughout the state. Private homes include some in metropolitan areas; some on the National Register; mountainside residences; ranches established in territorial days that have adobe guest quarters; some houses bordering national forests and others near the Grand Canyon. Apartments, condominiums, and a few students' specials also available. Most listings have pools, unheated in winter. Many have golf-course frontages. Directory $3.
Rates: Singles $20–$50 (one home is $110); doubles $25–$50. Minimum stay of two nights preferred. Weekly and monthly rates available.

Reservation services are listed alphabetically within each state according to the community in which they are based.

California

Educators who would like to stay with California educators can make their own direct bookings. See page 29.

California host lists that are published for **travelers who arrange their own bookings** are described on pages 41-42.

Accommodation Referral

San Francisco, CA
Phone: 415/346-5454; or in California toll-free: 800-833-1111 Jean Keenan. *This is not a booking service.* It is a telephone service (only) that not only can tell you where in California there is a B&B inn that suits your fancy, but also has up-to-date information on vacancies. The service is free (to guests). Guests make their own reservation directly with the B&B.
Listings: Throughout the state of California. Over 200. Mostly B&B inns. A few homes and some small unique hotels.
Rates: $40–$235 per night.

Eye Openers Bed and Breakfast Reservations

P.O. Box 694, Altadena, CA 91001
Phone: 213/684-4428 Ruth Judkins and Elizabeth Cox
Listings: About a dozen when service began in early 1983. Active and growing as a personalized service. Currently in Los Angeles/Pasadena area but expect to be expanding into adjacent areas of southern California.
Rates: Singles $30–$55, doubles $35–$60. $5 one-time membership fee. MasterCard and VISA accepted at a slight surcharge.

Digs West

8191 Crowley Circle, Buena Park, CA 90621
Phone: 714/739-1669 Jean Horn
Listings: About 45. In private homes, apartments, and condominiums in Orange County, Los Angeles County, and San Diego County.
Rates: Singles $25–$36, doubles $30–$48.

Homestay

P.O. Box 326, Cambria, CA 93428
Phone: 805/927-4613 Alex Laputz
Listings: At least 30 private homes, apartments, condominiums, and vacation homes (unhosted), with ocean views, in pine woods, or in village resort settings. Located on the central coast in Hearst Castle country and Santa Barbara.
Rates: Singles $20, doubles $30–$40. $5 for extra person. Groups can be accommodated. Three- and seven-day rates available. MasterCard and VISA accepted.

California Bed and Breakfast Inn Service

P.O. Box 1256, Chico, CA 95027
Phone: 916/343-9733 Lynn Morgan
Listings: At least 25 private homes, mostly in northern California. Variety includes a remodeled 130-year-old ranch house and homes in the pines near hiking trails.
Rates: Singles $20–$25, doubles $35–$55.

Bed & Breakfast of San Diego

P.O. Box 1006, Coronado, CA 92118
Phone: 602/952-9383 Bill and Louise Jacques
Listings: Private homes that vary from moderate to luxury to resort settings. A few are considered students' specials.
Rates: $35 and up. Minimum reservation: two nights.

Hospitality Plus

Box 336, Dana Point, CA 92629
Phone: 714/496-7050 Deborah Sakach
Listings: Over 100 homes all over California, including many coastal locations.
Rates: Singles $15–$35, doubles $20–$50, family $25–$40, deluxe $55–$80. Package B&B tours along the California coast including stays in San Diego, Laguna Beach, Ventura, Santa Barbara, Cambria, Monterey, and San Francisco.

Home Suite Homes* **

1470 Firebird, Sunnyvale, CA 94087
Phone: 408/733-7215 Rhonda Robins, Roberta Rosen
Listings: Around 250 in private homes, apartments, and some condominiums. Many exceptional homes throughout the United States including Hawaii and Alaska. Foreign sites are in India, Japan, Pakistan, England, France, Germany, Mexico, Netherlands, North Wales, and Spain.
Rates: $20 membership fee for one year plus nightly rate of $16–$30 for singles, $30–$60 for doubles. Screened members are eligible for hosting and traveling.

New Age Travel's "International Spareroom" Bed & Breakfast* **

P.O. Box 460, Helena, MT 59624
Phone: 406/449-7231 Corinne Elliott
Listings: About 300 including homes, apartments, condominiums, inns, and home exchanges. Some in Arizona, California, Colorado, Florida, Hawaii, Iowa, Louisiana, Montana, Maryland, Nevada, New Mexico, Ohio, Oregon, North Carolina, Texas, Virginia, Washington, Wisconsin, and Wyoming. And there are a few in northeastern states: New Hampshire, Vermont, New York, and Pennsylvania. Beyond that there are some in Canada, Great Britain, Scotland, Wales, France, Portugal, Mexico, Australia, New Zealand, Virgin Islands, and Bermuda.

*Some B&B's in states outside of California
**Some listings in foreign countries

Directory: $4. Name of host sent after 50 percent of rate has been sent for reservation.

Rates: Vary according to location and accommodation. Singles $19.50–$39, doubles $28–$60. Minimum reservation: two nights.

Rent A Room International — Bed and Breakfast

11531 Varna Street, Garden Grove, CA 92640
Phone: 714/638-1406 Esther MacLachlan
Listings: About 25 private homes and guest houses, all in California, located from Santa Barbara to San Diego, with many clustered around Los Angeles, Disneyland, Newport Beach, Laguna Beach, and San Diego.
Rates: Singles $25–$30, doubles $30–$50. Special rates for children or third person. Minimum reservation: three nights.

Bed & Breakfast International (San Francisco) *

151 Ardmore Road, Kensington, CA 94707
Phone: 415/525-4569 or 527-8836 Jean M. Brown
Listings: Approximately 300 by an organization that is one of the oldest (1978) B&B reservation services in the United States. There are a few hosts in Hawaii and in some major cities in various parts of the country. Most B&Bs are in California (all areas) and they range from apartments in the city to spacious homes in residential neighborhoods. Included are a houseboat, a penthouse, and a mountain site too.
Rates: Singles $20–$40, doubles $28–$60. A few are higher. Family rates available.

B n' B Megan's Friends **

1768 Royal Way, San Luis Obispo, CA 93401
Phone: 805/544-4406 Megan Backer
Listings: Private homes; a few apartments, condominiums, and private guest cottages. They may be on the seacoast, in wooded areas, or on hilltops. All have vistas or are "close to nature." Some exclusive listings with antique furnishings or the opportunity to sleep in an orchid solarium. California areas: Monterey, Pine Canyon, Cayuccos, Cambria, Los Osos, San Diego, San Luis Obispo, San Juan Islands, Rancho Palos Verdes, and Solvang.
Rates: $10 membership for one year. Nightly rates: singles $25 up, doubles $35 up.

Bed-By-The Bay

1155 Bosworth Street, San Francisco, CA 04131
Phone: 415/334-7262 or P.O. Box 902, Sausalito, CA 94966
Phone: 415/383-7430 Don Stanke and Patt Shea
Listings: In San Francisco area in private homes, some apartments, condominiums, and small B&B inns. This is a gay bed and breakfast agency that also welcomes nongay guests.
Rates: Singles $24–$45, doubles $36–$57. Monthly rates available.

*Some B&B's in states outside of California
**Some listings in foreign countries

California Bed 'n Breakfast

P.O. Box 8785, Newport Beach, CA 92660
Phone: 714/951-1530 Anthony James
Listings: Seven private homes, apartments, and condominiums in southern California.
Rates: Singles $35–$45, doubles $45–$55.

California Bed and Breakfast **

P.O. Box 1551, Sacramento, CA 95807 Barbara Stoltz
Listings: At least 130 in private homes, apartments, and condominiums and over 200 small family-owned inns — all with hosts in residence. Locations throughout California and some in New Zealand, Japan, Australia, and Puerto Vallarta, Mexico. All arrangements made by mail only.
Rates: $15 for one year's guest membership. Singles $20 and up, doubles $25–$80.

Bed & Breakfast Exchange

P.O. Box 88, St. Helena, CA 94574
Phone: 707/963-7756 Andee Beresini
Listings: Private homes, farmhouses, estates, guest cottages, and small inns in Napa and Sonoma Counties. Descriptive directory: $5.
Rates: $35–$165. Less December through February. Weekly and monthly rates available. Some have a two-night minimum on weekends.

Carolyn's Bed & Breakfast Homes in the San Diego Area

P.O. Box 84776, San Diego, CA 92118
Phone: 619/435-5009 and 481-7662 C. Waskiewicz
Listings: About 50 including private homes, suites, and cottages. Descriptive directory: $6.
Rates: Singles $20–$60, doubles $28–$70. Suite or cottage $55–$125. Required membership fee: $1.

American Family Inn/Bed & Breakfast San Francisco

2185 A Union Street, San Francisco, CA 94123
Phone: 415/931-3083
Listings: Approximately 100 private homes and several apartments. Included are some of the large mansions and yachts in the area. Located in San Francisco, Marin County, Carmel, Monterey, the wine country, and Lake Tahoe.
Rates: Singles $35–$50, doubles $35–$55. Yachts $80–$100 per night.

Christian Bed & Breakfast of America***

P.O. Box 388, San Juan Capistrano, CA 92693
Phone: 714/496-7050 Deborah Sakach
Listings: At least 250 homes nationwide, including many in the Northwest, Hawaii, and Alaska. Also included: India and Ecuador. Directory: $3, credited toward lodging.
Rates: Singles $15–$35, doubles $20–$50. Weekly and monthly rates available.

Wine Country Bed & Breakfast

P.O. Box 3211, Santa Rosa, CA 95403
Phone: 707/539-1183 Helga Poulsen
Listings: In 15 private homes. Varied selection from modest to luxurious, including a modern ranch, a restored Victorian, or maybe one near the vineyards with a pool and deck. All in northern California in the Sonoma-Napa-Mendocino wine country. Personalized service featured.
Rates: Singles $35–$45, doubles $45–$65.

California Houseguests, International***

6051 Lindley Avenue #6, Tarzana, CA 91356
Phone: 213/344-7878 Trudi Alexy
Listings: Around 1000, primarily in Greater Los Angeles area. Others are in Orange County, Monterey, Carmel, and the San Francisco and San Diego areas, and represent the wide range of settings possible in the state. Included are private homes, apartments, condominiums, mansions, chalets, and inns. Ms. Alexy networks with B&B organizations all over this country and with the United Kingdom, France, Canada, Australia, and New Zealand.
Rates: Singles $30–$70, doubles $35–$75. Membership fee $5 per person. Weekly and monthly rates available. Most hosts have a minimum stay requirement of two nights.

Bed and Breakfast of Los Angeles

32127 Harborview Lane or 32075 Waterside Lane, Westlake Village, CA 91361
Phone: 213/889-7325 and 889-8870 Peg Marshall and Angie Kobabe
Listings: About 85 including private homes, apartments, condominiums, and inns. Variety of accommodations throughout the Los Angeles area from Ventura to San Clemente.
Rates: Singles $24–$45, doubles $30–$75.

The following organizations and publications do not provide a matching service. They publish information on California B&Bs and the *traveler books directly with the listed hosts*.

Bed & Breakfast Almanac

Box 295, St. Helena, CA 94574
Phone: 707/963-0852 Janet Konhaus Strong
Listings: The 50 Napa Valley B&Bs include many small inns, briefly described in booklet that also has touring suggestions. $4.50 ppd.

*Some B&B's in states outside of California
**Some listings in foreign countries

Bed and Breakfast Inns of Sacramento

Sacramento Innkeepers Association,
2209 Capitol Avenue, Sacramento, CA 95816
Phone: 916/441-3214 Sue Garmston
Listings: Five inns in downtown Sacramento. Restored homes; some furnished with antiques. Write for free descriptive booklet.
Rates: $45–$75, single or double occupancy. Credit cards accepted.

Bed & Breakfast Homes Directory by Diane Knight

Knighttime Publications, P.O. Box 591, Cupertino, CA 95014
Listings: About 140, most in California. A few include Oregon locations. The directory and summer supplement cost $6.95 plus $2 for air mail and foreign orders.

Napa Valley Bed and Breakfast Reservations

P.O. Box 2147, Yountville, CA 94599
Phone: 707/257-1051 Jim and Carol Beazley and Carol Knight
Listings: About 25 Napa Valley B&Bs. The association lists all the rooms in its computer and links guests with their choice. Most places are of architectural and historical significance. A few are in the city of Napa and the rest in the countryside.
Rates: $50–$125. Some require a two-night stay if Saturday night is booked by the traveler.

Colorado

Bed & Breakfast — Rocky Mountains

P.O. Box 804, Colorado Springs, CO 80901
Phone: 303/630-3433 Kate Peterson
Listings: Over 75 hosts in around 25 cities in Colorado and New Mexico. Modest homes to elegant mansions in the European tradition. Located in scenic mountain towns and ski areas; near hiking, fishing, river rafting, and gold panning; and in major cities. Directory: $1 with self-addressed, stamped envelope.
Rates: Budget $15–$25, comfort $25–$35, exclusive $40 + . Seasonal rates in some ski areas. Many hosts offer seventh night free.

Bed & Breakfast Colorado

P.O. Box 20596, Denver, CO 80220
Phone: 303/333-3340 Rick Madden
Listings: Throughout Colorado. At least 50. Mostly private homes, a few small inns. And a few that are considered students' specials. Range includes an historic mansion overlooking a ski village, an apartment in the heart of a city, or a small cottage. Directory: $2.
Rates: $20–$40. Inns $40–$60. A few are higher. Weekly rates available. Rates are seasonal at ski-area homes. VISA and MasterCard accepted.

Connecticut
(Please see page 330.)

District of Columbia
(Please see page 482.)

Florida

Sun and Fun Accommodations

3604 S.W. 23rd Street, Ft. Lauderdale, FL 33312
Phone: 305/583-5157 Joanne Hewitson
Listings: About 100 private homes. Some in tropical settings, some with river views.
Rates: Singles $25–$40, doubles $30–$50.

Bed and Breakfast of the Palm Beaches

P.O. Box 322, Jupiter, FL 33468
Phone: 305/746-2545 Eliza Hofmeister
Listings: Private homes, apartments, condominiums, and a few students' specials. Settings range from mobile homes to luxury accommodations with private sitting rooms and sun decks.
Rates: Singles $18–$40, doubles $25–$85. Monthly rates available. $5 surcharge for one-night stay.

Bed & Breakfast of the Florida Keys, Inc.

5 Man-O-War Drive, Marathon, FL 33050
Phone: 305/743-4118 year round; 201/223-5979 (New Jersey) mid-July–early September Joan E. Hopp
Open: Mid-September until mid-July; during other months reservations are taken by call-forwarded telephone.
Listings: Approximately 100 in private homes, as well as apartments and efficiencies. Most hosts are located on the water. Some are on ca-

nals; a majority are on the ocean. Directory: $1.
Rates: Singles $15–$35, doubles $25–$60. Apartments up to $100 per night. Ten percent discount off-season on some rooms. Weekly and monthly rates available.

Suncoast Accommodations **

P.O. Box 8334, Madeira Beach, FL 33738
Phone: 813/360-1753 Bobbi Seligman
Listings: In 66 Florida communities and 50 countries. Private homes, apartments, condominiums, and inns, as well as some students' specials, health lodges, and dormitory accommodations. Most hosts (modern townhouses to Victorian homes) are located in residential neighborhoods and are convenient to points of interest. Most of the foreign listings are residences, but some are referral services based in another country.
Rates: Singles 20 percent less than doubles, which run from $24 to $85. Monthly rates available. Many hosts require a minimum stay of two nights. Inns have their own rates and vary according to season. No credit cards.

Bed & Breakfast Co.

1205 Mariposa Avenue #233, Miami, FL 33146
Phone: 305/661-3270 Marcella Schaible
Listings: Private homes, apartments, condominiums, houseboats. Wide range of settings from urban and suburban communities to private islands. Many host families are multilingual, with French, German, and Spanish the major second languages.
Rates: From mid-December through April: singles $28–$54, doubles $32–$65. Some monthly rates. $5 per night surcharge for less than three nights. Other months: singles $20–$48, doubles $24–$44.

Florida Suncoast Bed & Breakfast

119 Rosewood Drive (P.O. Box 12), Palm Harbor, FL 33563
Phone: 813/784-5118 Carol J. Hart
Listings: At least 75 on the Gulf of Mexico and throughout Florida.

**Some listings in foreign countries

Private homes, some with swimming pools and beach cottages. (Rental apartments and condominiums are not hosted.) Various surroundings range from restored homes filled with antiques in St. Petersburg to one in coastal community of Long Boat Key on the Intracoastal Waterway which includes two bicycles for use on seven-mile trail. Directory: $3. **Rates:** Singles $20–$35, doubles $24–$40. Minimum reservation: two nights in most host homes.

A&A Bed & Breakfast of Florida, Inc.

P.O. Box 1316, Winter Park, FL 32789
Phone: 305/628-3233 Brunhilde G. Gehner
Listings: All private homes. Most are in the broad central Florida area with its many tourist attractions. Several are on the beach. Hosts prefer at least two nights' stay.
Rates: Singles $25 and up, doubles $35 and up. A few exceptional homes $60–$75.

Georgia

Bed & Breakfast Atlanta

1801 Piedmont Avenue, N.E., Atlanta, GA 30324
Phone: 404/875-0525 Jane Carney, Madalyne Eplan, Paula Gris
Listings: About 60 in urban and suburban settings. Most are in private homes; a few are in apartments, in the city's most desirable and often historic close-in neighborhoods. There are also some hosts in the mountains of northeast Georgia. This is one of the older (1979) reservation services in the country.
Rates: Singles $24–$40, doubles $28–$44. A few run up to $60. Surcharge of $4 for one night's stay.

Savannah Bed & Breakfast

117 West Gordon Street, Savannah, GA 31401
Phone: 912/238-0518 Robert McAlister
Listings: About 20 in private homes and garden apartments. All in

restored 1850s houses in the heart of the historic district of Savannah, near the river, shops, museums, restaurants.
Rates: Singles $24–$44, doubles $28–$48. VISA, MasterCard, and American Express cards accepted.

Intimate Inns of Savannah

19 W. Perry Street, Savannah, GA 31401
Phone: 912/233-6890 Barbara Hershey
Listings: Eight garden apartments and carriage houses in restored properties, all in the historic district of Savannah. Some hosts offer tours of their homes to guests.
Rates: Singles $50–$68, doubles $50–$75. Two couples $65–$125. Weekly and monthly rates are available December through March.

Hawaii

Bed & Breakfast, Hawaii

P.O. Box 449, Kapaa, Kauai Island, Hawaii 96746
Phone: 808/822-1582 Evie Warner and Al Davis
Listings: Over 75 private homes, apartments, and condominiums on all Hawaiian islands. Range includes sea-cliff settings, the hills of Hilo, tropical beaches and lush rain forests, the edge of a volcano, ranch country, metropolitan Honolulu, and an authentic teahouse by the sea.
Rates: Annual membership of $5 includes directory of listings. Singles $15–$30, doubles $20–$45. Some weekly and monthly rates available.

Pacific-Hawaii Bed & Breakfast

19 Kai Nani Place, Kailua, Oahu, Hawaii 96734
Phone: 808/262 6026 or 254 5115
Listings: At least 80 in private homes, apartments, condominiums, and cottages. Some students' specials. Locations are in downtown Honolulu and the heart of Waikiki as well as in Kailua and on the islands of Molokai, Hawaii, and Maui. Several hosts speak German, Spanish, and French. Directory: $2.
Rates: $18–$100. Monthly rates available. Minimum reservation: three days.

Illinois

Bed & Breakfast/Chicago, Inc.

P.O. Box 14088, Chicago, IL 60614-0088
Phone: 312/328-1321 Janet Remen and Mary Shaw
Listings: At least 80. From elegant to budget in Chicago, suburbs, and nearby vacation areas. Private homes, apartments, condominiums, and unhosted executive suites available, plus some that are considered students' specials.
Rates: Singles $25–$60, doubles $30–$70. Weekly and monthly rates available.

River Country Bed & Breakfast

Based in Missouri, this service also has listings in Western Illinois. Please see page 53.

Kansas

Kansas City Bed & Breakfast

P.O. Box 14781, Lenexa, KA 66215
Phone: 913/268-4214 (evenings and weekends)
Listings: Hosts in private homes in "the center of the United States" are offered by this service begun in the spring of 1983.
Rates: Singles $25–$35, doubles $30–$45.

Kentucky

Kentucky Homes Bed & Breakfast

1431 St. James Court, Louisville, KY 40208
Phone: 502/635-7341 Jo Dubose Boone and Lillian B. Marshall
Listings: At least 60. Mostly private homes. The variety includes a mansion in saddle-horse breeding country, restored Victorian homes, a log house, and lakeside cottages. Directory: $1.
Rates: Singles $22–$28, doubles $36–$44. Rates double during three-day Kentucky Derby weekend. Weekly: seventh night free. Minimum reservation of two nights.

Louisiana

Southern Comfort Bed & Breakfast Reservation Service

2856 Hundred Oaks, Baton Rouge, LA 70806
Phone: 504/346-1928 or 926-9784 Susan Morris and Helen Heath
Listings: About 100 private homes. Directory: $1.
Rates: Singles $25–$95, doubles $30–$100. Fees may differ during Mardi Gras. Weekly and monthly rates available.

Bed & Breakfast, Inc.

1236 Decatur Street, New Orleans, LA 70116
Phone: 504/525-4640 Hazell Boyce
Listings: In French Quarter and throughout New Orleans. Private homes, apartments in private homes, and guest houses included. All offer continental breakfast and are close to public transportation.
Rates: Singles $15 up, doubles $25 up. Fees differ during Mardi Gras and Sugar Bowl. Weekly and monthly rates available. No credit cards.

New Orleans Bed & Breakfast

P.O. Box 8163/3658 Gentilly Boulevard, New Orleans, LA 70182
Phone: 504/949-6705 Sarah-Margaret Brown
Listings: Over 50 in New Orleans area. Many in French Quarter. Currently expanding to cover the entire state. All types of accommodations from budget to deluxe, including private homes and apartments as well as unhosted and group arrangements.
Rates: $20–$125. Rates are lower in summer. Weekly rates available. No credit cards.

River Rendezvous

Based in Tennessee, this service also has some listings in Louisiana. Please see page 60.

Maine
(Please see page 76.)

Maryland
(Please see page 482.)

Massachusetts
(Please see page 167.)

Michigan

Betsy Ross Bed & Breakfast

3057 Betsy Ross Drive, Bloomfield Hills, MI 48013
Phone: Norma Buzan 313/646-5357; Roberta Howell 313/647-1158
Listings: About 25 all over Michigan, north to Cheboygan, south to
Kalamazoo, east to Port Huron, and west to Muskegon. Mostly private
homes in the suburbs of Detroit, in university towns, in historic small
towns, and in recreational areas. Some inns.
Rates: Singles $20–$50, doubles $20–$70.

Minnesota

Bed & Breakfast Registry

This service has nationwide listings. Please see page 27.

Uptown—Lake District B&B League

2648 Emerson Avenue South, Minneapolis, MN 55408
Phone: 612/377-7032 Trilby Christensen
Listings: Six private homes in one neighborhood. All are large Victorian residences.
Rates: Singles $15 up, doubles $35 up. Some hosts have weekly and monthly rates.

Mississippi

Natchez Pilgrimage Tours

410 N. Commerce Street, Natchez, MS 39120
Phone: 601/446-6631 or 800/647-6742
Listings: All 16 in historic residences built 1790–1857, all privately owned. Some have accommodations in the main house, some in guest cottages. One is an 1840 inn on the Mississippi River. Most are intown. A couple are about six miles out. Although some have managers, others are hosted by the owners. Tours in many.
Rates: $60–$90. $105 for four people in available two-room suites. Off-season rates in January and February at some homes. Weekly and monthly rates available. VISA, MasterCard, and American Express accepted.

Missouri

Gateway Bed & Breakfast

16 Green Acres, St. Louis, MO 63137
Phone: 314/868-2335 Evelyn Ressler
Listings: About 25 in the St. Louis area, both central city and suburbs, in private homes and condominiums. Free descriptive listing available; send stamped, self-addressed envelope. Advance reservations preferred.
Rates: Singles $20–$40, doubles $30–$50.

River Country Bed & Breakfast

#1 Grandview Heights, St. Louis, MO 63131
Phone: 314/965-4328 Ms. Michael Warner
Listings: About 25 all over Missouri and the western parts of Illinois, many in college towns and river towns. Hosts are in private homes, apartments, condominiums, and cabins and on boats. Directory: $3.
Rates: $30–$45. Monthly rates available.

Montana

Western Bed & Breakfast Hosts — Montana

P.O. Box 322, Kalispell, MT 59901
Phone: 406/257-4476 Sylva B. Jones
Listings: About 20 and growing. Private homes, apartments, condominiums, and ranches located between Glacier Park and Yellowstone. Many hosts are bilingual (Spanish, French, and German).
Rates: Singles $18–$30, doubles $22–$50.

Nebraska

Bed and Breakfast of Nebraska

1464 28th Avenue, Columbus, NE 68601
Phone: 402/564-7591 Marlene Van Lent
Listings: Around 20 private homes throughout the state; on farms and ranches, in villages and cities.
Rates: Singles $15–$25, doubles $30–$45. Weekly rates available. Major credit cards accepted.

New Hampshire
(Please see page 110.)

New Jersey
(Please see page 408.)

New Mexico

Bed 'n Breakfast of the Southwest

P.O. Box 1357, 103 Aspen Circle, Ruidoso, NM 88345
Phone: 505/257-9888; toll-free number (for use in Texas, Oklahoma, Colorado, Kansas, Nebraska, Wyoming, Utah, Arizona) 1-800-443-8649
Dee Williams
Listings: About 17, including a small number of homes in the Ruidoso area, but many more apartments, condominiums, and cabins. Arrangements can be made in unhosted places for up to 60 people.
Rates: Singles $20–$55, doubles $25–$150. For most there is a three-day minimum stay. VISA and MasterCard accepted.

Bed & Breakfast of Santa Fe, Inc.

218 E. Buena Vista Street, Santa Fe, NM 87501
Phone: 505/982-3332 Star Jones
Listings: Around 30 in private homes, plus apartments, condominiums, and guest houses. One students' special. Accommodations range from modest to elegant and are located from downtown Santa Fe to country areas. Many are in adobe homes with shady patios.
Rates: $25–$80.

New York

(Please see page 348.)

North Carolina

Bed & Breakfast of Asheville

217-B Merrimon Avenue, Asheville, NC 28801
Phone: 704/259-9537 Ken Lawson
Listings: All private homes, made available through this matching service established in September 1981.
Rates: Singles $25, doubles $35.

Ohio

Chillicothe Bed & Breakfast

120 West 5th Street, Chillicothe, OH 45601
Phone: 614/772-6848 Katie Mallison
Listings: Just three private homes. All represent the architectural heritage of the area. Service established September 1982.
Rates: Singles $20–$30, doubles $24–$35. Weekly rates available.

Private Lodgings, Inc.

P.O. Box 18590, Cleveland, OH 44118
Phone: 216/321-3213 Jane H. McCarroll
Listings: About 20 homes with hosts. Accommodations include a Tudor-style mansion minutes from downtown Cleveland and a modern house with watchtower on a cliff overlooking Lake Erie. Some unhosted houses and apartments are also available.
Rates: Singles $28–$45, doubles $25–$60.

Columbus Bed & Breakfast

763 South 3rd Street, Columbus, OH 43206
Phone: 614/444-8888 or 443-3680 Fred J. Holdridge
Listings: Currently 10 private homes in historic German Village, a registered national historic area close to downtown Columbus.
Rates: Singles $26–$32, doubles $36–$56.

Buckeye Bed & Breakfast

P.O. Box 130, Powell, OH 43065
Phone: 614/548-4555 Don and Sally Hollenback '
Listings: About 30 and growing. Located in all parts of the state. At least 13 communities represented. Directory with full descriptions published; send SASE for a copy.
Rates: Singles $17–$28, doubles $28–$55. A few in the $15–$22 range. Five percent discount possible at some for two or more nights.

Oregon

Gallucci Hosts Hostels, Bed and Breakfast

P.O. Box 1303, Lake Oswego, OR 97034
Phone: 503/636-6933 Betty Gallucci
Listings: Around 25. Mostly private homes. A few apartments. Range of settings: urban to country estates to mobile homes. Directory: $1, plus large self-addressed, stamped envelope.
Rates: Singles $12–$20, doubles $16–$40. Weekly rates available.

Northwest Bed & Breakfast* **

7707 SW Locust Street, Portland, OR 97223
Phone: 503/246-8366 Laine Friedman, Gloria Shaich
Open: Monday through Saturday (closed Sundays).
Listings: Approximately 300 homes (a few apartments, condominiums, and guest inns) from British Columbia through the states of Washington, Oregon, California, and Idaho. Limited listings in Hawaii, Arizona, Nevada, Montana, Illinois, and Florida. B&B tours and golf B&B tours in England, as well as specially planned self-drive B&B holidays on west coast. A directory describing all homes costs $5, an amount credited to membership.
Rates: Guest membership is $15 for one, $20 for a family and is valid one year from date of payment. Overnight stays range from $14 to $25 for singles and $18 to $40 for doubles. And family rates are available.

Pennsylvania
(Please see page 431.)

Rhode Island
(Please see page 304.)

*Some listings in other states
**Some listings in foreign countries

South Carolina

Historic Charleston Bed and Breakfast

43 Legare Street, Charleston, SC 29401
Phone: 803/722-6606 Charlotte D. Fairey
Listings: About 40 private homes and apartments. All accommodations are historic (c. 1720–1890) and all are in Charleston's historic district.
Rates: Singles $30–$100, doubles $35–$100. Weekly and monthly rates available. $5 surcharge for one-night stay.

South Dakota
(Please see page 52.)

Tennessee

Tennessee Southern Hospitality, Inc.

P.O. Box 9411, Knoxville, TN 37920
Phone: 615/577-8363 Katie Reily, Jane Felker
Listings: A selection of 20 private homes in Knoxville and surrounding (30-mile) area. The directors chose these hosts from the hundreds who had B&Bs during the World's Fair.
Rates: $23–$35. Weekly and monthly rates available.

River Rendezvous

P.O. Box 240001, Memphis, TN 38124
Phone: 901/767-5296 Mimmye Goode
Listings: About 15 hosts in cities along Mississippi River from Memphis to New Orleans.
Rates: Singles $20–$32, doubles $25–$40. Weekly and monthly rates sometimes available.

Nashville Bed & Breakfast and Bed & Breakfast in Memphis

P.O. Box 150651, Nashville, TN 37215
Phone: 615/327-4546 Betty Cordellos; P.O. Box 41621, Memphis, TN 38104
Phone: 901/726-5920 Helen V. Denton
Listings: At least 50 in Nashville, about 25 in Memphis area. Both offer mostly private homes with a few apartments and detached guest houses. Both have a variety of intown, surburban, lakefront, and country homes, and include an adapted church, a country estate, and horse farms. Hosts speaking French, German, and Spanish are available. Guests may book for both Nashville and Memphis through either office.
Rates: Singles $21–$34, doubles $27–$40. Some weekly and monthly rates available. No minimum stay in Nashville, but two-night minimum (or $5 surcharge for one-night stay) in Memphis. VISA and MasterCard accepted.

Texas

The Bed & Breakfast Society of Houston

4432 Holt, Bellaire, TX 77401
Phone: 713/666-6372 Debbie Seigel
Listings: Among the dozen or more homes are quaint cottages in old established neighborhoods, high-rise condominiums, and suburban homes with swimming pools and tennis courts.
Rates: Singles $16–$50, doubles $21–$60.

Sand Dollar Hospitality

3605 Mendenhall, Corpus Christi, TX 78415
Phone: 512/853-1222 days, 512/992-4497 or 853-8953 evenings. Pat Hirsbrunner, Maureen Bennett, Margaret McGeagh
Listings: About 25 in private homes, in condominiums, or in guest cottage on host's property. Some homes have up to four rooms available.
Rates: Singles $25–$40, doubles $30–$50. Twenty percent discount for weekly stays.

Bed & Breakfast Texas Style

4224 W. Red Bird Lane, Dallas, TX 75237
Phone: 214/298-8586 and 298-5433 Ruth Wilson
Listings: About 50 in private homes, apartments, and inns. Settings include restored Victorians, log cabins, historic homes, lake cottages, and ranches. Directory: $2.
Rates: Singles $20–$35, doubles $25–$50. A few $40–$60.

Bed and Breakfast of Fredericksburg

330 West Main Street, Fredericksburg, TX 78624
Phone: 512/997-4712 Jean Jennings and June Kaderli
Open: Monday through Saturday (office closed Sundays).
Listings: About 25 hosts in private residences and guest houses in a city known for its Texas-German heritage in the Texas hill country. Great variety of styles (and personalities) represented. Fachwerk, Sunday Houses, and extra-thick limestone houses are included. Many are in town within walking distance from "Hauptstrasse" (main street). Others are pioneer farms or typical Texas ranches.
Rates: Singles $25, doubles $35. VISA and MasterCard accepted.

Bed and Breakfast Hosts of San Antonio Home Lodging Services

166 Rockhill, San Antonio, TX 78209
Phone: 512/824-8036 Lavern Campbell and Vicky Campbell
Listings: Currently 25 hosts in private homes, apartments, and condominiums. Settings range from a garden home with swimming pool to a restored Victorian in historic area. Most homes have special amenities such as a hot tub.
Rates: Singles $25, doubles $35. $25 extra for exceptional homes. VISA and MasterCard accepted.

Vermont
(Please see page 132.)

Virginia

Blue Ridge Bed & Breakfast

Route 2, Box 259, Berryville, VA 22611
Phone: 703/955-1246 Rita Duncan
Listings: All 20 are in private homes. Range of settings includes homes on the National Register, mountain retreats, small town locations, and houses in scenic horse and farm country. They are all 25 to 75 miles west of Washington, D.C.
Rates: Singles $25, doubles $35.

Guesthouses Bed & Breakfast Reservation Service

P. O. Box 5737, Charlottesville, VA 22905
Phone: 804/979-7264 or 979-8327 Sally Reger
Open: Monday–Friday year round; April–October 10–5, November–March 12–5. Closed weekends, holidays, and Christmas week.
Listings: About 125 in well-established intown neighborhoods and on

country estates in the foothills of the Blue Ridge Mountains within 20 minutes of Charlottesville. Directory, available for listings in the $48–$72 range, describes many that are on the Virginia Garden Week tour. Originally, this service was set up for Bicentennial guests in 1976, making it the oldest existing B&B service in the country. This program is thriving with emphasis on letting guests experience the area by staying in lovely Virginia houses and cottages, meeting the owners, and enjoying the lifestyle evident in these homes.

Rates: Singles twenty percent less than doubles. Budget doubles are $36 and require a two-night stay. Others run from $40 to $72 a night, with cottages in the $80–$100 range. Reductions for weekly/monthly visits and during winter months, when rates are determined by length of stay and number of persons in party. Lesser priced housing is available from $10 a night (for a monthly stay). MasterCard and VISA accepted.

Bensonhouse of Richmond

P.O. Box 15131, Richmond, VA 23227
Phone: 804/321-6277 or 804/648-7560 (24-hour answering service)
Lyn Benson
Listings: About 45 in private homes, apartments, and estate guest cottages. Many have been on district tours or Virginia Garden Week tours. All are "historically or architecturally unique" and are in and around the city of Richmond.
Rates: Singles $22–$48, doubles $30–$60. Estate homes are higher. Reduced rates for longer-term stays. MasterCard and VISA accepted.

The Travel Tree

P.O. Box 838, Williamsburg, VA 23187
Phone: (Evenings and weekends only): 804/229-6477 or 565-2236
Sheila Zubkoff and Joann Proper
Listings: Private homes in residential neighborhoods of Williamsburg.
Rates: Singles $20–$44, doubles $25–$55. Some weekly rates available.

Washington

Travellers' Bed and Breakfast

P.O. Box 492, Mercer Island, WA 98040
Phone: 206/232-2345 Jean Knight
Listings: Around 60 in private homes, apartments, condominiums, small guest houses, and inns located in Seattle/Puget Sound, Tacoma, Gig Harbor, Bainbridge Island, Vashon Island, Whidbey Island, Port Townsend, and Port Angeles; and Vancouver and Victoria in Canada. One, ten minutes from downtown Seattle, reached by a floating bridge, has an antique four-poster bed with 72 yards of fabric cascading from the ceiling. Breakfast served by candlelight if you wish on the patio adjoining that room with a garden and trickling waterfall. Directory: $3.00
Rates: Singles $25 up, doubles $30 up.

Pacific Bed & Breakfast

701 N.W. 60th Street, Seattle, WA 98107
Phone: 206/784-0539 Irmgard Castleberry
Listings: About 70 private homes and apartments in Seattle, the Puget Sound area, and many other locations in the state of Washington. This organization, which stresses personalized service, has an affiliate in Hawaii. Some hosts are bilingual. Directory, not necessary for bookings, is $3.
Rates: Singles $16–$40, doubles $26–$40. MasterCard and VISA accepted. Family rates and discounts for longer stays available.

Wisconsin

Bed & Breakfast in Door County

Route 2, Algoma, WI 54201
Phone: 313/743-9742 Eileen Wood
Listings: About 20 through new service begun in April 1983. Along Lake Michigan and Green Bay Waters in private homes and apartments in waterfront settings, on farms, and in towns near water access.
Rates: Singles $30, doubles $35. $10 extra per night for B&Bs on water July–Labor Day. Ten percent discount for seven nights or more. Child in room with parents when space permits, $5.

EASTERN CANADA

Labrador

Newfoundland

Quebec

Prince
Edward
Island

New
Brunswick

Nova Scotia

Québec

Montréal

Ontario

Atlantic Ocean

Picton

Toronto

United States

Stratford

London

N

EASTERN CANADA

Reminder: Allow weeks for round-trip mail.

New Brunswick

New Brunswick Department of Tourism

P.O. Box 12345, Fredericton, N.B., Canada E3B 5C3
Phone: Toll-free number May through September: 1-800-561-0123
Listings: A brochure entitled *New Brunswick Farm Vacations and Bed and Breakfast Program,* issued by Canadian Country Vacations Association, lists mostly farm vacation places and a few B&Bs. Each is described with location, name, address, and telephone. A book-your-own arrangement.

Newfoundland

Province of Newfoundland and Labrador Tourism Branch

Department of Development, 1460148 Forest Road, P.O. Box 4750, St. John's, Newfoundland A1C 5T7, Canada
Listings: Annual pamphlet lists basic information for about 30 Hospitality Homes located in coastal communities (mostly) and rural villages. Included are private homes, cottages, cabins, lodges, and inns. All have been inspected and approved by the Tourism Branch. This is not a reservation service; *travelers book directly with hosts.*

Nova Scotia

Two organizations publish book-your-own directories. The quickest way to obtain free copies may be to call the toll-free number of the Nova Scotia Tourist Bureau, 1-800-341-6096 (1-800-492-0643 in Maine). They are located at 129 Commercial Street, Portland, ME 04101. The two directories are issued by:

Cape Breton Bed & Breakfast

c/o Cape Breton Development Corporation, P.O. Box 1750, Sydney, Nova Scotia B1P 6T7, Canada
Phone: 902/539-6300
Listings: In this 10th year of operation, the program has 60 homes in all areas of Cape Breton Island. The program started with five in the northern part where there were no accommodations. Basic information in the free brochure includes the name of host, location, number of rooms, and phone. *Guests book directly with hosts.* Most B&Bs are open May–October, but some operate year round. And some offer the option of lunch or dinner.
Rates: Singles $18, doubles $24 per night.

Farm & Vacation Association

c/o Mrs. Sandra Houghton, RR 3, Centreville, Kings County, Nova Scotia B0P 1J0, Canada
Phone: 902/678-2329
Listings: Approximately 40 hosts describe their locations and facilities in the booklet "Nova Scotia Farm and Country Vacations and B&B Homes." Some are on the water, some in villages or on farms. Although the season may be short for some, others are open year round. *Guests book directly with hosts.*
Rates: Singles $15–$25, doubles $20–$30.

Prince Edward Island

Tourism Industry Association of Prince Edward Island

P.O. Box 2050, Charlottetown, P.E.I. C1A 7N7, Canada
Phone: 902/892-2457. Toll-free May through September 1-800-343-0812; for Maine residents 1-800-322-7004
Listings: Approximately 50 B&Bs and some country inns fully described in free brochure. Names, addresses, phone numbers, and rates included. *Traveler books directly with host.*

Quebec

Montreal Bed & Breakfast

5020 St. Kevin, Suite 8, Montreal, Quebec H3W 1P4, Canada
Phone: 514/735-7493 or 738-3859 Marian Kahn
Listings: About 40 hosts in all sections of Montreal including the west-end community of Notre Dame de Grace, the old and elegant section of Outremont, the Université de Montréal area, the villagelike community of Lower Westmount, and the fashionable Upper Westmount. All private homes.
Rates: Singles $25–$30, doubles $35–$45. Full breakfast included. Family rates available when occupying more than one room. Discount after first week.

Gite-Québec (Bed & Breakfast)

3729 Ave. LeCorbusier, Ste-Foy, Quebec G1W 4P3, Canada
Phone: 418/651-1860 Thérèse Tellier
Listings: About 25 private homes. All offer a full breakfast and are convenient to the city's attractions by good public transportation.
Rates: Singles $25–$28, doubles $35–$40.

Ontario

Kingston Area Bed & Breakfast

10 Westview Road, Kingston, Ontario K7M 2C3, Canada
Phone: 613/542-0214 Ruth MacLachlan
Listings: All 15 are private homes located in Kingston, at the east end of Lake Ontario, 185 miles from Montreal and 165 miles from Toronto. Short-notice placements possible. Directory (not necessary for reservations): $1.
Rates: Singles $22, twins $32, doubles $29. Some weekly and monthly rates available.

London Area Bed & Breakfast Association

720 Headley Drive, London, Ontario N6H 3V6, Canada
Phones: 519/471-6228 Serena Warren
Listings: There are 10 B&Bs in the London area, between Toronto and Detroit, on the printed list that includes each host's name, address, and phone, and a description of location and house. Guests may book directly or through the service.
Rates: Singles $18–$20, doubles $22–$30.

Ottawa Area Bed & Breakfast

P.O. Box 4848, Station "E," Ottawa K1S 5J1, Canada
Phone: 613/563-0161 Suzan Bissett or Al Martin
Listings: About 50 private homes.
Rates: Singles $18–$22, doubles $25–$30, three people $30–$35, four people $35–$40. Weekly rates available. VISA and MasterCard accepted.

Country Host

RR1, Palgrave, Ontario LON LPO, Canada
Phone: 519/941-7633 Grace Cronin
Listings: A selection of 20 homes (10 available year round) located 35–90 miles from Toronto. Cater primarily to skiers and hikers on the famous Bruce Trail, which most hosts live on or close to. Also offered: a car jockey from one host home to another so that hikers needn't carry extra gear and clothing. Most homes — Victorian, modern, and working farms — have from two to four rooms. At some, donkey and hayrides available in summer, sleigh rides in winter.
Rates: Singles $25, doubles $35.

Bed & Breakfast Prince Edward County

P.O. Box 1500, Picton, Ontario KOK 2TO, Canada
Phone: 613/476-6798 Ann Walmsley
Listings: Approximately 10 in the area between Toronto and Montreal on Lake Ontario across from Rochester, New York. Some rural, some in the town of Picton, others on or overlooking the water. The reservation service matches host and guest.
Rates: Singles $25–$30, doubles $30–$35.

Stratford Area Bed & Breakfast Association

c/o The Secretary, 30 Shrewsbury Street, Stratford, Ontario N5A 2V5, Canada
Open: May through October.
Listings: About 20 private homes and guest homes. The Association distributes a brochure with a list and sketches of the homes, addresses, phone numbers, and in most cases the hosts' name and rates. *Guests book directly with hosts.* Accommodations range from Victorian to modern. Some are only blocks away from the Festival Theatre on Lake Victoria in Stratford.
Rates: Singles are mostly $18–$20, doubles $25–$35, suites $35–$55. Weekly and monthly rates available by request.

Toronto Bed & Breakfast

P.O. Box 74, Station M, Toronto, Ontario M6S 4T2, Canada
Phone: 416/233-3887, 416/233-4041 evenings and weekends Randy Lee
Listings: About 30 hosts in private homes, apartments, and condominiums, located in various areas of Toronto, all near good public transportation. Many of the hosts speak several languages (Ukrainian, German, Polish) in addition to French and English. Annual directory ($2) published in April describes B&Bs. *Guests book directly with the hosts.*
Rates: Singles $25–$30, doubles $35–$45.

Metropolitan Bed & Breakfast Registry of Toronto

12 Danzig Street, West Hill, Ontario M1E 2K8, Canada
Phone: 416/282-8855 or 282-2280 Elinor Bolton
Listings: About 80 hosts, mostly private homes, are registered. Wide range of locations and accommodations in Toronto. Directory ($2) lists them all with name, area, description, rates, and telephone number. *Traveler books directly with host by phone.* Last-minute reservations are accepted.
Rates: Singles $20–$25, doubles $32–$45.

MAINE

MAINE

N

CANADA

MAINE

NEW HAMPSHIRE

19

14

9

3

15   17

4   16

10

21   5

13

20   1

2   12

7   Monhegan Island

8

11

18   6

Atlantic Ocean

The numbers on this map indicate the locations of B&Bs described in detail in this chapter.

MAINE

MAINE

Reservation Services

Bed & Breakfast Down East, Ltd.

Macomber Mill Road, Box 547, Eastbrook, ME 04634
Phone: 207/565-3517
Established March 1983
Listings: About 20 all over the state, in communities including Bar Harbor, Cumberland, Eastbrook, Ellsworth, Foreside, Gouldsboro, Hancock, Kittery Point, Plymouth, Prospect Harbor, Southwest Harbor, Sorrento, Surry, Trenton, and Winter Harbor. Restored farmhouses and beautiful old homes are among the B&Bs. Some are in villages, on ridges overlooking lakes, or on the ocean. One host, a lobsterman, offers half or full days aboard his boat with opportunities to observe sea life, birds, and coastal sights, and to have island picnics. Write or call Sally Godfrey. If you would like a directory (not necessary for bookings) of all her listings, send $1.
Reservations: Advance preferred, but last-minute callers may be accommodated.
Rates: Singles $20–$35, doubles $30–$45. Some weekly rates available. MasterCard and VISA accepted.

Bed & Breakfast Registry of Maine

32 Colonial Village, Falmouth, ME 04105
Phone: May through September 207/781-4528 (Portland) other months; 617/277-2292
Established May 1983 as a subsidiary of Bed and Breakfast, Brookline/Boston, page 221.
Listings: About 40 coastal accommodations in Portland, Yarmouth, Freeport, Brunswick, Bath, the Boothbay area, Damariscotta, Rock-

land, Camden, and other coastal villages and nearby islands. Ellie Welch's service includes arrangements for entire families, handicapped persons, and pets.

Reservations: Advance preferred, but last-minute callers can often be accommodated.

Rates: Singles $30–$45, doubles $40–$60. MasterCard and VISA accepted.

Pineapple Hospitality

This service has hosts in Acadia National Park area, Auburn, Camden, Bath, Cape Neddick, Deer Isle, Kennebunk, Pemaquid, Rockport, Sheepscott, Winthrop (Augusta area), and Wiscasset. Please see page 170.

Bed and Breakfast Associates Bay Colony

This service has a few in southern Maine. Please see page 220.

New England Bed & Breakfast

This service is spreading into the state with a growing list. Please see page 224.

Some of the reservation and referral services with listings throughout the country, pages 26-29, have a few hosts in Maine.

B&Bs

BAR HARBOR

The Hearthside Inn

7 High Street, Bar Harbor, ME 04609
Phone: 207/288-4533
Location: On a quiet street in downtown area, near but away from all the hubbub.
Host: Lois Gregg
Open: Late June through Labor Day.

"An innkeeper's lifestyle is different from any other's. We see people at their best — in a vacation mood — and they see us at our best — doing what we always wanted to. We love it."

The pretty Victorian summer cottage that was built in 1909 by a doctor who intended to practice here, had already become an inn by the time Lois Gregg bought it in 1979. She knew Maine from vacation days with her children and thought this would be a good place to live. The house provided an outlet for her talents in decorating and making changes. Every room has a different feel. "By the time I get through, it's time to freshen up the first room!" Draperies, dust ruffles, slipcovers, paint . . . and so it goes. Along the way more changes have come in Lois's professional life; while she is working on her thesis in counseling psychology, hosting is limited to the summer months.

Restrictions: Children should be at least 10 years old. No guests' pets please.
Bed: Ten rooms on three floors. All have double beds; some also have one or two twin beds. Most rooms have private baths. Two have fireplaces.
Breakfast: Continental served in music room.
Plus: Grand piano. Inviting parlor with fireplace, games, books.
Rates: $32 single with shared bath. For two people, $44–$46 with shared bath, $50–$56 with private bath. Additional person in room $10. MasterCard and VISA accepted.

BATH

Grane's Fairhaven Inn

North Bath Road, Bath, ME 04530
Phone: 207/443-4391
Location: Three miles from Bath center on same river (the Kennebec) in country setting.
Hosts: Jane Wyllie and Gretchen Williams
Open: Year round. Two-night minimum stay during the summer.

Two medical technologists in the Boston area worked and saved to buy a country inn. What they bought in 1979 was a homestead with many add-ons since its origin in 1790. The previous owners had spent nine years refurbishing it and were also responsible for adding the surrounding 27 acres to the estate. Jane Wyllie and Gretchen Williams converted the "pretty inside and out" home to an inn, keeping such treasures as the needlepoint rug that is on the back stairway. Most of their furnishings are colonial. Many — including some beds, quilts, clocks, tables, dressers, and lamps — are antiques.

California guests write that their fantasies of the East have been fulfilled. Canadians have written a seven-stanza poem that includes
Yes we've been to London
And we've been to Spain
But we've not found a chef
Better than Jane.
Now we've redefined
Our notion of heaven
A big comfy bed
In "cherry" room seven.

In residence: Three cats: Cleo, a Maine coon cat; Tuppins, a blue Siamese; and Foxy, their white flame-point Himalayan.
Restrictions: Small, well-behaved pets may be allowed with advance notice.
Bed: Nine rooms. One queen with private bath. Eight share three baths. One single, one with twin beds, one with queen, and five with one double bed in each. Rollaways and crib available.
Breakfast: Continental. Or, for $2 extra per person, a full breakfast including fresh fruit; hot and cold cereals; and an entrée that could be ham-and-cheese soufflé, scrapple and eggs, quiche, French "tipsie toast," finnan haddie. . . . Served in two breakfast rooms; one has a fireplace.

Plus: Library and BYOB tavern, each with a fireplace. Patio. Lawns with picnic table and lawn furniture. And, if you'd like, help in planning your day (hiking, swimming, golfing, picnicking, concerts, museums, restaurants — Bath, Brunswick, Wiscasset, Boothbay Harbor).
Rates: June–October, $30–$32 single, $39–$42 double, $44-$49 queen. Rollaway $14. November–May, about $5 less. Crib $3.

We were lucky. We just happened to hear about Grane's and knocked on the door. It's a home away from home, a delightful change from the usual hospitality.   A. S. Osmond, Cincinnati, Ohio

BETHEL

Bed and (Continental) Breakfast

Star Route Box 90, Bethel, ME 04217
Phone: 207/824-2229
Location: On U.S. Route 2, a little over a mile from the village; 72 miles from Portland, Maine, 180 miles to Montreal, 30 miles to White Mountain National Forest in New Hampshire.
Hosts: Dana and Barbara Douglass
Open: Year round. Reservations required during ski and holiday seasons.

Good timing! Barbara had thought about her B&B stays in the British Isles. And she thought the idea might be a good solution toward meeting the terrific oil bills. "And it has proved thus!" Barbara retired in the summer of 1982 from 25 years as a social worker for the state of Maine. The first B&B guests arrived in August. "The people have been marvelous and seem to enjoy their visit though it's usually brief. We enjoy them too."

Dana is a semiretired self-employed surveyor. The Douglasses bought this house in 1950 and brought up four daughters here. They are the only other family who has lived in it since the original Twitchell family built their first home in the early 1790s. By 1890, Twitchell descendants were prosperous farmers and they put on a Victorian addition. Later the 20-room home for years was a summer boardinghouse operated by the Twitchell sisters.

Whether guests come for antiquing, skiing, hiking, or foliage, they seem to turn in early.

In residence: Husband occasionally smokes ("Shouldn't!").
Foreign language spoken: A little French.
Bed: Five rooms, each with twin beds. Plus a large upstairs living room with a sofa bed and plenty of room for rollaways or sleeping bag. Cot and crib available.
Breakfast: Continental, 7–11. Tends to be leisurely except for skiers.
Plus: Attractive gazebo. Collection of menus from area restaurants. Tour of barn that is pegged and huge.
Rates: $20 single, $28 for two. Cot $10. Crib $5. Sorry, no credit cards accepted.

What a thrill to be once more in the home built and lived in by five generations of my ancestors. It was heartwarming to see it so beautifully cared for by a charming host and hostess. I can't wait to go back.
Roxanne Twitchell Sly, Princeton, New Jersey

It was a delightful pleasure to feel at home in our immaculate comfortable room (with a chaise lounge). We shared a refreshing visit with our hostess in the gazebo, surrounded by a spacious grass area and 100-year-old trees. . . . I'll go out of my way to return to this unique B&B.
J. W., Hawthorne, California

BRIDGTON

The 1859 Guest House

60 South High Street, Bridgton, ME 04009
Phone: 207/647-2508
Location: On Route 302, main route from Portland to New Hampshire and Vermont.
Host: Mary Zeller
Open: All months except December. Reservations necessary.

The Zellers have had a cottage on a nearby lake for 15 years, but they have been in this house just since November 1981. And is Mrs. Zeller enjoying the sharing! Her daughter lives in Seattle where B&B is very popular. "Last year she suggested that I would love B&B and she was right." The Zellers have lived in six states, locations for Mrs. Zeller's primary role as homemaker and secondary one as hostess. In Bridgton she has become immersed in community activities. The last time we spoke she mentioned that she had just spent the day planting 300 plants around the town monument.

At home, between B&B guests, there has been painting, papering, and restoring as well as other kinds of hosting. When the heat goes off in church, groups may meet here. And there have been local committee meetings and benefit musicales and luncheons.

The foundation of the house (and what was a tavern) was put in in 1821. After a fire the present house and barn were built in 1859. Furnishings come from both families; a feature is an extensive clock collection. The inviting kitchen has a fireplace and a rocking chair.

In residence: Mary's husband, Dr. Zeller.
Restrictions: No pets allowed.
Bed: Three rooms. Two with twin beds, one with double. Crib (no charge), air mattresses, and sleeping bags available.
Breakfast: At guests' convenience. Mary says grace before the full meal which includes hot or cold cereal, homemade coffee cake and jellies, maybe waffles or pancakes with Maine maple syrup or Pennsylvania Dutch scrapple. Hostess is likely to join you for coffee. Served with china and silver at kitchen table (made from a door from the old barn) or (in warm weather) in the sun room filled with plants.
Plus: House tour includes furniture and clocks; usually takes place after breakfast, if you'd like. Large front porch for sitting.
Rates: $35 per night per couple.

BRISTOL

Brannon-Bunker Inn

Route 129, South Bristol, ME
Mailing address: HCR 64, Box 045, Damariscotta, ME 04543
Phone: 207/563-5941
Location: About 4½ miles south of the village of Damariscotta on the road to Christmas Cove. Three miles from "a sporty golf course" and 10 minutes from the ocean and public beach.
Hosts: Char and Dave Bunker
Open: April/May (depending on when spring decides to arrive in Maine) through Columbus Day in October. Minimum reservation of two days for weekends July–October.

When the Bunkers acquired the Cape Cod–style house with attached barn in 1978, they hadn't thought about having paying guests. (In Illinois Char had, for 20 years, co-owned a dress shop with her mother. Dave was, and still is, a banker.) They did know that the barn had seen use as a dance hall, La Hacienda, in the 1920s, and that later it was converted into an overflow facility for a nearby inn. Because the demand for tourist housing is so great in this area, the Brannon-Bunker Inn just "sort of happened." Five years and an additional building later, Dave is in the kitchen making muffins every morning at 6. Many guests are repeaters, people who enjoy the rooms that are decorated with comfortable old pieces — such as pineapple-post, spindle, and pencil-post beds; Empire bureaus; and vintage desks. They remember the warm welcome (starting with posted names of guests on slate by the front door), the comfortable ambiance, the setting, White Cloud's "good morning," conversation, and answers to dozens of questions. "They kiss you goodbye! Can you imagine that happening if I had a hotel or motel?"

In residence: Their goose, White Cloud, a year-round resident in the man-made pond between the house and the river. Maynard, the Maine coon cat ("she even gets fan mail"), and Topsy, a regular coon, but shy and elusive of guests. "Both of our daughters are married and live in Maine; they often come up on weekends to help out."
Restrictions: Pets allowed only in ground-floor rooms in the carriage house.
Bed: Six rooms. Two twins with private bath, one with shared. One double with private bath, two with shared. Two of the rooms are on ground floor of remodeled carriage house. Cots and crib available.
Breakfast: Available 8–10 but at other hours by request. Continental including homemade baked goods. Served at table overlooking pond. Usually leisurely if you're not off to catch a ferry.
Plus: "Publyck Room" with fieldstone fireplace. Books everywhere. Television. The Damariscotta River, complete with seals at low tide, is a five-minute walk through the meadow by the home of White Cloud. Unscheduled snacks. Kitchen privileges. Tea or coffee always available. Lawn chairs. Picnic tables.
Rates: $30 single with shared bath, $35 for twin or double with shared bath, $40 for twin or double with private bath. Cot $8. Crib $5. MasterCard or VISA accepted.

Each visit makes us feel as though we are returning home. Char and Dave have "our" room, the one with a 19-century sleigh bed, prepared with fresh wildflowers gathered from the surrounding countryside. Char and Dave are innkeepers in the very finest sense. You leave their inn feeling you have left a part of yourself.
Patrick and Nancy Bell, West Bridgewater, Massachusetts

ELIOT

High Meadows Bed & Breakfast

Route 101, Eliot, ME 03903
Phone: 207/439-0590
Location: On a country road. Eight miles to Portsmouth, N.H. Near beaches and historic sites.
Host: Elaine Raymond
Open: Year round. Advance reservations strongly recommended for summer weekends.

We have visited New England many times and have always enjoyed the B&B atmosphere. However, no visit can compare to our weekend at High Meadows. It captures all the charm and grace of a bygone era . . . and is definitely the best of both eras . . . .
                                        Mr. and Mrs. R.A.E., Hayward, Wisconsin

    And the grandmother who has lived here for 20 years thinks her only "claim to fame is being the author of two cookbooks!" B&B travelers have been coming since 1981 to this antique-filled home built in 1736 by a merchant shipbuilder and captain. Last summer northern and southern Californians who are in the same business met for the first time here. And Maine residents, too, offer recognition:

The down-east ambiance that surrounds a visitor to High Meadows makes a stay there an unforgettable experience. The sparkling personality of the hostess (not to mention her excellent cooking) will instantly make the traveler feel he has discovered a home away from home.
                                        F.A. McIntyre, Skowhegan, Maine

In residence: Teenage son in summer. Two dogs — Willoughby, a Yorkie, and Eden, a golden retriever.
Restrictions: Children should be at least 14. No guests' pets.
Bed: Three rooms. Two with twin beds in each, one with double bed. One full bath upstairs. "A lavatory downstairs is available in case of a rush. Even with a full house last summer, no bottlenecks."
Breakfast: Usually 8–9. Fruit compote, juices, homemade muffins, beverage. On porch or patio in summer.
Plus: Beverage in late afternoon or evening. Attached party house.
Rate: $50 per room.

KENNEBUNK

Pineapple Hospitality Host #ME 401

Location: In historic district. Short walk to village. Three miles to beaches, shops, and Kennebunkport.
Reservations: Available year round through Pineapple Hospitality, page 170.

This couple (he is retired from the graphic-arts business) love to share their 1750 sea captain's home, one that has only had two previous owners. They usually give a tour and will fill you in on the Victorian furnishings and heirloom antiques. The host's grandmother did the 19th-century paintings. The host's mother upholstered many of the chairs with her crewel and needlepoint. The kitchen and bathrooms were renovated in 1974.

"Little luxuries" such as fresh-air-dried sheets and electric blankets are provided. What else do guests appreciate? "After a day of touring they sometimes take moonlit walks on our soft sandy beaches."

In residence: One who smokes a pipe. A Great Dane lives in the cottage behind the house and is penned up in the yard, not brought into main house.
Restrictions: Smoking allowed on first floor only.
Foreign language spoken: Some Swedish.
Bed: Two rooms. One with twin beds, one with a single. Crib and cot available. One guest bath.
Breakfast: Served 8–10 at attractively set table in Victorian dining room. Includes Swedish coffee bread.
Plus: Cheese and crackers in late afternoon. Beach parking pass.
Rates: $27 single, $35 double, $5 for crib or cot.

Beautiful home, comfortable beds, wonderful hospitality, friendly, helpful, quiet area and easy to park . . . safe . . . yummy Swedish rolls.
The Weisses, Wheaton, Maryland

KENNEBUNKPORT

1802 House, Bed and Breakfast Inn

Locke Street, Box 774, Kennebunkport, ME 04046
Phone: 207/967-5632
Location: On a side road in a residential historic district within walking distance of Dock Square. Next to an 18-hole golf course. Trolleys stop just around the corner.
Hosts: Bob and Charlotte Houle
Open: Year round. Two-night minimum stay July–October and on all weekends.

The list of "regular" guests includes addresses from all over the country and Canada, so one might think that the Houles were professional innkeepers of long standing. Maybe it's all just an extension of the way the Houles themselves were received when they first came to Kennebunkport in 1975. They found an "honest-to-goodness small-town spirit, one that's contagious, with down-to-earth 'Mainiacs' who have hearts of gold."

The family came from a small town in Massachusetts when the government funding was discontinued for Bob's woodworking design workshops. Charlotte had been an activities coordinator for nursing homes. They bought an apartment building that had something torn apart in every room. Bob put all of his woodworking talent to work and Charlotte helped with decorating. And for three more years it was an apartment building. Local residents who were aware of the transformation encouraged the Houles to become B&B hosts.

In a way history is repeating itself. The original part of the house with walnut staircase was built by a sea captain in Waterboro in 1802 and was brought by oxen to Kennebunkport. It became the lodging for men who worked on the locks on the Kennebunk River.

The decor is colonial with reproduction furniture and wallpaper. The atmosphere is cozy. Housekeeping is meticulous. The new careers are established. "I love the job of managing the inn. Bob loves the custom woodworking opportunities that are endless here. It's gratifying to see the pleasure our guests have received from our efforts. We have made many long-lasting friendships."

In residence: Bob Jr., all-around helper in summer. Laura-Lyn, age 15, gives a big hand. Daughter Debra, married and a mother, comes to take over when Mom and Dad need a vacation. Grandaughter Dorian, not yet two, frequently visits with grandparents (and guests) during the day.

And you may get to meet her uncle, the oldest Houle son — Bruce, a draftsman. Laura-Lyn's cat Moxie and Char's apricot poodle, Boy Boy.
Restrictions: No guests' pets. Children should be at least 12.
Foreign language spoken: Some French.
Bed: Eight rooms, all with wall-to-wall carpeting and private baths. Some have working fireplaces. Cots available.
Breakfast: Two sittings, at 8:30 and 9:30, at the sound of the ship's bell. Char is chef. Bob Sr. is a very popular waiter. "We go out of our way to please our guests whether it be a birthday party or fish fry!" Could be fresh fruit cup or strawberry yogurt and homemade granola topped with strawberries, plus pineapple French toast with pineapple sauce, or sour-cream scrambled eggs with a delicate flavor of herbs, or walnut pancakes with real maple syrup.
Plus: Common room with pot-bellied stove, books, games, sofas with big pillows. Umbrella tables and chairs for outdoor relaxation. Crackers and cheese (BYOB) from 5:30 to 7:30. For each guest, a map of area, advice if sought, and answers. Cross-country skiing at the door, followed by mulled cider or hot chocolate.
Rates: July 1–October 31, $44 single, $54 double or twin beds; $60 double with fireplace. Off-season rates $4–$5 less. Special winter package available. Cots $10 per person. MasterCard and VISA only for two or more days.

Our breakfast was exceptionally good and the warmth of the home and its hosts was equally impressive.　　　Janice T. Dalzell, Natick, Massachusetts

KENNEBUNKPORT

The Chetwynd House

Chestnut Street, Box 130, Kennebunkport, ME 04046
Phone: 207/967-2235
Location: In the village. Across the street is the busy Kennebunk River marina. Dock Square, "the village hub," is two blocks away. Galleries all around.
Host: Susan Knowles Chetwynd
Open: Year round.

Whether you join the tourists in this lovely seaport during the summer, or as your host does, put on your foul-weather gear and join the natives for an outdoor look at a dramatic angry winter ocean, you'll be well fortified for the day after an exotic Chetwynd breakfast, often a two-hour event shared with travelers from all over the world.

Since coming here (with her library that you are welcome to read) in 1971, Susan, a former English teacher in Connecticut, has become immersed in the history of the seaport. She's fascinated with the early citizens and their activities. Her tall-windowed blue-shuttered home, not a mansion by Kennebunkport's standards, was built around 1840 for a sea captain. In the early 1900s it was the home of an artist, Abbott Graves. Its wide pine floorboards are graced with antique and traditional furnishings. Blue, a favorite color, is tastefully introduced throughout. (Some knowledgeable guests check for markings on the Meissen-like breakfast china!)

"Many a fine friendship began with talk about the favorite dishes served in area restaurants and moved on to the offerings in the art galleries. We talk about our efforts to understand the school of art of black squares and harmony of colored stripes on canvas, and confess we buy paintings of the sea and harbor, and village scenes — and we ponder why that is. We ponder about a lot of things. That's nice."

Restrictions: Sorry, no children in season. No pets.
Foreign languages spoken: Some French and Italian.
Bed: Five double rooms with four-posters; two with private baths. Two shared baths. Cots available.
Breakfast: At 9 a.m. Fresh fruits, blueberry muffins, maybe egg dishes, fillet of sole or haddock, crabmeat soufflé, quiches, or oyster stew (in season).
Plus: Living room/library. Small garden bordered by flowering shrubs and lilacs. Late-afternoon wine and cheese. "Before evening activities there is a quiet checking around to see if anyone plays bridge." Fans, if needed. Tea or hot chocolate.
Rates: For two, effective June 10–November 1, Christmas, and other holidays: Private bath $65. Rooms with shared bath: $39–$52. Winter rates are about $5 less. Cots $15.

I never thought that I would be sending a thank-you note after having paid for the experience. It was a delightful stay.

Karen Jane Taylor, Toronto, Ontario, Canada

KINGFIELD

The Country Cupboard Guesthouse

Route 27, North Main Street, Kingfield, ME 04947
Phone: 207/265-2193
Location: On scenic highway, ¼ mile from town. A 45-minute drive to Canadian border, 2½ hours to coast. Eighteen miles from Sugarloaf, 10 miles to tennis; golf available as of 1984.
Hosts: Sharon and Bud Jordan
Open: Year round except mid-April through mid-May. Two-night minimum stay on weekends and during winter.

The farmhouse, built in the 1800s, was the first B&B in the area in 1957.

Sharon knew the B&B world from her own travels here and abroad. In 1975, when she left her swimming and ice-skating teaching in the Washington, D.C. area, she worked on the renovations and redecorating here, doing all the cosmetic work herself — with the goal of providing a home atmosphere, "not a fancy hotel, just a warm friendly place without planned entertainment." What has happened? "People really unwind here!"

The B&B is mostly her project, but Bud helps with breakfast. He works for a large construction company, and (happily) is a "tinkerer, mechanic and general fixit person with many talents."

In residence: One teenage son. Heidi, a five-year-old St. Bernard. Fritz, another dog, and Kitty the cat.
Restrictions: No guests' pets. Smoking allowed, but not in rooms please.
Bed: Seven rooms, all carpeted, some with yesteryear furniture, some colonial. One single, two with two twin beds in each, two with double beds. One with two double beds. One with four bunk beds (used for groups), rustically furnished, with private entrance. Two shared guest baths.
Breakfast: Available 7–10:30 in peak season. Full with homemade breads, muffins, pancakes, bacon and eggs, sausage, bagels, home fries or grits. Served in dining room.
Plus: Deck, 18-foot swimming pool. Screen house. Cross-country skiing at the door. Some rooms are air conditioned. Baby-sitting possibilities.
Rates: Spring through fall, $25 single, $30 double, $46 for two people in room with two double beds in summer. Bunk room is less per person;

rate depends on number in room. Winter (November 15–April 15) rates are higher; B&B offered weekdays, two meals offered weekends and holidays. MasterCard and VISA accepted.

Comfortable beds, great food and wonderful people.
Shirley W. Sullivan, Philadelphia, Pennsylvania

Delightfully charming with all the comforts of home, complete with outstanding hospitality.   Ralph and Ginger Colarusso, Brockton, Massachusetts

NORTH EDGECOMB

Channelridge Farm

358 Cross Point Road, North Edgecomb, ME 04556
Phone: 207/882-7359
Location: Between Wiscasset and Damariscotta, 2½ miles from U.S. Route 1. Ten miles to Bath Maritime Museum or Boothbay Harbor, 20 to Reid Park's long beach, 32 to Camden. Located on 50 acres that include a pond in the woods.
Hosts: Phillip and Eleanor Goggins
Open: May through mid-September. Reservations recommended.

If you want to stay with a native, this is the place. Eleanor, a Red Cross girl in World War II, and Phil, a technical sergeant from Montana, met overseas. He became a marine biologist and she a teacher. For 27 years they have lived in this New England saltbox with long ell, built sometime before 1741 and on the National Register. "I hope our house isn't more interesting than we are, but it does outdate us by a few years." Ask about the history and you'll get a fascinating account of Aunt Carrie, a tale that includes some maritime history — and maybe ghosts too. Furnishings? "If guests are from Charleston, South Carolina, tell them we have some antiques. Guests from Billings, Montana, might say we are almost completely furnished with antiques."

As (recent) retirement approached, they considered the Peace Corps, but "decided not to leave our much-loved house for two years." Nonpaying guests have been coming here for years. "We were too liberal with invitations on those Christmas cards when summer seemed far off." Actually, those guests were the ones who encouraged official B&B hosting.

Both Gogginses are quite involved locally. Eleanor is a Great Books leader in one school, teaches some English classes at a nearby boys' school, and is a member of several historical societies. Phil has a long list of church activities and key positions with civic groups.

In residence: "Emma, the cat, stays mostly in the barn or in the pasture where a neighbor keeps her horse. Lisa, an ancient toothless papillon, stays inside when accompanied by a human."
Restrictions: Pets allowed if they stay outdoors. Smoking allowed only in downstairs main living room.
Foreign language spoken: High-school French.
Bed: Three rooms. Two with double beds and fireplaces. Cot available. One small single. Two shared baths.
Breakfast: "Phil is the better cook." Usually served 8–9 at attractively set family dining-room table. Fruit or juice, cereal, bacon or sausage and eggs, toast or homemade muffins and jam.
Plus: Living room (originally the kitchen) with huge fireplace. Extensive grounds, wooded paths, small lake.
Rates: $25 single, $30 double. $20 for the small single room. Cot $5.

OGUNQUIT

Blue Shutters

8 Beachmere Place, Ogunquit, ME 03907
Phone: 207/646-2163
Location: On quiet street, within walking distance of everything. Three-minute walk down wildflowered path to ocean beach. One minute to bus stop for trolley bus that travels around Ogunquit and Perkins Cove.
Hosts: Ronald and Jean Dahler
Open: April through October 12. Four-day minimum stay, and reservations required mid-June through Labor Day.

The rooms have all been redecorated with a particular color theme. The Dahlers are doing just what they set out to do eight years ago — to be near the ocean, involved with people, and have an income by providing clean and comfortable accommodations. Jean was a secretary and Ron an engineer at Xerox in Rochester, New York, when they decided to change their lifestyle. They are both originally from England where B&B "has been an accepted thing since heaven knows when."

The hosts are good with directions and suggestions. Guests sometimes come into the kitchen to chat and there are moments for evening conversation, but there seems to be so much to do in town that guests spend very little time in the house.

When Ron isn't working on a Blue Shutters project, he may be repairing some fisherman's boat. Jean can tell you that there's never a dull moment. "The gratitude expressed makes it all worthwhile."

In residence: People who smoke.
Restrictions: No pets allowed.
Bed: Five rooms, each with twin beds (can be made into king) and private bath. Four overlook the ocean. Two have fireplaces. Cot available.
Breakfast: Continental includes homemade muffins and breads. Served with silver and English china. Choice of tray service at your door or on deck.
Rates: $50 per night double occupancy. Reduced rates before mid-June and after Labor Day.

PEMAQUID FALLS

Little River Inn

Route 130, Pemaquid Falls, ME 04558
Phone: 207/677-3678
Location: On Route 130, with view of salt cove across the fields. On the way to New Harbor (fishing port) and Pemaquid Point; 9.5 miles south of Newcastle/Damariscotta. Within a few miles of white-sand bathing beach, Pemaquid Lighthouse, restored colonial fort with ongoing archaeological digs, and art galleries.
Hosts: Jeffrey and Judi Burke
Open: Year round. Reservations strongly recommended in July and August.

Locally it is known just as Bed and Breakfast, the place (they say) where you have to sleep to eat. Little River Inn grew naturally — from Judi's experiences as a guest in California B&Bs, and from their first guests placed here as overflow from inns in town. The antique Cape house had never had paying guests, but the Burkes bought it with that intention.

Judi is used to beautiful and tranquil countryside because she grew up on Cape Cod. In California she had a career as an elected union official for a large corporation. Jeffrey, a woodworker with his shop in the barn, teaches and does some model making for a local design company, and is responsible for inn changes and additions. He has been a social worker. And Judi and Jeffrey were in the Peace Corps in Venezuela when their first child was born.

Because the family loves the host role, it is easy for guests to feel at home. Within a three-day stay one 80-year-old gentleman became a Parcheesi partner for the Burkes' son Matthew and was also a cast member on the inn's float in the community parade.

When you are enjoying the now-famous breakfast in the dining room overlooking the river that winds out of a blue-spruce forest, you forget that the house is across the street from a lumber yard. The old stone works for the original water-driven sawmill are still in place. And it is possible to follow the river down the short walk to the saltwater cove, a spot famous for the spring alewives (herring) run.

In residence: Peter, age 15. Dawn, age 13. Matthew, age 8. Maggie, a Great Dane. Buffy, a collie mix.
Restrictions: No guests' pets.
Foreign language spoken: Spanish.
Bed: Eight double rooms. Half are old fashioned with traditional and antique furnishings. One has a fireplace and a view of waterfall. Other half are rustic barn style with skylights and high ceilings. One room has a private bath. Three rooms are at ground level without steps. Cots available.
Breakfast: Served 8–10. Entrée may be quiche, Italian frittata, Swiss baked eggs. Always included are fresh fruit, homemade breads and muffins, Judi's original granola, juice, coffee, good music, and pleasant surroundings.
Plus: Piano. Books and games. Album of local menus. Sitting areas inside and out. Barbecue by river. A short walk through the forest brings you to the door of the community library. Bedtime serenade of the river cascading down to the salt cove.
Rates: $35 for room with shared bath, $40 for private bath. Cot $5 for under age 12, $10 for 12 years and older. MasterCard and VISA accepted.

Warm, friendly, clean. . . . Freshly baked homemade bread each morning. . . . The large room with a woodburning fireplace and a view was superb.   M.J. Legome, M.D., Mission Viejo, California

A completely delightful experience. Could not have been better, including joining with the family in their entry in the parade to Fort William Henry. Excellent breakfast — and wine in the late afternoon — great! Jeffrey and Judi Burke deserve to succeed.   Charles Mee, Barrington, Illinois

PROSPECT HARBOR
(ACADIA NATIONAL PARK)

Carilam

Location: Off the beaten track near Schoodic Point section of Acadia National Park. In a quiet coastal town, 5 minutes' walk to sandy beach and magnificent ocean views, 30 minutes to Ellsworth, an hour from Bar Harbor.

Reservations: Available year round through Bed & Breakfast Down East, page 76.

The 20-year-old reproduction Cape home is hosted by a great-grandmother who has traveled B&B in Britain. She "just knew" that she would enjoy sharing her home, gardens, wooded landscape, and knowledge of "this lovely area" with guests. Her volunteer work in the "very adequate small-town library a mile from home" helps to make her a particularly good resource for visitors.

In residence: Two cats.

Restrictions: No guests' pets.

Foreign language spoken: High-school French.

Bed: Two rooms. One with two twin beds and one with a double, one twin, and a crib. One shared guest bath.

Breakfast: Available 8–9. Fresh-picked blueberry (in season) muffins, fishcakes, homemade doughnuts. A relaxing time in the family room or kitchen.

Plus: "The run of the house and grounds." Books, puzzles, games, lawn furniture.

Rates: $25 single, $35 for two, $5 for additional twin bed or crib. $60 for both rooms as a suite.

RANGELEY

Viola's Guest House

Pleasant Street, Route 16, Rangeley, ME 04970
Phone: 207/864-5409
Location: Right in the heart of town. In lake and mountain (skiing) country.
Host: Mrs. Viola Kunz
Open: Year round.

Viola started coming to Rangeley from New York over 40 years ago, but she has "only" lived here for 22. In 1974 she decided to have guests in her "old-fashioned well-built brown shingled house" and now close to 1500 vacationers have enjoyed her Maine blueberry pancakes. The grandmother of nine does everything herself. And lately she has added a gift shop with her own handmade items including pillows, tablecloths, potholders, and placemats.

Restrictions: No smoking or drinking in bedrooms.
Bed: Four rooms. One with double bed, two with twin beds in each, one with double and bunk beds. One and one-half shared baths in the house. Cots available.
Breakfast: Continental, 7:30–noon. Extra charge for blueberry pancakes. Served on glassed-in porch.
Rates: $12.50 per person in summer, $15 per person in winter. $1 off for hikers. Cots $3. Travelers' checks, but no personal checks, accepted.

READFIELD

Pineapple Hospitality Host #ME 402

Location: A half mile in on a dirt road, 2½ miles from Readfield Center, 15 miles from Augusta. Waterfront location.
Reservations: Available weekends June and September. All July and August. Book through Pineapple Hospitality, page 170.

One of a kind.
What was for 50 years the main lodge (rec hall) for a luxury summer camp has been the summer residence for this family since 1981. It's

one of those wonderfully built rustic places from the late 1920s with open ceiling, massive beams, and lovely natural-finished floors. The nine-foot fieldstone fireplace is the only source of heat. The second floor is bordered by a 10-foot-wide balcony that overlooks the main eating area. Furnishings are simple and functional.

"People kept asking if we lived here all by ourselves. With four teenagers and college years approaching, we knew this was a place to share. Our very first guests were two so-called senior-citizen friends who put us all to shame with their endless energy and enthusiasm. (They also sent us off packing when they discovered it was our wedding anniversary and did the dishes themselves.)"

The family has lived in Maine for 14 years. The host is a project manager in a semiconductor facility and the hostess has been a nursery-school owner-director for 11 years.

In residence: Four teenagers and Gram. Host joins family on weekends. And there are two animals: a very quiet female beagle and a cat you seldom ever see.

Restrictions: No smoking. No drinking.

Bed: Three rooms. One with double bed. One with a single and a double. One family room with half bath. One full bath shared by all guests. "A quaint little tub on legs and a neat little makeshift shower." Crib available. Sometimes guests' children bunk in with hosts'.

Breakfast: Generally 8–9. Cereal selection, homemade granola, sometimes blueberry pancakes, frequently hot muffins, occasionally eggs, homemade jellies and jams. Hostess and Gram cook. Everyone seems to help thereafter.

Plus: Something cool to drink in late afternoon. Fruit available in evening. Two canoes for guest use, tennis courts, swimming beach and warm lake water, woods for hiking, field for baseball and soccer, basketball courts. Ping-pong, games, and puzzles. "Guests who are here during strawberry or blueberry season may go picking and we'll help them make jam if they're new to it." And baby-sitting is available.

Rates: $25 single, $30 for two, $5 extra for each person up to a total of six in family room.

To enjoy the calls of the loons and to canoe on water disturbed only by the ripples made by my boat was a relaxing experience which surpassed any previous flight from the city.

Judy Haynes, Glastonbury, Connecticut

A comfortable, warm, and informal atmosphere. The hosts make you feel like you're part of the family. We really enjoyed our stay there.

Joseph D. Golden, Ft. Lauderdale, Florida

ROCKPORT

Sign of the Unicorn Guest House — Bed & Breakfast

191 Beauchamp Avenue, Box 99, Rockport, ME 04856
Phone: 207/236-4042 or 236-8789
Location: Steps from Rockport Harbor. Within walking distance of galleries, restaurants, concerts, classes, and woods for jogging and picnicking. Two miles from Camden.
Host: Winnie Easton
Open: Year round.

The Unicorn is an environment — and a unique one at that. It has been a bed-and-breakfast place, "a nurturing, caring, spontaneous, immaculate one with comfort and good-humored wit" for four years without advertising or a sign. Word of mouth brings guests who are looking for informality, peacefulness, maybe participatory possibilities, maybe some inspiration in a creative atmosphere.

What does all this mean? Original art — by professionals and guests — is displayed. For youngsters there are crayons, building materials, clay, paper. (Young guests frequently correspond with hosts through the winter.) Books! Fine arts books, mystery books, children's books, photography books, and over 100 cookbooks. Unplanned music making may occur for hours on any given evening with people who have never met before. The grand piano is available as are five recorders and harmonicas. Some guests arrive with their own instruments; this summer a young woman is coming with her harp. Storytellers or chamber-music players come to town for the Rockport Opera House.

And what if all you want to do is sit on a rock and read? Or walk through a wildlife refuge? That's fine, as long as the hosts are allowed to live up to their motto, "We spoil you rottener than you are." Winnie Easton's welcoming co-host is a model-maker and cartographer. His fun map of Rockport shows how much there is — culturally and recreationally — to do in this small picturesque village.

And how did the proprietor, a Pennsylvania lady, land in Rockport seven years ago? That's a long story that involves an unlimited-destination 30-day bus ticket and a multitude of happenstances and coincidences — that link her roles as mother, teacher (of French, music, young children, English), day-camp director, professional photographer, and B&B traveler abroad. She has continued to grow in Maine — first at the Maine Photographic Workshop and now as a watercolor and oil student (for the first time) and as a tutor with Literary Volunteers. And she had always wanted to be an architect; the Unicorn has provided an opportunity to try out some of her ideas.

In residence: There are no animals.
Restrictions: Nonsmokers preferred; considerate smokers welcomed. No guests' pets please.
Foreign language spoken: French.
Bed: Four rooms. One suite-like room with white carpeting, a double bed and a twin bed, a grand piano, antiques, built-in bookcases and a semiprivate bath. One double with loft, rough-sawn pine walls, sliding glass doors looking out onto harbor. One with twin beds; carpeted; wicker love seat, pine chests, and plants; shared bath. One with double bed, carpeted, antiques, books, flowers, shared bath.
Breakfast: Full, served for the first four days of any guest's stay. Muffins, homemade bread, cold cereal, and coffee always available thereafter, along with full kitchen privileges through the day.
Plus: Wine and cheese, and fruit bowl. Places to sit inside and out. Barbecue. Washer and dryer available. Hosts enjoy taking guests on rides to share scenic surroundings and to meet artisan friends. Babysitting possibilities. With advance notice pick-ups can be made at bus stops and airports. Sailing, fishing, and theater expeditions arranged.
Rates: Summer rates start May 20. $35–$45 single, $40–$50 for two. $8 for additional person in room. Weekly and group rates vary according to season. Long-term arrangements made too.

SEARSPORT

Homeport Inn

Route 1, East Main Street, Searsport, ME 04974
Phone: 207/548-2259
Location: On the main street of the village. Inn grounds extend to the seashore.
Hosts: Dr. and Mrs. F. George Johnson and Sally Johnson Wilson
Open: Year round. Reservations recommended.

When the Johnsons decided to become innkeepers in 1977, they bought and restored this sea captain's house that is listed on the National Register of Historic Places. It has been such a good match that changes are ongoing. There has been an addition to the main house, and the carriage house now has guest rooms. Beyond "what's where," the hosts find that many of the questions from guests focus on the lovely home that is furnished with family heirlooms and period antiques, all shared with guests.

Dr. Johnson is a down-easter who comes back home on weekends from his dentistry practice in Massachusetts. Mrs. Johnson has worked in the health profession and Sally has experience in the teaching world. They are all quite familiar with the state. When I asked how long they had been here, they replied, "We are Maine people of Scottish descent."

Dozens of antique shops are in the area. And there's a long list of recreational and cultural opportunities.

In residence: Dr. Johnson smokes a pipe. Christy is their golden retriever and Joshua is a big yellow cat.
Restrictions: Sorry, no guests' pets. Smoking allowed on first floor.
Bed: Eleven rooms, elegantly furnished. Six have private baths. Crib available.
Breakfast: Served 8–9 in the formal family dining room or on the sun porch overlooking Penobscot Bay. Includes juice, fresh fruit, and freshly baked muffins and breads. Full breakfast is an extra charge. A leisurely time.
Plus: Packed lunches can be provided. High tea served in afternoon. Dinner as an option for guests.
Rates: $20 single with shared bath, $24 private. $40 for two with shared bath, $44 private. $12 for additional person sharing room, $6 if under age 14. Crib $3. Holiday and weekend specials offered fall through spring. MasterCard, VISA, American Express, and Diners Club/Carte Blanche accepted.

SOUTH BERWICK

Tatnic B&B

RFD 1, Box 518A, South Berwick, ME 03908
Phone: 207/676-2209
Location: Half in Wells and half in South Berwick. In a secluded and quiet spot. Five miles west of Route 1 in Wells, 6 miles from Ogunquit's beaches, 15 miles to Kennebunkport, 15 miles to Dover and Durham, N.H.
Hosts: Tin and Jane Smith
Open: May–October.

"We built our passive-solar modified shed-roof styled home with the help of all our friends in 1978–1980. It is 2000 square feet and heats with about 3½ cords of wood in the winter. There is no backup heat. Hot water is solar in summer, heated by wood stove in winter. Even *Better Homes and Gardens* has been here. It's almost maintenance free and is a great example of what you can do yourself with a little forethought and a tight belt."

Jane's dad calls this "pink cloud living." "I love that image and work hard to cultivate it. I love living here in this house, being home, and doing what I love to do."

For 10 years she was a home economics teacher. During that time Tin was a marine biologist in lobster development technology. Now he sells greenhouse supplies by mail, is a local director of Maine Organic Farmers and Gardeners, and as a marine biologist is working on the establishment of the Laudholm Farm National Estuarine Sanctuary, a 2500-acre site in Wells. Jane is a professional quiltmaker/designer/teacher.

Since the summer of 1982 B&B vacationers have been part of the casual, informal scene.

In residence: Poppi, a friendly black dog who barks at everyone coming across the bridge. ("Even she's a vegetarian!")

Restrictions: No smoking.

Bed: Two rooms. One single and one with twin beds. Shared bath. Cot and two sofas available.

Breakfast: Generally at 9. Fresh fruit from garden (berries, apples, peaches); homemade bread and corn pancakes made with freshly ground flours and served with locally produced maple syrup. Homemade granola or fresh eggs. Honey from own beehives. Eat in dining room overlooking garden.

Plus: Insulation and cross-ventilation keep house cool "like a cave" in summer. Good exercise possible with a 2.8-mile walk "around the block." Lawn and outdoor furniture (and maybe mosquitoes too). Sometimes hosts and guests have dinner and/or an evening swim at Ell Pond, seven miles away. Guests are welcome to help in the big garden and to join neighbors Tuesday evenings for quilting bee — right here and free.

Rates: $20 singles, $30 double. Extra person in room $5.

Enjoyable, peaceful, relaxing. The house is comfortable and unique; the food generous and wholesome; and the hosts warm and knowledgeable in many areas. It is one of my favorite places in Maine.

Roger L. Taylor, New Orleans, Louisiana

STRATTON

The Widow's Walk

Main Street at Rangeley Road, P.O. Box 150, Stratton, ME 04982
Phone: 207/246-6901
Location: On main street of small village that is 8 miles from Sugarloaf Mountain, 25 from Saddleback, ¼ mile from Flagstaff Lake, 19 miles from Rangeley Lake.
Hosts: Mary and Jerry Hopson
Open: Year round.

Since buying the Victorian (1892) home in 1978, the Hopsons have been restoring and remodeling. The house is on the National Register of Historic Places and has original woodwork, fireplace, and mantel. The Hopsons have old photos as some documentation. It's one of those places with enough turrets and dormers — and a tower too — to be dubbed "the castle" by some local residents. Tourists have been known to stop just to take a picture of it.

Mary teaches swimming and Jerry has exchanged his U.S. Customs chemist's hat for one of handyman-about-the-house.

In residence: One teenage daughter. Three cats — Oliver, a 15-pound grey short-haired one; Tigger (T, for Trouble); and Peachy, gentle mother of Tigger. Two dogs — Freckles, 9-year-old St. Bernard; and Princess, 17-year-old beagle /terrier.
Bed: Six rooms, each with twin beds. Semiprivate baths. Cot and crib available.
Breakfast: Served 7:30–9. In summer it's juice, bacon and eggs, toast, and beverage. Added in winter: Jerry's ultralight pancakes or spicy French toast. Served in dining room overlooking Stratton Brook and view of Bigelow Mountain. Can be quick service, if that's what you want.
Plus: Dinner option, December–April, for guests only.
Rates: $20 per person during ski season; $10 at other times. No credit cards accepted.

Friendly, warm, informal . . . it's like visiting a favorite aunt and uncle. Whether swapping ski stories around the fire or enjoying Mary and Jerry's home-cooked specialties, in my opinion the Widow's Walk can't be beat!   M. Marchev, Hallowell, Maine

TENANTS HARBOR

Martinsville Guest House

Star Route, Box 772, Tenants Harbor, ME 04860
Phone: 207/372-8477
Location: Across from Ridge Road on Route 131, south of Thomaston. In a rural area on a beautiful saltwater cove. Three miles south of Tenants Harbor, 2 miles north of Port Clyde (departure point for Monhegan Island ferry), 1 mile from public beach, 15 miles from Rockland, 14 miles from Owls Head, 25 miles from Camden Snow Bowl.
Hosts: Paul and Betty Koelle
Open: Year round. Reservations recommended.

After hearing the "where is there a place to stay around here" question for about four years, the Koelles started B&B in 1981.

They have been restaurateurs for 15 years. Their most recent (Maine) location was recognized in the book *Road Food.* They have also been residents of Oregon, in Paul's forestry days. And Betty is the author of a cookbook.

Since they acquired this big comfortable home six years ago, both the house and the barn have been moved onto new foundations and a new connecting section has been built. Some passive-solar features have been added.

Many successful B&B hosts talk of friends who were guests first. The Koelles have some heart-warming experiences to relate — about a 90-year-old from Florida and about the many parents who come to visit back-to-the-land young people.

Restrictions: Pets may possibly be allowed. Nonsmokers preferred.
Bed: Three rooms, each with an ocean view and a southern exposure. One double, one with twin beds, and one with two twin beds and two bunk beds. One and one-half shared baths.
Breakfast: Continental.
Plus: Use of deck on south side, screened porch on north side. Two and one-half story greenhouse with small balcony off living room. Wood stoves in both living and dining rooms. Electric heaters in bedrooms and baths.
Rates: $18 single, $25 for two, $35 for four people.

TENANTS HARBOR

Mill Pond House

Box 640, Martinsville, Tenants Harbor, ME 04860
Phone: 207/372-6209
Location: On Route 131 south, two miles from the Monhegan Island ferry.
Host: Marilyn Korpinen
Open: Year round.

When Marilyn, a Tenants Harbor resident for 46 years, found that she had an empty nest, "everyone asked what I was going to do with the big old house. I decided I would keep it and fill it with guests who would provide the joy, laughter, and fun that I was used to. I called the local inns and they were more than nice in sending me their overflow. Last summer I had a lot of repeats and have made some wonderful friends. . . . I have never advertised. . . . A lot of guests who are artists love painting my view of the ocean."

Marilyn makes a point of visting with her guests — while juggling responsibilities in her beauty shop (located in a wing of the rambling Victorian house) five days a week. Beyond what she has hoped, "lots of interesting things have happened." All curious frustrated innkeepers might inquire!

In residence: No one who smokes. Princess is the collie and Penny the cat.
Restrictions: Sorry, no children. No pets. Smoking allowed on first floor only.
Bed: Three rooms. One with twin beds, two with double beds. One shared guest bath.
Breakfast: Generally 7:30–9. Continental with homemade muffins.
Plus: Front porch and back deck.
Rates: $20 single, $25 for two. Weekly rates available. No credit cards honored.

WISCASSET

Maggie's Farm

RFD 1, Box 110, Wiscasset, ME 04578
Phone: 207/882-7877 (8–noon and 5–7 are best)
Location: A little over a mile north of Route 1 on 11 acres along the Sheepscot River.
Host: Maggie Rogers
Open: April through October, special arrangements for other times.

In 1971, Maggie, an executive in Connecticut, came in search of a charming place "that just said Maine." And here it is, a farmhouse converted from a carriage house in the early 1900s after it was moved "by six oxen and a jug of rum" from downtown Wiscasset.

In 1978 Maggie left all this for an 18-month sail around the world — crewing on a traditional schooner that had no running water or electricity. Upon return she decided to have the world come to her doorstep. She spent three intensive weeks putting her plan to work. Ever since, guests have been enjoying the site of a former dairy farm furnished with country pieces and folk art collected from all over the world, together with the view of six miles "over to the hills" — complete tranquillity just 20 minutes away from bustling Boothbay Harbor.

In residence: One old English sheepdog, four cats.
Restrictions: Pets reluctantly accepted.
Foreign language spoken: Very little French.
Bed: Two rooms. One double (with extra bed for child) and one room with twin beds. Connecting bath.
Breakfast: Served 8–10. Could include eggs Benedict or blueberry pancakes, freshly ground coffee, herbal teas, homemade raspberry jam. Served on English china in dining room with fresh flowers in summer; early or late in season could be in kitchen with wood stove burning.
Plus: Private entrance to sun porch with wicker furniture and plants. Extensive library. Grand piano. No television. Your own picnic or cookout on front lawn.
Rates: $25–$30 single, $35–$40 for two. Cot $15.

WISCASSET

The Roberts House

P.O. Box 413, Wiscassett, ME 04578
Phone: 207/882-5055
Location: Right in the village, two blocks from shops.
Hosts: Alice and Edward Roberts
Open: June through October or by chance.

When the 1799 Federal home was scheduled for replacement by the local bank, depositors raised an effective fury. The house — with five working fireplaces — was on the market in 1973 at just about the time the Robertses were looking for a home in a small community. By now they know many folks in town and their children have grown up.

Alice did some research at the courthouse, at the historical society, and in the attic (where she found a diary from one of the long-time owners). The bedrooms now have names of the previous owners on them. The kitchen is one of those big country ones, complete with a beautiful oriental rug. The antiques, rugs, silver, and china are from both Alice's and Robert's families. It's a comfortable, homey place.

Very congenial. Full use of home. Excellent country breakfast. What made it nice was the final morning when Mr. Roberts sat down and joined us for a good discussion of current topics.

Mr. and Mrs. Tom Jones, Paxton, Massachusetts

Alice is a professional home economist with experience as an associate food editor for *Family Circle* magazine in New York and as a publicist for Sunkist in Los Angeles. Ed, a native Californian, heads a high-school English department.

In residence: Sometimes daughter's Labrador retriever is here. One host smokes "when not working."
Restrictions: Check if you want to bring children or pets.
Bed: Three rooms, two with fireplaces. One with twin beds, two with doubles. Two shared baths, one with shower and the other with shower and tub. Rollaway bed available.
Breakfast: A full country meal usually includes Maine blueberries, apples, or rhubarb from the full freezer. Freshly made breads and muffins. Eggs in one of a half-dozen styles. Served on Wedgwood bone china in formal dining room with fireplace and Oriental rug.
Plus: Living room, magazines, books, piano for spontaneous sing-

alongs, cable TV, flagstoned screened porch.

Rates: $28 single, $35–$38 for two. $5 for rollaway. Seventh night free for one-week stays. Surcharge of $5 for one-night stays on July and August weekends.

NEW HAMPSHIRE

NEW HAMPSHIRE

VERMONT

MAINE

N

7

14

5

3

North Conway •

9

2

1

10

Hanover •

4

• Laconia

8

Concord •

NEW HAMPSHIRE

Portsmouth

11

• Keene

6

13

12

Atlantic Ocean

Nashua •

MASSACHUSETTS

The numbers on this map indicate the locations of B&Bs described in detail in this chapter.

NEW HAMPSHIRE

New Hampshire

Reservation Services

The whole state is covered by:

New Hampshire Bed and Breakfast

RFD 3, Box 53, Laconia, NH 03246
Phone: 603/536-4347. Established: September 1982.
Listings: About 50 (from a start of just 12). A few are small inns and guesthouses.
Reservations: Advance reservations preferred. Same-day reservations may be possible.

At press time hosts who have listed with Martha Dorais's fast-expanding service are in Ashland, Bedford, Belmont, Canterbury, Center Harbor, Dublin, Goffstown, Georges Mills, Hillsboro, Laconia, Loudon, Meredith, Milton Mills, Moultonboro, New Hampton, Ossipee, Peterborough, Sanbornton, Wolfboro Falls, and Whitefield. Directory: $1. Almost all hosts offer a full breakfast. The wide range of accommodations and locations is reflected in the range of rates (below).
Rates: Singles $15–$30, doubles $20–$65. Weekly and monthly rates available.

Pineapple Hospitality

This service matches guests with hosts all over New England. Their New Hampshire listings are in Ashland, Barnstead, Concord, Conway, Center Harbor, Center Sandwich, Jaffrey, Laconia, Northwood, Peterborough, and Temple. Please see page 170.

American Bed & Breakfast in New England

This service has book-your-own arrangements for hosts in Fitzwilliam on the southern border, near Dartmouth College in Hanover, and a little further north on the Vermont border in Woodsville. Please see page 132.

Christian Bed & Breakfast of America

This service has hosts in Durham, Northwood, and Salem. The service is based in California but the New Hampshire homes can be booked through eastern representatives: Myra and Dick Wilmot, P.O. Drawer D, Middleboro, Massachusetts 03456.
Phone: 617/747-2356 or 947-1230.

*

Some other reservation and referral services with listings in many states throughout the country, pages 26-29, have a few hosts in New Hampshire.

B&Bs

ASHLAND

Cheney House

40 Highland Street, Ashland NH 03217
Phone: 603/968-7968
Location: Within walking distance to village center, recommended restaurant, and tennis courts.
Hosts: Mike and Daryl Mooney
Open: Memorial Day through Columbus Day.

There are good reasons for the professional style that makes the gracious hosting here look so easy. Mike has been in hotel management for over ten years; and before moving into this home the Mooneys together managed a Dartmouth College conference center for four years, with Daryl being chef. Before that Daryl was a home-economics teacher and home decorator.

The Victorian (1895) house is on a country street with an old stone wall and pasture right across the road. Since 1976 the Mooneys have worked on the gardens, restored the hardwood floors, and tastefully decorated with country furniture and crafts.

Vacationers take advantage of the town beach just a mile away, or drive 15 minutes to the White Mountains or to Squam Lake or the Lake Winnipesaukee area.

In residence: Cameron, age three, and their 1983 arrival, Shannon.
Restrictions: Nonsmokers preferred. No pets please.
Bed: Three rooms, each with a double bed. One guest bath.
Breakfast: Full, 7:30–9. Popovers or homemade muffins, egg dishes, maybe French toast with peaches. Served in unusual and beautiful foyer that has wainscoting, stained glass windows, and carved balustrade.
Plus: A flock of hens that produce fresh breakfast eggs.
Rates: $24 single, $30 for two.

Truly the best house we found in our travels — in comfort, hospitality and above all, food. Delicious! I want to stay here next time I make it back east. With all the people we've told about Cheney House, we should probably make reservations now.

Merribrook Havener, Walnut Creek, California

CHOCORUA

New Hampshire Bed & Breakfast Host #107

Location: At the top of a dirt road in a very beautiful private area.
Reservations: Available May through November through New Hamsphire Bed & Breakfast, page 110.

Because a son had such marvelous experiences staying with families when he traveled all over the world with a performing company, this couple decided to try B&B in their large, traditionally furnished home.

One of their early guests was so pleased with her visit that she left with the thought that a weekend here would be the perfect Christmas gift for her daughter and son-in-law.

What do guests do in this lovely mountain region? "They go to summer theater, to factory shopping outlets, and they love sports — hiking, canoeing, rock climbing, golf, tennis. After dining out they usually relax in our living room. They are wonderful people!"

The host is an engineer and his wife was in banking before they moved from Massachusetts to this permanent residence six years ago. Before that, they had known the area from frequent visits to their New Hamsphire vacation home.

In residence: Of their six children (two are married), probably just the youngest, a 17-year-old daughter.
Restrictions: Children should be at least ten. Sorry, no pets allowed. Smoking not permitted in bedrooms.
Bed: Three guest rooms, all stenciled by hostess and one of her daughters, share two full guest baths. One large room has a double bed. One room with two twin beds has an adjoining room with one single bed.
Breakfast: 7-9:30. Juice, homemade muffins with bacon and eggs, or pancakes or French toast with sausage, beverage. Served in breakfast room or in fireplaced dining room with views of mountains and lake.
Plus: Plenty of privacy, large screened porch, large fireplaced living room with piano, television, many books and games. Clay tennis court, badminton, croquet, horseshoes. Hot mulled cider or other beverage in late afternoon or evening.
Rates: $30 single, $40 double.

EASTON

New Hampshire Bed & Breakfast Host #110

Location: In Robert Frost's Easton Valley. Six miles south of Franconia, ten miles southeast of Littleton. On a main road, situated in the woods on eight acres on the western edge of the White Mountains.
Reservations: Available year round through New Hampshire Bed & Breakfast, page 110. Advance reservations strongly recommended late September through mid-October.

Informality reigns in this new post-and-beam house that was built with reclaimed beams from an old barn. After living here for a year, the host couple, a landscape designer and a patent attorney, decided that "B&B just made sense for two people in such a large house."

Guests have the run of this comfortable residence. Its two-storied living room has a large fireplace that is enjoyed by guests who often write about returning, or as one couple from California said, "At least sharing you with our good friends."

"Guests have surprisingly varied backgrounds and interests. We have yet to have a sourpuss come here." The hosts' own interests include the outdoors, of course, and scuba diving, sailing, and travel too.

In residence: Hugo, their standard poodle. And you may meet Monty, seven-year-old grandson who visits frequently.

Restrictions: Children should be at least six. Sorry, no pets. Non-smokers preferred.

Bed: Four rooms. One large room with queen-sized bed. One with twin beds. Two rooms with double bed in each. Two guest baths; one can be private. Cot available.

Breakfast: Full. Served 7-10 by whomever is handy, even guests, at a trestle table in dining area overlooking mountain range. Blueberry pancakes with local maple syrup. Home-produced honey, when available, on muffins.

Plus: Other meals by arrangement. Guests may pack their own lunches and contribute to the cost of dinner. Coffee any time. Use of two decks; there may be more by this summer. Small sauna in the house. Possibility of movie on VCR. Laundry facilities. Plenty of local information, including menus from nearby restaurants. Arrangements can be made for a son, a naturalist/guide, to take no more than six people for a full day or overnight backpacking trip; fee charged.

Rates: $30 single, $40 double. Cot $15.

ETNA

Moose Mountain Lodge

Moose Mountain, Etna, NH 03750
Phone: 603/643-3529
Location: About seven miles east of Dartmouth College (Hanover),
high on the western side of Moose Mountain, overlooking the Connecti-
cut River valley and the Green Mountains beyond.
Hosts: Peter and Kay Shumway
Open: Year round except April, May, and December. Minimum reserva-
tion: both Friday and Saturday for weekend reservations.

*It's not possible to be objective about Moose Mountain Lodge. It has
been part of our family tradition for almost 11 years. Like most guests,
we were introduced to its charms by friends, and except for two years
when we were in Northern California, we've journeyed back from wherever we were to rejuvenate our spirits and to add to our memories. We
usually tell our special friends: Imagine a big old log cabin with stone
fireplaces to the ceiling, homemade breads, homegrown vegetables,
homemade soups, access to the Appalachian and Dartmouth Outing
Club trails, open meadows, logging roads, an active beaver pond — all
nearby; hosts that you have to hug, who make their cookies with your
children, who start your car, who teach you to knit, play a genteel
game of "kill hockey." . . . They usually go and then almost always tell
their special friends.*

  Irmhild, Matt, Peter, Ursula, and Stefanie Liang, West Newton, Massachusetts

The rustic building was built as a ski lodge in the 1930s. The rope
tows have gone, but the Shumways have come (Peter was in the whole-
sale lumber business in New York State) as hosts who are "relaxed, easy
going folks who have time to listen." That knitting wool is homespun
from their sheep. Much of the furniture, including couches and four-
poster beds, is made from logs. Days are usually spent in outdoor pursuits. Evenings are made for talking, reading in front of the fireplace,
and sleeping.

In residence: Ulla, a grey weimaraner, who loves to go for long walks.
Restrictions: No pets. Children should be at least five years old. Smok-
ing in living room only.
Foreign languages spoken: French, some Spanish and Swedish.
Bed: Twelve rooms. Shared baths.
Breakfast: Huge country breakfast cooked and served 8–9:30 by Kay

and Peter. Always a leisurely meal. Could include homemade granola; fresh farm eggs; bacon or sausage; hot cereals made with applesauce; raisins; sunflower seeds; or pancakes served with the hosts' own maple syrup.

Plus: Option of lunch and dinner (extra charge). Hiking and cross-country ski trails. Cross-country ski equipment and snow shoes available (extra charge). Huge porch with 100-mile panoramic view. No television or radio.

Rates: $30 single, $40–$60 for two. $15 for children 13 and under when sharing room with parents.

HAVERHILL

Haverhill Inn

Dartmouth College Highway, Haverhill, NH 03765
Phone: 603/989-5961
Location: On main route NH 10, half a mile from the Common, with wonderful view of Connecticut River Valley and Vermont hills. It's a half hour (south) to Dartmouth College and within an hour's drive of five major ski areas.
Hosts: Stephen Campbell and Katharine DeBoer
Open: Year round except for a few weeks in March during mud season.

The Haverhill Inn is a gracious period New England home, lovingly transformed into a beautiful inn, a place you can't wait to get to, or bear to leave. It is plainly run for its guests, not its owners, with delicious food, charming guest rooms and the feeling that it is yours while you're there.   Brook and Molly Kindred, Scarsdale, New York

A partial list of interesting features in this 1810 Federal house includes wide-board floors, painted-grain interior doors, solid panel interior (Indian) window shutters, old kitchen hearth and bake oven, and the warmth of antique furnishings.

If you are interested in a complete history of the house, there are two volumes to peruse. For a perspective on the area, there's a collection of antique maps. The hosts are familiar with cultural and recreational resources and frequently help guests plan day trips.

It's a balanced (and full) life for these newcomers (in their thirties) to B&B. "Steve took a year off from computing to manage an inn in 1976 and got the bug to have his own place. Met (1979) Katharine who promised to be an enthusiastic partner. Purchased Haverhill house (1980) and were married here (1981). We have done much of the preparatory work and all the decorating ourselves. This summer we will be open to the public on a House Tour. We continue our separate professions — Steve is an independent programmer who works at home most of the time. Katharine, a concert soprano, teaches voice in her Hanover studio. Her heaviest concert seasons are less busy innkeeping times, so the schedules are complementary."

In residence: Pets that are not allowed in guest rooms or parlor — "two venerable cats who are shy of people and two affectionate puppies."
Restrictions: Children should be at least eight years old. Smoking in parlor only.
Foreign languages spoken: Katharine speaks reasonable French. Steve knows some Spanish.
Bed: Four large rooms. One with twin canopy beds, one double, one queen, and one with pair of double beds. Each room has a fireplace and private bath.
Breakfast: Served 8–9. On Sundays 9–10. Always a full meal. Fresh bakery, locally smoked bacon, and freshly ground coffee are part of it. Sundays it's more of an exotic brunch. Steve is chef. Katharine serves.
Plus: Tea is served in afternoon. Decanter of sherry sits on the hall desk. Other meals provided for canoeists who participate in a planned inn-to-inn program. Cross-country ski trails at the door.
Rates: $50 for two, $10 less for single. $10 more for each additional person (up to two) in room with two double beds.

Steve and Katharine greet guests as long-lost friends. You join a select family.   Kay and Bob Higgins, San Diego, California

JAFFREY

Margaret C. Gould

Prescott Road, P.O. Box 27, Jaffrey, NH 03452
Phone: 603/532-6996
Location: About 2½ miles from Jaffrey off Route 124E on 100 acres with a terrific view of Mount Monadnock.
Host: Margaret herself
Open: Year round. Advance reservations required.

When Margaret retired in the summer of 1982 from her nursery-school position in Pennsylvania, she came right back to this marvelous farmhouse that has been in the Gould family since the 1770s. Most of the furnishings are antiques that have been accumulated over several generations. The beautiful appointments include antique rugs.

Walls and woodwork have been freshly painted. The bedroom floors have been refinished, and the doors are open for B&B. Margaret brings her zest and enthusiasm to hosting. It's a traditional arrangement — with guests pretty much taking in the area during the day, rather than treating the home as an inn.

In residence: A Rhodesian ridgeback, a friendly dog named Lily.
Restrictions: Sorry, no guests' pets. No smoking, but summer guests may smoke on the porch.
Bed: Two rooms. One with twin beds, a private entrance, and a private bath. One with double bed and shared bath. Cots available.
Breakfast: Full and simple. Juices, fruits, toast, muffins, eggs, cereals, jams and jellies. Served in dining room or upstairs sitting room.
Plus: Radio and television. The property has accessible woods, fields, hiking possibilities, and a rough trail around the pond.
Rates: $25 for double-bedded room, $30 for room with twin beds. Cot $5.

LITTLETON

Beal House Inn

247 West Main Street, Littleton, NH 03561
Phone: 603/444-2661
Location: Steps from the town center, but quiet.
Hosts: The Clickenger Family—Doug and Brenda, Alisa, and Alison
Open: Year round.

This is a living antique shop. Except for the sign outside it looks like a typical rambling "added-on-to" upcountry Federal style home, circa 1833.

It's just three years since the salesman and his cartographer wife came from St. Petersburg, Florida, looking for an inn that would offer a new family lifestyle. The search involved 10,000 miles of driving. What they have now attracts repeaters who make it a point to visit the Clickengers at holiday time; local residents who book their own visitors here;

and newcomers who think they have stumbled into a lost era. It's a comfortable home with the mix and match of the current collection of antiques. Everything — the canopied beds, Windsor chairs, mirrors, clocks — is for sale. Browsers find more in the barn shop.

Along with the redecorating (period papers), upgrading, and accessorizing (handmade quilts) has come a style, one that has made their breakfasts (see below) somewhat famous. In the old tradition, the Beal House Inn is a family business. "Everyone does just about everything." Thirteen-year-old Alison capped one discussion with a comment that would warm the heart of any parent: "It's really fun to work together. And we get to meet all these wonderful people."

Littleton is not a cutesy or touristy place (some find that an advantage) but the Clickengers have become experts on the four-season attractions of the White Mountains.

In residence: Two teenage daughters.
Restrictions: No pets. Smoking not allowed at the breakfast table.
Foreign languages spoken: Alisa and Alison know some French and Spanish.
Bed: Fourteen rooms as twelve units. (Two are two-room suites.) Shared and private baths available.
Breakfast: Served in dining room 7:30–9:30 (8–10 on Sundays) with candlelight and fireplace, red and white tablecloths, and Clickenger women in long dresses. Homemade breads, popovers, waffles with pure maple syrup, maybe creamy scrambled eggs served in glass hen dishes, meats, 26 varieties of tea — all prepared by Doug. You might meet a few locals who come for breakfast too.
Plus: Tea and popcorn in late afternoon or evening. Sitting rooms with fireplaces, backyard picnic tables, glassed-in porch with mountain views, deck overlooking woods. Kitchen privileges and baby-sitting available.
Rates: Singles $22–$30 with shared bath, $28–$45 private; doubles $27–$30 shared bath, $35–$45 private. All major credit cards accepted.

. . . A family-owned inn that makes you feel a part of the family if you wish, and at the same time doesn't smother you if you feel like being very private. Tremendous sensitivity to individual preference.
Howard W. Long, Okemos, Michigan

LOUDON

Pineapple Hospitality Host #NH 510

Location: A rural setting high on a hill, ten minutes from Shaker Village in Concord, N.H.; an hour from mountains and ocean.
Reservations: Available year round except spring mud season through Pineapple Hospitality, page 170.

The copper tub with a tin wash and the original wood paneling are the big hits here. In addition there is New England hospitality together with oral history that starts this way, "The land was bought in English pounds by my great-great-great-grandfather in 1782. His son, my great-great-grandfather, came here with his bride in 1824." The hostess entered the picture in 1963 when she came for the summer. "And I'm still here. We always seem to be in the process of restoring. I feel I'm taking care of an elderly relative. I love it dearly." The picture-postcard property has provided the inspiration for gardening pursuits; birding; and just recently, basketmaking. The host is in the field of two-way radio communications and is a volunteer fireman.

While working at the New Hampshire Historical Society the hostess discovered that tourists were looking for personalized accommodations. Both her great-grandmother and her grandmother had had paying guests in the "continuous architecture" farmhouse. Since the fall of 1982 B&B travelers — antiquers, day trippers, and those en route north or south — have found that this is an experience, a great place to unwind.

In residence: Nonsmokers, three dogs, two cats, and sometimes one or two grown children home from school.
Restrictions: Nonsmokers preferred. Well-behaved children are welcome.
Bed: Four rooms. Two with double beds, one single adjoining a double. Two guest baths. A guest area with private entrance has sitting room, room with two twin beds, and a room with a double bed and ¾ (no tub) bath. Cot and portacrib available.
Breakfast: Available 5 a.m. on (really!). Full. Possibilities include French toast or pancakes served with local maple syrup. Homemade bread.
Plus: Beverage, crackers, fruit in late afternoon or evening. Screened porch, badminton, croquet, fields and woodlands for walking and birding. Canoe available for use in pond two miles down the road; swimming there too.

Rates: $27 single, $32 for two. Cot or crib $5.

Comfortably restored ancestral home . . . unique hilltop view. . . . The history surrounding the house and furnishings within were extremely interesting. . . . Prior to our arrival we requested that a birthday cake be ordered. It was there and all joined in the celebration!

Carolyn A. Jackson, Spring, Texas

LYME

Loch Lyme Lodge

RFD 278, Route 10, Lyme, NH 03768
Phone: 603/795-2141
Location: On Route 10, one mile north of the village of Lyme, on Post Pond — a spring-fed lake surrounded by hills. Eleven miles from Dartmouth College, four miles from Dartmouth Skiway.
Hosts: Paul and Judy Barker
Open: As a bed-and-breakfast establishment from mid-September until mid-May. Closed Thanksgiving and Christmas Day. Advance reservations appreciated.

"After being here a few days one memorable guest commented, 'You really live life in the slow lane up here.' We thought that was a great compliment."

In 1784 Loch Lyme was a farmhouse. Over the years it slowly grew and sprawled, until in 1923 it became part of a boys' camp and a lodging place for campers' parents and tourists too. It was being run strictly as a summer resort by Judy's parents when, in 1977, Judy, a real Lyme native, and Paul, originally from New York State, decided to leave their teaching careers and offer B&B in other than summer months.

"Immediately after Labor Day we close the cabins, move all the tables and chairs out of the dining rooms (which become our living room and piano room), move from the barn (the location of our summer apartment) into the Lodge, and reopen as a bed and breakfast.

"We really enjoy both of our seasons. In the fall and winter it is a much quieter way of life. Family members or local friends stop by. We have more time to spend with our guests and enjoy the chance to go skiing with them.

"Hopefully some day we'll be filled with antiques. For now guests are comfortable with our family furniture."

In residence: Jon Paul (J.P.), age two. Paul smokes a pipe. And Willie is the name of their cat.

Restrictions: No guests' pets. Smoking is not generally encouraged.

Foreign languages spoken: Paul speaks Spanish. Judy speaks a little French.

Bed: Four rooms. Three rooms have two twin beds each. One has a double. Cots available. Shared guest baths.

Breakfast: Full country breakfast. Leisurely meal, served 8–9 (or anytime if notice given previous night) family style on sun porch. Busy birdfeeder in view.

Plus: Living room with fireplace. Piano room. One hundred acres of woodlands, fields, and lake shore. Skating and night cross-country-skiing possibilities. Informal cross-country lessons and tours available; equipment rentals can be arranged with advance notice. Beverage (cider in fall) in late afternoon or evening. Baby-sitting possibilities.

Rates: $18 per person. $11 ages 8–12, $6 ages 7 and under. Cots $6–$10.

Comfortable quiet accommodations in a homelike lodge beautifully situated. Best of all is the friendly hospitality of the Barkers.

Doug and Karen Rumble, Chevy Chase, Maryland

Once discovered, Loch Lyme Lodge is a place people go back to year after year. We are no exception.   The Freemans, Brooklyn, New York

OSSIPEE

New Hampshire Bed and Breakfast Host #1

Location: On a quiet dirt road with no visible neighbors. Ten miles to Whittier, Moose, and Ossipee Mountains. Nine miles to Lake Winnipesaukee, 25 miles to North Conway.

Reservations: Available year round through New Hampshire Bed and Breakfast, page 110.

"We have been restoring this center-entrance colonial for a long time. The house had seen 50 years of neglect by the time we bought it. It has taken us 20 years to get this far. With much more to do, we love it!"

The land, first settled in 1786, became by 1820 one of the largest farms in the area. What was the hosts' summer residence became their year-round "simple, quiet and peaceful country place" in 1978. They have made it into a working farm once again, with sheep, turkeys, pigs, hens, and a small herd of beef cattle. The house has the original Indian shutters in the dining room, six fireplaces, some antique furnishings, and a warm atmosphere. Their hosting style? "We think people need a little pampering." And that means fresh flowers in the rooms, mints on the pillow, coffee in your room before breakfast if you would like — attention to detail.

In residence: One cigar smoker. Two cats. One dog.

Restrictions: Children should be at least 10 years old. Small pets only please. Smoking on first floor only.

Bed: One large double-bedded room (together with a small single on request).

Breakfast: Fresh fruit from local growers. Own pork products smoked without nitrates or preservatives. Own farm eggs, homemade jams, bread, and muffins. "More if you wish." Served anytime in dining room or garden.

Plus: Sitting room, television, porch, garden.

Rates: $45. $15 for single, available only with double.

Our bed was turned down for us — comfy and warm. Cream sherry was on our table. The breakfast of homegrown bacon, sausage, and eggs — also superb. The hosts — very outgoing and helpful.

Jack and Mitzi Hill, Holliston, Massachusetts

PORTSMOUTH

Portsmouth has become once again a thriving city on the Piscataqua River. There is much to do and see: Strawbery Banke, a historic waterfront neighborhood and museum, is preserving one of the nation's oldest urban sites. . . . Prescott Park has a full summer festival of performances. . . . Shops, antiques, and crafts are in the old harbor area. . . . There's a professional resident theater company. . . . Many historic houses are open to the public. . . . Walking tours are offered. . . . Harbor trips are regularly scheduled. . . . And the list of more than 50 restaurants includes many outstanding ones.

PORTSMOUTH

The Inn at Strawberry Banke

314 Court Street, Portsmouth, NH 02801
Phone: 603/436-7242
Location: In historic district, within walking distance of downtown, restaurants, shops, Prescott Park.
Hosts: Mark and Kerrianne Constant
Open: Year round.

A young couple, still in their twenties, stayed at a guest house on Nantucket and mused about duplicating the setup back in Portsmouth. They returned home on a Wednesday, saw this 1790 colonial on Friday, and had their offer accepted that Sunday! The house had been rental property for 10 years. Most of the work to be done was cosmetic — refinishing hardwood and pine floors, papering, and painting.

They opened in the fall of 1981 with comfortable mix-and-match furnishings — some colonial reproductions, some antiques. Rugs are hooked and Oriental. If a floor creaks that's considered part of the charm by guests who have come to sense a bygone era. An artist friend's paintings are on display and for sale. Fresh flowers in the rooms are in porcelain vases that are made by another friend and also for sale.

Mark and Kerrianne juggle their time and tasks. He works in a restaurant. She is a part-time fund-raiser/public-relations person. As this book was going to press, they were expecting their first child. Their property abuts Strawberry Banke (no official connection) and the Governor Langdon Memorial.

In residence: Two dogs — Kemo, a husky, and Maggi, a collie.
Restrictions: No guests' pets.
Bed: Four rooms, all with double beds. Two shared guest baths. Cots available.
Breakfast: Continental with homemade bakery.
Plus: Air conditioner and gas heater in each bedroom. Sherry in the sitting room. Small secluded yard and garden with wrought-iron furniture overlooking the rose trellises of restored property. Bicycles ($5 per day) available.
Rates: $35 single, $40 for two. Cot $5. MasterCard and VISA accepted.

PORTSMOUTH

The Inn at Christian Shore

335 Maplewood Avenue, Portsmouth, NH 03801 Mailing address: P.O. Box 1474, Portsmouth, NH 03801
Phone: 603/431-6770
Location: On a main street, a 10-minute walk or 2-minute drive to downtown and harbor area, 20-minute drive to Ogunquit (Maine) beaches.
Hosts: Charles Litchfield, Louis Sochia, Thomas Towey
Open: Year round. Confirmed advance reservations required.

Although you may come here just to enjoy the ambiance of a restored Federal house that was built around 1800 as the home of a sea captain, you may become a house-restoration buff on the spot. The three owners, former antique dealers — and before that they wore separate hats of electronics supervisor, accountant, and credit manager — have restored five other homes, but this is the first they have opened as a B&B (1977). If you are interested (and it's hard to spend time in Portsmouth and not be), they have before-and-after pictures and fascinating sagas to relate about additions, now removed, that had been built without foundations; about hidden fireplaces and wainscoting; and about a removed, but now replaced, back staircase. At one time the house was a candy store and at another a two-family residence.

The inn has been furnished with antiques, reproductions, and decorative accessories of the period.

In residence: Agatha and Muffins, the cats. Boston and Clover are two rabbits that live in an outside pen but are "brought inside if a guest is curious."
Restrictions: Children should be at least 10 years old.
Bed: Five rooms. Each has air conditioning, color TV, and wall-to-wall carpeting. Single, twin-bedded, and double-bedded rooms available.
Breakfast: Served 8–9, earlier if requested beforehand. Full and attractive. Fruit juice, fruit cup, eggs, meat, home fries, vegetable, homemade sweet breads, homemade jams. Served in a tavernlike room with beamed ceiling, huge fireplace, and Windsor chairs.
Plus: Wine in late afternoon or evening.
Rates: $25 single, $40–$45 for two. Additional person in room $10 extra. MasterCard and VISA accepted.

RINDGE

The Tokfarm Inn

Wood Avenue, Box 229, Rindge, NH 03461
Phone: 603/899-6646
Location: On a dirt road, 5 miles from Rindge village and Cathedral of the Pines, 5/8 mile from Route 119, 10 miles from Fitzwilliam.
Host: Mrs. Ev Nottingham
Open: April–November. Reservations preferred. Minimum stay in foliage season is two days.

"The most noise here is the chirping of birds in the morning and/or the wind in the trees when it's windy."

It's a 150-year-old farmhouse originally built as a private home, extended over the years to a 23-room inn on the Boston-to-Keene stagecoach road. The Nottinghams bought it as a summer place 30 years ago. In addition to being a B&B now, it is an active tree farm. If guests are in the mood, there are opportunities to plant Christmas trees (in May) or to prune them (anytime). There's a tri-state (Vermont, Massachusetts, New Hampshire) view from the site, a great vantage point for watching sunsets or, on moonlit nights, fireflies.

Mrs. Nottingham has a background filled with zest and diversity. Born in Holland and educated in Canada, she had a career in New York City and was one of the first ten women to receive an MBA (when most schools wouldn't take "girls"); and she has hosted a radio program in Dutch. She and her husband ran a ski lodge in Stowe, Vermont, for 10 years. At times she can be talked into showing slides and home movies of the exotic and not-so-exotic places she has been to.

Outdoor activities, sightseeing, and antiquing possibilities are boundless in this area.

In residence: One cat, "The Plumber."
Restrictions: No children. No pets. No smoking.
Foreign languages spoken: German, Dutch, French, Spanish.
Bed: Six rooms. One with king-sized bed, two with two twin beds, two doubles, and one single. All share two baths.
Breakfast: In farm kitchen, 8–9 a.m. Continental, native honey included.
Plus: The 100-acre tree farm with woodland trails for hiking, natural spring-fed pond for swimming.

Rates: $15 single, $28 twin beds, $25 double bed, $27 king.

I found Tokfarm to be very interesting with a casual atmosphere, comfortable and clean accommodations.   R.H., Cambridge, Massachusetts

RYE

Rock Ledge Manor — Bed and Breakfast

1413 Ocean Boulevard, Rye, NH 03870
Phone: 603/431-1413
Location: Right on the ocean. About a 10-minute drive to Portsmouth and within a half hour of York or Ogunquit, Maine.
Hosts: Janice and Norman Marineau
Open: Year round. Reservations recommended.

The Marineaus have just celebrated their first anniversary as B&B hosts. What they have is a prime location (many guests walk the coastline before the memorable breakfast) and a marvelous home that was part of an old "gingerbread" resort colony built around 1880. Janice and Norman have been New Hampshire-based apartment-house owners and caterers with personal interests in the arts, running, and racquetball. Now most of their energy goes toward making this property the landmark it once was. As travelers they recognized the importance of the hosts' role, so their natural instincts have created a friendly relaxed atmosphere.

Restrictions: Children should be at least 10 years old. No smoking permitted in breakfast room.
Bed: Four double-bedded rooms, each with a private bath and an ocean view. Cots available.
Breakfast: Served 8–10:30 in mahogany-ceilinged room that overlooks the ocean. Full brunchlike menu could include crêpes, meats, vegetables. Table set with linens.
Plus: Air conditioning and paddle fans. Sunbathing areas on property. Minutes' walk to two beaches. Porch; library; music room (when redecorated) too. All-day parking even after check-out.
Rates: Mid-May through mid-October $37.50–$45 single, $45–$50 double. Off-season about $10 less.

SUGAR HILL

Southworth's Bed & Breakfast

Main Street, Sugar Hill, NH 03585
Phone: 603/823-5344
Location: On Route 117, across from Town Meeting House. Close (15 minutes) to Cannon and Loon Mountains, Bretton Woods. About three miles from Franconia.
Hosts: Amy and David, Judy and Bruce
Open: Year round. Advance reservations preferred.

You are likely to meet several Southworths, but for now Amy and David are the main hosts, establishing the B&B "as a very relaxed operation." The location is so convenient that guests from all over the country and the world have stayed a day or two while trying to "take in all of New England." In the winter, skiers find it central enough for trying various slopes.

Since opening in August 1981 the Southworths have redecorated the traditional two-story house, achieving a country look with antiques and older furniture. This is definitely a family effort. The senior Southworths (Judy and Bruce) may be around, or another son, Robert, may take over on occasion. Amy, formerly a floral designer, is the official greeter. David, a builder when he was in Pennsylvania, now has his own maintenance business.

In residence: Two dogs — Shamu's Shadow, mixed black, age one, and Choo Choo, a Shih Tzu, white, age two.
Restrictions: Children allowed but not encouraged.
Bed: Three rooms. One with twin beds, two with brass double beds.
Breakfast: Continental, at 7:30 or 8:30. Usually includes homemade coffee cake. Used to be served in dining room, but moved to big homey kitchen at guests' requests.
Plus: TV room with backgammon and chess, beverage in late afternoon or evening.
Rate: $30 double occupancy.

Hosts were most cordial . . . well informed about places of interest in the area. Their lovely home was spotless and full of interesting antiques. . . . Having "bed & breakfasted" our way around England several times, we're happy to see the concept catching on in the U.S. Southworth's is doing its part to uphold the tradition.

Barry and Sally Dorn, Richardson, Texas

VERMONT

VERMONT

CANADA

10

15

8

9 13   23   5

VERMONT

1

24   2

• Middlebury

22   3   20   19

18

21   14   27

• White River Junction

4

6

17

7   25

NEW HAMPSHIRE

• Manchester Center   11

16

26

12 • Brattleboro

N

NEW YORK

MASSACHUSETTS

The numbers on this map indicate the locations of B&Bs described in detail in this chapter.

VERMONT

VERMONT

Reservation Services

American Bed & Breakfast in New England

Box 983, St. Albans, VT 05478
Established June 1980
Listed: About 50. Although most listings are in Vermont, several are in other New England states.

Bob Precoda, a former Peace Corpsman, likes the people-to-people concept of B&B. He started by just knocking on rural doors in Vermont. Now his selected people-oriented hosts are listed in a directory ($3) that includes names, addresses, and phone numbers. *Guests book directly with the hosts.* About 2/3 of Vermont hosts have signs in front of their homes; they may be the only private home B&B signs in America.
Rates: Singles $18–$25, doubles $24–$35.

Pineapple Hospitality

This service has hosts in Bellows Falls, Bethel, Burlington area, Dorset, Pawlet, Stowe, Waitsfield, and Woodstock. Please see page 170.

*

Some of the reservation and referral services with listings in many states throughout the country, pages 26-29, have a few hosts in Vermont.

B&Bs

BARNET

Old Homestead Inn

P.O. Box 35, Barnet, VT 05821
Phone: 802/633-4100
Location: On Route 5 in picturesque village, with views of Connecticut River and mountains of New Hampshire; 25 miles from Burke Mountain ski area.
Hosts: Robert and Mary Gordon
Member: American Bed & Breakfast in New England, page 132.
Open: Year round.

In what is considered the most remote — and perhaps the most beautiful — countryside in the state, is a home that greets B&B vacationers who seem to come principally for the countryside. Hikers, experienced bicyclists (it is *very* hilly), and photographers appreciate the peace and quiet. The 100-year-old colonial inn has been home to the Gordons since the summer of 1980. Robert is a retired postal worker and Mary paints in oils.

In residence: One son. One family member who smokes. Three dogs — Buffy, part collie; Schatze, a Gordon setter (Scottish); Kelly, German shepherd. Three cats — Smoky, Snowball, and Lucky.
Restrictions: No guests' pets.
Bed: Five rooms. Two doubles have private baths. Two singles and one double share a guest bath. Two cots and one crib available.
Breakfast: Continental, 7:30–10.
Rates: $18–$25 single, $29 double.

BARRE

Woodruff House

13 East Street, Barre, VT 05641
Phone: 802/476-7745
Location: Near the center of the city, on a quiet park. Near the state capital (Montpelier) and the largest granite quarries in the world. In ski country.
Hosts: Robert and Terry Somaini
Member: American Bed & Breakfast in New England, page 132.
Open: Year round. Advance reservations essential during foliage season.

Woodruff House is a delightful echo from a gentle past, presided over by a jovial and gracious host. Bob Somaini is as fascinating as his surroundings. An evening's conversation with this young squire, fueled by his homemade bread, cheese, fruit, and his own blend of teas was the highlight of a memorable fall weekend in Vermont.
Dr. and Mrs. D.F.S. Crowther, Portland, Connecticut

"Our home is an 1883 Victorian, blueberry with vanilla trim and cranberry shutters, filled with antiques of all styles. It is warm, cozy, a bit Edwardian. Our eclectic collection is ever changing and being added to. Must be experienced to appreciate fully."

Robert, a native Vermonter, is an interior consultant and in sales work. Terry is a teacher at a Christian School.

In residence: Katie, age eight.
Restrictions: No pets allowed. No smoking.
Bed: Two rooms, each with a double bed. One shared guest bath.
Breakfast: At 8 (sharp) weekdays, 9 on weekends. Menu varies from simple to fancy. Cooked and served by Robert in one of two dining rooms filled with antiques.
Plus: Three living rooms, shelves of books, piano, television, radio. Quiet times by the fire. Beverage and dessert often served in the evening.
Rates: $22 single, $30 for two.

BRANDON

Stone Mill Farm

P.O. Box 203, Brandon, VT 05733
Phone: 802/247-6137
Location: One mile from village, off Route 73, over the bridge, up the lane to total seclusion. Five miles from the Long Trail.
Hosts: Eileen and Charles Roeder
Member: American Bed & Breakfast in New England, page 132.
Open: Year round. Advance reservations preferred.

When Salmon Farr built the farmhouse in 1786, so the story goes, he painted it black and orange because his wife and daughter couldn't agree on what color it should be. Now it is white and home to two former antique dealers (and their teenagers) who came here just three years ago from New Jersey. Restoration "to the charm of the old with amenities of the new" is complete with antique colonial furnishings.

In two years of hosting they have had a wide range of guests. Some prefer to be alone and some like to sit on the doorsteps and help shell peas. "One family from Connecticut visits with us twice yearly. Their four-year-old invariably forgets to close the barnyard gate and has to share the pool with our ducks and goose."

The Roeders raise all their own produce and meats.

In residence: Patrick, age 17. Aimee, age 15. Some family members smoke. On the farm — ducks, chickens, beef cattle, geese, pigs.
Restrictions: "Considerate pets only please."
Bed: Three rooms in a separate ell with their own ground-level entry. One with double bed; one with double bed, woodburning stove, and glass door; one room with a double and a single bed. Cot available.
Breakfast: At guests' convenience. Continental featuring Charles' cast-iron-baked cornsticks and homemade jellies and jams. Served in dining room furnished with country antiques in winter; on porch in summer, overlooking barns and dooryard.
Plus: Tour of house. Bowl of fruit in room. In-ground swimming pool. Common room in guest wing. Baby-sitting. Opportunities to help feed, or watch the care of, stock. Gather berries (in season) and eggs. Walk on logging trail to third tee of Neshobe Golf Course.
Rates: $18 single, $28 double. $35 for double and single in same room. Cot $7.

BROWNSVILLE

Bed & Breakfast Brookside

Brownsville, VT 05037
Phone: 802/484-5072
Location: On Route 44, three miles from the village on wooded property. Near Dartmouth College; no more than 20 minutes from all major central Vermont ski areas.
Host: P. Gavin Wenz
Open: Year round.

The setting and B&B experience inspired one New York City guest to write a poem that begins this way —

by a green sprinkled window
runs a snow covered stream
through an ice frozen woods
from a brass laden dream

in a hundred year corner
sits a spinning wheel still
with the threads bare to run it
on a pictured window sill

on a trunk full of toys
that once danced with delight
rests on bath water basin
that still warms every night

R.S., New York, New York

With her architecture and interior-design background, Pat, a New Jersey resident until 1973, had a grand time converting the 150-year-old peaked-roof Vermont horsebarn ("it looked like a garage with a big drop in back where the horses had been kept") into a wonderfully cozy seven-room, two-bath house. Furnishings combine lovely antiques with contemporary pieces.

"The Country Mouse" sometimes answers the phone. In the last couple of years the hostess has established a business that does everything from catering to house sitting, from house cleaning to plant and pet care.

In residence: Nonsmokers.
Restrictions: No pets. No children.

Foreign languages spoken: Greek, German, French.
Bed: Two rooms, each with a double bed, telephone, and television. Two open loft rooms, each with a single bed. Two shared baths. A separate entrance by a spiral staircase leads to the lower-level double room with a ceiling-to-floor slate fireplace. The other double room has an antique brass bed and bay window overlooking brook. The two loft rooms are completely furnished and quite charming.
Breakfast: Available 7–9. Continental. Served beautifully in beamed, cathedral-ceilinged kitchen/dining area with fine china and pewter coffee service.
Plus: Many books and magazines. Deck and patio. Hiking trails. Man-made pond, probably about five feet deep at the most, for some swimming. The historic Mill Brook flows behind the house and is reputed to be the best trout stream in the state.
Rates: $35 for two. $20 for one in loft room.

CRAFTSBURY

Gary-Meadows Dairy Farm

RR1, Craftsbury, VT 05826
Phone: 802/586-2536
Location: Off the beaten path, 500 feet off Route 14, two miles from picture-book Craftsbury Common, one mile from Craftsbury village. Pick-up and delivery ($5 each way) to and from bus station in Morrisville, 17 miles away.
Hosts: Gary and Nioka Houston
Member: American Bed & Breakfast in New England, page 132.
Open: April, if warm. May – October.

This was our very first American B&B. The style was European. After calling from the village store for directions we pulled up to the 1884 Cape Cod–style farmhouse on an unpaved road and were greeted by hundreds of cows, dozens of calves, and a real B&B sign on a post. We wondered what country we were in!

Nicki is a cheerful ex-teacher (now a substitute) who seems to be doing three things — successfully — at once. She feeds the calves before you get up, and she has probably fed her three young children by then too. Seven-year-old Megan joined us in the country kitchen for our morning meal, a time when we heard about the changes in farming. It's a computerized business now. Gary started with 12 holsteins. Of today's 700, half are milkers. In the last dozen years Nicki has changed too. She'll tell you how she "helped" during her first visit with Gary's family: she let the cows out all right, but quickly learned that she had, unknowingly, also released the bull.

And we learned a little about the community from various perspectives. Nicki is involved with the local dramatic group. "It's always a sellout." Gary, originally trained as a mechanical engineer, is a member of the local school committee.

In residence: Megan, age seven; Joseph, five; Jesse, two. Gary's mother stops by frequently. Nicki commented, "She's a terrific woman who travels a lot and I draw on her mind." No one in the house smokes (but smoking is allowed).
Restrictions: No pets.
Bed: One large room with a double bed. Refinished wide pine floorboards, attractively arranged Shaker pieces, and a bed covered with a glorious starburst-pattern quilt made and sold locally. The "information shelf" includes all you need to know about attractions in the area plus some news clippings on how to resist the temptation to sell the farm.
Breakfast: Available 6:30–11:30. Full country breakfast with wide variety served in country kitchen or on sun porch. This time, Nicki's favorite part of the day, is "my payoff, my reward, for all the housecleaning I do before guests arrive."
Plus: Beverage in late afternoon or evening. Electric blanket. Black-and-white television. Kitchen privileges. Baby-sitting ($1 per hour per child). Use of iron, hair dryer, gas grille, lawn chairs, sandbox, even lawn mower, if you'd like! Complete farm tour — barns, cows, manure, equipment, milking being done. And hints on cycling routes (beautiful and hilly).
Rates: $24 single, $28 for two. Cot or crib $5.

Their house was very comfortable and the food excellent, but also they were a very interesting and stimulating couple and for a short time we felt part of the neighborhood. Our children enjoyed meeting American children, not to mention playing with their toys!

J. and A. Alexander, Dynnyrne, Tasmania, Australia

CUTTINGSVILLE

Maple Crest Farm

Box 120, Cuttingsville, VT 05738
Phone: 802/492-3367
Location: Near Rutland on main road in town of Shrewsbury. Farm setting with marvelous views. Near Killington and Okemo ski areas.
Hosts: Donna and Bill Smith
Open: Year round. Two-night minimum reservation.

Guests comment about "true Vermont hospitality" or "a step into the past." Bill is the fifth generation to live and farm here. Except for the first 20 years, when it was run as a tavern, this 1808 landmark has been a private home with each generation having guests on a small scale. The major activities are dairy farming and sugar making. The traditional furnishings and personal treasures reflect Smith activities and their lifestyle through the years.

"We wish to share our Vermont way of life with others. Guests are part of the family and this is their home away from home. This is the way B&B started. If I have to be commercial, I don't want to stay in B&B." Donna's interests go beyond the farm. She serves as town treasurer and is a bank director.

In residence: Grandfather, and 17- and 22-year-old sons. Charlie is the cat and K-C is a Labrador retriever.
Restrictions: No guests' pets.
Bed: Four large rooms, some with wood stoves. Three on second floor with a double and a single in each. One room with a double bed and half bath on first floor. One full shared guest bath. Cot and crib available.
Breakfast: Full country meal with bacon and eggs, pancakes with maple syrup. Served 8–9:30 in kitchen or dining room.
Plus: Flowers in season. Beverage in late afternoon or evening. Tours of farm and maple sugaring operation. Cross-country skiing and hiking right here.
Rates: $15 single, $25 for two, $30 for three in a room. Cot or crib $5.

DORSET

The Little Lodge at Dorset

Route 30, Dorset, VT 05251
Phone: 802/867-4040
Location: On a hillside facing Spruce Peak. It's on a "rather quiet main road," a block from village green. Not far from craft and antique shops, summer theater, concerts; 20 minutes to Bromley, 30 minutes to Stratton.
Hosts: Allan and Nancy Norris
Open: Year round, except for part of November and April. Advance reservations preferred.

The Little Lodge was created by adding the personal charm of Allan and Nancy Norris to a warm, clean, and comfortable private home. Conveniently located across the street from one of New England's oldest golf courses, and adjacent to hiking and cross-country ski trails, it even has a small pond for winter ice skating. Most importantly, our children, aged five and seven, felt so "at home" during our stay that they asked us to bring dinner back to enjoy in front of the fireplace in the spacious den rather than go out to eat.

Sandy and Jim Wilbur, Plainfield, New Jersey

Restoration had taken place when the Norrises bought the private home in 1981. The original part, c. 1810–20, was moved here in the 1930s from Hebron, New York. Two additions were subsequently made. Now it's filled with antiques, and hosted by a couple who moved here from Baltimore, Maryland. Allan, formerly a wholesaler, was ready for a change in occupation. Nancy had had years of active volunteer work and motherhood. "This is something we had considered doing when our children were all out of high school, which is when we did it." After reading guests' testimonials about "the friendliness of proprietors who have the perfect spot for a vacation," and after listening to the enthusiasm of the hosts, I can believe that the midlife career change was the right choice.

In residence: College daughter in summer and during holidays. And "one fantastically friendly Doberman named Trillium, after the wildflower, whom everyone, even if they come here afraid of dogs, adores."
Restrictions: Pets not usually allowed.
Foreign languages spoken: Some French and Spanish.
Bed: Five rooms, three with private baths, two with shared. Each room

has two twin beds that can be made up as kings. Cots and crib available.
Breakfast: Served 8–9:30. Juice, cereals, homemade breads, muffins, and beverage. Both Allan and Nancy cook and serve in the dining room or on screened porch.
Plus: The barnboard den has picture window looking out on trout pond and mountains. Refrigerator and wet bar (BYOB) for guests. Dartboard, books, puzzles. Living room with wood stove, stenciled wallpaper, wide board floor, and braided rug. Beverage and cheese and crackers usually served in late afternoon. Terrace and lawn chairs in summer. Wildflowers around outside, lovely arrangements inside. Barn, complete with horse stall, used for storing bikes and skis.
Rates: $35–$40 for two with shared bath. $45–$50 with private bath. $12 for third person in room. American Express cards accepted, preferably for deposit only.

EAST BURKE

Blue Wax Farm

Pinkham Road, East Burke, VT 05832
Phone: 802/626-5542
Location: On 326 acres adjoining Burke Mountain ski area, 2.5 miles from small village and Route 114. Not far from Lyndon State College. Wonderful views.
Hosts: Kenneth and Ingrid Parr
Open: Year round. Advance reservations preferred.

Since the Parrs "retired" in 1970, they have just about completely redone the 1862 farmhouse. They began taking overflow guests from a nearby inn in 1981 and enjoy providing "friendly comfort on a lightly traveled road" to "skiers, hikers (lazy and aggressive), bicyclists, sightseers, and people who 'wind down'."

Many items in the house reflect 17 years of overseas living in the Middle East and South America. The hosts have been in educational and personnel work for institutions and corporations in several states and many countries.

The grandparents (of grown grandchildren) are quite occupied with their large experimental orchard that has about 150 kinds of apples, other fruits, and berries. And then there's always woodcutting and the lawn.

In residence: "Man, our aging dog, loves children and people in general — and loves to wander away." The Parrs do not smoke, but smoking is allowed.
Restrictions: No guests' pets.
Foreign languages spoken: Spanish, Finnish, and some French and Arabic.
Bed: Three rooms. Two with twin beds, one double. Two guest baths. Crib available.
Breakfast: Continental.
Plus: Piano, lots of books, open fireplace in large living room. "Ubiquitous TV." A large collection of classical and other music for hi-fi. Cross-country skiing right here. Collection of area information; restaurant menus and their own "anonymous confidential" ratings. Outdoor sauna; robes furnished. Maybe an arborist's tour for tree identification with Ken as leader.
Rates: $12 per person per night. Crib $3.

A very comfortable, relaxing stay in a quiet but beautifully scenic area. . . . Good food, lively conversation, and genuinely warm hosts provide a delightful, homey atmosphere. Once discovered, return visits are sure to follow.   C.W.B., Smithfield, Rhode Island

ESSEX JUNCTION

Pineapple Hospitality Host #VT 608

Location: About six miles from Burlington, two miles from village.
Reservations: Available year round through Pineapple Hospitality, page 170.

Two years ago this energetic family bought a builder's field house, did it all over inside, and landscaped the outside. They are very involved in camping and outdoor activities.

In residence: One son, age 8, and one daughter, age 11. Two cats.
Restrictions: No smoking. No guests' pets.
Bed: One room with twin beds. Cot and crib available.
Breakfast: Continental. Available 7–9.
Plus: Picnic table. Enclosed patio.
Rates: $27 single, $32 for two. Crib or cot $5.

My visit to Burlington was enhanced by staying with a friendly family in a lovely neighborhood. Our every need was met. Our room was on a lower level and apart from the family bustle. The whole house was clean and well ordered.   C.H.B., Brookline, Massachusetts

ESSEX JUNCTION

Varnum's

143 Weed Road, Essex Junction, VT 05452
Phone: 802/899-4577
Location: Just off Route 15. Twelve miles from Burlington. On 10 acres overlooking mountains.
Hosts: Todd and Sheila Varnum
Open: Year round. Advance reservations preferred.

When Sheila, a professional cook, and Todd, an engineer, transferred here from New York state three years ago, they were true newcomers. But they are doing their darnedest to become immersed in Vermont life. While tracing the history of their home — a 1792 cedarshake farmhouse "lovingly renovated" — they learned from a neighbor that way back when it was a stagecoach stop.

Bartering is a way of life here and Sheila knows how to do that. She plans to apprentice with a neighbor who has 18,000 taps for sugaring. She's into crafts and needlework, and is learning how to play the piano. Through the hosts' membership in a folk coop, they can lead guests to great music and dancing.

B&B links all their interests. Already returnees request the same room or a repeat menu.

Sheila works cooperatively with Sue Eaton, page 148, through their new referral organization, Vermont Bed & Breakfast.

In residence: Sammy, a Labrador retriever, and Cherpy, the cat.
Restrictions: No guests' pets. No smoking. Not really an ideal place for active children.
Bed: Two rooms, both freshly decorated. One with pine double bed. One with brass-and-iron double bed. One shared guest half bath plus solar shower located in hot-tub room with plants.
Breakfast: At guests' convenience. Continental, Vermont style. Good food! Leisurely. Served on patio (summer), or in country kitchen (winter) with view of Mt. Mansfield. Sheila usually joins you for coffee.

Plus: Beverage — maybe cider or hot chocolate — in late afternoon or evening. Usually fruit in rooms. Living room that faces mountains. A reference library of all local attractions including folk and classical concerts and theater. Turned-down beds at night, cookies on the pillow.
Rates: $25 single, $30 for two.

We thoroughly enjoyed the quaintness of the surroundings. . . . Beautiful and exceptionally fine accommodations. The little extras were apparent. . . . The host and hostess displayed a definite interest in their guests and added to the comfort of our visit.
Howard and Helen Norris, Kenosha, Wisconsin

Four of us arrived quite late on a snowy evening. . . . welcomed, shown around . . . invited to visit around the wood stove with our hosts. It was a delightful stay in a cozy, warm atmosphere. . . . Delicious breakfast served and shared with our hosts — now our new friends.
Mr. and Mrs. J.H.P., Red Bank, New Jersey

Even under the circumstances of a loss of electricity Sheila arranged for everything to run smoothly.   E.M.A., Laguna Hills, California

FRANKLIN

Fair Meadows

Route 235, Franklin, VT 05457
Phone: 802/285-2132
Location: In the land of "big sky," minutes from the Canadian border, 3 miles west of Franklin, 12 miles from I-89, 60 miles from Montreal.
Hosts: Terry and Phil Pierce
Member: American Bed & Breakfast in New England, page 132.
Open: Year round.

Fortunately the hills were too much for our planned cycling route! We had a further destination, but my legs decided that we would never make it. So the welcome B&B sign was in the right place at the right time. And it meant we met the Pierces.

Here we were, seemingly in the middle of nowhere, at a farm that had been in the family since 1853. On the hall wall was a mounted window frame with family pictures that told of the widespread younger generation. The five children, educated at five different colleges, are now in five different states. One has been in the Peace Corps. We met daughter Jane (then in banking, now in graduate school) home from New York City — enjoying Mom's blueberry pie.

Dad's sense of humor came through. And so did his perspective; he is concerned about the next generation's surviving or even establishing themselves in the dairy business. Hostess Terry offered some practical gardening advice and a new recipe for muffins.

The farmhouse was comfortable and immaculate. Flowers and views were everywhere. We left the next morning with renewed spirit and energy.

In residence: Maybe one son during the summer. Phil smokes. Two German shepherds. The farm has 95 cows.
Restrictions: Pets should be well behaved.
Foreign language spoken: French.
Bed: Four rooms, each with a double bed. One has a private half bath. One full bath shared by all. Two cribs available.
Breakfast: At guests' convenience. A real farm breakfast including homemade muffins and butter. Served in pine-paneled room off kitchen, overlooking meadow.
Plus: A large living room that has the one piece of furniture, a wicker-seated chair, that survived an 1896 fire. Television. Bicycles can be put in the barn.
Rates: $20 single, $26 for two.

While drawing in the Franklin landscape, my extended visit was enhanced by the genuine warmth of the Pierces. Their colorful plant-filled farmhouse is charming. Terry's expertise in baking and gardening and Phil's wise tales as a fifth-generation farmer fascinated me. Both, hard workers, still had time to treat guests as family members. H. Putnam, Somerville, Massachusetts

GRAFTON

The Hayes House

Grafton, VT 05146
Phone: 802/843-2461
Location: In the village, next door to an 1870 covered bridge. An easy and pleasant walk to village center. Not far from Grafton Village Cheese Company (visitors welcome), Grafton Historical Society Museum, an-

tique shops, printmaking workshop, ski shop and trail system, and country store.
Host: Margery Hayes Heindel
Open: May through March.

"I was a summer kid from Cambridge, Massachusetts, when this first became 'home.' I fell in love with my town then — and I'm still in love." Today Marge is chairman of the Board of Selectmen, but 20 of the in-between years were filled with 28 moves while she was wife of a naval officer and mother "of two great children."

The house, built in 1803, is "cluttered, clean, and welcoming. It's furnished with many Oriental things that fit in well with old pieces — including me!" Marge doesn't spend too much time on the front porch rockers. "I am a gardener (flowers and vegetables), and good cook, enjoy arranging flowers, knit, sew, do stitchery, read far too many books — and I'm grateful to my cleaning lady because I hate to vacuum." In addition she is a registered occupational therapist and Story Lady at the local library.

In residence: Chibi and Velva, two Chesapeake retrievers that give you a real welcome, and Polly and Tyl, two fuzzy double-pawed cats. Marge does not smoke, but smoking is permitted.
Restrictions: Dogs are the only guests' pets allowed.
Bed: Four rooms. One double on first floor with four-poster bed high enough to need the stool provided for climbing into it. Working fireplace and private bath. On second floor, one single, one with twin beds, and one double share one full guest bath (plus a half bath spring through fall).
Breakfast: Continental with homemade breads, muffins, jellies, and jams. Served 8–11, family style in dining room. Leisurely.
Plus: Fruit and cookies in rooms, flowers in season. Sound of babbling brook at night, if windows are open. "A new guest is always told to consider the house theirs while they are here. If I've got it, they can have/use it." Back porch overlooks vegetable garden and large meadow. Rockers on front porch. Kitchen privileges in winter months, a season when homemade soup is available, self-served, after 2 p.m. Suggestions for back road routes. Baby-sitting arranged with advance notice.
Rates: $25 single, $30 twin or double with shared bath, $40 double with private bath.

GUILFORD

Capt. Henry Chase House

Hinesburg Road, Guilford, VT Mailing address: RFD 4, Box 282, West Brattleboro, VT 05301
Phone: 802/254-4114
Location: About six miles from Brattleboro in an agricultural ("breathtaking") valley. Written directions are sent to guests.
Hosts: Pat and Lorraine Ryan and teenage daughter, Laura.
Open: Year round. Advance reservations preferred.

"It's the kind of place where few people seem to be in a hurry. Some linger. Some just jog along the road. Very few are on a schedule."

It's a bit of a treasure hunt to find the 185-year-old farmhouse, but guests frequently comment on the "lovely house, friendly people, and beautiful area." Explorers discover an old-fashioned watering hole, a covered bridge, and a waterfall dam.

The Ryans have lived here for four years. Pat is a telephone-company technician; Lorraine is a realtor. The family finds time to walk in the hills and fish in the river on the farm and to be active in both the historical society and church activities.

In residence: (all in the barn): Katy, Laura's horse. Gilly, the dog. Four cats. April and Emma, the goats. Chickens, ducks, and "whatever other creature may find a home in the barn at any given time."
Restrictions: No guests' pets. No smoking in bedrooms.
Bed: Two air-conditioned rooms, each with a double bed. One shared guest bath.
Breakfast: Vermont style complete with pancakes and maple syrup made from trees on the farm. Served in dining room with original hearth and cabinets.
Plus: Very large family living room with 10-foot hearth, beehive oven, cauldron that swings, wide floorboards. Private upstairs living room. Large screened summer room. Kitchen and laundry privileges. Evening refreshments. Baby-sitting possibilities.
Rates: $20 single, $30 for two.

JERICHO

Eatonhouse

Box 139, Browns Trace, Jericho, VT 05465
Phone: 802/899-2354
Location: On a quiet main road in a pastoral setting with mountain views. Three miles off I-89. Twenty minutes from Burlington. Eight miles from Sherman Hollow cross-country ski center. Forty-five minutes from Shelburne Museum.
Hosts: Sue and Dave Eaton
Open: Year round. Advance reservations preferred.

Shortly after being completed in 1978 this reproduction saltbox was on an Old House Tour! It was designed by one of the Eatons' sons when he was an architecture student. (The artwork of another son can be seen throughout the house.) Overall a cozy country feeling prevails, with wide board floors, open fireplaces in old brick, and colonial colors.

The family, grown now, spent their earlier years on a chicken farm in Maine. Sue was a practicing nurse. The farm had 20,000 layers — and four growing children. Here Dave is an agency manager for an insurance company. Sue works cooperatively with Sheila Varnum, page 142, through their new referral organization, Vermont Bed & Breakfast.

In residence: Jacyn, five-year-old kitty.
Restrictions: Sorry, no guests' pets. The Eatons do not smoke but smoking is allowed.
Bed: Two rooms, each with a double bed. One shared 3/4 guest bath. Cot available.
Breakfast: Available 7–9. Full with plenty of juice, homemade muffins, fruit cup, and an entrée that may be bacon or sausage with eggs, homemade waffles, frittata, or some exotic casserole. Served in dining area in front of fireplace and view of Adirondack Mountains.
Plus: Study/library with books and television. Laundry facilities available. Workbench for waxing skis. Two guest garage spaces (appreciated in winter months). Tour of house that has details such as square-headed nails, wrought-iron latches and hinges, paneling, chair rails, door curtains made from a 1770 bedspread, and a back stairway.
Rates: $20 single, $28 for two. Extra cot in room $5.

Everything is as neat as a pin. . . . Breakfasts made from scratch. . . . Eatonhouse is unique in the personal attention you get and the very

*real home atmosphere. It is our favorite B&B either in Britain or any-
where we have found so far in the States.*   S. and M. Talbot, Chicago, Illinois

*After a rigorous day of cross-country skiing at Sherman Hollow, the
Eatonhouse offers a relaxing taste of New England hospitality.*
Jack and Nancy Heiden, Madison, Wisconsin

KILLINGTON

Mountain Morgans

McClallen Drive, Box 138A, RD 1, Killington, VT 05751
Phone: 802/422-3096
Location: On Killington Mountain, a little off a main road, near
Killington ski area.
Hosts: Jeffrey and Susan Hiers
Member: American Bed & Breakfast in New England, page 132.
Open: Year round.

*Our stay at Mountain Morgans was certainly a "peak" experience. . . .
We had planned a vacation to include various sites in New England . . .
expected to stay with the Hiers for one night . . . warm and gracious
family . . . breakfast with fresh eggs from the barn. . . . Jeff's tour-
guiding skills were offered without hesitation as he outlined our itiner-
ary of Vermont sites that we mustn't miss. . . . With this homespun
service, pure New England hospitality, and beautiful, lush Vermont
countryside, we didn't care to leave. In fact, we stayed six days and
nights. This Killington location was a central location from which to
take leisurely day trips. We now feel we have friends whom we look
forward to visiting again sometime in the future.*
Julia L. Lavin, Baldwinsville, New York

The Hiers live in a duplex; the "other half," a fully equipped home,
is for B&B guests. Families are welcome and are particularly comfortable in the unusual arrangement.

Because Jeff has been an official tour guide in the area, he can direct
guests to museums, historic sites, outdoor activities, covered bridges,
and marble exhibits. Now he is pretty much full time at the farm except
for conducting sleigh rides in the winter or carriage rides for tourists in
the summer. Susan is a registered nurse with hours that allow her to be
around to "share the Vermont we love." The Hierses had been coming

from New Jersey to this part of Vermont for 13 years before they became full-time residents four years ago.

In residence: Joanna, age 6, and Lisa, 2 1/2. Two donkeys, sheep, a pony, two calves, two horses, rabbits, and chickens.
Restrictions: No guests' pets.
Bed: Two rooms, one with two twin beds and one with double bed. Cots available. One guest bath.
Breakfast: Provided by hosts. Prepared by guests in own kitchen. Juice, fresh farm eggs, English muffins, beverage.
Plus: Guest duplex has full kitchen, living room with fireplace and TV. Picnic table, barbecue. Swings for children. Lots of room for running. Horses to ride. Baby-sitting possibilities. Tours of Killington ski area by horseback, horse-drawn carriage, or car.
Rates: $20 single, $30 for two. No charge for children (if in same room).

MILTON

Hummel Haus

RD 2, Milton, VT 05468
Phone: 802/893-4667
Location: At Four Corners in small village 17 miles north of Burlington; close to Lake Champlain, Smugglers Notch, and Mount Mansfield.
Hosts: Jack and Ruth Hummel
Member: American Bed & Breakfast in New England, page 132.
Open: Year round.

Behind the tall maple trees and post-and-rail fence is the site of the first town meeting held in 1789. The house was originally a Burlington-to-Montreal stagecoach stop. Since the Hummels arrived 11 years ago they have restored the center-entrance colonial with its beamed ceilings and wide board floors "in a rather formal manner."

Jack is a meteorologist. Ruth is a former registered nurse. The family raises cattle here.

In residence: Daughter Betsy and son Jack, a high schooler. Ben, the dog, and Molly, the cat.
Restrictions: No guests' pets. No smoking.

Foreign language spoken: Betsy and Jack know some German.
Bed: Two rooms. One with twin beds, one double.
Breakfast: At guests' convenience. A full breakfast with a variety of homemade breads and muffins. Served in dining room.
Plus: Use of in-ground pool. Tour of house if you'd like. Cool beverage in late afternoon or evening during summer months.
Rates: $20 single, $30 for two.

The warmth and consideration of the Hummel family to our needs made us feel very much at home. Our room was very comfortable and spotless and our breakfast appetizing and bountiful. We feel we have made great friends. Bess and Gil Albert, Fairfield, Connecticut

NEWFANE

Hobby Hill

Newfane, VT 05345
Phone: 802/365-4038
Location: Four miles from Newfane. Two miles off a blacktopped road, uphill on a dirt road that is plowed eventually in the winter.
Hosts: Marion and "Red" Chaffee
Open: Year round, sort of. Written reservations always preferred. Fall reservations made long in advance.

Once you arrive you know you are "home." The 1790 farmhouse, home for Marion for the last 23 years, is just what you would expect (or hope) to find along an old stagecoach route. "It's comfortable, cozy, and filled with our old things. We welcome family, friends, and new acquaintances in small doses, so that it's not like a zoo."

Marion knows all about numbers of people. She ran a boarding-house on Long Island for 27 years. Her grandchildren now total 17, from age 36 down to infants. She and Red worked for many years at the Republic Aviation Corporation on Long Island. Here in Vermont they get involved in local activities and enjoy gardening, reading, embroidery, woodworking, and the "winter wonderland." They get a kick out of "sharing Vermont" with young people and old acquaintances alike; and from all I hear, it's pretty mutual.

Restrictions: Preferably no pets. Nonsmokers preferred.

Bed: Three rooms. One with a single bed, two with double beds. Shared bath.
Breakfast: Continental. Usually served in kitchen where the big old iron stove is. "We finished redoing the dining room five years ago, but the regulars prefer the kitchen."
Plus: Plenty of rest and relaxation, reading, and music.
Rates: $18 single, $36 double.

What a delight to be able to return to such a beautiful spot. It's what I think heaven will be like. The hospitality made our vacation a delight.

J. K., Long Beach, California

NORTH RUPERT

Pineapple Hospitality Host #VT 610

Location: On a main road, 4 miles from two villages (Dorset and Pawlet), 10 miles from town (Manchester), 30 miles from city (Rutland). Adjoining dairy farms. Beautiful mountain and valley views. Near many ski areas including Bromley (17 miles).
Reservations: Available year round through Pineapple Hospitality, page 170.

A first bed-and-breakfast stay for us. We were so comfortable, content, and charmed by both our hosts and our surroundings, we wanted to write a thank-you note. It is a "must stay" kind of place.

Betty and Earl Somers, Chapel Hill, North Carolina

It started out to be a dairy farm in 1790. The house was enlarged in 1850. The farm operated until 1975. Along the way the North Rupert Post Office was housed here. For the last five years the property with its guest house, nonoperating cow, pig, and horse barns has been home to this couple who moved from Connecticut. Their antiques and Oriental rugs fit perfectly.

"After our four sons left we found ourselves with the perfect home for B&B." They also hike, cross-country ski (right from the door), and swim. The hostess is a fabric-store owner and the host, a former bank trust officer, is in real estate.

In residence: One dog. No smokers here, but guests may smoke.
Foreign language spoken: Swedish.

Bed: Three rooms, each with private bath. One single, one with twin beds, and one sofa-bedded double. Cot available.

Breakfast: Juice or fruit, homemade muffins, tea or coffee. Hot oatmeal with Vermont maple syrup in winter. Served in breakfast room adjoining country kitchen with fireplace.

Plus: Beverage in late afternoon or evening. Tour of barns, house, river. Private beach on river. Excellent river fishing. Join hosts in living room or on marble terrace under awning.

Rates: $27 single, $40 double. Cot $5. $10 higher in foliage season.

. . . Mountains covered with beautiful colors to be seen out every window. But the big plus was in the personable host and hostess. They were friendly, interesting, and interested in helping us to make the best choices of where to go and what to see. And they provided us with much information about history of the area and their lovely home. They really made a big difference in our trip.

Steve and Connie Michaelson, Jeffersonville, Pennsylvania

NORTH THETFORD

Stone House Inn

Route 5, Box 47, North Thetford, VT 05054
Phone: 802/333-9124
Location: Along the Connecticut River near Dartmouth College and Lake Fairlee. A secluded setting in a small town that has a general store, post office, and garage.
Hosts: Art and Dianne Sharkey
Open: Year round. Two-day minimum reservation during foliage and football weekends.

A visit to the Stone House Inn is like coming back home to old Vermont. The accommodations are spotlessly clean. . . . The best part is the food — home-cooked meals and baked goods. The owners' interesting backgrounds and varied experiences both here and overseas give the Inn a "touch of class" that's hard to duplicate anywhere.

Karl C. Gruen, Ridgefield, Connecticut

After teaching in California, North Dakota, Idaho, Massachusetts, the Washington D.C. area, Pittsburgh, France, England, and Greece, the Sharkeys decided to blend their experiences and their love of cooking in another profession. Art grew up in Philadelphia, has a degree in educational media, and teaches English at the high-school level. Dianne is from Los Angeles and is now at the inn full time. There are plenty of opportunities to utilize her quilting and sewing interests. She used her silk-screening talents to reproduce a *Moby Dick* motto for the kitchen! "O, Time, Strength, Cash and Patience!"

Furnishings are mostly Victorian. Some large brass rubbings from England are admired by many. And the tin ceilings are, of course, original. The stone walls date from 1835, but the house was rebuilt after a fire in 1906. What has been considered the most imposing house in the area has been a guesthouse/inn with four different owners since 1957. Since the Sharkeys acquired it in 1979 some guests have booked the entire place for themselves. Others have held their weddings here. The inn is home; hosts and guests share the living room. The entire family gets involved. As Dianne says, "We love it here."

In residence: Two capable and "not shy" kids — Katie, age 11, and Adam, age 8. Three cats — Podge, Bibsie, and Fido. The Sharkeys do not smoke but smoking is allowed.

Restrictions: No guests' pets. No minimum age for children but they should be "well behaved."

Foreign languages spoken: A little French and Spanish.

Bed: Six rooms. Two twin beds are in two rooms. Four have doubles. All have comforters. Views to the mountains, river, or pond. Cots available. Three shared baths.

Breakfast: Continental with homemade muffins, breads, and/or croissants. Served family style on plant-filled sun porch overlooking pond in summer; in dining room other seasons.

Plus: Rockers on screened veranda, armchairs by fireplaces, log benches by the pond. Dinner by reservation (for a total of about 20) on Friday and Saturday in July and August. They are stop #3 on their Inn-to-Inn Canoeing Program that goes north to south along a 55-mile section of the Connecticut River.

Rates: $22 single, $30 for two, $10 cot. MasterCard and VISA accepted.

Lovely host and hostess . . . bedroom with windows on three sides . . . music of the brook beyond. . . . It was fun to listen to the whistle of the Boston and Maine Railroad as it sang through the night. . . . The food was delicious. . . . One night was just too short a time in this charming home on the Connecticut River.   B.S.L., Glen Rock, New Jersey

POST MILLS

The Lake House

Route 244, P.O. Box 65, Post Mills, VT 05058
Phone: 802/333-4025
Location: In the Connecticut River Valley where "it's quiet" on a state secondary road. Pretty rural territory, 300 yards from the shores of Lake Fairlee, home to five summer camps. Near facilities for boating, swimming, fishing, tennis, golf, and cross-country skiing.
Hosts: Ralph and Lea Easton
Open: June through October. Plus weekends and holidays only November through May. Two-night minimum stay on holiday weekends.

"We got into B&B on a whim after visiting a wonderful guesthouse in the Berkshires where a 70-year-old lady had 10 rooms and did just about everything herself. In looking for a business that we could both participate in and do at home, we found this wooden clapboard farmhouse that was built in 1871 as an inn complete with dancehall and barn. It was a private home when we bought it in 1979."

The Eastons, originally from Massachusetts, went to work on the decor, and have been greeting passers-by, foliage-season tourists, and camp personnel and parents ever since. Ralph is a federal employee. Lea is an accounting supervisor. With the part-time help of a local woman and their son and daughter, they do as they planned — everything.

Horses and buggies that carried square dancers to the dancehall (now a storage area) no longer "park" in the barn. Photographs in the living room show how the house looked in the early 1900s.

In residence: Andy, age 15, and Pam, age 9. Judge is their golden retriever and Sophie is a black-and-white cat. None of the Eastons smoke, but smoking is allowed.
Restrictions: No guests' pets.
Bed: Six rooms. One single and five doubles. Three shared baths. Cot and crib available. Rooms are decorated with white ruffled curtains, chenille bedspreads, and comfortable old furniture.
Breakfast: Available 8–9:30. Choice of poached egg, cereal, or French toast. Sunday special is homemade waffles with Vermont maple syrup. Served in dining room or on screened porch.
Plus: Living room with fireplace (in use during cooler months), open veranda, screened porch. Tour of house if you'd like. Posted menus of area restaurants. Apple picking in season at orchard 15 minutes away.
Rates: $22 single, $32 double. Cot $10. MasterCard and VISA accepted.

RANDOLPH

Windover House

RFD 1, Randolph, VT 05060
Phone: 802/728-3802
Location: On Route 66, 1¼ miles from I-89. One mile from village, ½ mile from Green Mountain ski touring center, 40-minute drive from Killington.
Hosts: George and Shirley Carlisle, Ian and Brian
Open: Year round. Two-day minimum stay for special holiday weekends.

Very nice comfortable bedrooms, a large lounge with a big log fire in the winter, very congenial hosts, and an excellent bacon-and-eggs breakfast. What more could one wish for? An excellent place to stay for a night or a week.
G. N. Walsh, Montreal, Canada

That's been the story since 1978 when a traveling training officer for the largest jewelry company in Canada and her motorcycle-dealer husband decided to seek a different lifestyle. While looking for a country store they stumbled on Windover House. They furnished it "simply and comfortably — not like a museum." The Carlisles find that some guests want to be left alone, while others are filled with questions and conversation.

Their two sons were used to big city schools. With friends miles apart here, they walk and use their bicycles. They have seen their parents rush pregnant ladies to the hospital in the middle of the night, conjure up baby formula and diapers for a young couple with infant caught in a snowstorm, and find a mechanic at odd hours. Ian and Brian take visiting youngsters tobogganing or to the swimming pool — and baby-sit too.

The big old house, built in 1800, has a checkered history. Guests are staying in the exact middle of the state, a fact determined about the time of World War I. Subsequently the then hotel was called Mid-State Villa. Even though it is miles from the sea, it once had a widow's walk, according to an old photo that the Carlisles have.

Shirley, originally from England, and George, from Ireland, met in Canada. In their Vermont community, George is a Rotarian and works with the scouts. Shirley is a volunteer with Environmental Learning for Future and is a church Sunday-school superintendent.

In residence: Brian and Ian, teenagers. One black Labrador retriever and one cat.
Restrictions: No guests' pets allowed inside.
Foreign language spoken: French.
Bed: Eight rooms, all with semiprivate baths. Some have double beds, some twins, some sleep three or four. Crib available.
Breakfast: Available 6:45–9. Full. (If you are a coffee or tea-only morning person, rate is reduced.) Served in kitchen/dining room by large picture window overlooking patio and huge old fir and maple trees.
Plus: Coffee and tea always available. Wood stove (made in nearby Randolph) in kitchen. Huge wide-open porch. Glassed-in porch with fireplace. Lounge with corner fireplace. Garden. Board with posted menus of area restaurants, concerts, museums, local attractions, and auctions.
Rates: $23 single, $31 for two, $8 for each additional person in room. Slightly less for nonbreakfasters. $5 for crib if linen used.

RUTLAND

Hillcrest Guest House

McKinley Avenue, Rutland, VT 05701
Phone: 802/775-1670
Location: Two miles from the junction of Routes 4 and 7; ³⁄₁₀ mile from U.S. Route 7.
Hosts: Bob and Peg Dombro
Open: Year round.

"Our Chamber of Commerce seasonally requests additional residential housing for tourists. We have traveled B&B in Britain and enjoyed that style of meeting people. . . . We like to think of B&B as hosting new friends, exchanging ideas, learning about other home towns, and sharing with guests our love of Vermont." After three years of successful hosting, they have the theme of "Mi casa es su casa."

The Dombros' rambling mid-19th-century post-and-beam farmhouse, no longer on a working farm, has been their home for 14 years. Their collection of country antiques enhances the New England flavor. Herb and vegetable gardens grow on the site of the old dairy barn. If you are looking for native Vermonters, a couple of their neighbors are frequently around.

Bob is executive director of the Vermont Achievement Center, a school and rehabilitation agency for exceptional children, and Peg is involved in community theater, gardening, and cooking.

In residence: Three cats.
Restrictions: No guests' pets. Smoking in downstairs living room only.
Bed: Three rooms. One single and two doubles. Furnished with antiques, handwoven rag rugs, and down comforters. Cots available.
Breakfast: Available 7–9. Continental, Vermont style, with homemade muffins, freshly brewed coffee. Served on screened porch in warm months, in country dining room in winter.
Plus: Usually some beverage in late afternoon or evening. Packed lunches can be arranged for bikers, hikers, and skiers. Dinner on special request for guests only.
Rates: $15 per person per night. Cot $10.

The rooms were nicely appointed. Our hosts were very pleasant and helpful with information on activities in the area.

Matt and Mary Beth Tucker, Tucson, Arizona

SHOREHAM

The Shoreham Inn and Country Store

Shoreham, VT 05770
Phone: 802/897-5081
Location: On Vermont Route 74 west, 22 miles north of Fair Haven, 12 miles southwest of Middlebury, 5 miles east of Fort Ticonderoga on Lake Champlain.
Hosts: Cleo and Fred Alter
Open: Year round.

The Alters are third-generation innkeepers; but until coming here 10 years ago they were in advertising, public relations, school teaching, graphic design, and publishing — in New York, Virginia, Connecticut, and Vermont. They run both the inn, where "breakfast is a great time," and the next-door country store (complete with bell that jingles as you arrive and depart) that was built in 1828. Their extensive collection of country-auction antiques has spilled over into a new sideline, a little shop in the inn.

The Shoreham was built in 1799 and has always been a public inn.

Remodeling and changes have taken place — the balustrade is from an old church in Shoreham — but the charm of a post-and-beam added-on-to structure is all there to be enjoyed. Although many guests have some association with area colleges, the list also includes bicyclists, skiers, hikers, fishermen — and a particularly memorable guest who arrived on horseback.

Restrictions: Sorry, no pets. Smoking allowed on first floor only.
Bed: Nine rooms — named for former owners, local notables, and one native Vice President of the United States. Some singles, some doubles, and some that can hold up to four in a room. Five shared baths. Crib available (no charge).
Breakfast: Usually 8:30–9:30. Juice, almond date granola, hot muffins, butter, preserves, cheese, fresh fruit, beverage. Served in beautiful dining room with exposed beams and open fire. Leisurely. Up to two hours? "Sometimes even longer!"
Plus: Extensive library, quiet sitting room, puzzles. Lawn games. Picnic tables (shared with country-store shoppers). Beverage with cheese and crackers in late afternoon or evening. Tours of inn. Maps and, if you wish, help in planning the day. Dinner for B&B guests by advance reservation only.
Rates: $25 single, $45 double.

STOWE

Guest House Christel Horman

Mountain Road, RR 1, Box 1635, Stowe, VT 05672
Phone: 802/253-4846
Location: On Mountain Road (Route 108), 1 mile from Mt. Mansfield, 5.5 miles from Stowe village.
Hosts: Christel and Jim Horman
Open: Year round.

Much of the old woodwork in this 1980 chalet-style house is from another lodge that was dismantled. Many of the decorative accessories, such as the kangaroo skin and the hand-painted ceramic plaques are from "home."

Jim was an auto mechanic and ski instructor in Australia. Christel was a secretary in West Germany. They met in Stowe, where they have lived for 16 years, when she was a waitress and he was a ski instructor.

Since, they have been host/hostess and manager/housekeeper. In 1980 they had the shell of their own guest house built and did all the finishing work and decorating themselves. The Hormans made corner benches, painted a mural of children sitting on a fence, constructed all the headboards, painted flowers on them, and did the stenciling. Jim still works for the Mt. Mansfield Company. Christel is here full time. Many a good conversation is had by the fire — while Christel knits magnificent ski sweaters.

In residence: Neil, age eight.
Restrictions: Sorry, no pets allowed.
Foreign languages spoken: German and a little Swedish.
Bed: Eight rooms, each with two double beds and private bath. Wall-to-wall carpeting and individual thermostats. Cots and crib available.
Breakfast: Full, 8–10. Served in living room that has a European feeling.
Plus: Living room with hearthstoned fireplace, books, magazines, and color TV. Cross-country skiing from the door. Swimming pool. Lawn games. Trout fishing in brook behind house. Nearby in summer — tennis, horseback riding, golf, theater, Alpine Slide. Baby-sitting possibilities. Coffee and tea always available.
Rates: $22.50 per person, double occupancy, in summer months. $24 other months. Cot $16. Crib $6. MasterCard and VISA accepted.

WAITSFIELD

Knoll Farm Country Inn

Bragg Hill Road, RR Box 180, Waitsfield, VT 05673
Phone: 802/496-3939
Location: Off the beaten track, on 150 acres a half mile up a hill away from main road (Route 100), with views of rolling farmlands and Mad River Glen, Sugarbush, and Sugarbush North ski areas.
Hosts: Bill and Ann Day Heinzerling, Harvey and Ethel Horner
Open: Year round except April and November. Reservations strongly recommended.

B&B travelers have been coming here since 1957, but many stay through the day and make it a real farm vacation, just as guests have been doing for more than 25 years.

Now Ann is an Audubon Society director, a member of the Poetry Society of Vermont, and a free-lance writer and photographer. Originally it was the ski business that brought her and her first husband, Frank Day, to Vermont from Massachusetts. In 1957 they bought the fixed-up 19th-century farmhouse that has had guests and been a working farm ever since. After Frank's untimely death in 1970 Ann continued the inn with the help of her two grown children. When Ann married Bill Heinzerling and they moved into a nearby contemporary house in 1979, the Horners became inn residents and co-hosts.

Maple floors, turn-of-the-century and older antiques, natural woodwork, and braided rugs enhance the authentic farmhouse feeling. With a total of 10 guests at most, camaraderie reigns. And so does relaxation — and rejuvenation. Returnees are many; summer reservations in particular can be hard to come by.

In residence: Jeannie Horner, a high-schooler, during college vacations Linda and her seeing-eye dog, and Michael, may be home. Three dogs. Five cats. And all the farm animals — 12 horses, 6 Scottish Highland cattle and calves, Araucana chickens that lay edible blue and green eggs, and a pig.

Restrictions: Children should be at least six. Smoking not allowed in dining or kitchen areas.

Foreign languages spoken: German (Bill) and a little French (Ann).

Bed: Four rooms. Three have double and a single. One has two twins. Cots available. One double is a pineapple four-poster, some are brass, one is a spool bed. Two full baths upstairs, one down, plus an additional shower room.

Breakfast: Full farm meal. Leisurely (very). Cooked cereals and their own bacon, eggs, sausage, and ham. French toast, maybe cornbread with apples. Blueberry pancakes on Sunday. Served in dining room or in cozy sun room overlooking pond, birds, animals, mountains.

Plus: Tea or hot mulled cider at the right moment in winter in kitchen/living room with wood stove; lemonade in summer. No television. Kitchen privileges. Option of lunch. (Dinner for guests only is $6 per adult and $4 per child includes entrée, farm-fresh vegetables, homemade breads, salad with maple-syrup dressing, and dessert.) Extensive library, puzzles, ping-pong, use of typewriter, piano, ornate antique pump organ, electric organ. Rowboat. Swimming in (or skating on) pond. Croquet, horseshoes, hiking possibilities, guided nature walks, horseback riding, buggy rides. Tours of farm and lots of opportunities to help with chores. Equipment available for snowshoeing, ice skating, cross-country skiing, and tobogganing. Transportation provided, if needed, to and from skiing or shopping, bus and train stations, and airport.

Rates: $28 single, $24 per person for double occupancy for B&B. $16 for children 6–12 years. Weekly rates available.

WESTON

The Darling Family Inn

Route 100, Weston, VT 05161
Phone: 802/824-3223
Location: Half mile north of village with panoramic view of surrounding mountains and farmland. Near Bromley, Stratton, Okemo, and Magic Mountains, summer theater, antiques and crafts, and art exhibits. Three miles from Weston Priory.
Hosts: Chapin and Joan Darling

Chapin and Joan have spared no effort in creating a warm and gracious atmosphere, which makes one want to return often. From the fresh orange juice in the morning to the freshly baked chocolate cookies on the night table, one is constantly aware of the many touches in this marvelous inn.   Steve and Peggy Morgan, Marlton, New Jersey

"The kids grew up. We were ready for a change from corporate (Connecticut life-insurance executive) life, and wanted to work together at something."

And they are enjoying their new occupation, which involves interaction with each guest ("an individual") as well as restoration work. (The kitchen is just about done.) They do everything themselves in the 150-year-old farmhouse that provides a wonderful backdrop for their early American and English antiques. Appreciative guests find lots to look at in the personalized decor. Joan paints on wood and tin items. The coffee table was once a wash bench. There are many comments on the thimbles painted with minute New England scenes that have discernible twigs on the trees. Chapin makes miniature and sophisticated wood items and has already restored several trunks.

The farmhouse was a private home until 1957, a guesthouse until the Darlings made it an inn in 1980.

In residence: Sam, the dog; Cinder, the cat. Perhaps any or all of the four grown Darling children might be visiting.
Restrictions: Children should be at least eight. Sorry, no guests' pets.
Bed: Five rooms. Two twin beds in two rooms; semiprivate baths. Three double-bedded rooms, one with canopied four-poster; one with private bath, two with semiprivate bath. Cots available.
Breakfast: Served 8–10. Chapin cooks. Joan serves. Juices; homemade breads; bacon, ham, or sausage; and beverage. Full country breakfast is $4 extra. All served by candlelight. Cloth napkins.

Plus: Swimming pool. Living room with wood stove. Chape's guitar accompaniment for impromptu sing-alongs. Candles in windows as a welcome to guests year round. Cross-country skiing at the door. Beverage in late afternoon or evening. Frequent exchanges of recipes. And many surprises "not to be printed so that they remain surprises."
Rates: $32–$42 per room with semiprivate bath; $38 private bath. Additional cot in room $10. Some special rates available for a stay of five or more nights.

. . . A charming, cozy yet elegant home away from home. The beauty of the antique-filled rooms, the outstanding meals, and the down-to-earth warmth of the hosts combine to make this a very special place.

Nancy Jean Gold, Watertown, Massachusetts

WILMINGTON

Darcroft's Schoolhouse

Route 100, Wilmington, VT 05363
Phone: 802/464-2631
Location: In Mount Snow area on main (two-lane) scenic road, four miles from town and shops. Within walking distance of restaurants, (free) pool, tennis, and golf.
Host: Doris Meadowcroft
Open: Year round. Availability limited December–March.

When the schoolhouse was built in 1837 it was the whole school district. In the late 1800s the town of Wilmington made it part of their school system. Along the way a second floor was added; and in 1979 Doris, a computer programmer in New Jersey, made it her home. She now works at the Mount Snow ski area.

What was the classroom is now the living room/lounge with fireplace, antiques, and paintings.

In residence: Cats Mister and Sassy, and the dog, Talk.
Restrictions: No guests' pets. (Kennel facilities are nearby.)
Bed: Two rooms, each with a double bed, plus an open (no privacy) loft area with three single beds sometimes used by cyclists (and skiers in winter). Crib available.
Breakfast: Continental including pastry and/or muffins and home-

made jam or jelly. Various seating arrangements possible, including an old ice-cream booth.

Plus: Kitchen privileges.

Rates: $25 for two in summer, $40 for two in winter. Sorry, no credit cards accepted. $15 per person for loft. Group rates available.

. . . Clean, comfortable and a pleasure. But Doris was the real topper. We enjoyed it immensely.   M.Z./S.Z., New York, New York

WILMINGTON

Holly Tree

Sterns Avenue RFD 1, Box 315A, Wilmington, VT 05363

Phone: 802/464-5251

Location: On a small lake, one mile from Route 9 along a dirt road at the end of a maple-lined avenue. Four miles from Wilmington, 8 miles from Mount Snow, 16 miles from Brattleboro.

Host: Norma Naudain

Open: Year round.

Here's real English hospitality with a family who established a successful B&B with the same name in the 1970s in Norma's native country — on the Welsh border. Before that the Naudains had lived in New Jersey and Florida. Their Vermont B&B, a barn-roof colonial that has a chalet-like exterior, was built in 1927 as an annex to a hotel. It has been their home for three years.

Norma enjoys sharing the lovely setting that remains "undeveloped." Her husband, Craig, works for a local inn.

In residence: No one who smokes. Three children — Rebekah, age 17; Lisa, age 15; Norman, age 12. Dudley is their basset hound.

Restrictions: No guests' pets. Smoking allowed on first floor only.

Foreign language spoken: French.

Bed: Two rooms. One double and one family room. One shared guest bath. Crib available.

Breakfast: Continental with homemade bread, coffee cake, and jams. Hot cereals in winter.

Plus: Piano. Trails for hiking. Berry patches and foundations of old farmhouses are up on a hill that was once sheep country.

Rates: $15 per person per night. Children under 12, $7.50.

Hospitality and friendship were offered so generously at the Holly Tree that I soon felt more like a visiting relative than a paying guest. . . . I was quick to make another reservation when I traveled through Vermont again that year, so I could enjoy the hospitality and see what was new with the family.   Ellen M. Grant, Alden, New York

WOODSTOCK

Three Church Street

3 Church Street, Woodstock, VT 05091
Phone: 802/457-1925
Location: In the picture-book village (without overhead wires) just two blocks from most restaurants and shops.
Host: Eleanor Paine
Open: All months except April. Two-night minimum reservation during Christmas holiday week and Washington's Birthday week, and from late September through the next-to-last week in October.

Since 1979 Eleanor has been "stressing informality — but we do stress service—in a relatively formal house. We call it elegant informality."

Eight Paine children have grown up in this house that is on the National Register of Historic Places. Antiques, paintings, and prints enhance the gracious brick residence. The original house has been added onto over the 150 years of its life. Eleanor has been here for 25 years. She is an outdoor and sports person, and before the days of B&B (and filling out forms such as those for *Bed and Breakfast in the Northeast*) she used to be an avid reader.

In residence: Three dogs — Abigail, a yellow Labrador retriever, and Nubbles and Fatso, Norwich terriers. The youngest Paines, college students, are here during school vacations.
Restrictions: Pets allowed, but shouldn't be left in guests' rooms when guests go out.
Bed: Of the ten rooms, five have private baths. Five rooms have twin beds, five have doubles. Crib (no charge) and rollaway available.
Breakfast: Generally 8–10:30. A leisurely time. Bountiful. Juices, fruits, cereals, meats, eggs, home fries, grits, pancakes or French toast, and then some pastries. Eleanor cooks and "a couple of staffers" serve.
Plus: Entire downstairs including two cozy sitting rooms with fire-

places and TVs, and a formal large sitting room. Extensive library in a room overlooking Ottauquechee River and Mt. Tom. Porch. Swimming pool and clay tennis court available May 15–September 15. Instant soups and beverages always available. Kitchen privileges (extra charge). **Rates:** $38–$48.50 per night. Single occupancy rate available only for stays of at least one week. Rollaway $8. MasterCard and VISA accepted.

MASSACHUSETTS

MASSACHUSETTS

N

VERMONT   NEW HAMPSHIRE

NEW YORK

MASSACHUSETTS

6

Boston

10   9   8   7   • Worcester   5

• Springfield

CONNECTICUT   RHODE ISLAND

4

1

2

3

Atlantic Ocean

The numbers on this map indicate the locations for which there are detailed maps in this chapter.

MASSACHUSETTS

Page numbers refer to pages on which regional maps appear.

MASSACHUSETTS

Reservation Services

The whole state is covered by:

Pineapple Hospitality, Inc.

384 Rodney French Boulevard, New Bedford, MA 02744
Phone: 617/990-1696 (Monday–Friday 8–5, Saturday 8–12)
Established January 1981.
Listings: About 150 hosts all over New England; about half of these are in Massachusetts.

What started out to be a reservation service for the historic whaling city of New Bedford has become a base for the whole New England experience, with booking possibilities in all six states. Because of Joan Brownhill's desire to keep personally in touch with everyone and to continue making careful matches, she doesn't expect to get much bigger. She now has two trained interviewers and inspectors who do the traveling necessary to maintain the service. Her directory, coded with basic details about each host, is available for $3.32 including postage.

Rates: Singles $20–$27, but $36–$52 in Boston and other high-demand areas such as Martha's Vineyard, Nantucket, and Newport, Rhode Island. Doubles $27–$40, but $40–$72 in high-demand areas. $5 for extra person in same room. $3 handling fee for one-night stays out of Massachusetts.

*

• Some of the reservation and referral services with listings in many states throughout the country, pages 26-29, have a few hosts in Massachusetts.
• Many Massachusetts educators who host others in the field can be reached through **Educator's Inn,** page 29.
• Many Massachusetts-based services concentrate on one area but have a few "other" hosts in one direction or another.

Other services going from east to west:

CAPE COD

Bed & Breakfast Cape Cod. Please see page 174.

House Guests, Cape Cod. Please see page 174.

BOSTON AREA

Bed and Breakfast Associates Bay Colony. Please see page 220.

Bed and Breakfast, Brookline/Boston. Please see page 221.

Bed & Breakfast Cambridge & Greater Boston. Please see page 222.

Bed & Breakfast in Minuteman Country. Please see page 222.

Boston Bed & Breakfast. Please see page 223.

Greater Boston Hospitality. Please see page 223.

Host Homes of Boston. Please see page 223.

New England Bed & Breakfast. Please see page 224.

University Bed and Breakfast. Please see page 224.

CENTRAL MASSACHUSETTS

Folkstone Bed & Breakfast Registry. Please see page 260.
Sturbridge Bed & Breakfast. Please see page 260.

CONNECTICUT VALLEY

Pioneer Valley Bed & Breakfast Network. Please see page 267.

HAMPSHIRE HILLS

Hampshire Hills Bed & Breakfast Association. Please see page 270.

BERKSHIRES

Berkshire Bed & Breakfast Connection. Please see page 278.

Covered Bridge Bed and Breakfast. Please see page 278.

CAPE COD, MARTHA'S VINEYARD, NANTUCKET AND SOUTHEASTERN MASSACHUSETTS

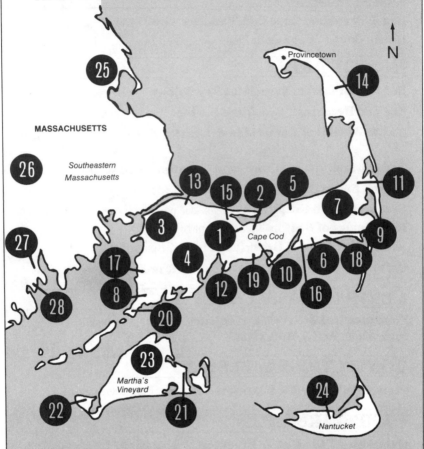

The numbers on this map indicate the locations of B&Bs described in detail in this chapter.

CAPE COD

MARTHA'S VINEYARD

NANTUCKET

SOUTHEASTERN MASSACHUSETTS

CAPE COD

Reservation Services
for Cape Cod, Martha's Vineyard, Nantucket

Bed & Breakfast Cape Cod

Box 341, West Hyannisport, MA 02672
Phone: 617/775-2772 Established December 1981.
Open: Year round, 9–5 Monday–Saturday, answering machine other times.
Listings: About 50 bed-and-breakfast hosts from all of Cape Cod, from Sagamore Beach to Provincetown.

Elaine Borowick and Kay Traywick, two former teachers (and Kay is a licensed real-estate broker), went to England in 1981 for the 10th anniversary of their gourmet dinner group. The idea for a service was born. Upon return they opened with a focus on friendly hosts in homes that they themselves would stay in.
Rates: Singles $24–$30, doubles $30–$50. Some hosts have reduced rates for long-term stays or in off-season. MasterCard and VISA accepted.

House Guests, Cape Cod

Box 8, Dennis, MA 02638
Phone: 617/398-0787 Established May 1981.
Open: Year round, 8 a.m.–8 p.m. April–October.
Listings: About 125 hosts are described in the directory ($1); they are located all over Cape Cod and Martha's Vineyard.

Allison Caswell aims to provide accommodations "from very simple to luxury for those who crave it." This year her in-season telephone staff consists of volunteers, her very own B&B hosts and hostesses.
Rates: Singles $20–$30, doubles $30–$50. Seventh night free. Three

nights for rate of two, September 15–June 15. Minimum reservation of two nights preferred for July, August, and holidays.

Pineapple Hospitality

This service also covers Cape Cod and the islands. Please see page 170.

*

Most of the Boston services, pages 220-225, have a few listings on the Cape.

B&Bs

Many Cape Cod hosts report that guests come to see all of Cape Cod in a weekend. "Please remind them in your book that Cape Cod is 90 miles long."

The following B&Bs are in alphabetical order according to the towns and villages where they are located. B&Bs on the islands of Martha's Vineyard and Nantucket are on pages 201-209.

BARNSTABLE

Bed & Breakfast Cape Cod Host #27

Location: On a street with wonderful old trees and stone walls. Tucked away with a beautiful view. Just a few steps from a beach.
Reservations: Available year round through Bed & Breakfast Cape Cod, page 174.

Everyone appreciates the setting high on a bluff overlooking tidal marshes of Barnstable Harbor. Sometimes guests go clamming with the hosts.

The house was originally built in 1960 as their vacation retreat. Since the host became a retired engineer four years ago, they moved from Connecticut and made this their permanent residence. He can give you some tips on gardening and fishing. She's a nursery-school teacher and a weaver, and loves handwork. Together they spent one winter building a dollhouse of exacting specifications. They have four grandchildren, ages four to six, and enjoy theater, literature, and travel.

In residence: People who smoke.
Restrictions: No pets.
Bed: Two rooms, each with a double bed. Shared guest bath. Crib available.
Breakfast: Continental with homemade bakery served 8–9.
Plus: Use of swimming pool, sitting area, screened porch. Small refrigerator for guests.
Rates: $30 single, $40 for two.

BARNSTABLE VILLAGE

Cobb's Cove

Route 6A (Mailing address: P.O. Box 208), Barnstable Village, MA 02630
Phone: 617/362-9356
Location: Overlooking Barnstable Village, the harbor, and ocean. Close to historic district. Five minutes from Hyannis.
Hosts: Evelyn Chester and Henri-Jean
Open: Year round.

In 1643 Deacon Henry Cobb built a stone fortification house here for defense against the Indian attack. About 300 years later, Evelyn, a librarian from New York, and Henri, a former engineering specialist from the United States and France, designed and built this marvelous post-and-beam saltbox with huge 12-inch beams in all the rooms and natural wood inside and out.

In residence: Two dogs, Annie Laurie and Beau. Vickie is the cat.
Restrictions: No pets. Nonsmokers preferred.
Foreign languages spoken: French, some Spanish.
Bed: Six rooms. One with twin beds, three with doubles, two with

queen-sized beds. Each room has a dressing room and a private bath with whirlpool tub.

Breakfast: Served 9–10. Fresh fruit, homemade bread, "special" crepes, cooked by host and served by hostess in keeping room at traditional trestle table in front of Count Rumford fireplace; or on terrace, weather permitting. Hosts often join you for coffee at the end of the leisurely meal.

Plus: Air conditioning. Library. Patio, gardens, grounds. Option of dinner by guests' request.

Rates: $78–$98 per couple.

Cobb's Cove has totally captivated us with its rustic charm and warm hospitality. We especially appreciate the relaxed atmosphere conveyed by the leisurely meals and delightful whirlpool baths. It is an inn in the true sense — a welcome haven for weary travelers.

Chris and Bill Vernau, Jermyn, Pennsylvania

BOURNE

Aboard A Sailboat
Pineapple Hospitality Host #148

Location: At Monument Beach, just over the Bourne Bridge in the upper part of Buzzards Bay.

Reservations: Available through Pineapple Hospitality, page 170. Bookings are taken for weekdays May through October.

"I love to live on a boat during the summer, especially on Cape Cod. To me it is clean air, water licking gently against the boat, and the peacefulness of the night. Some evenings we sit in the cockpit of the boat and sing while I play the guitar."

The 41-foot Morgan Out Islander sailboat is identical to the boat that led the parade of the Tall Ships in 1976. The well-maintained two-master boat has been up and down the east coast and has been the host's summer home for seven summers. Last year the host became licensed to take out charters and this year she has added B&B at the dock next to a public beach and the Cape Cod Canal.

In residence: A friendly dog who could "go home for the night" if guests request in advance.

Restrictions: Smoking allowed in cockpit. Children should be able to swim.
Bed: Forward stateroom with two extra-wide full-length berths. Queen-sized bed in main salon. Full bath with shower only.
Breakfast: Full. Available 7–9; could be later if there is no charter scheduled for the day.
Plus: Color television, stereo.
Rates: $37 for one or two.

COTUIT

Bed & Breakfast Cape Cod Host #33

Location: On main street of village, close to public tennis courts, free golf (1 1/2 miles away) and three lovely beaches within three miles. Falmouth: 10 miles. Hyannis: 8 miles.
Reservations: Available year round through Bed & Breakfast Cape Cod, page 174.

The hostess is almost a native. Her husband, a high-school ecology teacher, has been here eight years. The young couple (in their early 30s) love Cape Cod and feel personally responsible for guests having a good vacation: "We even feel badly if it's a cloudy or rainy day when guests had planned to go to the beach."

There are no bogs on the one-acre property, but the restored Victorian cranberry farmer's house, circa 1882, is shaded and cooled by large trees, a rarity in the area.

In residence: One three-year-old daughter. Two Dalmatians.
Restrictions: No guests' pets.
Bed: Four rooms. One single, one double, one with twin beds, one with king-sized bed. Cots and cribs available. Two shared baths.
Breakfast: Continental with homemade pastry available any time in the morning.
Plus: Picnic table. Six bicycles (no extra charge) for guests.
Rates: $25 single, $35 doubles. $5 less October 15–May 15. Cot or crib $5.

. . . Comfortable accommodations with the charm and coziness of braided rugs and New England style architecture . . . congenial and

helpful host and hostess. . . . We liked it so much we have returned three times.   Paula and Justin Grimes, Natick, Massachusetts

The true flavor of Cape hospitality and quaintness is evident. We were close enough to the beach to use the bikes available to guests as transportation. Truly recommended!
                         Rosemary Orsi and Clint Holland, Peterborough, New Hampshire

COTUIT

House Guests, Cape Cod Host #C1

Location: In a quiet village within walking distance of beaches and just 10 miles in three directions to Sandwich, Falmouth, and Hyannis.
Reservations: Available year round through House Guests, Cape Cod, page 174.

What had been a summer home for 25 years has been redecorated and restored as a year-round residence by this warm couple, grandparents of five. The house, a big old Victorian with a large porch, was built around 1900. Some family members of the first owner still live in town.
"Most everyone takes a trip to Provincetown, Martha's Vineyard, and Nantucket. Here in Cotuit we have a playground nearby, tennis courts, a lifeguarded beach, and one of the top teams in the Cape Baseball League. (Big League scouts come to all the games.) We give tours of the town — beaches, homes of famous people, the oyster company."

Restrictions: Pets (and children too) should be well behaved. Non-smokers preferred.
Bed: Three rooms. One single with shared bath. One room wih twin beds and private half bath. One double-bedded room with trundle (single) bed and private bath. Crib and cot available.
Breakfast: Full country meal with fresh fruit, blueberry muffins, and one of many specialties — maybe ham and egg on English, or waffles.
Plus: Sometimes a snack in late afternoon or evening. Bicycles available for guests. Baby sitting possible. Lawn, card and board games, toys, TV in most rooms.
Rates: $30 single, $40 doubles. Cot $5. Crib $2. Seventh night free. Three nights for rate of two off-season.

DENNIS

House Guests, Cape Cod Host #D7

Location: Right on a 15-acre pond.
Reservations: Available year round through House Guests, Cape Cod, page 174.

The world of nature can be literally in the palm of your hand here. The rotating population usually includes squirrels — red ones with names beginning with *R* and grey ones with names beginning with *S*. Gulls have names that start with a *G*. "Chipmunks eat peanuts from our hands. And right now we have a duck who thinks he is a goose! We usually have two or three Canada goslings and some mallard ducklings. In the summer when the pond is 'people busy' the white China geese are in a pen in the yard."

The hosts, active members of the Cape Cod Museum of Natural History, are the only year-round residents on the pond, "so we 'own' it for nine months each year." With only eight cottages on the pond, thick woods, and no power boats, it is pretty "Capey" even in the summer.

Foreign students have been coming here for years, and now B&B travelers are lucky too. "Some do have the idea of doing the Cape in a day. Some day-trip and some find our place is what they want. We've had guests who had never hung clothes on a line before. We thought B&B would be fun and it is!"

The house is "sort of a Cape Cod cottage, one that has been added to and is filled with stuff we've collected on our travels."

In residence: Two cats, one Siamese and one Maine coon.
Restrictions: No guests' pets. "And the house is not child-proofed."
Foreign language spoken: A little German.
Bed: One double-bedded room. One single room. One guest bath.
Breakfast: Served until 10 a.m. Guests' choice. "I make my own cranberry juice, jellies, jams, breads, waffles, pancakes — own honey. I like to cook except scrambled eggs throw me." Eat in plant-filled dining room complete with telescope by huge picture window overlooking lake and birdfeeders.
Plus: Patio, terrace, dock, great swimming in a lake "that is a kettle hole (formed by a glacier), gently sloping down to 30-foot depth." Use of sailboat, canoe, and "a neighborhood paddle boat."
Rates: $22 single, $36 double. $10 extra per person. Seventh night free. Three nights for rate of two off-season.

. . . Extremely knowledgeable about all aspects of Cape Cod life. They gave generously of their time to answer our questions and recommend places to visit which we would otherwise have missed. Every morning we were served a different, sumptuous breakfast. As we ate we watched the wildlife on what, to us, was a beautiful lake, to our hosts "a pond." . . . Above all, the warmth of the welcome made this a most memorable vacation.   John and Eileen Cawley, Glenside, Pennsylvania

DENNISPORT

House Guests, Cape Cod Host #DP1

Location: Ten-minute walk to town, beaches on the warmer, south side, bicycle rentals, and restaurants.
Reservations: Available May–October through House Guests, Cape Cod, page 174.

The weaver host has restored — and still finds projects in — this Cape Victorian that she came to four years ago.

A visiting professor of Russian wrote that it certainly isn't a typical B&B. A potter felt very much at home. Swedish guests enjoyed conversing in their own language and being treated to familiar bakery. Two-week visitors wrote about the relaxing atmosphere.

In residence: One cat. And a teenage son.
Foreign languages spoken: Swedish and Spanish.
Bed: Two rooms. One with twin beds, one with double. Shared bath. Cot available.
Breakfast: Continental with homemade cranberry or blueberry muffins made in wood stove. Served in country kitchen.
Rates: $22 single, $36 double. Weekly: $132, $210. Three nights for rate of two in off-season.

EAST HARWICH

House Guests, Cape Cod Host #EH1

Location: Near enough to Route 6 to get here easily; far enough for no traffic noise. Ocean, bike paths, shops, crafts fairs, tennis, and golf all within minutes.

Reservations: Available May–November through House Guests, Cape Cod, page 174.

He's a school administrator turned woodcarver. She's a school supervisor turned quilter. (Craft demonstrations gladly given.) After vacationing on the Cape for over 30 years, they moved here 8 years ago.

Peace. Quiet nights. Wake up to birds singing at the edge of the woods. Enjoy flower and vegetable gardens. Nearby pond with great sunsets. Hosts offer help with reservations at tennis courts; restaurants; boat trips; bicycles (1 to 10 speeds, with child carriers); lots of organized and categorized information; hand-drawn maps; detailed directions. Continental breakfasts and lots of extras. Happy hosts who aren't in a hurry and are thrilled to have guests feel relaxed.

"We found out how warm an experience it can be to stay in a B&B home in our travels in England, Scotland, Ireland, and Wales. We love being hosts and returning the favor." But there have been some surprises. "Some of the younger couples call me Mom. And imagine people who make their beds when they don't have to!"

In residence: One pipe smoker.
Restrictions: No pets. Children should be at least 10.
Bed: Two rooms on main floor of the roomy saltbox. Each has twin beds. One private bath between them.
Breakfast: Full. Homemade everything. Served whenever, on deck or in country kitchen overlooking birdfeeder. Could include scones or coffee cake, eggs or pancakes. "The morning belongs to the guests."
Plus: Welcoming and bedtime snacks. Fruit or candy in the room. Deck and patio. Living room, TV, outside hot-and-cold shower. Fan is offered "but has never been needed." Changing room available after check-out time on beach days.
Rates: $25 single, $40 for two. $72 for party of four in both rooms. Seventh night free. Three nights for rate of two in off-season.

FALMOUTH

House Guests, Cape Cod Host #F3

Location: Right across the road from the beach. Not far from ferry.
Reservations: Available June through early October through House Guests, Cape Cod, page 174.

Just friendly, comfortable, and fun. That goes for the house and the hosts. They love theater and sometimes guests are theater people, but they have had honeymooners, singles, professionals — "diverse personalities. You get attached to people. Last year we took pictures of each one."

The sizable cottage — not fancy — is about 110 years old and is filled with Victoriana: wicker, iron beds, oak furniture, a big glass china cabinet in dining room. This has been the summer residence for the family for 16 years.

In residence: One who smokes. Thumper, a real hounddog.
Restrictions: No guests' pets. No children.
Bed: Four rooms. Three with twin beds, one with double. One bath up and one down shared by all.
Breakfast: Continental on weekdays. On weekends "it's eloquent. I love cooking, so they might get eggs Benedict."
Plus: Porch with rockers, two living rooms, sun room.
Rates: $28 single, $40 for two. Seventh night free. Three nights for rate of two in off-season.

FALMOUTH

Mostly Hall

27 Main Street, Falmouth, MA 02546
Phone: 617/548-3786
Location: In Falmouth's historic district on the village green. Set back from the road on over an acre of lawn, practically hidden by bushes. One mile to many town beaches, two blocks to bus and train station.
Hosts: Jim, Ginny, and Suzi Austin
Open: Year round. Reservations strongly suggested.

For something completely different, here's Mostly Hall, named by an owner's child decades ago when the youngster first saw the inside of the new family home. The four-storied Mississippi-style residence was originally built as a wedding present by a sea captain for his bride in 1849. They say it was the only way the New Orleans belle would come to Falmouth.

Since 1980, Mostly Hall has offered Southern elegance together with hospitality provided by a former airline stewardess who had summered on the Cape in her childhood; her husband, a management consultant who grew up in Michigan; and their teenaged daughter. The tone is set with their guest book: it's really called a friendship book.

The Austin treatment of those 13-foot-ceilinged rooms is so well received that many guests inquire about help with their own decorating problems! There are fabric-covered walls, four-posters and sleigh beds; much art; lots of comfortable antiques; and some use of blue, Ginny's favorite color, in every room. This year's most popular (and reasonably priced) room is new, thanks to about a hundred guests who asked that the widow's walk be turned into a bedroom. As Jim says, "It's an experience."

Imaginative suggestions abound. Hungry? Try this seafood place because guest reports from this very week indicate that the chef is at his/her best. Or at the other place *not* on the water you should order the children's portion. Or how about kale soup even if you haven't ever tried it before?

Something very Capey to do? Take Mostly Hall's "Mom and Pop" bicycles along the flat, carless 3.2-mile trail past bird sanctuaries and ocean views to the docks in Woods Hole.

In residence: Suzi, a senior in high school. Solo, their nine-year-old sheltie who loves to be patted. "Tuasha is our mostly Siamese cat and is less friendly."

Restrictions: Children should be at least 16. No guests' pets.

Bed: Seven rooms. Three with double beds and private baths. Four with twin beds, two with private baths, two with shared. That widow's-walk room has 10 windows, two iron beds, hardly any space or closets, but a wonderful view of the village green.

Breakfast: "The whim of the innkeeper." Long-term guests try to trick Ginny into doing the same thing twice. Repeaters try to trick Jim into divulging the surprise menu. You might have creamed eggs and popovers; or crêpes with exotic fillings; or cheese, ham, and mushroom gratiné; sweet bread; sometimes fruit soups. Of course if you're a vegetarian or have a kosher diet, just mention that ahead of time. Everyone is served at 9 a.m., on the porch in summer, in lovely living room with fireplace at other times.

Plus: Covered porch on all four sides. All that lawn and gardens too. A good-sized gazebo. Use of four three-speed bicycles. Fresh fruit or nuts, tea or lemonade at just the right time. Tours of the house are best 12–2 or in off-season. Shared recipes.

Rates: In season (July through September 15) $33–$50. December through April $30–$39; spring and fall $30–$49.

Some things should never change. Mostly Hall is one of them.

Barbara Salladin, Timonium, Maryland

I dream of returning again and again to find a little bit of myself in the quiet homey moments. Mostly Hall is the memory of Massachusetts that I take home with me.   Philip James Herman, Palisades, New York

HARWICHPORT

Bed and Breakfast Associates
Bay Colony Host #771

Location: Just two blocks from the beach. In a town that allows you to "go either way" to see the Cape.

Reservations: Available through Bed and Breakfast Associates Bay Colony, page 220, June through September, but the season may be extended in 1984.

An interior decorator and a business executive, parents of four grown children, recently bought this retirement home, a marvelous Victorian with twists and turns, bays, and gingerbread too. It is the kind of place that prompts passersby to stop and take a picture. And invariably B&B guests ask for a tour, much to the delight of the hosts.

Both previous owners — and there have only been two in a century — made changes to the kitchen. At this very moment a solar room is being completed by the new owners. It is added to the kitchen which is being updated but "keeping the 100-year-old look."

Although the Cape is known for its beaches, the many first-year guests here were real sightseers. Several arose at dawn to see the sunrise from the jetty at the nearby beach. And they gratefully accepted suggestions of noncommercial attractions — Chatham Lighthouse, cranberry bogs, National Seashore — and hints for scenic routes away from the highway.

The hosts think about traveling the country via B&B; and many of their guests, inspired to become hosts, hope that they have the opportunity to switch roles with this outgoing couple.

In residence: One Irish terrier.
Restrictions: No smoking. No pets.
Bed: One single on first floor, shared bath. Three doubles, each with two twin beds, on second floor, shared guest bath.
Breakfast: "We're breakfast people." Always includes cranberry nut bread. Pancakes sometimes. Served no later than 10 in dining room or solar family room.
Plus: Yard and porch. Baby-sitting possibilities.
Rates: $35 single, $40 doubles. $5 surcharge for one-night stay.

HYANNIS

Bed & Breakfast Cape Cod Host #4

Location: Residential neighborhood, ½ mile from Main Street; one mile from ferries to islands.
Reservations: Available year round through Bed & Breakfast Cape Cod, page 174.

The host, an avid reader (and listener), has lived in this central location for two years. The house is a weathered shingled ranch. The yard is landscaped with colorful gardens. "It's not historical or unusual, just a friendly, cheerful, light and bright place."

Restrictions: Nonsmokers preferred. Pets allowed if under guests' control.
Bed: One room with a double bed and private half bath.
Breakfast: Full. Includes homemade coffee cake, maybe grilled tomatoes, pancakes, or eggs Benedict. Served whenever.
Plus: Use of garage for day-trippers to the islands.
Rates: $26 single, $36 for two in season (June–Labor Day); $24 and $32 in off-season.

ORLEANS

House Guests, Cape Cod Host #02

Location: A mile and a quarter from Route 6A, 1 mile to town, two short blocks to Cape Cod Bay beach, ½ mile to Cape Cod Bike Trail, 3½ miles to Cape Cod National Seashore ocean beach.

Reservations: Available year round through House Guests, Cape Cod, page 174. Minimum two-night reservations preferred.

Three years ago they were looking for an inn in Maine or the Berkshires or the Cape. But the librarian (was and is) and the former dean of a private school (now working in a wine-and-cheese store) from Connecticut fell in love with this restored farmhouse. They have made a few changes and some day may do something with the convertible barn, but "for the moment this is just right."

Most B&B guests seem to be seeking the quiet life that is here.

Restrictions: No children. No pets.

Foreign language spoken: A little French.

Bed: One double room with one double and one twin bed. Private bath and private entrance.

Breakfast: Continental with homemade muffins. Served on enclosed porch overlooking huge yard and birdfeeder.

Plus: Will meet bus and plane. Use of screened porch, picnic table, grill, badminton, grounds. Use of refrigerator and kitchen for making day-trip lunches.

Rates: $28 single, $42 for two. $252 weekly rate for two.

ORLEANS

Bed & Breakfast Cape Cod Host #37

Location: About 10 minutes from the village, 10 minutes to National Seashore headquarters at Eastham.

Reservations: Available year round through Bed & Breakfast Cape Cod, page 174. Minimum reservation: two nights.

If you come in the spring, you are greeted by the blooms of a 200-year-old apple tree that is taller than the house. "The front is Gothic structure. The rest is Cape Coddy." It has been the hosts' home for 40 years.

He's an ardent golfer. She scouts garage sales to add to the collected collectibles. The flower beds are her pride and joy. At the moment she wonders if her poppy seeds are coming up in the garden of a New Hampshire guest. She's been known to exchange recipes also.

In residence: One dog, "a lovable cuss."
Restrictions: No guests' pets. Children should be at least 10.
Bed: One room with twin beds and private half bath.
Breakfast: Full. Available 7–10.
Plus: Use of grounds and picnic area.
Rates: $24 single, $38 for two.

OSTERVILLE

Bed & Breakfast Cape Cod Host #34

Location: Within walking distance of beach and pond with lifeguards.
Reservations: Available year round through Bed & Breakfast Cape Cod, page 174.

The architecture, furnishings, and hospitality are all traditional here. Wine, cheese and crackers, and mints are in your room upon arrival. And someone will greet you between 5 and 6 between your "fun day" and "fun night."

The host, a 15-year resident, always seems to be involved in some adult-education course and finds each guest different and interesting. There has been a 6'2" folk-dance teacher who spent a rainy day in her rec room practicing for classes he was going to give at a festival. One family included a 20-year-old son who acted as interpreter for French friends who accompanied them. Other guests ended up house-sitting while the host went to a wedding. Some have gone deep-sea fishing, cleaned their catch, and then barbecued it in her backyard. It's a pretty flexible household.

Bed: Two rooms. One upstairs has twin beds, a double bed and a private bath. Downstairs room has twin beds and shared bath.
Plus: Kitchen privileges. Yard with badminton and barbecue. Babysitting possibilities.
Rates: $24 single, $36 twin room. Upstairs room is $36 for two, $48 for four.

SANDWICH

Bed & Breakfast Cape Cod Host #22

Location: In the center of a village that has maintained its Cape Cod look and feel, yet has enough attractions within walking distance so that you may choose to forget the car for at least a day and easily more.
Reservations: Available year round through Bed & Breakfast Cape Cod, page 174.

If you are curious about the inside of a sea captain's house, here's a host who is all-willing "to drag the unsuspecting" from the cellar to the attic. You can see the captain's name chalked under a roof beam, the name and date of a subsequent owner etched by diamond on a window-pane, and the early precursor to the Franklin stove in the master bedroom. Antique furnishings are throughout.

In September 1982, after having lived 10 miles down the road for 14 years, the family moved into this hip-roofed Federal house built in the early 1800s. Since moving, the host (a social-studies teacher) and his wife have repaired plaster walls and refinished floors. Already they have had guests whose children have exchanged telephone numbers with theirs. Others have come to celebrate "the end of January" and returned from dinner for wine, popcorn, and conversation.

In residence: Two daughters, ages 9 and 12, one son, age 4. One cat, a neighborhood feline that took up residence when they purchased the house.
Restrictions: No guests' pets.
Foreign language spoken: French, "less and less fluently as the years pass."
Bed: Six rooms. Four double rooms with new private baths; two have twin beds, one has twin ¾ beds, and the other a double. Two single rooms with shared bath.
Breakfast: Continental. Served 8–10 in dining room.
Plus: Use of family living room and den.
Rates: $26 single, $36 for two.

TRURO

Bed & Breakfast Registry Host #02666

Location: In the center of this tiny beautiful town not far from Provincetown and the beautiful beaches of the Cape Cod National Seashore.
Reservations: Available year round through Bed & Breakfast Registry, page 27.

The house has been in the family since 1920. It has wide painted floorboards and family antiques — both English and New England — and a hostess who rounds out the feeling that vacationers are looking for. She spent all of her own childhood summers and a number of winters in the homestead. In 1980, after a career of story-department work in film and television in New York and California, she returned to restore the lovely old Cape residence. "There will always be something else to do. The outside will be painted some day, but right now I'm working on the gardens to bring them back." She loves this wonderful place and the casual lifestyle and is delighted to find that B&B travelers do too. Her new career is centered on work with the local Council on Aging.

In residence: Two cats. One is 18 years old.
Restrictions: Sorry, no children, because of noise factor in an old house. No guests' pets allowed.
Bed: Three rooms. One single. Two rooms with double beds; one with two three-quarter beds. Extra mattresses on floor available. Two shared guest baths.
Breakfast: Available 8–9:30 (more or less). Continental with fruit, a variety of breads, jams and jellies, cold cereals — in dining room.
Plus: Parlor with color TV, screened porch, grounds, and lawn chairs.
Rates: $35 single, $40 double. $10 less in winter. $10 for extra mattress. One-night surcharge $6. No credit cards accepted.

WEST BARNSTABLE

Bed & Breakfast Cape Cod Host #3

Location: Not far from the mid-Cape highway, close to "most everything" but still on a dead-end street where all seems peaceful.

Reservations: Available year round through Bed & Breakfast Cape Cod, page 174.

The host's relatives have been on the Cape for several generations, but this couple summered here for two decades before building this marvelous contemporary house six years ago. They enjoy sharing both the history of their antiques and their high vantage point and deck with a spectacular view of Cape Cod Bay, Sandy Neck Beach (two miles away), and Barnstable Harbor and marshes.

The hostess is a folk artist who specializes in country painted objects. Her husband, a sailor, is in the insurance business. They are well prepared with touring and restaurant hints.

In residence: One 12-year-old dog.
Restrictions: Children should be in their teens. No guests' pets.
Bed: A two-room suite. Each room has two twin beds and a private entrance through sliding glass door on terrace. One guest bath.
Breakfast: Full. Includes homemade muffins and their own jellies. Served in large informal room with view of dunes and ocean.
Plus: Laundry facilities. Terrace. Deck. Sitting room with television. "Ice box in unfinished room."
Rates: $32 single, $46 for two, $22 for child.

The host being an ex-hardware wholesaler and myself an ex-hardware retailer, we had many things in common to talk about — such as his antique hardware collection.   D. Butler, Marina Del Rey, California

WEST BARNSTABLE

Bed & Breakfast Cape Cod Host #24

Location: One mile from Sandy Neck Beach, high on a bluff with grand view of salt marshes and Barnstable Harbor.
Reservations: Available June through September through Bed & Breakfast Cape Cod, page 174.

He is a teacher who enjoys body-surfing and clam digging. She is a pediatric nurse who finds time for the arts and cooking. And they both love the Cape and the casual lifestyle.

Their family is grown and for five years they have spent weekends and summers in this marvelous reproduction antique half-Cape. Inside it's a beam-studded contemporary with stucco and American Indian decor in the living room, traditional in the bedrooms.

In residence: People who smoke.
Restrictions: No pets.
Bed: Three rooms. One double with private bath. One room with single bed and one room with trundle bed that sleeps two; share one bath.
Breakfast: Full. Served until 10 a.m. on the sun porch or in the wonderful kitchen/family area.
Plus: Laundry privileges.
Rates: $24 single. $36 trundle room. $44 double room.

WEST DENNIS

House Guests, Cape Cod Host #WD1

Location: Just a half mile from West Dennis center, in historic district. Secluded and beautiful.
Reservations: Available May through September through House Guests, Cape Cod, page 174.

Three years ago the business executive and his accountant wife, both in their 30s, were looking for an escape away from their city residence. They just happen to love space and company, so they settled on this 11-room house, which has since become their hobby. Originally built in the 1950s, the Cape style house has had several additions, each with an entrance: there's privacy for everyone. The somewhat exotic setting is bordered not only by conservation land but by the Grand Cove with its salt water swimming at high tide and sea life to explore at low tide.

Much of the furniture comes with a story: Grandma's wicker set, an old sofa from the Ritz, antique brass beds from cousin Ed's bargain hunting, and organ bench and table from. . . .

In their first year of B&B the hosts found that many came with programmed days, so hospitality was limited to helpful hints during the extraordinary breakfast. They hope that more guests will plan to stay and enjoy the facilities right here!

In residence: People who smoke.
Foreign languages spoken: A little Spanish and Lithuanian.
Bed: Three rooms, all with water views. One with twin beds and one

with a double share a bath. One has a queen-size bed, balcony, air conditioning, and a private entrance.

Breakfast: Whenever. Host and hostess attempt to outdo each other. Could include fresh fruit, cheese omelets, homemade breads, or blueberry pancakes. Served in fireplaced country dining room with glass sliding doors or on patio.

Plus: Landscaped patio. Dock with sailboat and rowboat. Shellfishing on Sundays. Feed ducks and geese. Bicycles available. Collection of restaurant menus with comments. Carafe of wine cooler prepared daily. Laundry facilities available.

Rates: $42 for twin or double-bedded room. $50 queen. Seventh night free for full-week bookings. Three nights for price of two off-season. Cots $5.

We have spent many vacations on Cape Cod (my family's summer home was there for 30 years) and we couldn't bear the thought of staying in a motel. The hosts offered all the comforts of home, cooked terrific breakfasts, and made us feel like special guests. A couple from London was with us. They had never been to New England. They loved it too! Mr. and Mrs. Justin McCarthy, Bethesda, Maryland

WEST DENNIS

Bed & Breakfast Cape Cod Host #32

Location: Near Bass River in the village off Route 28, near shops and restaurants, ½ mile from beaches.

Reservations: Available April through September through Bed & Breakfast Cape Cod, page 174.

Although this, the oldest house in the village, is just 300 feet away from the village center, it is secluded, nestled among lilacs and cedars.

The host is a walking encyclopedia of outdoor activities who became intrigued with B&B as a traveler. Now that she's into B&B hosting, she dreams of doing this full time in a larger place — some day. Meanwhile, she has restored the outside of the house (her residence for six years), and is in the process of doing the interior, as well as hiking, biking, swimming, baking (all her own breads), cooking, gardening, sewing, and playing the piano.

In residence: One cat. No smokers, but smoking is allowed.

Restrictions: Children should be at least nine years old. No guests' pets.
Bed: One room with steep staircase access (hang on to the rope!). Twin beds. Private half bath.
Breakfast: Continental on weekdays 7:30–8:30. On weekends full, available 7:30–10, with a fruit compote and a choice that may include pecan waffles or banana fritters.
Plus: Small refrigerator in bedroom. Fan. Yard for sunbathing. Clothesline for wet beach clothes. Use of one 10-speed and one 3-speed bicycle.
Rates: $30 single, $40 for two.

I relaxed in a home atmosphere, enjoyed delicious home breakfast . . . even went blueberry picking with my hostess.

Nancy Sheppard, Albany, New York

WEST FALMOUTH

Bed & Breakfast Cape Cod Host #13

Location: On a small pond in a lovely rural residential setting. Five minutes from Old Silver Beach, 7 miles from Falmouth, 11 miles from Woods Hole.
Reservations: Available year round through Bed & Breakfast Cape Cod, page 174.

Peace on a pond is enjoyed and shared by Scottish hosts, a marine biologist and a professional caterer. They have restored and redecorated the 250-year-old Cape Cod cottage in their 10 years of residence. In the downstairs rooms you'll see 18th-century paneling, and the living room ceiling is beamed.

Sometimes the hosts tell the story of how the house was moved in 1921 by a woman who wanted her mother's house to be close to hers. Then the road was called Mother's Lane.

In residence: One large black dog.
Restrictions: Children should be at least 12. No guests' pets.
Foreign language spoken: French.
Bed: Two rooms reached by narrow steep stairs. One double-bedded room and one with twin beds. Decorated with baskets and fans, an evening bag and gloves, antique chests and chairs, hooked rugs. Down quilts. Shared guest bath with claw-footed tub.

Breakfast: Full. Homemade. Special. Includes fresh fruit, bacon or sausages with eggs, mushrooms, tomatoes, croissants, breads and scones, marmalade, jams, butter. Served in sitting room with antiques everywhere.
Plus: Fresh flowers in rooms. Use of dock, pond (which can be fished), and sailboat.
Rates: $30 single, $44 double.

WEST FALMOUTH

Sjöholm Bed & Breakfast Inn

17 Chase Road, P.O. Box 430, West Falmouth, MA 02574
Phone: 617/540-5706 or 548-5070
Location: "In a residential area known for its magnificent coastline and beautiful homes. One-quarter mile from the ocean as the crow flies."
Hosts: Karen and Alan Cassidy
Open: Year round. Closed just for a short time in February. Reservations strongly recommended in summer.

"I guess you could call it an old farmhouse with many add-ons. Furnishings are mostly early Cape (1920–1950) interspersed with some antiques and clocks. We're doing lots of redecorating and attempting to maintain the homey charm which our guests tell us the rambling house has. Ultimately we would like to replace much of the furniture with antiques."

They bought Sjöholm in 1982 (the year of their marriage) and immediately had a "sold-out" season; they are still fascinated, excited, and grateful for all the new friends who have extended invitations to California, Australia, Florida, Switzerland, and New York. The Cassidys exude enthusiasm for a personalized style of hosting that is a challenge with a full house. Such joie! May it sustain.

Alan, now the full-time host, is a licensed pilot who had spent 18 months commuting to Boston when his employer, a large architectural engineering company that builds power plants across the country, decided to move operations to Colorado. That seemed to be the time to "take a gamble" and do what he had been dreaming about since he first bought a home on the Cape in 1970. Karen teaches special-needs children at the junior-high-school level and is involved in several substance-abuse programs.

Restrictions: No pets. Generally, children should be at least 10.
Foreign language spoken: French.
Bed: Thirteen rooms. Two singles, four with twin beds, six doubles. Porch room has one double and two twin beds. All shared baths.
Breakfast: Offered 8–10:45 in summer, but early ferry passengers start about 6. "We don't clean up until 11 and the refrigerator is never closed." Buffet usually includes fresh fruit cup, occasional quiches, muffins, Danish, bagels and cream cheese, cheeses, cereals, yogurt.
Plus: Use of the whole house including large screened and glassed porch. Use of outdoor shower after check-out for beachers. Bicycles for rent on the premises.
Rates: $22–$25 singles, $27–$39 twins, $30–$40 doubles. Porch room is $39 for two, $44 for three, $49 for four. About 25 percent lower in fall, 33 percent lower in spring, lower still in winter.

It truly allows its patrons an "escape to the Cape" feeling of relaxation and pace. The Cassidys really welcome you "home."

S. E. Anderson, Dedham, Massachusetts

The hosts are not only very knowledgeable about their area — places to eat, entertainment, bicycling on Martha's Vineyard — they are also two of the most engaging people we have met. While never interfering, they were always available for assistance or conversation; like old friends, we still correspond. Michael and Bridget Borato, Cleveland, Ohio

Their warmth and genuine concern were instrumental in making our visit to the Cape a fairy tale honeymoon.

Geri Grayson Weinberg and Harold Weinberg, East Windsor, New Jersey

WEST HARWICH

Bed & Breakfast Cape Cod Host #18

Location: In residential area on two acres of pine and oak trees. Ten-minute walk to Nantucket Sound beach. "Maximum 30 miles from everything."
Reservations: Available year round through Bed & Breakfast Cape Cod, page 174.

For two years now the hosts have been living their dream of being on the Cape in an old home as a backdrop for their antiques — "while still in our fifties with good health and lots of energy." The host (an early retiree from the food-service profession) and his wife vacationed for 25 years in this area. Their five grown children have settled from Florida to western New York.

The shingled and shuttered main house of the property (there are also eight cottages) was built as a summer home about 200 years ago. Through the years it has expanded to about four times its original size and for the last 20 it has been a guest house.

"B&B brings the world to our doorstep. We seem to find things in common with all our guests, treat them like family, and sincerely enjoy them. We try to think of the extras that 'feel good' and find guests very responsive."

In residence: One setter, loved by all.
Restrictions: No guests' pets.
Bed: Three rooms with wide floorboards — refinished or repainted — "that slant slightly up or down." One twin with spool beds and braided rugs; private bath. One double with four-poster; private bath. One double with shared bath. Cot and crib available.
Breakfast: Full. Fresh fruit, muffins, maybe egg crisps, quiche, or cheesecake. She cooks and serves. Host pours nonstop coffee. In dining room with everyone seated at one long, elegantly set table.
Plus: Beverage in late afternoon or evening. Patio. Barbecue. Publick Room with books, games, television. Large living room with fireplace.
Rates: $45 single, $50 for two. Cot or crib $5.

WEST HYANNISPORT

House Guests, Cape Cod Host #WH 1

Location: In a quiet neighborhood, 500 yards from an ocean beach, near private beach safe for children, ½ mile to Craigville Beach; 1½ miles to Hyannis.
Reservations: Available year round through House Guests, Cape Cod, page 174.

When the elementary-school principal took early retirement in 1980, he and his wife, a teacher, moved to their ranch-style vacation home and made changes so that now it looks "Capey in addition to still being homey." They do all those things that people say they'll do when they retire — read; garden; and enjoy music (piano), theater, and dining out.

B&B guests are really on vacation here. No rules, all choices, and many personal touches such as tours and extended stays for your car.

In residence: One grandmother and, in summer, one adult daughter.
Restrictions: No pets. No smoking.
Bed: Three rooms. One single with shared bath. One with twin beds that is large enough to take two cots has a private half bath. One with queen-sized bed and private bath.
Breakfast: Full; hostess's handwritten menu gives choices including host's omelet special.
Plus: Fresh fruit in rooms. Outside (as well as inside) shower. Yard. Barbecue. Screened porch with TV. Option of tour of area that encompasses Kennedy Memorial and Kennedy compound. If you're taking the ferry, host will drive you to ferry and your car remains at "home" off the street.
Rates: $28 single, $32 double with shared bath, $44 double with private bath. Seventh night free. Three nights for rate of two off-season.

WOODS HOLE

The Marlborough

320 Woods Hole Road, Woods Hole, MA 02543
Phone: 617/548-6218
Location: In a residential section, on a main road, on a secluded, wooded ½ acre ("a little Brigadoon"). One mile from center of town and from private beach with parking. Two and one-half miles to Falmouth. One mile to bus terminal for New York and Boston. (Arrange for pick-up service.)
Host: Patricia Morris
Open: Year round. Reservations strongly suggested.

It was a snowless January when we spoke, Patricia taking time out from covering a wall with fabric. "Yes, many guests are inspired and want to know how to do it." She has redecorated her authentic full Cape reproduction in the style of English designer Laura Ashley, with sheets and comforters that match walls, and color-coordinated carpeting and tissues too. Furnishings include antiques, collectibles, and some handmade spreads.

During the 10 years that Patricia traveled B&B in California, she took notes on what she liked. Professionally she was an interior designer and teacher there — one who also spent time managing an inn. Her updated story is possibly a B&B classic.

"I have always loved home and all it symbolizes — warmth, tastefully cooked foods, fireside conversations, comfort, pleasing decors — and began dreaming about how I could stay 'home' and still earn my living.

". . . In May 1980 I came east to see my older daughter graduate from college, after which I decided to come to the Cape for a rest. A certain guesthouse kept beckoning to me as I searched for the right place to spend my holiday. I spent the next few days there and each morning that I awoke I felt so positive — the bright sunlight pouring in my windows, the new green leaves on the maples. I began prowling the rooms (I was the only guest) planning how I could make them look. I wondered if the young man would consider selling, but decided against asking him as I was already considering a similar venture in Montreal. As I was warming up my rented car to leave, the owner tapped on my window and said, 'Did you know this place is for sale, Mrs. Morris?' There was no sign posted. I had not told him of my interest in buying a B&B. I made him an offer, he accepted, and two days later I owned the Marlborough. On June 30 I became an innkeeper with a full house of guests. What a shock, but what an adventure. I have loved every moment (well, almost) of it since.

"I am repeatedly amazed at how many lovely people there are in this world. I learn about their professions (do you know we may be entering another mini-ice age?) and often their families and sometimes even their problems!"

Although Patricia will never pass as a native, her enthusiasm for all the Cape has to offer rates with the best of them.

In residence: Maybe a daughter or two at holiday time. P.K. (Pretty Kitty), a 14-year-old Siamese.
Restrictions: Pets rarely allowed.
Foreign language spoken: "Je parle français un petit peu."
Bed: Six rooms. One single, one with twin beds, two triples. Shared baths. One triple with private bath. One family suite with private bath sleeps five. Cots available.
Breakfast: Available from 5:30 on. Menu varies "as the spirit moves the chef." Includes juice, fresh fruit, cereal, eggs, hot breads, perhaps scones or fruit loaves, even small quiches occasionally. Breakfast in bed, outside in garden, or in the parlor at table set with cloth napkins and fresh flowers.
Plus: Pool, available 9–3. Croquet, hammock, rope swing, picnic facili-

ties. English paddle-tennis court. High tea in winter by the fire.
Rates: $32.50 single, $35 twin, $42 double, $47.50–$50 triple, $60 suite. Ten percent discount for five days or longer in season, 30 percent in winter. Cots $5.

Pat has successfully fashioned comfortable rooms into a charming Cape environment. And of course you always look forward to her breakfasts.   Arthur Purcycki, Brookline, Massachusetts

MARTHA'S VINEYARD

B&Bs

EDGARTOWN

Phillip and Ilse Fleischman

off Planting Field Way, Box 1176, Edgartown, MA 02539
Phone: 617/627-5411
Location: Secluded, down a sandy pine-treed road, just a 10-minute walk to Main Street.
Hosts: Phil and Ilse
Open: Year round.

We have returned time and again to the Fleischmans'. Their mini-apartments are decorated with European charm and provide every comfort. They are located in the woods, yet are in easy walking distance to Edgartown. Best of all the Fleischmans are great hosts, both helpful and welcoming!   N. Levin, Lexington, Massachusetts

The Fleischmans designed and built their German country-style house themselves 10 years ago. It's built in post-and-beam style and has many European details.

Phil is an architect now, but he has been a yacht captain and boat builder. Ilse was a kindergarten teacher in her native Germany, and also in Greece; here she is a travel agent and an exuberant hostess.

In residence: Mietze, a large (13-pound), very friendly cat.
Restrictions: No guests' pets.
Bed: Two rooms. Each has a double bed and a private bath.

Breakfast: Continental. At guests' convenience. Probably not hosted, but there are many other hours when you experience the warmth of hospitality.
Plus: Horseshoes and bocce. Use of hibachi.
Rates: $65 June 15–September 15. $40 off-season.

GAY HEAD

Pineapple Hospitality Host #MA 134

Location: Away from the down-island towns. Secluded in oak woods, on a small hill. Atlantic Ocean and Menemsha Pond are 5 minutes by car and Vineyard Sound is about a 10-minute walk.
Reservations: Available through Pineapple Hospitality, page 170, mid-June through mid-September at least.

"Thirteen years ago we designed the house with a large living and dining room and deck for our family (six children), so there is nothing precious. It's simple and modern, not elegant.

"We do aim to make our guests feel like invited rather than paying guests. I think they love, as we do, our seclusion. We are surrounded by woods, and in front of the house there is a small meadow where we have a large variety of wildflowers when I can restrain my husband and his tractor. Right now we are engaged in making a new approach to the house, building a barn, and making a garden.

"The Vineyard is the loveliest of places. Its greatest magic lies in its being an island — and Gay Head is its farthest place. My children, when they were small, used to ask when we were going back to America."

The hosts also have B&B guests in their Providence home, page 322.

In residence: One who smokes "if I don't manage to quit by next summer." Others? "When the living is best, some of our sizable tribe of sons and daughters and various in-laws and in-loves who accompany them." And there are two pets, "a Doberman/pussycat and a real pussycat."
Restrictions: Children should be at least 10. No guests' pets.
Bed: Three rooms. One with queen-sized bed, one with double, and all three with double-decker bunk beds. One full bath, one half bath, and one outside shower with wonderful hot water shared by all.
Plus: "When guests go clamming we all eat the harvest." Use of Sunfish on pond by qualified sailors. Charcoal barbecue grill. Dinner option.

And "last year we made ferry reservations when our guests couldn't get through by phone. We collected and discharged guests at the airport, provided transportation to beaches, sewed on a button or two, generally did whatever met our guests' special needs."
Rates: $45–$60 double. Bunk bed $35, $10 for second person.

. . . Warm, helpful and inviting . . . homey, lived-in atmosphere. The host offered to take us to the ferry or assist us if our bicycles, our only transportation, failed en route. They also went to dinner with us and their other B&B guests, providing transportation and tourist info!

J. St. Clair, Culver City, California

VINEYARD HAVEN

David and Judy Federowicz

122 Main Street, P.O. Box 423, Vineyard Haven, MA 02568
Phone: 617/693-5544
Location: In historic district. Five-minute walk from the ferry; two blocks from business district, public transportation, bike rentals. Two minutes to public tennis courts, beach, and evening band concerts.
Hosts: Dave and Judy
Open: April through October. Minimum reservation: Two nights.

This magnificent home has Palladian windows and a large central hall which immediately brings a wedding to mind. It is neither a museum nor a public inn. Guests experience the warmth of a family that finds joy in sharing their year-round residence with visitors. An effort is made to provide specialized information that allows each guest to become acquainted quickly with the island.

The house was originally floated to Vineyard Haven in 1815 and pulled up the hill by oxen. In 1856 it was moved further back and enlarged.

Before coming to the Vineyard in 1981, when Dave became hospital administrator here, the family lived in Newburyport (Massachusetts) where they had restored a 10-room 18th-century house. Hosting blends Judy's broad experiences — in teaching, small-business managing, and the worlds of interior decorating and real estate.

Memorable guests? "Last summer was an especially wet season. One morning a caller inquired about an opening. He was on his honeymoon — camping — and he and his bride had been washed out by the deluge from the night before. We told him to come. In less than five minutes the newly wedded bedraggled couple was on our doorstep . . . sneakers sloshed . . . hot coffee, warm showers. . . . We prepared a basket of champagne wrapped in a linen napkin which we presented to them when they came downstairs, and then sent them on their way to the cliffs of Gay Head to watch the sun set over the Elizabeth Islands. The rest of the week was indeed a success. They are planning to return to celebrate their first anniversary."

In residence: Sean, 15; Kristen, 13; Ehren Blaine, 10; Katie, 8. Snowflake, an affectionate, white, long-haired house cat. No one smokes, but smoking is allowed.
Restrictions: Children should be at least five. No guests' pets.
Bed: Two rooms. One with fireplace has twin four-poster beds that can be made into a king-size bed. One queen-sized bed in two-room suite with harbor view. Private baths. Handmade quilts, white eyelet curtains and dust ruffles. Cot available.
Breakfast: Continental, 8–9:30, with fresh fruit, homemade bakery and jam. Morning newspaper. Judy usually serves with assistance of Ehren and Katie in fireplaced bedroom or on the porch. Option of sun room for suite occupants.
Plus: A welcome cool drink upon arrival. Fresh baskets of flowers. Fluffy beach towels. Storage place for bicycles. Baby-sitting possibilities.
Rates: June 15–Labor Day, suite $75, fireplace room $55. May 15–June 14 and Labor Day–October 12, $55, $45. Off-season: Suite not available. Fireplace room $35. Cot $10. Ten percent charge for credit cards.

VINEYARD HAVEN

Haven Guest House

278 Main Street, P.O. Box 1022, Vineyard Haven, MA 02568
Phone: 617/693-3333
Location: In a residential neighborhood, a half mile beyond the edge of the village, one mile from ferry landing.
Hosts: Karl and Lynn Buder
Open: Year round. Minimum of two-night reservation for weekends May–October.

Here is peace for guests (mostly couples) in the fireplaced living room, on the screened-in porch, and on the grounds with big old trees.

And there's peace, too, for a busy, contented host who thoroughly enjoys his new career. The 1918 house, built for the son of an industrialist, had been a guest house for 10 years when the Buders bought it in 1981. Karl, a marathon runner, put his master's degree in public administration in one pocket and his title as a probation officer in another, and became a carpenter for a winter. Together with his father he supervised and was involved in installation of new baths, designing, and redecorating. Lynn is responsible for creating the charming and comfortable decor. There are turn-of-the-century lamps, claw-foot tubs, chestnut headboards, some brass beds — each room different, with furnishings from colonial, early and late Victorian, and even late art-deco periods.

For two summers Lynn has commuted on weekends from her executive position with a Connecticut insurance company. (News: Now she is full-time hostess and mother. Alex was born about the time this book went into a third printing.)

"We were tourists before we became innkeepers and we haven't forgotten the pain of a tourist trap. We will give you more advice and directions than you will ever need!"

In residence: Two cats, Antigone, a calico female, age eight; and Lysistrata, a British blue male, age five.
Restrictions: Smoking allowed in guest rooms only. Children should be at least 13. No guests' pets.
Foreign language spoken: Fluent French, "but that was in college 15 years ago."
Bed: Nine rooms with double beds. Two have private entrances. All private baths. One cot available.
Breakfast: Available 8–10 on screened porch. Continental with homemade bread and muffins, and morning paper.
Plus: Living room with fireplace, piano, TV, yard with lawn furniture. Use of bath for beachgoers after check-out time.
Rates: In season, $60–$70. Mid-May–mid-June and after Labor Day–mid-October, $45–$55. Off-season, $30–$40. Cot $10. MasterCard, VISA, and American Express accepted.

It is the type of place where we find ourselves falling in love all over again.   Nancy Autumno, New Britain, Connecticut
. . . A perfect blend of comfort, friendliness, proximity, and economy.
                                                M.M., Trenton, New Jersey
The peaceful quiet of the night gives way to bright and lively conversation in the breakfast room. . . . We have met many wonderful people before heading out for another adventure on the island.
                                        J.K. and P.T.A., Boston, Massachusetts

NANTUCKET

Nantucket's unique characteristics have always been appreciated by its residents. Since others have discovered the island, it has become increasingly popular. Reservations in season are strongly recommended.

Prices vary and tend to be expensive. Since real-estate values have skyrocketed, bed-and-breakfast places with less expensive rates may be those that have been in business for a while.

Food is a feature on the island — but not in B&Bs! Some offer their own special muffins, but lovers of a full breakfast take a short walk to one of the many restaurants.

Because of the popularity of Nantucket combined with the limited number and size of B&Bs (and guest houses), a (frustrating) series of long-distance calls can be a common summer experience. Nantucket Accommodations, 617/228-9559, solves that in part with its listings. When you call (and it is sometimes difficult to get through in season) they put you on hold while they call around to see where they can book you.

The Steamship Authority (phone 617/540-2022) services the island from Hyannis and Woods Hole. Bicycles (extra charge) are allowed. Advance reservations for cars are essential (B&B guests may find little need for them), and are often made months before the summer season.

B&Bs

NANTUCKET

The Carriage House

4 Ray's Court, Nantucket, MA 02554
Phone: 617/228-0326
Location: On a quiet country lane, two half blocks from Main Street, in historic district.
Hosts: Jeanne and Bill McHugh
Open: Year round. Minimum reservation of three nights during busy times.

On the McHughs' first trip together to Nantucket in 1972, their host encouraged them to open a guest house. The McHughs were from Brooklyn, via Long Island, and knew they were tired of the electronics and insurance worlds, but enjoyed entertaining and paying attention to details in the home. Now they are the ones who can tell about two guests who have subsequently become hosts.

Since becoming proprietors in 1973 they find that they can do more than "take from their adopted island" that gives them the different kind of life they sought. She's currently president of the Nantucket Women's Club and is involved with Amnesty International and the nuclear freeze movement. Bill spends time as an officer of Rotary and a trustee at church and participates in the Nantucket Chamber of Commerce.

"Bill's really the intellectual one and I guess I'm everyone's idea of what a mother should be," says Jeanne. Bill has a warm touch too. Guests usually comment on his handwritten personal answers sent in response to any and all inquiries.

The Victorian Carriage House was originally just that for a wealthy sea captain and owner of a large lumber yard. It became a guest house in the 1950s. McHugh changes include the private baths, full-length drapes in the rooms, (reproduction) pine furniture in the parlor, and impeccable housekeeping.

Restrictions: No pets. Children should be at least five.

Bed: Eight rooms. All have private baths. Two have twin beds, four have double, one queen, one triple.

Breakfast: Continental with homemade muffins. Cereal for children. Served 8:30–10 in old-fashioned guest living room or on patio. Leisurely and social. Hosts usually join guests.

Plus: Guest refrigerator, small fenced-in landscaped patio, game room. And if you are there at the right time there may be an opportunity to join Bill at a Rotary meeting, a town meeting, or a church festival.

Rates: Vary according to season. $60–$80 per room. $5 additional for triple bed.

The warmth of Jeanne and Bill McHugh's hospitality plus their superb knowledge and love of the island not only make guests comfortably welcome, but insure return visits.

Sandy and Mike Unger, Livingston, New Jersey

NANTUCKET

Phillips House

54 Fair Street, Nantucket, MA 02554
Phone: 617/228-9217
Location: A six-minute walk to Main Street.
Host: Mary Phillips
Open: Year round. Reservations strongly recommended for summer months.

"Restored by many over the last 200 years, it's a (former) whaler's house with comfortable antiques." Mrs. Phillips had spent many summers on Nantucket before she decided to work for herself in her "pure Quaker-style home." As a year-round resident she loves the fog and mist of the "Grey Lady's" winters and finds the fall "perhaps the most beautiful of all seasons here." In the quieter times she makes baskets. Then guests cycle, walk the beaches, "do the island in about two days" and enjoy the peace in general.

Restrictions: Guest's well-behaved pets accepted.
Bed: Four rooms. One with twin beds. Three with double beds; one has a private bath.
Breakfast: Served mid-June through mid-October. Continental with

homemade cranberry or blueberry muffins.

Plus: Wood stove in living room in winter.

Rates: $30–$45. $50 for private bath. "Favorable winter and early-spring weekly rates for summer job seekers."

NANTUCKET

Pineapple Hospitality Host #MA 143

Location: In historic district, 1½ blocks from Main Street shops, three blocks from ferry. Beach is within cycling distance.

Reservations: Available year round through Pineapple Hospitality, page 170.

This exuberant hostess moved here from Philadelphia three years ago. One day a friend who had a guest house needed room for the overflow. And ever since B&B travelers have been stepping through this Federal-style doorway and onto Oriental rugs, random-width floorboards, and hand-hooked stair carpets. The house, built in 1807 by a whaling merchant, has eight fireplaces, a red living room, and stenciling on the dining room walls.

The hostess loves to share information about the island's history and doings. Her own specialty is using her own herbs to make her herb vinegar.

Restrictions: Children should be at least six. No pets. Nonsmokers preferred.

Foreign language spoken: "Un peu de français."

Bed: Two rooms. One with twin beds. One with twin beds that together can be a king-sized bed. Private baths. Also a small extra room with sofa bed for young people. Cot available.

Breakfast: Continental. Juice or fruit in season, homemade muffins, real coffee. Served in kitchen with fireplace or in dining room.

Plus: Use of porch and flagstone terrace.

Rates: Season is mid-June through Columbus Day. Two per room in season $72, one in room $57. Off-season: two per room $57, one in room $42. Cot $15.

Staying here was like staying at a favorite aunt's. Her home is full of Nantucket charm. . . . and very comfortable. The morning muffins were terrific!   Tom and Susan Ela, Milwaukee, Wisconsin

SOUTHEASTERN MASSACHUSETTS

Reservation Services

Bed and Breakfast Associates Bay Colony

This service has hosts in Brockton, Hingham, Kingston, Plymouth, and Westport. Please see page 220.

Pineapple Hospitality

This service has hosts in Assonet, Attleboro, Dartmouth, Duxbury, Easton, Fall River, Fairhaven, Lakeville, Mattapoisett, New Bedford, North Dartmouth, Onset, Plymouth, South Dartmouth, and Wareham. Please see page 170.

B&Bs

DUXBURY

Pineapple Hospitality Host #MA 98

Location: Southeast of Boston. One mile from village in quiet residential area among towering pines. About six miles from Plymouth, 35 minutes to Boston.
Reservations: Available year round through Pineapple Hospitality, page 170.

Every hour is announced from hither and yon from the host's wonderful collection of antique clocks. They come in all sizes and shapes — including a grandfather one, a mantel version, a carriage clock. From the garden the hostess gathers fresh flowers in the summer and dries some for winter arrangements. The appraiser and educator, grandparents of four preschoolers, love their Cape home with blue shutters; and yes, of course they'll show you through the antique-filled residence.

The enthusiastic hosts enjoy giving touring hints. Some guests come for beaches. Some are on their way to Boston or the Cape. Among memorable B&B guests: a southern politician and his wife — the daughter of a minister — and their family, here to take the Pilgrim's walk in Plymouth at Thanksgiving time.

Restrictions: Nonsmokers preferred. No pets.
Foreign language spoken: Some French.
Bed: Three rooms on private second floor for guests. Two rooms each have twin beds. One single room. One shared guest bath. Crib available.
Breakfast: Continental with homemade muffins, served 8–9:30 in formal dining room with mahogany furniture, Orientals, and silver.
Plus: Terrace. Porch.
Rates: $27 single, $35 for two. Crib $3.

DUXBURY

Pineapple Hospitality Host #MA 195

Location: Thirty-five-minute drive (without rush-hour traffic) southeast of Boston; ten minutes to Plymouth. One block from the bay where the view is fantastic. One mile from a nine-mile beach and one mile from shopping.

Reservations: Available year round through Pineapple Hospitality, page 170.

Built around 1900, this is one of the few Victorians in Duxbury. (Most historic homes, and there are many here, are colonial.) It has stained-glass windows and period furniture. After one family owned the 10-room house for 65 years, it was restored and updated with a new kitchen and baths.

"We have five children. Four are adopted and of different races. The teenagers have many friends and part-time jobs and are not at home very much. Our playroom is in the basement, so the rest of the house is quiet." The host is an executive in a large company. The hostess, an unemployed registered nurse, knows the area well and finds that guests usually go to Plymouth, the beach, boating, restaurants, and "small beach-type pubs."

In residence: Dad smokes. Of the five children, one is six years old and four are in their teens. And there's an Irish setter.

Restrictions: Children should be at least four.

Foreign language spoken: Two of the children speak Spanish.

Bed: One room with double brass bed (formerly a grandmother's) with an old-fashioned spring. Connecting private bath. Two cots available.

Breakfast: Available 7–10. Includes homemade bread, many cereals. Served in large dining room.

Plus: Air conditioning. Baby-sitting possibilities.

Rates: $25 single, $35 for two. $5 for cot.

It was interesting and fun. We enjoyed the large Victorian house and the occupants very much.   Betty J. Stackhouse, Monrovia, California

LAKEVILLE

Pineapple Hospitality Host #112

Location: One mile from Route 140 on a picturesque country road. Set in a two-acre pine grove fronting on a scenic lake that has islands and no commercial development.

Reservations: Available year round through Pineapple Hospitality, page 170.

Where do I start to describe this B&B — on the outside, with the lakeside setting and all that it offers; on the inside, with its furnishings and facilities ("we are sybarites and love comfort"); or with the effervescent hosts? "Bed and breakfast has taken care of our itchy feet to travel. We're hooked." There's a breakfast worth talking about and guests find a banner with their name on the door proclaiming their welcome.

The host is an electrical contractor. The hostess is a business consultant. Before 1979 this custom-designed 12-room brown barnboard house with pistachio green shutters and much glass was their second home. It is fully carpeted and soundproofed. Furnishings are upholstered in velvets, silks, and deep piles. Walls are covered in silk moiré. Color is an important part of the decor, even with the plants — Christmas cacti, gardenias, jasmines, impatiens, and dozens of African violets. There is help to keep things going.

It's a great "escape place" to use as a base for sightseeing, to be outdoors or indoors.

In residence: No smokers, but guests may smoke. A well-behaved intelligent beagle, "one who senses who wants to play," is not allowed in the house; she has her own private kennel.

Restrictions: Children? "We love 'em." Pets? "We have a private kennel on the property for guests to use."

Foreign language spoken: French.

Bed: Four rooms, each with a name and different features (facing lake or the treetops; sunny; one is furnished in antiques). One has a king-sized bed and private bath. One has a double with shared guest bath and refrigerator. Another is a double with shared guest bath. And there's a single with shared guest bath. Bed chairs that open to a single bed available. Every room has color TV, radio, telephone, fan, electric blanket, and intercom.

Breakfast: A gourmet brunch available 7–10. Fresh fruit ("today's included persimmons and kiwi fruit"), blueberry or apple strudel, coffee cake, ham or maple-seasoned sausage, eggs a million different ways, maybe quiche made with homegrown herbs, and some cheese from daughter and son-in-law's farm in Wisconsin.

Plus: Something cool and frosty in warm months, maybe a hot mulled drink by the fire in other seasons. Use of the 28-foot living room with fireplace, dining room, solarium, laundry room, sewing room, office equipment, tape recorders. Swimming, good fishing and boating. Use of a rowboat, 15-foot powerboat, barbecue grill, picnic tables, dock. Two guests may sleep on the powerboat on the lake if they choose. In winter skating, ice boating, and ice fishing may be possible.

In the woods are hundreds of lady's slippers, lily-of-the-valley, mountain laurels, and lowbush blueberries.

Rates: $38 king, $30–$32 doubles, $25 single. $5 bed chair.

. . . Beyond expectations. Our meals were creative, original, and excellently prepared. The warmth of our hostess was the highlight of our vacation.   D. Erhardt, Towson, Maryland

All the comforts of home and more . . . like being with your favorite relative. They spoiled us.   Ron and Carolee Singley, San Jose, California

NEW BEDFORD

Pineapple Hospitality Host #120

Location: Near park in attractive residential area, one mile from downtown historic district.

Reservations: Available year round through Pineapple Hospitality, page 170.

During my research for this book many hosts told me that as travelers they were "very fussy." They frequently offered their own evaluations of other hosts. One "very fussy" host, who gave some negative reviews in her list, made it quite clear that this was an outstanding B&B.

Other happy guests include California travelers who asked the reservation service for a B&B New England experience. They were booked into this lovely 80-year-old Georgian colonial home hosted by a teacher and her business executive husband. Because there wasn't a huge amount of family communication about travel plans, it was a total surprise to everyone to find that the visiting couple and the hosts had mutual relatives.

In residence: Two teenage sons. One affectionate dog.
Restrictions: No guests' pets.
Bed: Three rooms. One single, one with twin beds, one with double extra long bed. One shared guest bath. Crib available.
Breakfast: Continental. Served in formal dining room with china, silver, and crystal. Available 6–10:30.
Plus: Baby grand piano you are welcome to play. Private sun room with television. Limited kitchen privileges. Laundry facilities. Use of patio, grille.
Rates: $25 single, $32 doubles. Crib $5.

NEW BEDFORD

Pineapple Hospitality Host #104

Location: Ten minutes from Route 195. In the city, about a 15-minute walk from the historic district. Bus stops near house.
Reservations: Available year round through Pineapple Hospitality, page 170.

In 1856, at the height of the whaling era, this Italian Renaissance house with a grand staircase was built for a judge and his new wife. More than a century later a young New Bedford boy dreamed of owning the house. In 1980 it happened.

The new owner, now a high-school English teacher in his 30s, has painted the exterior with the approval of the local historical society. Landscaping is in progress. Because 10 owners have each made alterations, the original interior layout is still a bit of a mystery. "Somewhere there must be a picture of what this house looked like, but it hasn't been found yet." The host does know that the original entrance was made into what is now a breakfast room.

"Many B&Bers come with a surprising amount of knowledge about New Bedford architecture and history. And they come from all over the country and the world. Some come by accident; one couple on bicycles missed the ferry to Martha's Vineyard so they stayed with me for a night."

Furnishings include some antiques, a baby grand piano, and a Pairpoint glass chandelier. Locally it is still possible to see glass being blown steps from the Whaling Museum and the cobblestoned streets.

In residence: One who smokes.

Restrictions: No pets. Children over age nine are welcome.
Bed: Two rooms, each with a double bed. One has a ceiling fan. One guest bath with tub on legs. Shower available in second bath.
Breakfast: Set out for you before host leaves. Continental at least. Eggs if desired.
Plus: Living room, television, stereo, porch, backyard. And every bureau has a top drawer filled with brochures and maps. Parking available on street.
Rates: $25 single, $32 for two.

SOUTH DARTMOUTH

Pineapple Hospitality Host #MA 81

Location: About a 10-minute drive from downtown New Bedford in a quaint village with lovely harbor.
Reservations: Available year round through Pineapple Hospitality, page 170.

Summer residents, sailors, and bridge fishermen know about this small community. But for some out-of-towners B&B is the perfect excuse to become acquainted with it. Parts are reminiscent of the Cape or the islands. It's a wonderful area for touring and cycling too.

A stay in this beautiful home is often called "the best part of our vacation" by B&B guests. It has a collection of antiques, whaling items, and marine paintings. The host is a retired professional. He and his wife are long-established residents who enjoy the evening visits with guests who "usually return exhausted from the local sights, outlet shopping, and dinner."

In residence: A big black dog, usually kept outside.
Restrictions: No guests' pets. No smoking in bedrooms.
Bed: Two rooms. One with twin beds, one with double. Shared guest bath.
Breakfast: Continental with muffins, served in dining room overlooking harbor.
Plus: Use of laundry facilities.
Rates $25 single, $32 for two.

BOSTON AREA, NORTH SHORE

N

12

13

10

North Shore

9

MASSACHUSETTS

Atlantic Ocean

14   11

4

5

3

1

6   Boston

2

8

7

The numbers on this map indicate the locations of B&Bs described in detail in this chapter.

BOSTON AREA

JUST A LITTLE WEST

NORTH SHORE

BOSTON AREA

Bed and Breakfast is very popular in Boston. Although some hotels and motels are now offering B&B package rates, at the moment all arrangements for B&B hosts are available only through reservation services. One small hosted inn in a Victorian home has plans to be the first "real" B&B in the city, but the proprietors are not ready to announce themselves.

While *Bed and Breakfast in the Northeast* was being written, the list of reservation services kept growing. The differences among services? Sometimes slight. All the suggestions about reservation services in general, pages 24-25, hold here. Correspondence can work but a telephone call can often give the best sense of attitude.

For many, the convenience of being in the city is primary. But it may be helpful to realize that because the Greater Boston area is compact, several hosts in "outlying" areas are actually closer to downtown Boston than many residents of Boston. If you have time to commute, many of these B&Bs are less expensive than those in the city. Public transportation routes are convenient. The schedules are not as dependable as those Europeans are used to, but the "T" is frequently recommended. Traffic and parking in the city can be time-consuming hassles.

Reservation Services

Bed and Breakfast Associates
Bay Colony Ltd.

P.O. Box 166, Babson Park Branch, Boston, MA 02157
Phone: 617/449-5302 (live 10–12 and 1:30–5, Monday–Friday; answering machine at other times) Established September 1981.
Listings: The 80 listings are in *Boston and Cambridge:* in the *western suburbs* of Brookline, Dedham, Framingham, Natick, Needham, New-

ton, Watertown, Wellesley, Weston, Westwood, Walpole, Holliston, and Hopkinton; in the *southern suburbs* of Braintree, Brockton, Duxbury, Hingham, Kingston, and Plymouth; and in the *north/northwestern suburbs* of Arlington, Belmont, Winchester, Bedford, Concord, and Acton. There are also a few listings on Cape Cod and in Maine, New Hampshire, and Vermont. The detailed directory ($1) is not required for bookings.

Reservations: A minimum 24-hour advance notice is usually needed for bookings.

Breakfast: Although only continental is required, some hosts offer a full breakfast.

Arline Kardasis and Phyllis Levenson first met when they were both complaint mediators in the Consumer Protection Office of Massachusetts. Together with Marilyn Mitchell they focus on minute details that even the experienced traveler may not think of. I found that every host independently and spontaneously spoke of the professional, personal, and efficient service that the agency performs.

Rates: Singles $25–$50, doubles $30–$60. $5 surcharge for one-night stay. MasterCard and VISA accepted.

Bed and Breakfast, Brookline/Boston

Box 732, Brookline, MA 02146
Phone: 617/277-2292
Established August 1982.

Listings: Most of the 25 hosts (the number goes up every time I check) are in downtown Boston, Cambridge, and Brookline. A few are in outlying communities and on Cape Cod. All B&Bs are hosted and some monthly placements are possible.

Ellie Welch's people-oriented professional life has taken an interesting twist. While coordinating services for the elderly for 10 years, she saw the lack of personalized pleasant places for people who came to Boston for medical reasons. She now provides that service, but finds that most guests are from the academic, professional, and business worlds.

Rates: Singles $30–$40, doubles $45–$50. $5 for extra person in same room. Some long-term arrangements are possible. MasterCard and VISA accepted.

Bed & Breakfast Cambridge & Greater Boston

73 Kirkland Street, Cambridge, MA 02138
Phone: 617/576-1492 (live at least 5–6 daily)
Established January 1983.
Listings: Although listings stretch from Maine to Cape Cod and the islands of Martha's Vineyard and Nantucket, most of the 100 hosts are in Cambridge and Boston. Metropolitan and outlying communities with hosts include: *To the west* — Acton, Belmont, Brookline, Concord, Dover, Framingham, Lexington, Natick, Needham, Newton, Southboro, Sudbury, Westboro. *To the north* — Malden, Medford, Marblehead, Winchester, Manchester, Ipswich, Haverhill. *To the south* — Hingham, Quincy, Falmouth.
Reservations: Telephone orders preferred.

Riva Poor, a management consultant, has opened the newest of the B&B reservation services as a full-fledged business with a staff prepared to offer everything. "You name it and we'll find it for you — from musical instruments to kosher kitchens, from access to sports and country clubs to special libraries." Her list of specialties includes homes accessible to handicapped guests. This agency, one of the largest in the country, offers "almost instant" placement capabilities every day of the year.
Rates: Membership fee of $5 per year. Singles $21–$50, doubles $28–$60. All major credit cards accepted.

Bed & Breakfast in Minuteman Country

8 Linmoor Terrace, Lexington, MA 02173
Phone: 617/861-7063
Established March 1982.
Listings: About 25 hosts. Most are in Lexington. A few are also in Bedford, Burlington, Cambridge, Concord, Harvard (Mass.), Winchester, and Woburn.

Sally Elkind and Judy Palmer offer some accommodations specifically for the tourist, and same-day reservations may be possible; but they specialize in short- and long-term B&B stays (with kitchen and laundry privileges) for those who are in the area for business along America's Technology Highway, Route 128.
Rates: Singles $35–$40, doubles $40–$45.

Boston Bed & Breakfast

16 Ballard Street, Newton Center, MA 02159
Phone: 617/332-4199
Established December 1980.

Cynthia Spinner and Elisabeth Moncreiff run an agency that emphasizes service for a particular audience. Bookings are not made for the general traveling public. Advance reservations (only) are taken from *professional people* and *visiting scholars* who are *attending courses, conferences, seminars, and other gatherings* in the Boston area. Travelers who have such an affiliation can book a B&B directly with Boston Bed & Breakfast. All host homes are within walking distance of major hotels or a maximum of 20 minutes by public transportation to Boston and Cambridge. The minimum reservation requirement is two nights.
Rates: Singles $37, doubles $55.

Greater Boston Hospitality

Box 1142, Brookline, MA 02146
Phone: 617/734-0807
Established 1983.
Listings: About 75. Most are in Boston and Brookline. Others are in Cambridge and Somerville, to the west in Needham and Newton, to the north in Marblehead, and to the south in Duxbury.

Last minute callers may be accommodated by Lauren Simonelli, but she prefers advanced bookings to allow time for a written application that avoids extensive phone interviews, and for receipt of deposit and mailed confirmation.
Rates: Singles $30–$45, doubles $35–$55. More for luxury accommodations.

Host Homes of Boston

P.O. Box 117, Newton, MA 02168
Phone: 617/244-1308
Established September 1982.
Listings: Of the 20 hosts, most are in Newton and all are within walking distance of public transportation (approximately 30 minutes into downtown Boston). A few are in Boston as well as in other Greater Boston communities. Suburban locations all are in single-family colo-

nial, Victorian, or contemporary homes.

Marcia Whittington offers a service that emphasizes personal attention. Most hosts are professionals who have grown families.

Rates: Singles $32, doubles $45. Seventh night free. Short-term rates available. MasterCard, VISA, and American Express accepted.

New England Bed & Breakfast, Inc.

1045 Centre Street, Newton Center, MA 02159
Phone: 617/244-2112 for evenings and weekends; answering service 617/498-9810
Established April 1980.
Listings: About 50, most just outside of Boston, in Brookline, Cambridge, and Newton. Several are in downtown Boston. A few are in other parts of Massachusetts, Maine, New Hampshire, and Vermont in areas of scenic or historic significance.

John Gardiner selects homes that believe that "bed and breakfast is a cottage industry designed to provide reasonably priced clean accommodations by friendly people." Advance reservations are preferred but last-minute bookings sometimes possible. New this year is the offering of tours with bookings from B&B to B&B in the four New England states covered by the service.

Rates: Singles $20–$32, doubles $33–$47.

University Bed and Breakfast, Ltd.

12 Churchill Street, Brookline, MA 02146
Phone: 617/738-1424
Established July 1982.

Ruth Shapiro and Sarah Yules accommodate *visiting professionals, accompanying spouses, and/or traveling companions* who are *coming to Boston primarily for academic reasons.* Bookings (unavailable for the general public) can be made directly with University Bed and Breakfast. Most hosts are accessible to public transportation or are within walking distance of universities and other meeting places. Advance reservations are preferred.·

Rates: Singles $32, doubles $50. Extended-stay rates sometimes available.

Pineapple Hospitality

This service has about 30 hosts in Greater Boston. In town their B&Bs are in Back Bay, Beacon Hill, and Charlestown. Area communities with Pineapple B&Bs, many near public transportation, are Arlington, Belmont, Cambridge, Chestnut Hill, Concord, Malden, Melrose, Newton, Somerville, and West Roxbury. Please see page 170.

B&Bs

BOSTON: BACK BAY

Bed and Breakfast Associates
Bay Colony Host #102

Location: Near Newbury Street shops, Charles River, and the Ritz too.
Reservations: Available year round through Bed and Breakfast Associates Bay Colony, page 220.

The two architects, both from large families, lived in various neighborhoods before they renovated this town house and moved into the penthouse that has utilized stairwell space and flights in interesting ways. Victorian detail has been preserved. Furnishings are eclectic — modern, antique, and refinished "finds."

"Where is . . .?" Stand in the bay window, look down Commonwealth Avenue mall to the Boston Garden (swan boat home), find the Park Street Church spire, check the host's map, and you'll know the Faneuil Hall Marketplace is just beyond. It's a good location for orientation and experiencing life in a city that is made for walking.

After 10 years in the area the hosts know the city well and they share guests' joy in discovering its rich resources. Their own professional lives spill over to their concern about protecting the architectural quality of their historic district. And when they get away from woodworking, painting, or sewing, there are moments ("not enough!") for canoeing, camping, sailing, wind-surfing, or cross-country skiing.

In residence: A well-behaved dog who loves attention and will take whatever is offered.

Restrictions: No smoking. No guests' pets.

Bed: One room on their third floor with view of John Hancock Tower. No elevator. Oversized twin beds made by host's father from one six-foot-high headboard.

Breakfast: Usually continental 7:30–9. Eat in sunlit dining room with antique grandfather's clock.

Plus: Roof deck with garden and view of city. Use of living room with piano. For parking, most guests use the Boston Common underground garage; $5 for 24 hours.

Rates: $45 single, $50 for two. $5 surcharge for one-night stay.

There is no way our visit could have been better fulfilled than by our friendly host and hostess in their gracious old brownstone. We were comfortable and safe and in a very warm atmosphere.

Gerald and Mary McKay, St. Paul, Minnesota

BOSTON: BEACON HILL

Beacon Hill Condo

Location: In the shadow of the State House, near Massachusetts General Hospital.

Reservations: Available most of the year through Bed and Breakfast, Brookline/Boston, page 220.

This former teacher from California and Santo Domingo, a New England native, now has time to enjoy her home and guests. "I like to listen to what they have to say and I honestly like to wait on people!"

She lives in a modern, quiet, secure building with views of the brick townhouses and sidewalks in this historic neighborhood. The condominium's decor is eclectic and picture perfect with white wall-to-wall carpeting in the living room and prominently displayed Japanese kimono, oil paintings, and artifacts from her travels.

The convenient central location has been appreciated by everyone from a west-coast travel agent to one exhausted business person who just wanted to sleep and recuperate.

Foreign language spoken: Spanish.

Bed: One room with queen-sized bed. Private bath.

Breakfast: Continental with special local muffins and the morning newspaper. Served on contemporary table under crystal chandelier.
Plus: Air conditioning.
Rates: $35 single, $40 for two. Seventh day free if staying full week.

BOSTON: CHARLESTOWN

Pineapple Hospitality Host #MA 153

Location: In historic district. One block from the Freedom Trail, 10-minute walk to USS Constitution, 15-minute walk or 10-minute bus ride to Faneuil Hall Marketplace.
Reservations: Available year round through Pineapple Hospitality, page 170.

"We moved here after living in the suburbs for 16 years. There are several differences. Here many of our neighbors are seventh-generation residents. I still have a garden but it is actually more private. Now I walk to work in Boston. And, as it has turned out, we are in a place that is perfect for B&B.

"About half our guests come with cars. We've had cyclists too. Even though I grew up in Ireland, I couldn't have imagined that hosting would leave you with the feeling of having friends rather than paying guests. There is a special sharing that is wonderful."

A marathon runner (cheered at the finish line by the hosts), Europeans who gravitate to the attractive courtyard, and an intern-to-be at a nearby hospital have been recent guests.

The hostess first came to America as an exchange student in 1956. Her permanent return to the United States was in 1965. Shortly after that she met her husband, an engineer who was born of Polish parents in India and brought up in Afghanistan. They have made some exciting changes while restoring their lovely new home, an 1846 brick townhouse. The room arrangement is perfect for B&B. And from the deck on the roof there is a wonderful view of the North End and Boston Harbor (and the forthcoming Tall Ships).

In residence: No one who smokes, but smoking is allowed.
Restrictions: Sorry, no pets allowed. And it's not an ideal place for children.
Foreign languages spoken: French, Polish, Turkish.
Bed: A suite on the second floor that has one room with a double bed,

adjoining sitting area, private bath. A room with double bed on third floor with shared bath. Rollaway available.

Breakfast: At guests' convenience weekdays; self-serve after 8. Continental with freshly squeezed orange juice and homemade cake, croissants, or Irish bread. Weekends you may have orange yogurt pancakes with strawberries in season.

Plus: Use of deck and garden courtyard. Storage area for bicycles. Parking on the street or in a nearby lot (no charge).

Rates: $36 single, $40 double. Rollaway $10.

BOSTON: GOVERNMENT CENTER

Bed and Breakfast Associates
Bay Colony Host #104

Location: Near Faneuil Hall Marketplace, boat rides on the Charles, Freedom Trail, North End . . . a long list of attractions right in the city; and steps from a subway stop.

Reservations: Available year round through Bed and Breakfast Associates Bay Colony, page 220.

From the balcony off the living room and guest room you can see the airport and ocean in one direction, the Charles River and Cambridge in another. The British hostess, a human-relations consultant and counselor, has traveled widely in Europe. She has lived here for several years and furnished her residence with English and early American antiques and English brass rubbings.

Restrictions: No pets. No smoking.
Foreign language spoken: Spanish.
Bed: One room, a single with a shared bath. Rollaway bed available.
Breakfast: Continental. Flexible. Maybe with hostess, depending on her schedule. Eat-in living room near window with a marvelous view of the city.
Plus: Air conditioning. Garage parking available, $5 for 24 hours.
Rates: $40 for one, $45 for two. $5 surcharge for one-night stay.

Not only inexpensive for a walk-to-everywhere in this popular section of Boston, but a hostess who provided information and all the comforts of a friend's home. It is now my first choice of the way to travel!

Mrs. Geraldine Stevens, Stamford, Connecticut

Because of the hostess's amiability and the lovely room, my trip to Boston was particularly enjoyable. At the end of the day I was able to share my experiences with a new friend.   B.P., New York, New York

BOSTON: SOUTH END

Bed and Breakfast Associates
Bay Colony Host #101A

Location: Just three blocks from John Hancock Tower (the best orientation spot for first-time visitors to the city).
Reservations: Available year round through Bed and Breakfast Associates Bay Colony, page 220.

She comes by her hosting naturally. "My family built and operated a large hunting and fishing resort in northern Minnesota during the '30s." Now the hostess is in senior management ("still in the people business") involved in the recruiting and training of women staffers and helping clients to solve financial problems. She's also an ardent golfer and loves to walk.

After living in the Back Bay for 12 years, she made the move to a new neighborhood, the most diverse in Boston, and to a new condominium that was constructed in the shell of a bowfront brick town house. "After looking at dozens of renovations all over the city, this is *it!*" For guests it's a relaxed, easy atmosphere.

There have been a variety of B&B guests here. "They attend conventions, lectures; visit hospitalized relatives; sightsee; eat in good restaurants; and then come home — exhausted."

Restrictions: Minimum age for children: teens. No pets.
Bed: One double room with shared bath.
Breakfast: Served until hostess leaves for work; self-serve after that. Includes fresh fruit dish, croissants or "great Danish" (a big hit) enjoyed at octagonal table in dining room with exposed brick.
Plus: Air conditioning. Maybe beverage in late afternoon or evening.
Rates: $40 single, $45 for two. $5 surcharge for one-night stay.

... A charming, warm, and cordial hostess. ... lovely renovated brownstone close (within walking distance) to many of Boston's great historical sites. She was so helpful in providing us with just the right

information regarding restaurants and places to see. Bed-and-Breakfast traveling is a perfect way to go!   L.F., St. Paul, Minnesota

BROOKLINE

The Parsonage

Location: On a tree-lined court two blocks from shops and subway. Ten-minute ride to downtown Boston.
Reservations: Available through Bed and Breakfast Brookline/Boston, page 221.

"I think I have found my metier as a concierge." She is a free-lance court reporter. Her husband is a college chaplain. "Through the years people of all ages in all situations have used our home for a variety of reasons. B&B is really an outgrowth of our interest in shared housing which is of long duration."

They live in a Victorian brick row house built just before the turn of the century at a time when Beacon Hill could be seen from here. Their four daughters are grown, but with the casual friendly lifestyle "you never know who will be here."

In residence: People who smoke.
Restrictions: No pets.
Foreign language spoken: French "poorly."
Bed: One room with twin beds — "my pride and joy, with top-quality mattresses and down comforters." One double room, also with comforters. Shared bath. Cot and crib available.
Breakfast: Continental.
Plus: Garden, patio.
Rates: $30 single, $45 for two. Cot or crib $5.

The warm hospitality and helpful hints for touring Boston were more than we ever expected. Hosts made this trip a very special memory.
Melina and Mary B., Seattle, Washington

BROOKLINE

Salisbury House

Location: One block from public transportation, 20-minute ride into Boston. One mile from Boston College.
Reservations: Available year round except the Christmas holiday week through Bed and Breakfast, Brookline/Boston, page 221.

The 1893 Victorian house is rather grandiose and the family is rather down-to-earth—"relaxed, supportive, and informative. We do a lot of entertaining anyway. We enjoy our house and enjoy having others enjoy it." The "others" have included a couple who were in town on a romantic getaway; a psychiatrist and his wine-merchant wife from France who invited the host family to visit them in Europe; and visitors from Nova Scotia (another sincere "come and see us" couple). Some seek the companionship of the entire family and others want privacy. The hosts' two-year-old was good company for a little one in town with his parents for an evaluation at a local hospital.

The husband, an Irishman who has traveled B&B throughout Ireland, is a marine consultant; his work takes him all over the world. Spain is one of the many countries the family has lived in. They share sightseers' enthusiasm for Boston and are members of the Museum of Fine Arts.

The house — "it's easy to get into the mood of it" — has an ornate hallway; nine fireplaces, each with a unique mirrored mantel; antiques; some furnishings from the Far East; and a carriage house.

In residence: Two teenagers, one preschooler, one cat.
Restrictions: No smoking.
Foreign languages spoken: French and Spanish.
Bed: Two rooms each with a double bed and TV. One has a brass bed and antique cradle. Crib and cots available.
Breakfast: Continental. Served in formal Victorian dining room.
Plus: Beverage when you arrive "to unwind." Game room in Victorian decor with pool table and card table. Baby-sitting possibilities.
Rates: $35 single, $45 for two. Crib or cot $5.

BROOKLINE

Country Comfort

Location: High on a hill, not far from main road, very residential. A 7-minute walk to public transportation, 15-minute ride to downtown Boston.
Reservations: Available year round through Bed & Breakfast in Minuteman Country, page 222.

"There seems to be a pattern to sightseeing activities, and by now we can tell who would like what restaurant in a certain price range." The experienced hosts are an assistant to a college president and her husband, a business executive. They live in a lovely brick home built in the late 1920s.

In residence: A pipe smoker.
Restrictions: No pets. Nonsmokers preferred.
Bed: Two rooms, each with twin beds. One guest bath. Both rooms have sliding glass doors that open onto patio. Both have use of a guest den.
Breakfast: Continental on weekdays 7–7:30, self-serve after that. More elaborate on weekends when hosts and guests usually eat together.
Rates: $38 single, $45 for two.

BROOKLINE

Victorian Row House

Location: Two blocks from 10-minute subway ride into Boston. Within walking distance of Museum of Fine Arts and Fenway Park, colleges and hospitals in Longwood area.
Reservations: Available year round through Bed and Breakfast, Brookline/Boston, page 221.

"The heart of B&B is being with guests on their arrival and at breakfast." That's the thinking of the host, "an outdoor person" who juggles hospitality and her home business in this 1876 house. Guests are welcome to use the entire house and they appreciate the spaciousness that spans the three floors. In one case a room was booked for a month because different members of the family had various reasons to be in Boston. And when we spoke a professional person from the Midwest was in town because of relocation.

Marble fireplaces, chestnut woodwork, and heirloom antiques are part of the charm here. The decor is enhanced by the handwork of the host's mother, a B&B host herself in another part of the state. Mother has made curtains, worked in needlepoint, upholstered, and created pressed-flower parchment lampshades. And there are some wonderful photographs from the hostess's extensive travels on three continents.

In residence: One cat.
Restrictions: Nonsmokers preferred. Children should be at least 12.
Bed: Three rooms. One cozy single. One with twin mahogany four-poster beds. One with antique walnut double bed. Two shared baths; one has Victorian tub and a brick wall, the other antique and brass accessories and new stall shower. Fold-out bed available.
Breakfast: Continental, usually with homemade breadstuffs and jam. Served in fireplaced dining room with bay window overlooking garden.
Plus: Deck off dining room. Beverage in late afternoon or evening. Television.
Rates: $30–$35 single, $45 for two. Fold-out bed $5.

Concern for the comfort and pleasure of the guests is paramount to the delightful hostess who is attuned to the needs of the traveler whether it be a quiet rest, advice on places to eat or to see, or an invitation to mingle after a long day of sightseeing. Use of anything from hair dryer to heating pad is offered. . . .   Lyn Van Vranken, Stockton, California

How often I've looked at these lovely homes and wondered just what they felt like on the inside. The hostess proved to be as gracious as the home. I had my privacy and at the same time felt myself to be a welcome and special guest.   Carol Heinz, Duluth, Minnesota

CAMBRIDGE

Harvard Square is not a square at all. It's a wide area of historic and cultural resources interspersed with shops that reflect the international flavor of the community. There are minimalls everywhere, bookstores every few feet, museums and events aplenty.

B&B hosts are in the square; 5 minutes' walk from the heart of the square; 10 minutes from the famous glass flowers in the University Museum; near MIT; or in a lovely suburban home just a 12-minute bus ride away. Hosts are singles, retired, families, widows, couples, professors, professionals, business-oriented people, consultants, world travelers, foreign-born, newcomers and old-timers — all friendly people who appreciate the diversity that surrounds them.

Practically every reservation service that has hosts in the Boston area has listings in Cambridge, a city that is only about six miles square and minutes by subway from downtown Boston. As I have said elsewhere, be specific with the reservation service. Maybe location is your number one priority. If it's pampering you're looking for, say so!

CAMBRIDGE

Harvard Square #1

Location: Right in the square, but on a side street.
Reservations: Available year round through Bed and Breakfast Brookline/Boston, page 221.

"Very few homes were built like mine in the area. It is a century-old three-story, three-family home with all rooms off a hallway. I have done extensive renovations on my top floor. Five walls were taken down to open up the living-dining and kitchen into one large warm area. From my front door you can see shops and boutiques; from my kitchen window there are backyards and trees! Through B&B I have been able to extend hospitality to people from all over the world."

The host, an entrepreneur since the age of 19, has been at this address for 15 years. She is an avid ocean sailboat racer and downhill skier.

Restrictions: No smoking. No pets.
Bed: Two rooms. One single and one double. One shared bath for apartment.
Breakfast: Continental.
Rates: $25–$35 single, $45 double.

CAMBRIDGE

Carol and Henry

Location: A 15-minute walk (north toward Harvard Law School and Porter Square) from Harvard Square.
Reservations: Available year round through New England Bed & Breakfast, page 224.

Their fourth-floor walkup residence is in a Queen Anne–style building, built in 1880, that is restored outside and renovated inside. Skylights, loft, wood stove, and balcony give it a warm, lovely, and spacious feeling.
The host is an educator and his wife is a social-policy researcher.

In residence: One son, age two.
Restrictions: Children should be no older than 2½.
Bed: One sofa that pulls out to a double bed. New private bath. Crib available.
Breakfast: Continental. Could be self-serve for late sleepers.
Plus: Garage parking. Baby-sitting possibilities.
Rates: $24 single, $37 for two. Crib $5.

CAMBRIDGE

Bed and Breakfast Associates Bay Colony Host #201

Location: Ten-minute walk from Harvard Square on a side street that I lived on 26 years ago. Three blocks from Harvard Law School.
Reservations: Available year round through Bed and Breakfast Associates Bay Colony, page 220.

A native! The hostess grew up in this neighborhood, one that has seen changes but still has many older residences. Her home, built in 1773, is a "workman's cottage" that has a history of two moves. "It is so tiny that you can almost see it all from the front hall." Although the hostess is retired, her time is filled with city politics, part-time work with the Nuclear Freeze movement, needlework (she was making a kilt the day we spoke), and museum going.

Most guests have full days planned. Sometimes, because of her own flexible schedule, she has been known to drive visitors to some distant museums. The B&B room always has a good collection of maps and information about current doings.

In residence: A 2½-year-old short-haired tabby with double front paws.

Restrictions: No smoking. Sorry, no children.

Bed: One large room with a twin bed and a rollaway.

Breakfast: Continental with croissants or muffins. Served 7–9 at cozy round table with floor-length tablecloth.

Plus: Air conditioning, if necessary. Fan available too. Street parking available.

Rates: $35 single. $45 for two. $5 surcharge for one-night stay.

The hostess and her 18th-century house are as much a part of our memories of Boston/Cambridge as the Freedom Trail, the Museum of Fine Arts, and the Glass Flowers. Her genuine interest in our interests, her hospitality, courtesy, and enthusiasm extended far beyond what we ever expected. Bob and Susan DuRar, San Mateo, California

CAMBRIDGE

Bed and Breakfast Associates
Bay Colony Host #203

Location: Four flights up (on foot) in a brick building. A 10-minute walk toward MIT from subway and Harvard Square. Two-block walk to bus.

Reservations: Available year round through Bed and Breakfast Associates Bay Colony, page 220.

After spending several years as a teacher and department coordinator at a well-known preparatory school, this host decided that a change was in order. At the moment she is completing her MBA and expects to be in marketing in the Boston area. Secretly, though, she would like to run an inn in southern France.

So careers and career change can naturally be topics of conversation. And so can Boston, a city that she thinks is special. Restaurant suggestions? "I love to cook and to eat and enjoy recommending restaurants to others." One B&B guest jogged with this marathon runner along the Charles River. Whatever, she greets every new experience with contagious enthusiasm.

Her condominium is furnished with a combination of modern, antiques, and art nouveau.

In residence: Three parakeets.
Restrictions: Nonsmokers preferred. No pets.
Foreign language spoken: Limited French.
Bed: Two rooms. One with a double bed and one with a single.
Breakfast: Juice, scrambled eggs, real coffee.
Plus: Plant-filled balcony.
Rates: $30 single, $40 double. $5 surcharge for one-night stay.

. . . Gave me insights into Boston that fellow conventiongoers did not have. My choice of bed and breakfast resulted from limited funds, but the next time I'll use it regardless of funds, just for the experience. My hostess was warm and outgoing and cared for me like family!

Cathy Ament, Rochester, New York

Just a Little West

BEDFORD

Brownstead

Location: On a main road between Lexington and Concord. Three miles (no public transportation) from Lahey Clinic and the Burlington Mall. Sixteen miles to downtown Boston.

Reservations: Available year round through Bed & Breakfast in Minuteman Country, page 222.

"Our house is an exploded ranch, an interesting exercise in remodeling and combining inherited goods."

Their hosting is an interesting blend too. Life experience is rich. They are grandparents of 10, ages 1–13. He is in professional placement (of engineers) and she is a librarian in a vocational-curriculum resource center.

Their guests have had the opportunity to explore the area on their own or with the family, and (at one New Zealander's request) to attend church functions. "We follow whatever they bring to us." Families of hospitalized patients find quiet and solitude, if that is appropriate — and supportive understanding too.

Restrictions: No smoking. Sorry, no pets.

Bed: Two rooms for a family or same party. One room with double bed and air conditioner. Other room has two twin beds that can be bunked. Cot, crib, and portacrib available. "Everything that grandparents need."

Breakfast: Up to 7:45 a.m. Chef's choice each morning. (He is apt to consult.)

Plus: Large yard, television, laundry facilities.

Rates: $35 single, $40 for two. $60 for one party in both rooms.

LEXINGTON

The Little Red Schoolhouse

Location: One block from historic center of Lexington and the Green, overlooking Belfry Hill.
Reservations: Available year round through Bed & Breakfast in Minuteman Country, page 222. Two-day minimum reservation.

The advertising executive, an avid sailor and downhill skier, recently moved from her waterfront address in Boston to this terrific condominium in a converted century-old schoolhouse.

She now knows about B&B as a newcomer from both points of view. Her very first guest arrived with a local friend who came to see what the alternative to impersonal housing (a hotel!) would be like. It was so successful (for everyone) that the host has subsequently had her own wonderful first B&B experience as a traveler. The day we spoke she was expecting someone from Sweden for a fortnight. Another host is launched.

Restrictions: Nonsmokers preferred. No pets allowed in building.
Bed: One room. Could be single or double. Share 1½ baths.
Breakfast: Continental weekdays. Full weekends.
Plus: Air conditioning. Kitchen privileges. Bicycle storage. Outdoor patio.
Rates: $35 single, $40 double.

LEXINGTON

The Minuteman Inn

Location: Within walking distance to Lexington center.
Reservations: Available year round through Bed & Breakfast in Minuteman Country, page 222.

The background of the 200-year-old home has a ring of a historical plaque: "Home of clock-maker, burned by British in 1775, rebuilt in 1780, house moved to current location in. . . ."

The hosts have had extensive travel experience and have always wanted "to do something to repay for magnificent situations we have had in Europe." As it turns out, they have found their guests as interesting as the hosts they met abroad. The hostess is an architectural designer and her husband is a professor.

In residence: One dog who loves children.
Bed: Private suite with two connecting bedrooms and private bath.
Breakfast: Served beautifully in a plant-filled area between study and living room, or in dining room. Fruit, homemade muffins, and cereals included. Pancakes or eggs on Sunday.
Rates: $35 single, $40 double.

While in town for a family wedding we found our B&B hosts gracious and considerate, providing comfortable quarters and a delicious breakfast. We had not tried B&B before in this country and would not hesitate to repeat the experience.   Dr. E. M. Kent, Lakewood, Colorado

LEXINGTON

A Doll's House

Location: Just off main street, at top of hill on way to Concord or Route 128. At bottom of hill is the town, full of tourist stops, old houses, graveyards, a lot of shops, good restaurants, and bus to Cambridge and Boston.
Reservations: Available year round (maybe not in December) through Bed & Breakfast in Minuteman Country, page 222.

With prompting, the hostess may talk about her own career history as an art director with a national magazine and with a major high-fashion retailer, but her guests may take the lead with their "experiences, ideas — even problems sometimes." Conversation is hardly a problem with interests that run from old trolley cars to houses, from political action to choral singing. B&B guests have included parents visiting their college students, job hunters, and tourists.

The hostess grew up in this area and returned about five years ago. "I plan to learn the history of my house. I do know that it was built in 1884, the same year, by coincidence, as the coal stove in the living room. The furniture is mostly worn Victorian with a few irreverent touches. There is a meadow in which I try to grow wildflowers with minimal success."

In residence: At least three cats, four if son has arrived for a visit.
Restrictions: No smoking. No guests' pets.
Bed: One room with a double bed. Shared bath.
Breakfast: "I have been told, urged, even commanded, to serve only continental, but. . . ." Eat in the small attached solar greenhouse.
Plus: Fans in summer.
Rates: $35 single, $40 for two.

LEXINGTON

Red Apple Inn

Location: One mile from center of town in woodland setting, surrounded by gardens and trees.
Reservations: Available year round through Bed & Breakfast in Minuteman Country, page 222.

The colonial house has been 30 years in the making and remaking. It is typically New England by plan. The builders, the hosts, researched everything carefully at Old Sturbridge Village.

Their appreciation for the late-1700s/early-1800s style can be seen in what has been built, refinished, and collected. Whatever talent or skill they haven't mastered is on their list to learn. Curtains and crewel work, braided rugs, cabinets and furniture, even a carved wood Noah's Ark have been done true to the period. Since the hostess has retired from being a nursery-school teacher and director of the Red Cross, she's taken tin-painting and watercolor lessons. Her husband, a teacher, recently made window seats in the summer kitchen (family room), added a greenhouse, and converted the garage to another bedroom.

Beyond living history right here, B&B travelers explore Lexington and Concord; and often, with the assistance of the hosts and their maps and knowledge, the home is used as a base for day trips that are launched complete with parking and age-appeal hints.

In residence: One black fluffy cat who loves children. Preschool grandchildren live nearby and have special day times with their grandparents.
Restrictions: No guests' pets. No smoking.
Bed: Second floor with two bedrooms and connecting bath. Twin beds in one room and a ¾ antique bed and cot in another. All traditional decor with appropriate fabrics and colors. Crib (the hostess's own) available.

Breakfast: Guests' choice, 7–10. Full. Includes homemade jams and maybe homemade bread. Served in colonial kitchen with brick floor, wood stove, birdfeeder at window.
Plus: Living room. Yard with garden, swing, sandbox. Own television and radio. Long-term guests have kitchen privileges; those with babies have laundry privileges.
Rates: $35 single, $40 for two.

NEWTON

Margaret's Bed & Breakfast

Location: In Newton Center, five-minute walk from shops and subway (25-minute ride into downtown Boston).
Reservations: Available year round through New England Bed & Breakfast, page 224.

The grandmother of 28, ages 8 to 30, has been in the at-least century-old home for 53 years. "We moved here just after getting married. I really should go to City Hall and find out about this house."

She used to house as many as 10 or 12 students when the nearby college dormitories were filled, but lately she has limited the guest list to B&B travelers.

In residence: One cat.
Bed: One room with two twin beds. Shared bath.
Breakfast: Continental with homemade muffins.
Plus: Porch, living room, off-street parking.
Rates: $26 single, $44 for two.

What a lovely discovery! The house is so warm and friendly . . . the breakfasts so delicious.
S.K., Stamford, Connecticut

Weekend great
Friends sublime
Bed superb
Breakfast divine!
Dr. Eileen R. Taska, Greenwich, Connecticut

NEWTON

Myra and Richard's Bed & Breakfast

Location: On a quiet residential cul-de-sac in Newton Center, one mile from shopping and public transportation, eight miles to downtown Boston.

Reservations: Available year round through New England Bed & Breakfast, page 224.

From the maps and directions to the umbrella when it rained, our stay in Boston was made most pleasurable through the advice and suggestions of our hosts.   Dale and Pam Johnson, Deerfield, Illinois

Other guests write about the "genial, helpful hosts in a delightful 1930s colonial home." And there are frequently notes about "keeping in touch and come visit us." Some guests, like the hosts, have had B&B experiences in England. Others are grateful for a "first, comfortable, fun, and adventuresome experience."

The hostess, a training consultant, and the host, a quality-control manager, are interested in "art, music, cooking, traveling, tennis, people, gardening, solar engineering — and all things beautiful."

In residence: Ashley, their baby girl. A Siamese cat. No smokers present but smoking is permitted.

Restrictions: No guests' pets.

Bed: One double room with private bath. Cot available.

Breakfast: Continental with homemade bakery, served in traditionally furnished dining room with collection of international artifacts.

Rates: $26 single, $44 for two. Cot $8.

Our very first B&B was highlighted with a knock on the door at 5 a.m. After putting us in charge of the house and explaining about breakfast our hosts departed for the hospital where the hostess gave birth to their first child, a daughter. As parents of two children it was exciting to be a part of such a special time.   Don and Jay Petro, Schenectady, New York

NEWTON

Waban One

Location: One mile from Waban Square, on a quiet street close to Route 128, Route 16, and the Massachusetts Turnpike.
Reservations: Available year round through Host Homes of Boston, page 223.

"Most guests seem to be busy from after breakfast until after dinner, but one of the delights of B&B, that human aspect of sharing, has been the opportunity to help with information and directions (for driving, public transportation, and bicycle); to talk about similarities and differences in lifestyles with Europeans; or even to compare the estimate for a roof repair with someone from Texas. And still, hosting requires a certain flexibility — recognizing that some guests prefer total privacy."

The host has lived in the comfortable and cozy brick center-entrance colonial for 17 years. She is a former actress and singer. Her home is filled with books and music.

In residence: One who smokes. College-age daughter at home summers. One cat.
Restrictions: No children. No guests' pets.
Bed: Two single rooms, one with private half bath, one with shared bath.
Breakfast: Full.
Plus: Living room with wood stove. Screened porch. Off-street parking on property.
Rate: $32 per room.

NEWTON

Windsor Hill

Location: Near Routes 128 and 16. In a quiet residential area, five minutes' walk from Waban Square and public transportation into Boston.
Reservations: Available year round through Host Homes of Boston, page 223.

"In my native England B&B has been mostly a business, maybe treated as an inexpensive hotel. It is interesting to see the movement take hold with variations in America. I have hosted business people, some here for a family celebration, and one who was scooped up daily by a realtor for condominium hunting. Wherever you are traveling, it's nice to know a native rather than having a stack of pamphlets in hand."

The family bought the Victorian (1896) home 16 years ago when they had four young children. Furnishings are more modern than traditional. The host, an X-ray technician in Boston, now has extra room and is happy to share the peace and quiet.

In residence: One teenage daughter. One cat.
Restrictions: No guests' pets.
Bed: Four rooms. Two singles on second floor share a bath. Two rooms on third floor: one single, and another room has twin beds and a telephone. Shared bath.
Breakfast: "A typical English breakfast!"
Plus: Swimming pool in summer. Off-street parking available.
Rates: $32 single, $45 double.

WELLESLEY HILLS

Bed and Breakfast Associates
Bay Colony, Host #376

Location: Fifteen miles west of Boston, within walking distance of commuter train, ¼ mile from shops, very quiet and private.
Reservations: Available year round through Bed and Breakfast Associates Bay Colony, page 220.

"I love my own creature comforts and get fun out of providing the same to others. People interest me, entertain me, and make me feel very alive and I like to do the same for them."

Her husband is in the hotel and food business. She is a former English teacher who now teaches swimming. The interests of this couple, grandparents to six, range from law, philosophy, and literature to tap dancing, theater, and outdoor activities. Their home was built in 1976 by an Italian in French (Normandy) style with castle effects for an English girl married to an Irishman. The builder preserved a teahouse, located in the woods and once used for watching tennis matches, and built a bridge from it to a deck that leads into the kitchen of the home built on the site of the tennis courts. "When we bought the property in 1977 we thought, and still think, of it as a beautiful example of synchronicity in ideas and taste. It is filled with sculpture, paintings, and artifacts collected through our years of travel here and abroad."

Most guests are busy during the day, come home to gracious hospitality late in the afternoon, rest, and go out to dinner.

In residence: No one who smokes, but smoking is permitted. Two (old) dogs. One older cat and one young cat.
Bed: Three rooms. One with a double bed and a single. One with two twin beds. One guest bath. And an auxiliary room with pull-out bed and private bath.
Breakfast: Usually continental with fresh fruit and croissant, but could be full. Served in fireplaced dining room with stained-glass collection, overlooking woods, or on deck in good weather.
Plus: Air conditioning. Use of teahouse, patio, beautifully landscaped grounds. Beverage in late afternoon or evening. Kitchen and laundry privileges available.
Rates: $40 single, $45 for two, three in one room $50. Auxiliary room with same party $15. $5 surcharge for one-night stay.

WEST OF BOSTON

Bed and Breakfast Associates
Bay Colony Host #557

Location: Thirty-five minutes west of Boston by car. Near Longfellow's Wayside Inn.
Reservations: Available year round through Bed and Breakfast Associates Bay Colony, page 220.

Even Boston area natives would feel as if they have had an Experience in this 1690 house on 150 acres. In addition to the gambrel-roof colonial, the property has a three-stall barn built 200 years ago; extensive gardens and lawns; country pine antiques — and a long-time resident who hikes two miles every day in the woods where hawks, owls, and deer are seen regularly. Snowshoeing and cross-country skiing (bring your own) are possible too.

Because the host is involved in town affairs, guests could hear about present-day concerns — or maybe attend a good old-fashioned Town Meeting if you're there at the right time.

The host, a former writer and public-relations person who did medical editorial work, now finds B&B is a natural extension of years of hosting foreign visitors in the authentically preserved home.

Restrictions: No pets. No smoking.
Bed: Three rooms. One with two twin beds. Two with a double bed in each. Shared guest bath. Cots available.
Breakfast: Whatever you would like.
Plus: "It's home for my guests." Fruit bowl. Gardens. Woodlands.
Rates: $35 single, $40 for two. $5 surcharge for one-night stay.

Our family including four teenagers was able to see unusual historical landmarks and exhibits in the Boston area because of the helpfulness of our host. With warmth and marvelous advice we were treated like a friend.   Halsted Welman, South Haven, Minnesota

The charm of this historic home is enhanced by its owner who makes you part of the family the moment you step across the threshold.
                                                    R.M.P., Ballwin, Missouri

NORTH SHORE

Reservation Services

All of the following have several North Shore listings:

Bed and Breakfast Associates Bay Colony

Please see page 220.

Bed & Breakfast Cambridge & Greater Boston

Please see page 222.

Pineapple Hospitality

Please see page 170.

B&Bs

ESSEX COUNTY

Bed and Breakfast Associates
Bay Colony Host #661

Location: Thirty-five minutes to Boston, 25 minutes to Gloucester, 35 minutes to Newburyport, 10 minutes to canoeing.
Reservations: Available year round through Bed and Breakfast Associates Bay Colony, page 220.

"Everybody unwinds here. Our friends come for R&R. . . . We have 30 acres, enough to get lost on."

Come for B&B and see what he means. The gracious 14-room house was built in the 1830s on stone foundations and with doors and fireplace mantels dating from 1660. Wide pine board floors, wainscoting, beehive ovens, eight working fireplaces, a large country kitchen, fine furnishings — all lovely and charming and comfortable.

It's perfectly all right to arrive in the dark and drive away after breakfast, but you may want to allocate time to explore the property on your own. Just pay attention to the official Rules of the House:

1) No smoking in house, barn, or outbuildings.
2) No feeding the animals, or monkeying with them without official supervision.
3) No spitting, swearing, or blasphemy except in barn basement.
4) If you find a gate open, leave it open; if you find it shut, leave it shut. If you can't find it, don't worry about it.
5) Don't take house towels to the pool. Help yourself to the swimming towels in the cabana at the pool.
6) No children under 12 in the pool without adult supervision.
7) Feel free to browse in the various libraries.
8) Personal services such as laundry, baby-sitting, and cracking jokes on company time are yours by private arrangement with Marie.
9) Your suggestions, complaints, and disputes will be handled out behind the barn.

The host, an investment advisor, is a journalist and author who writes a dispatch devoted to humorous aspects of farm life. His wife, the farm manager, is a horticulturist and an accomplished equestrian.

Foreign languages spoken: French, Spanish, German.
Bed: Three double rooms share a bath. One single shares another bath. Two sleep sofas and cot available.
Breakfast: Join the hosts for a real farm breakfast at 8. Everything homegrown. Fresh eggs. Vegetables in season. Blueberry pancakes. Zucchini marmalade for bread or muffins. Herbs from garden. Milk from down the road.
Plus: A tour of the house is quite possible. Guests may use the pool (May 30–Labor Day), tennis court, and hiking trails. Self-guided tour of barn, chicken house, sheep shed, rabbitry, spectacular greenhouse and gardens. In season pick-your-owns from the 850 highbush blueberries are sold to whomever.
Rates: $45 single, $55 double. Family rate, $85 for four persons. $5 surcharge for one-night stay.

My daughter and I shared a spacious room on this beautiful estate. The hosts were gracious but never intrusive. Our special requests — where to find the nearest good seafood restaurants, where to run a few miles before dinner, and how to get most quickly to upper Manhattan the next day — were speedily gratified.   Gretchen Kreuter, St. Paul, Minnesota

GLOUCESTER

Williams Guest House

136 Bass Avenue, Gloucester, MA 01930
Phone: 617/283-4931
Location: On Good Harbor Beach, on scenic drive, 1½ miles from Gloucester center, 5 miles from Rockport. View of beach, salt marshes, or the ocean from every window.
Host: Betty Williams
Open: May–November.

Betty agrees with all her guests who think that she is lucky to live in this big old house by the ocean. It was just what was needed for five growing children, but in 1968 when the youngest left for college, she started renting rooms. And for 11 years it has been a bed-and-breakfast arrangement. Now that her husband is retired, he gives a hand too.

Hints? Maybe plan on more time! Because there is so much to see and do in the area, many who have come from a distance frequently comment that their planned one-night stay isn't sufficient.

Restrictions: Children should be at least four years old.
Foreign language spoken: None really, "but I have loads of fun using my high-school French and trying to understand my French Canadian guests."
Bed: Four rooms. One with a double bed and one with twin beds share a bath. Private baths for a room with a queen-sized bed and a single bed and another room with twin beds. Cot available.
Breakfast: Continental, 7:30–10:30; includes homemade muffins.
Plus: Use of picnic table and barbecue grille overlooking beach.
Rates: $30 single, $40 for two. Off-season rates are $5 less.

MARBLEHEAD

Pineapple Hospitality Host #MA 188

Location: Coastal town north of Boston. On main street near historic district with shops and villages ⅔ mile away. Forty-five minute ride to Boston by car or bus.
Reservations: Available year round through Pineapple Hospitality, page 170.

Our hostess shared her house, her knowledge of the area, her friends, and her own personal warmth. We had come to a seaport but we discovered a friend.   B.S.S., Lexington, Kentucky

The hostess's great-great-great-grandfather helped George Washington cross the Delaware during the Revolutionary War, so she loves to bring guests into Town Hall to see the "Spirit of '76" painting. Sightseeing with her includes a special viewing point for watching boats from around the world in the beautiful harbor, and walking along the winding streets with historic homes, lanes, and hidden old-fashioned gardens.

After touring nearby communities filled with art colonies, history, fishing fleets, and lobster boats, guests of all ages frequently visit with the hostess in her comfortable traditional home. She is a 35-year resident with three grown children and is involved in community activities and the arts.

Even though our stay was less than 24 hours, we actually have feelings of "homesickness" for Marblehead and the lady we fell in love with — at first sight!   Bill and Marty Martin, Ponte Verda Beach, Florida

In residence: A nonsmoker, but smoking is allowed. One dog, "a sweet loving golden retriever."
Restrictions: No guests' pets. Children? "I love them!"
Foreign language spoken: Wee bit of German.
Bed: One large room with double bed with adjoining single room. Cot available.
Breakfast: Full with homemade muffins, served at guests' convenience.
Plus: Fan. Dining room with piano. Television. Outdoor patio. Good chance of guided tour through the town.
Rates: $27 single, $37 for two. $5 for cot in same room. Adjoining room: $20 for an adult, $10 for child.

NEWBURYPORT

Morrill Place

209 High Street, Newburyport, MA 01950
Phone: 617/462-2808
Location: On historic High Street within walking distance of restored waterfront area. Five-minute drive to nine-mile beach at the Parker River National Wildlife Refuge on Plum Island.
Host: Rose Ann Hunter
Open: Year round.

In the last six years Rose Ann Hunter has established two personalized inns and retained her sense of humor. She was a Midwesterner with experience in advertising, public relations, and inns, and decided to be her own boss in a community that needed an inn. Two years after creating the Benjamin Choate House (six rooms and one common room) in Newburyport, she acquired this 1806 26-room mansion — stripped, without a book in the library, a lighting fixture, or a rug. It did come with architectural features: 12 working fireplaces, 96 windows, a graceful double-hung stairway with six-inch risers, Indian shutters on the first two floors, and chair-rail and wainscoting on the second. Mrs. Hunter has designed and supervised all the redecorating, trying to be as true to the period as possible. Refurbishing is constant, auctions are attended at least once a week, and every dealer in the area knows the inn and its needs.

Morrill Place is used for functions as well as B&B guests. If you happen to be there when a wedding, a dance with baroque music, or a mayor's reception is scheduled, you are invited!

Eight-year-old Kristin may be the country's youngest experienced innkeeper. Since the age of two she has attended all meetings and conferences. On occasion she checks guests in, serves them tea, and describes restaurants (from first-hand knowledge); and only once has she booked the same room to two different parties. She, like her mother, is writing a play based on the years of living in an inn. If one of the scripts is eventually produced, you might recognize a fellow guest (or yourself) as a character. From what I understand, material is plentiful. ("How much advance notice do you need for a funeral?" a caller once asked.)

In residence: Daughter Kristin, age eight. Chubby, the rabbit, may be hopping about. Lepra is their bird. Monroe and Tyng are two cats. The cocker spaniel, Pooh, was born in early 1983.

Restrictions: No children during winter season.

Bed: Ten guest bedrooms. Some private baths. In summer some rooms are made into suites for families. Every room has at least a double and a twin bed. Cot and crib available. The Daniel Webster Room has an antique mahogany four-poster. Different moldings are in every room on the first two floors but the former maids' quarters on the third floor have exposed beams and plaster walls that lend themselves to country decor.

Breakfast: Continental, 8–10.

Plus: Music room with square grand piano and a 1910 Steinway. Library, front parlor, 2½ acres of grounds. And interesting items such as a daguerreotype collection and hair wreaths in oval frames. Guests are frequently given tours at check-in (4 p.m. and after) and others may have tours at 3 by appointment.

Rates: $38–$48. Additional cot in room: $5 for children, $10 adults. American Express card accepted.

NEWBURYPORT

The Windsor House

38 Federal Street, Newburyport, MA 01950
Phone: 617/462-3778
Location: Downtown, within walking distance to the harbor and shops.
Five minute drive to the ocean and Parker River Wildlife Refuge.
Hosts: Judith Crumb and Jim Lawbaugh

There is an old New England feeling to the former residence/chandlery that has Federal and Colonial furnishings. Warmth, hospitality, and charm are epitomized here by Judith and Jim, innkeepers, who offer that special blend that invites returnees.

Judith was director of career counseling at the Museum of Fine Arts in Boston at the time that she converted the 16-room-mansion into a bed and breakfast inn with each room distinctively different. The three-story brick building, across from Newburyport's Old South Church, was completed in time for the wedding of Aaron Pardee and Jane, his new bride. The house was built by ship carpenters and has an exquisite combination of Colonial, Georgian, and Federal styles of architecture. The huge country kitchen in the former chandlery shipping and receiving room has a high beamed ceiling and a welcoming oak table "where we spend a great deal of time talking and sharing and often laughing."

One guest wrote me an enthusiastic five-page handwritten letter. Excerpts from it:

Judith greeted us with one of those bear hugs. . . . The roaring fire draws everyone to the kitchen which is the hub of life at the inn. . . . There is a graciousness here. . . . A Federal mansion tastefully decorated with Her Majesty Queen Elizabeth II reigning supreme over the fireplace in the Commons. . . . Two nights, too short a visit. . . . We hope to buy an inn ourselves.

Pauline O'Reilly Weakland, Cranford, New Jersey

In residence: Lilabet Silver Jubilee, "our toy 'guard' poodle," and two cats, Sir Thomas More and Lord Merlin.
Restrictions: Pets should be well trained. All children welcomed.
Foreign languages spoken: A little French, less German.
Bed: Six rooms, each with a name and a story behind it. Three with private baths. One shared bath for other three rooms. Some rooms have Sheraton four-posters or sleigh beds, single beds as well as double. Window seats and Federal shutters in three rooms. One room has

Indian shutters with "gun slits." Trundle beds available.

Breakfast: A celebration. Watch preparations and chat with Judith and Jim. Served 8:30–10, earlier by arrangement. Fresh breads and muffins, eggs cooked with homegrown herbs, homemade sausage, own brew of coffee.

Plus: Tour that sometimes goes into the warehouse and attic where the original hoist is stored. The Commons (formal living room), courtyard, and small patio. A hand-drawn map with suggested back roads. Option of dinner by advance reservation.

Rates: (includes tax and service charge): May 1–November 1, shared baths $67 single, $73 double. Private bath $72 single, $79 double. 10% less out of season. Trundle bed: $12. MasterCard and VISA accepted.

ROCKPORT

The Inn on Cove Hill

37 Mt. Pleasant Street, Rockport, MA 01966
Phone: 617/546-2701
Location: One block from village, harbor, shops. Bus servicing Cape Ann goes by the inn. One mile to train to Boston; pick-up service provided.
Hosts: Marjorie and John Pratt
Open: Washington's Birthday weekend in February through October. Reservations strongly recommended in summer and fall. Two-night minimum reservation on weekends from Memorial Day through October.

We discovered The Inn on Cove Hill by accident and have been return-ing for many years because of the relaxed atmosphere there. The rooms are beautifully decorated, comfortable, and always clean. The breakfasts with muffins baked by John are delightful, especially in the warm weather when served outside under yellow umbrellas. . . . I want to write more about the hospitable innkeepers. . . . John and Marjorie Pratt make their guests feel very important. . . . They listen with inter-est to all tales of their guests. . . . When we found out more about them and their lives, we were astounded. . . . We reserve a room in Rockport even when we are just going to Boston.

Howard and Ingeborg Schwab, Pompton Lakes, New Jersey

Five years ago John, a civil engineer specializing in soils and foundations, and Marjorie, a registered nurse in public health and home care, took a trip around the world. They stayed in many homey, clean B&Bs (and also hiked in the Himalayas, Switzerland, and the Pacific Northwest). John had an aunt who was once an innkeeper, and the idea of a "being together, sharing a business in a lovely location" had strong appeal. Since 1978 the Pratts have been restoring the classic square, three-story, 200-year-old Federal-style home that has a welcoming picket fence, granite walk, and attractive doorway. This year cedar shingles are replacing the asphalt roof. Inside, the architectural details include pumpkin pine floorboards, H and L hinges, dentil molding, and a spiral staircase with 13 steps symbolizing the original 13 colonies. Furnishings are some fine Pratt family antiques, some reproductions, and original paintings, including one done in 1881 of an ancestor's clipper ship.

The Pratts like to feel that they offer a friendly atmosphere and the option of privacy. When a guest writes, "I came to the sea for peace and escape and found it at your inn," it's a good feeling — for everyone.

In residence: One cat named Thai. First Pratt child, due any day now, will, with parents, move into the main house when sleeping through the night. And help is on the way.

Restrictions: No guests' pets. Children should be at least 10.

Bed: Eleven rooms, eight with private bath. Eight have double beds and two of those rooms have an additional single bed. One with queen canopied bed. One with queen canopied and a trundle bed. One with twin four-posters.

Breakfast: Continental includes one of seven varieties of muffins (full recipe sheet shared). Served 8–10 in daisy garden or in living room.

Plus: Guest refrigerator. Third-floor porch with view of harbor and ocean. Hot spiced cider during fall and winter months. Blackboard with events of interest. Tour complete with saga of how the mansion was built with legendary pirates' gold.

Rates: $23 single year round. Rates for two depend on bath arrangement and vary according to season. $35–$49 twin, $23–$40 double, queens and triple $35–$49. Third person in room for two: $5.

SALEM

The Suzannah Flint House

98 Essex Street, Salem, MA 01970
Phone: 617/744-5281
Location: Five-minute walk from train stop to Boston. Within walking distance of historic sites, museums, Pickering Wharf.
Host: Charlotte Post
Open: March–November.

When the time was right for Charlotte to start B&B, she researched the history of her house and named it after an 18th-century owner. Since May of 1981 she has had guests from all over the world in her cheerful home that has wide-board floors, plants, and antiques acquired from local auctions. Because she has a full-time job as volunteer coordinator at a Council on Aging, she may not be there when guests leave on weekdays. One of her bowlful of notes reads, "Thanks for your oasis. I felt far away from my usual busyness."

In residence: Three (timid) cats, not allowed in guest area, but they are allowed in garden.
Restrictions: Sorry, no guests' pets.
Bed: Four rooms, all air conditioned. Two rooms that each have twin beds. One double. One with double and a twin. Cot available. One shared full bath and a half-bath.
Breakfast: Continental with four kinds of fresh fruits, homemade breads. Served in sitting room with wicker furniture, fireplace, wood stove. Leisurely. "Guests sometimes make plans to tour the town together."
Plus: Garden, shade trees, sea breeze.
Rates: $45 per room. Cot $10. MasterCard and VISA accepted. Ten percent less for weekly stays.

CENTRAL MASSACHUSETTS, CONNECTICUT VALLEY, AND HAMPSHIRE HILLS

N

VERMONT

NEW HAMPSHIRE

⑥

②

Connecticut River

MASSACHUSETTS

⑦

⑧

• Amherst

⑤

④

Worcester •

③

• Springfield

①

CONNECTICUT

The numbers on this map indicate the locations of B&Bs described in detail in this chapter.

CENTRAL MASSACHUSETTS

CONNECTICUT VALLEY

HAMPSHIRE HILLS

CENTRAL MASSACHUSETTS

Reservation Services

Folkstone Bed & Breakfast Registry

P.O. Box 131, Boylston, MA 01505
Phone: 617/869-2687
    After a year of hosting through a regional B&B reservation service, Margot French saw a need for a local registry that would match hosts and guests. Her hosts are all in the Worcester area and include a Federal-style home in Grafton and a converted artist's studio in West Boylston.
Rates: $25–$30 singles, $30–$50 doubles.

Sturbridge Bed & Breakfast

43 Main Street, Williamsburg, MA 01096-0211
Phone: 413/268-7244
    Tim and Mary Allen, organizers of Berkshire Bed & Breakfast Connection, page 278, are interviewing hosts within a 15-mile radius of Sturbridge. At the moment they have selected 10 and will probably have more in the very near future.
Rates: $20–$30 singles, $25–$40 doubles.

Pineapple Hospitality

This service has homes in the Sturbridge and Worcester areas. Please see page 170.

B&Bs

HOLLAND

Pineapple Hospitality Host #MA 169

Location: On Lake Milton, 1½ miles from I-86, six miles from Old Sturbridge Village, four miles from Brimfield Flea Market.
Reservations: Available April–December through Pineapple Hospitality, page 170.

Travelers looking for overnight accommodations were always stopping into the restaurant that the host used to own. He's now in the heating business, is a solar dealer — and is the town's building inspector. Their six children are grown. And so rises another B&B in the right place at the right time.

The hostess is always surprised if guests clear the table or make their own bed. But some just take to the homey atmosphere in the country setting in that way. Maybe it's the huge stone fireplace in the family room combined with happy hosts who think this is the best thing that they have ever done.

In residence: People who smoke.
Restrictions: No guests' pets.
Bed: Five rooms. Twin beds are in two of the rooms. Three have doubles. Two rooms per bath. Cot available.
Breakfast: Full with pancakes or French toast or home fries and eggs. Eat in dining room overlooking lake.
Plus: Some rooms are air conditioned. Beverage in late afternoon or evening. Maybe a light snack. Baby-sitting possibilities.
Rates: $25 single, $35 for two. Cot: under age five, no charge; over age five, it is $5.

My daughter and I both felt the friendly warmth extended to us and other guests. . . . It was an atmosphere of close friends as we sat around the fireplace.   Cathy Cellamare, North Windham, Maine

TOWNSEND

Wood Farm

40 Worcester Road, Townsend, MA 01469
Phone: 617/597-5019
Location: On a main road, on a corner 15-acre lot, on the bank of Squannacock River. One-half mile from the center of a small New England town. Near antique and craft center, Harvard Shaker Village, 15 miles from summer stock theaters, 20 miles from the hiking trails of Mount Monadnock in New Hampshire, and ten from Mount Watatic in Ashby. Within a half hour's drive to downhill skiing at Nashoba Valley and Mount Wachusett in Massachusetts and Crotched Mountain and Pheasant Run in New Hampshire.
Hosts: Debra Jones and James Mayrand
Open: Year round. Advance reservations preferred.

Although the sheep may steal the show here, the residents of this historic home are kind of fun too.

Debra and Jim, both electrical engineers and natives of the area, bought the center chimney cape-with-an-ell in 1983 with the idea of hosting. They were married by the hearth of the new-to-them home, the residence of many generations of the Wood family until 1964. This was the first house in town, built around 1716, as part of the original King's Grant.

Extensive restoration efforts have included the refinishing of all those wideboard pine floors. Jim grew up in a family that is in the construction business. Debra's mother is a recognized interior decorator. Ideas abound here. This year's project may be an herb garden.

The weaving room is the setting for another one of Debra's avocations, one that allows her to use wool from her own sheep. By the time you read this, there should be at least two dozen sheep on location. "Each has its own name and personality. Kids are welcome to hold them." Lambing season is April and May. Shearing takes place on Memorial Weekend with the assistance of Debra's uncle who lives nearby.

Wood Farm has four fireplaces, two wood stoves, and a relaxing atmosphere. Its location is really perfect for the diverse interests of Debra, Jim, and their guests. There are country antiques to be found. The hosts are active bicycle racers, cross-country skiers, and runners. You are welcome to join them on a local tour. (Bring your own equipment.)

In residence: Hawkins, "a stately Lab" always bedecked in a red bandanna, and Beannie, a cute, cuddly, and confused cockapoo.

Restrictions: Children are welcome if supervised by parents. No guests' pets, please, but horses or barn animals are allowed. Sorry, no smoking permitted. Check-out time: 10 a.m.

Foreign languages spoken: A little French and Spanish.

Bed: Four second-floor rooms in a guest ell. One has a queen-sized bed. Three have double beds; one of these rooms faces the river and a waterfall. All carry out the country theme and have quilts made by Debra. Some even have stenciled canvas rugs she has made. Two shared guests baths, one with large claw-foot bathtub.

Breakfast: Large country meal. Possible features: apple/walnut quiche, smoked slab bacon and fresh bread, fresh fruit and eggs Benedict, or an herb souffle, sausage, and croissant. Served in the keeping room that has an eight-foot open hearth, or in dining room with fireplace, or, in summer, on patio along the river. Available 6:30–8 on weekdays, 7:30–9 weekends when it tends to be a more leisurely meal.

Plus: A welcoming beverage. Use of a separate B&B living room or join the hosts in theirs. Bedroom fans available. Use of library, weight training room (for adults). Pond for swimming and skating. Plenty of literature about area attractions and a good sampling of menus from nearby restaurants. Complete tour of house and 250-year-old barn along with a visit to resident sheep.

Rates: $25 single, $30 double. $35 for queen room. Cots $10.

WARE

The Wildwood Inn

121 Church Street, Ware, MA 01082
Phone: 413/967-7798
Location: Midway between Old Sturbridge Village and historic Deerfield on a quiet street with former mill owners' homes, ¾ mile up the hill from the center of town. Old stone walls are on the two acres of land that lead back into woods and the river.
Hosts: Margaret and Geoffrey, Heather and Lori Lobenstine
Open: Year round. Reservations strongly recommended. Minimum reservation for holiday weekends: three days.

A beautiful home where guests feel welcome. Serenity, warmth, "country yummies," and a four-poster bed! It's perfect.

Linda Lynch, Valencia, California

Other guests are inspired to write songs, poems, and ditties, even adaptations of the 23rd psalm and "Home On the Range." Some return for their wedding — and some have been known to name their children after the hosts.

The town fathers weren't quite sure what a B&B was when the Lobenstines applied for a license four years ago. The Lobenstines weren't quite sure what Ware was when they stumbled upon it by taking a wrong turn during a New England trip. And if you're not quite sure who would come to a B&B in this relatively unknown community, consider five (often overlapping) types: "literary people, historic people, nature people, college hoppers, guests who only wish to relax and do absolutely nothing."

Maybe the host family really did discover Ware. Whatever, they have put it on the map. Zest combined with caring! Geoff, a former postal worker, is now a social worker in Springfield. Margaret is living her dream of being in a big house with a wraparound porch, just like the one she read about years ago in *Little Women*. She has taught remedial reading, been in early-childhood education, and worked in the post office; and she has long been involved in community, political, and women's issues. Peace is always on her list of concerns. Now she also enjoys letting folks who dream of innkeeping get "hands on" experience in her innkeeping apprenticeship program, possibly the first and maybe the only one of its kind in the country.

The house? A lovely Victorian, filled with American primitive antiques. Many comment that it combines the fascination of a museum with all the comforts of home.

In residence: Heather and Lori, both age 16. They may serve you a breakfast, beat you at a game, invite you to play basketball, or answer questions about being twins. Spoofer is their beagle mutt; he has an adorable face, but he still isn't allowed in the parlor or guest rooms.

Restrictions: Children should be at least six. No guests' pets allowed but there is a recommended heated kennel in town. No smoking above first floor and not during breakfast.

Bed: Five rooms with primitive antiques and dual-control electric blankets. The three doubles have heirloom quilts. One with twin beds has a four-window bay. The one with a queen-sized four-poster and a beautiful embroidered quilt has a four-window bay and air conditioner. Shared baths.

Breakfast: "One of the magic times of the inn." Served at hour arranged with guests the night before. Continental included in rate with freshly homemade bakery, maybe popovers, peach butter. For slight charge ($1) your menu will include one of Margaret's "country yummies," maybe something with the name of "chipmunk pie."

Plus: So much to do here, combined with the good location for day trips, that guests are often sorry they haven't booked a longer stay. A partial list includes the parlor ("meant to be used") with century-old log-cabin quilt on the wall, carpenter's chest full of games, beautiful old cradles, wooden music box. Canoe available to guests without charge. Short paddle to area with wildlife. Swimming in brook-fed swim hole in a lush setting and with a tree rope swing too. Ice skating on the river in winter. "Private" cross-country skiing on about five miles of groomed trails, just one mile from inn (at a friend's) through virgin woods. And maybe a welcoming hug from Margaret.

Rates: They differ according to room, season, and events in the area. The range for doubles is $25–$40. Twins: $32–$40. Queen: $37–$45. MasterCard and VISA accepted.

Superb; friendly; real; heartwarming; all-around homey, caring, open feeling.   Sam Weintraub, New York, New York

WESTBOROUGH

Heywood House

207 West Main Street, Westborough, MA 01581
Phone: 617/366-2161 or 366-7440
Location: Minutes from the Massachusetts Turnpike, Routes 495, 20, 9, all near high-technology headquarters. On a curve of what is now a main suburban road, 1½ miles from center of town, three miles from Willard House and Clock Museum, 20-minute drive to Worcester, 30 minutes west to Sturbridge Village and east to Wayside Inn.
Hosts: Mary and Doug Heywood
Open: Year round. Advance reservations required. Two-night minimum stay July and August weekends.

"During the spring and summer the birds sing in symphony. If you don't like this kind of music, avoid these seasons. Try our fall instead; foliage at its best without even driving."

Doug admits to being a frustrated innkeeper, professional travel consultant, and former student of hotel and restaurant management. His family came to town in the mid-1800s and settled in this center-hall colonial farmhouse that had been built around 1729. Gnarled trees are vestiges of the orchard that once was. Inside the house there are some exposed beams and rounded corner walls.

When Mary, a Wisconsin native and occupational therapist, and Doug moved into the homestead a couple of years ago, it was with the specific intention of having a B&B. During the first eight months of their marriage, they both had full-time jobs and redid the whole house themselves, "keeping the old flavor." Each guest room is decorated in a different color scheme.

It didn't take long before the Heywoods reaped the big reward: the feeling of having family in the house all the time. Heywood House has been discovered by many travelers including honeymooners, and has been booked for family reunions and wedding parties. Some guests take Doug's recommendations for back roads to covered bridges, to Indian burial grounds, and by historic taverns and homes. My husband and I are among the cyclists who have pedaled along these marvelous byways.

In residence: Helcha, their golden retriever, "looks forward to meeting all who wish her greeting."

Restrictions: Smoking only in first-floor sitting room. Children should be at least 10. Check-out time: 11 a.m.

Bed: Four second-floor carpeted rooms. One with twin beds and one with a double bed share a bath. One double-bedded room has a full private bath, and another has a private bath with shower only.

Breakfast: Juices, homemade muffins and breads, cereals, beverage. Served in dining room that overlooks back yard and woods. Available 7–8:30 weekdays, 8–9:30 weekends and holidays; exceptions by arrangement.

Plus: A welcoming beverage. Fireplaced living room with piano and a good supply of books and magazines, games and puzzles. Outdoors: Badminton, croquet, horseshoes, and grill (bring your own charcoal). "We specialize in fiery sunsets." Cleared trails on many acres for walks and cross-country skiing. And a tour of house, if you would like.

Rates: Single $25 with shared bath, $30 with private bath. Double $35 with shared bath, $40 with private. Cots $10 extra. Weekly rates available.

CONNECTICUT VALLEY

Reservation Service

Pioneer Valley Bed & Breakfast Network

43 Main Street, Williamsburg, MA 01096-0211
Phone: 413/268-7244
Listings: About 15 hosts are located in the Amherst-Springfield area including the communities of Amherst, Belchertown, Buckland, Chicopee, Greenfield, Holyoke, Springfield, and Wilbraham.

Mary and Tim Allen, directors of both Sturbridge and Berkshire bed-and-breakfast reservation services, may link those two and Pioneer Valley as one organization covering western Massachusetts. Essentially, between their three services, that is what they do now.
Rates: Singles $20, doubles $25. A few are higher.

B&Bs

NORTHAMPTON

The Beeches

Hampton Terrace, Northampton, MA 01060
Phone: 413/586-9288
Location: Overlooking the valley and hills. Six-acre estate that is ¼

mile from downtown Northampton and Smith College.
Hosts: Daisy Mathias and Robert Nelson

When Daisy and Bob decided to move to New England ("land of independent, down-to-earth, and friendly people") they hoped to find a place that would be big enough for B&B guests. What they recently located was one of Calvin Coolidge's homes, the one he retired to after the presidency. It is a gracious 16-room shingled Tudor with a wonderful library room. And the new owners are just about moving in, so they wonder if the first guests will help decide where to hang pictures! Furnishings are antiques from both hosts' families. Hosting is intended to be welcoming and elegant in space that allows for privacy.

Bob is originally from Kansas and is involved in administrative work. Daisy lived in the Boston area for 10 years and is a speech and language pathologist.

In residence: Sugar Plum, their 10-year-old cat. Ida Mathias, Daisy's mother, is here during wintertime.
Restrictions: No pets.
Bed: Three rooms. Two have fireplaces. One room with twin beds and one with a double share a bath. One double has a private bath and dressing room.
Breakfast: Full with fruit, homemade bakery, omelets, waffles with maple syrup from Daisy's sister's farm in Vermont. Eat in dining room or on terrace or sunporch.
Plus: Laundry facilities. Coffee—anytime—in front of parlor fireplace.
Rates: $45 per room with shared bath. $55 for a private bath. Ten percent discount on stays of four nights or more.

NORTHFIELD

Centennial House

94 Main Street, Northfield, MA 01360
Phone: 413/498-5921
Location: In a small "but not provincial" town that has a two-mile stretch of Main Street with lovely old frame homes set back on beautiful lawns; a couple of antique shops; gas stations; and the grocery, drug, and country stores. House has large lawn in front and terrific views in back.

Host: Marguerite Linsert Lentz
Open: Year round.

Was it fantasy to think that there were still small communities in the east that could offer a nonsuburban lifestyle? Marguerite Lentz had fond memories of her schooldays in Northfield. In the 1970s she experienced the writer/editor/proofreader professional life combined with parenthood in suburbia. Then in 1982 she bought Centennial House, built by a wealthy lawyer in 1811 and most recently part of the Northfield Mount Hermon School. Now it is hard for her to imagine a house without a constant stream of wonderful guests who understand the casual arrangements. Sometimes they help themselves to breakfast. Sometimes they choose the kitchen for eating instead of the dining-room setting with its candles and silver. Frequently they say goodnight to young Erika or chat with Kristina, a student at her mother's alma mater. And in Northfield Marguerite Lentz has seen her fantasy become a reality.

Because of the location, many guests have some association with the school. The Northfield Mountain Center with its extensive network of groomed cross-country trails is just five miles away, so that skiers, too, have discovered the residence that has a place on the National Register of Historic Places.

In residence: Kristina, age 16; Erika, age 4. "Kitty is our large and daring cat."
Restrictions: Pets maybe; check with host. Nonsmokers preferred.
Foreign languages spoken: Very little German and Spanish.
Bed: Six rooms. One with twin beds, three with doubles, two with queens. Three and one-half shared baths. Cot and infant crib available.
Breakfast: Continental, 6:30–9:30. Includes homemade bread served in dining room.
Plus: Front parlor, magnificent living room with hand-hewn beams and huge fireplace, dining room, large glassed/screened porch with rockers, lawn with view of the sweep to the Connecticut River. Baby-sitting possibilities.
Rates: $30 doubles, $35 for twin beds and queens. Crib $2.50. Cot $10.

HAMPSHIRE HILLS

The Hampshire Hills area encompasses the "in between" towns. To the north is Vermont; the Berkshires are to the west; Jacob's Pillow is south; Northampton, Amherst, and the five-colleges region are east. Within the picturesque pocket of hill towns are New England villages, farms, a major general store, craftspeople, and restaurants.

A Book-Your-Own List

In an effort to promote tourism and maintain the area's rural character, families have been encouraged to offer bed and breakfast. A free brochure with brief descriptions and direct booking arrangements is sent to those who mail a self-addressed stamped (long) envelope to **Hampshire Hills Bed & Breakfast Association**, P.O. Box 17, Chesterfield, MA 01012. The 19 hosts live in Chester, Chesterfield, Cummington, Goshen, Huntington, Plainfield, Westhampton, Williamsburg, and Worthington.

B&Bs

CUMMINGTON

Cumworth Farm

Route 112, Cummington, MA 01026
Phone: 413/634-5529
Location: On a secondary state highway, 3½ miles from town center. Forty-five minutes to Tanglewood or Williamstown.

Hosts: Edward and Mary McColgan
Open: Year round. Advance reservations preferred.

As a youngster Ed worked on potato, dairy, and tobacco farms. He grew up to have a series of careers — as college history professor, director of the Bicentennial celebration for the state of Massachusetts, state legislator, and executive with the Department of Public Health. Ed and Mary have both been city councilors in Northampton. Four years ago they bought this 200-year-old farmhouse and acquired a workhorse, chickens, pigs, ducks, and a big vegetable garden plot. Mary still works as a planner with the area agency on aging, but as a full-time farmer Ed always has a new thing going. Their sugarhouse produced over 600 gallons this last year. The wool from the sheep is spun into blankets sold at farmers' markets. The new barn roof went on in one weekend, thanks to friends and a big barbecue.

Visiting parents of summer campers, Tanglewood concertgoers, hikers, balloonfest people, and skiers usually come with a planned day; but there are other possibilities for B&B guests here. As Ed says, "Whatever happens at Cumworth Farm happens spontaneously. Some people choose to be by themselves. Others join in herding the sheep in the morning. Some couples have returned with their children just to have the opportunity for the kids to sleep in a real barn. In the spring they watch the activity in the sugarhouse. One couple helped sort and grade carrots and ended up buying ducks to bring home!"

In residence: Sons Michael and Daniel, both 14. Two dogs — Benjy, a St. Bernard, and Michael, a Border collie. No one smokes, but smoking is allowed.
Restrictions: No pets allowed in house.
Bed: Five rooms. One single, two that each have twin beds, two with doubles. Three shared baths; two have showers. Crib and cot available.
Breakfast: Continental. Full is $2 extra. Eat in kitchen, in dining room, or on patio in warm weather.
Plus: Beverage in late afternoon or evening. Inviting wood stove in stone-floored kitchen. Plenty of sightseeing hints and ideas from these folks, who know the area well.
Rates: $20 single, $25 double. Cot $5.

CUMMINGTON

Tom and Ginnie Caldwell

Main Street, Cummington, MA 01026
Phone: 413/634-5556
Location: On main street in village, half way between Pittsfield and Northampton, 45 minutes to Tanglewood or Williamstown.
Open: Year round.

The red-and-white four-dormer Cape, circa 1812 (as the plaque reads), is the second-oldest house in the village. During World War II it was used as a refuge for church-sponsored Austrian refugees. A film, *Cummington Story*, featured the house and the integration of the refugees into village life.

Tom, a salesman, and Ginnie, a secretary and office manager, have lived here for 30 years. They both get involved in town politics. Tom does furniture restoring and caning and is a photographer. Ginnie is responsible for most of the gardening and likes to see the countryside on foot and cross-country skis. They have grandchildren who live just a few miles away.

Among their memorable B&B guests have been couples from France and Japan with only the wives speaking any, and not much, English. "We made out just fine."

In residence: Jasper, a black cat. Greta loves people; she's a large black dog, St. Bernard and Labrador retriever combination.
Restrictions: No guests' pets. Smoking permitted, but not in bedrooms.
Bed: Two rooms, one single and one with a double bed; and a two-bunk-bed cottage (that uses house facilities) with fireplace. Cot available.
Breakfast: Full, 8:30. Menu varies: "You have what we have." Served in large comfortable kitchen.
Rates: $25 single, $30 for two. Cot $5.

Our whole family had the most delightful weekend. Tom and Ginnie are gracious hosts; we felt at ease in their home. The children had a wonderful time playing croquet in the lovely backyard while I worked on a book and my husband painted village scenes.

Nancy K. Robinson, New York, New York

WILLIAMSBURG

Helen and Donald Gould

4 Nash Hill Road, Williamsburg, MA 01906
Phone: 413/268 7314
Location: Within walking distance of, and on a hill overlooking, the village center, eight miles west of Northampton.
Open: Year round.

The Greek Revival house, built in 1812, has been in Helen's family since 1919. For the last four years it has been home to the Goulds. Their art, artifacts, and antiques were collected during seven years of seafaring and 25 years in the diplomatic service. African ceremonial masks, pottery, weavings, wood carvings, brass, and copper are among items that are set against white walls, refinished floors, and stripped woodwork. One visitor commented that a stay here is like taking a journey around the world.

In residence: "One gabby parrot. And an impertinent beagle named Cleo."
Restrictions: Nonsmokers preferred.
Foreign languages spoken: Spanish, French, Portuguese.
Bed: Three rooms. One double, one single, and one with twin beds. "However, we prefer to have one party for all so that a private bath is available for the group." Cot and crib available.
Breakfast: Served until 9:30. Donald is official chef and offers a big and interesting choice. Beautifully served in formal dining room with large fireplace or in great remodeled country kitchen.
Plus: Sherry in room.
Rates: $25 single, $30 double. Cot or crib $8.

Exceptional! A fascinating home filled with warm hospitality. Wake up to the aroma of freshly baked muffins and other delicious surprises! We have made reservations far in advance to return for various Smith College activities.   Bob and Betty Reid, Atlanta, Georgia

The hosts are charming. The bedroom has every imaginable comfort and the breakfast food is gourmet.
                    Anne W. Higgins, Roosevelt, Long Island, New York

WILLIAMSBURG

Twin Maples

106 South Street, Williamsburg, MA 01096
Phone: 413/268-7925
Location: Two and one-half miles from village, 7 miles from North-
ampton, 7 miles from I-91 interchange, 25 miles to Springfield.
Hosts: Eleanor and Martin Hebert
Open: Year round. Two-night minimum reservation.

Since the Heberts arrived in 1963 they have restored the wonderful
old farmhouse, now about 200 years old. There are wide pine floors;
exposed beams are in the ceiling of the dining room; the kitchen has a
large fireplace with Dutch oven; and there are a total of four working
fireplaces in the house. Because B&B is so new in the area (and the
country), Eleanor notices that some guests aren't quite sure what to
expect — but by the time they leave they want to return!
Martin is a design engineer. Eleanor is a librarian. The youngest of
their three children at home is 16.

In residence: Jennifer, Mark, and Michael. Their three dogs — Panda,
Prince, and Toby — are all outdoor pets.
Restrictions: No smoking. No guests' pets.
Bed: Three rooms, freshly decorated with attention to colonial theme.
One with twin beds, two with doubles. Shared bath. Antique brass and
brass and iron beds. Electric blankets in winter. One room has a fire-
place. Crib available.
Breakfast: Full, 7:30–9 weekdays, until 10 weekends. Include home-
made maple syrup, breads, and jams. Table set with hand-crafted pot-
tery in dining room or on screened porch.
Plus: Fresh flowers in season, beautifully arranged. Sitting room with
games, puzzles, stereo. Porch. Swing set for children, charcoal grille,
and picnic table. Baby-sitting possibilities.
Rates: $25 single, $30–$35 for two. Crib $5.

*A very comfortable stay in a nicely furnished colonial home. Warm
flannel sheets for cold evenings and superb breakfast served up on
white linen tablecloths. Excellent hosts!*   Heidi Johnson, Gainesville, Florida

BERKSHIRES

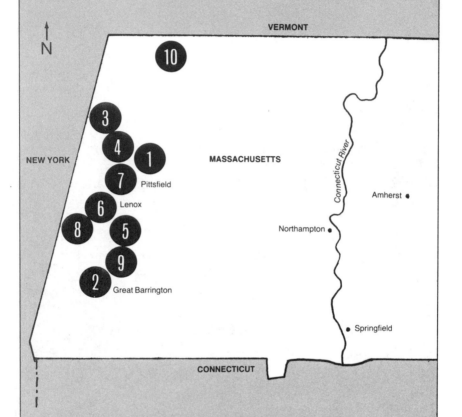

The numbers on this map indicate the locations of B&Bs described in detail in this chapter.

BERKSHIRES

BERKSHIRES

Reservation Services

Berkshire Bed & Breakfast Connection

43 Main Street, Williamsburg, MA 01096-0211
Phone: 413/268-7244
Established April 1980.
Listings: About 30 hosts in Lee, Lenox, Stockbridge, and Williams-town. Also Cheshire, Clarksburg, Dalton, Great Barrington, Lanes-borough, Pittsfield, Richmond, Sheffield, West Stockbridge.

Tim and Mary Allen serve a pastoral area that reminds them of Ireland, one of the countries they have experienced as B&B guests. Their concern for B&B standards has led them to network with other agencies. "Homes don't have to be elaborate, but they do have to have a host-in-residence, a friendly one who has clean, pleasant accommodations."

Tim is a systems analyst for an insurance company and Mary is a school counselor. They are the parents of two preschoolers, children who may hold the record for the number of experiences at American B&Bs.
Rates: Singles $16–$30, doubles $20–$45. MasterCard and VISA accepted for deposit ($20) only.

Covered Bridge Bed and Breakfast

This service is the newest service to match hosts and guests in the (southern) Berkshires. Please see page 330.

Pineapple Hospitality

This service has hosts in Pittsfield, Williamstown, and near Tanglewood. Please see page 170.

B&Bs

DALTON

The Dalton House

955 Main Street, Dalton, MA 01226
Phone: 413/684-3854
Location: On the main street of a small town that has a few basic stores and is home of the company that makes all the paper for U.S. currency.
Hosts: Gary and Bernice Turetsky
Open: Year round. Two-night minimum reservation on summer and holiday weekends.

"I was a B&B before I knew there was a name for it," says transplanted Gary Turetsky. "It's really fun."

When the Turetskys came here from Freehold, New Jersey, in 1971, it was the flower business in a quaint town that attracted them. Then there was a gas shortage that resulted in changed customer habits. A visit to innkeeper friends in Vermont provided the inspiration to think differently about their four-season Massachusetts location and their 1810 colonial home. The flower shop is still in business (some repeat guests even sell plants to customers if the hosts are out); but now they also offer hospitality in their meandering place (main house with wing, greenhouse, and converted carriage house) complete with fireplaced common room.

In residence: Three daughters aged 14, 18, and 20. When they are home, they host too. And they have a cat, Pumpkin.
Restictions: No guests' pets.
Foreign languages spoken: One daughter speaks French, another knows Hebrew.
Bed: Ten carpeted rooms all with private baths. Four rooms each have twin beds. Six have doubles. Cots available.

Breakfast: Continental with muffins. Buffet-style in dining room. Often part of the "experience" for a first-time B&B traveler not used to morning conversations with other guests.

Plus: Air conditioning. Living room with loft, piano, and television. Patio. Picnic area in woods.

Rates: $48 (for two) in summer, $38 fall through spring. Cot $8.

A delightful combination of warm hospitality and the charm of old New England.   T. M. Jones, Beloit, Wisconsin

My Tanglewood weekends without Dalton House would not be as pleasurable by half!   S. W., Forest Hills, New York

GREAT BARRINGTON

Berkshire Bed & Breakfast Connection Host #2

Location: On a main street, five minutes' walk from town center. Bus stop nearby to New York City and points north and south.

Reservations: Available year round through Berkshire Bed and Breakfast Connection, page 278. Two-night minimum stay preferred on summer weekends.

Musician, teacher, chef, general manager of a restaurant, counselor to adolescents, antique dealer — what have I missed? The three hosts have individually or collectively worn all those hats. Two are siblings and the third worked for them when they operated the family restaurant with "the madness of 35 employees."

At first the thought was to have an antique business (only), and then this 1820 Greek Revival house seemed to be just right for B&B, "a more intimate way of earning a living. I guess it's worked out that way. Sometimes not always, we feel guilty about taking money from guests. Repeaters can seem like family.

"It's a nice old house. A couple of the rooms have wide floorboards. Nothing is perfectly straight of course. Cosmetically we've done some things that were necessary; but others such as the wonderful wallpaper in one room — not new but it gives a good feeling — will wait a bit. Restoration work is ongoing. We have traced the history of the house, most recently a private home, but don't yet know what kind of classes once took place on the second floor."

Two seven-foot grand pianos are in the hosts' quarters. Unscheduled practice times result in wonderful impromptu concerts.

Recipes are happily shared.

In residence: Three dogs. One small Collie-type mongrel who loves to be the center of attention; a large shepherd with the personality of a puppy; and another shepherd, a gentle and extremely well-behaved seeing-eye dog.

Restrictions: No guests' pets.

Bed: Five rooms. Four with double beds, one with twins. Crib and cot available. Two shared guest baths.

Breakfast: Hosts usually join guests for this event in their dining room. Menu includes "bran muffins from grandmother's recipe, a variety of egg dishes, stewed tomatoes and bacon on toast, or a variety of other selections as the spirit moves."

Plus: Television/sitting room; picnic tables and lounge chairs in yard during warm months. Beverage in late afternoon or evening.

Rates: $30 single, $40 for two, Memorial Day through Labor Day. $20 single, $24 for two, off-season. $10 for additional person.

The congenial hosts provide a relaxed atmosphere in pleasant surroundings. I particularly enjoyed the beautiful breakfasts.

Ann M. Rover, New York, New York

GREAT BARRINGTON

Elling's Guest House

250 Maple Avenue, RD 3, Box 6, Great Barrington, MA 02130
Phone: 413/528-4103
Location: On five acres of lawns, gardens, and wooded areas, 300 feet from state road, one mile from town center. Half hour to Tanglewood. Close to Butternut Basin and Catamount ski areas.
Hosts: Josephine and Raymond Elling

Through their decade of ownership the Ellings have noticed that the appeal of their kind of place has widened. "Younger people have discovered us too." They think that such accommodations should be reasonably priced and aim to keep things that way.

"Such accommodations" are in the second-oldest lived-in house in Great Barrington. It was built in 1746 for a woolen-mill owner. When Jo and Ray originally bought it as a summer home they furnished it with family possessions. "Our pride is our 1820 tall clock which strikes each hour." Jo's mother's stove, used during the winter months, is a conversation piece too. It wasn't long before their summer address became a nonpaying guest house; so they decided to turn it into a paying guest house by inviting 175 coworkers and friends to come once (only) for free. Now the Ellings can say that "running the B&B together makes life more interesting and rewarding."

Ray, a former corrections officer in New York, is involved with the local historical society and is a do-it-yourself buff. Jo was full-time mother to their four sons and now is active with a barbershop chorus and does much of the gardening.

Restrictions: No pets allowed, but kennel boarding is close by. Maximum of two children per visiting family.
Foreign language spoken: Some Italian.
Bed: Six rooms, each with a view of cornfields, mountains, or woodlands and lawns. Two have private baths. Four share baths. Cots available.
Breakfast: Buffet-style continental, 8:30–10:30. Jo bakes, Ray brews coffee. In summer eat on porch or lawns. Morning paper available.
Plus: Swimming just three minutes away in river, one that runs through cornfields and at a bend forms a small pool and beach. Swing on shade tree. Guest refrigerator. Fans, if needed. Baby-sitting possibilities. And an invitation to see the original cooking fireplace and colonial carpentry in the Ellings' part of the house.
Rates: Vary according to season, holiday, day of week, and whether with private or shared bath. For two in a room in season $38–$45. Out of season: $35–$40. Cots $5–$7.

Jo and Ray Elling are the warmest, friendliest people in many a long mile. This is really "home from home" where you can feel comfortable and be yourself. The rooms are spotlessly clean and comfortable, all with lovely views.
                                                    Anthea McKinley, England

GREAT BARRINGTON

Seekonk Pines

Route 23 and Seekonk Cross Road, Box 29AA, RD 1, Great Barrington, MA 02130
Phone: 413/528-4192
Location: On main road, bordered with pine trees. Two miles west of town and Route 7, 15 minutes from three state forests.
Hosts: Linda and Christian Best
Open: Year round. Two-day minimum reservation for summer and holiday weekends.

They met while playing the lead roles in *Damn Yankees*. Both are paid soloists at a local church and they still study voice. Chris, a self-described "people-business" person, and Linda, a watercolorist, are the first to have paying guests in the 1830s house, a structure that expanded as several generations lived in it. The Bests "refinished, repaired, rebuilt, reinterpreted, and furnished comfortably and eclectically" what was once a country estate and before that a working farm.

They live in the former servants' quarters and do everything themselves. Repeat visitors see changes because Linda's watercolors exhibited in the house are for sale. Auction acquisitions emerge in a reconditioned state from Chris's barn workshop and they may be reupholstered or slipcovered by the professional seamstress-in-residence, Linda.

Before coming here, Chris was a sign repairman. He specialized in cheering up customers who were unhappy about their sign problems. He loves his new title of host and gets a kick out of telling about some of their first guests (in 1978) who eventually opened their own B&B.

Blueberries are harvested from the nearby mountainside and the garden produces black raspberries, strawberries, rhubarb, and yellow squash (eventually cooked with apples) for breakfast jams and jellies.

In residence: Two dogs. Bear is a shepherd/collie and Toby a dachshund mix.
Restrictions: Smoking limited to public rooms. No guests' pets.
Bed: Seven rooms. Handmade quilts on all beds were sewn by Linda, her grandmother, or her great-grandmother. All upstairs rooms have wide floorboards. Upstairs there is one large room with double bed and one twin, sitting area, and private bath. Three rooms with double beds, one room with twin beds, and one room with one queen and one twin bed share two baths. Downstairs there is one room with twin beds,

private entrance, and shared bath. Cots available.

Breakfast: Continental with homemade muffins. Full (extra charge) with pancakes, omelets, or granola. Very leisurely meal in formal dining room.

Plus: Large common room with fireplace, piano, chess, puzzles. Pool. Wildflower meadow, extensive lawn area, picnic table. Unscheduled performances could include recitals with classical and popular music sung by Linda and Chris. "Last year we had a concert pianist who completely overwhelmed our modest instrument."

Rates: For two: summer, holidays, and October, $38 shared bath, $45 private bath. Out of season, $30 shared bath, $40 private bath. $7 for additional person in room.

GREAT BARRINGTON

The Turning Point Inn

Route 23 and Lake Buel Road, RD 2, Box 140, Great Barrington, MA 02130

Phone: 413/528-4777

Location: Just down the road from Butternut Ski Basin, on a well-traveled road, 15 minutes from Tanglewood.

Hosts: Irving and Shirley Yost

Open: Year round. Three-day minimum reservation for three-day holiday weekends; two days for weekends in summer and fall.

The children, now all in their 20s, were the first Yost vegetarians. When it became a family style of cooking and eating, there was thought of having a vegetarian restaurant. In 1976 Irv, an architect, and Shirley, a teacher, bought this place ("a mess then") to fulfill that goal. A restaurant permit wasn't allowed, so they established a B&B in July 1981. The match was right. In the fall of 1982 the Yosts, heretofore summer and weekend residents, moved from New Jersey so they could share their home with guests year round.

While converting "the mess" into an inviting home they uncovered a beehive oven in the old kitchen and two Rumford fireplaces. From the old chestnut boards found in walls taken down, two large breakfast tables were made. The Yosts have traced the history of the house, have discovered on one of the chimneys the signature of the owner in its tavern/inn days, and can declare that Daniel Webster has slept here.

The Turning Point guest list includes honeymooners; a couple who came to celebrate their 50th wedding anniversary; another given the weekend as a gift for their 25th; and family members who have come from opposite directions for a get-together.

In residence: One black cat, Cassandra. Four-year-old granddaughter visits frequently. And maybe one of the junior Yosts ("all excellent cooks").

Restrictions: Children welcome as long as they sleep through the night and are well behaved. No guests' pets. No smoking.

Bed: Seven rooms, moderate size, attractively furnished with "19th- and 20th-century furniture." One room with private bath has two twin beds that can be a king. One single room, four doubles, and one twin-bedded room share three baths. Crib and cots available.

Breakfast: Two seatings, 8:30 and 9:30, but other arrangements can be made. In one of two kitchens or in dining/common room. Menu could include Irv's special blend of whole-grain hot cereal; bran and whole-wheat pancakes; eggs with veggies; or Shirley's hot baked fruit, apple crisp, bran muffins, or zucchini and date bread. Tofu and tofu salad too.

Plus: Fresh fruit bowl always available. Fireplaces in three common rooms. Piano. Library. TV and stereo. Refrigerator. Laundry facilities. Picnic tables, hammocks, outside swing. Nature trails on 11 acres. Baby-sitting available.

Rates: Weekends: $35 single, $50 twin or double, $65 for twin (or king) with private bath. Sunday–Thursday $5 less. (Another $5 less out of season.) One-night stay, if available, $5 extra. Crib $5. Cot $10 under age 12, $15 over age 12.

The warmth of a visit with friends — plus the independence to go off "at wish" to enjoy the Berkshires' best. . . . With Irving's cooking and Shirley's baking — using the fresh bounty of their garden — breakfast is a four-course feast. The beauty and comfort of the restored rooms is hard to leave, but the lush countryside lures. I'll be back.
                                        Ms. Alice Costantini, New York, New York

The food was abundant and delectable, especially for a vegetarian. It was like walking into my mother's kitchen! The home was gracious, centrally located for a late walk on a back road or a beautiful bike ride. Room was clean and homey. . . . This place is a real jewel.
                                        Larry Hoffman, Bridgeport, Connecticut

HANCOCK

Berkshire Bed & Breakfast Connection Host #7

Location: Really in Stephentown, New York, just a mile over the border, but "everyone comes here for the Massachusetts Berkshires." On a busy road, 15 miles from Pittsfield, 19 miles from Tanglewood, and 30 miles from Albany. Four and one-half miles from Jiminy Peak, 9½ miles from Brodie Mountain.

Reservations: Available year round through Berkshire Bed & Breakfast Connection, page 278.

"About four years ago someone I grew up with mentioned that this farm was for sale. I left my job teaching geography at the University of Pittsburgh, bought the farm with him and learned how to be a farmer. My friend is in Florida now, but I do have help in the sunup-to-sundown season. What's it like to make such a change? I've never been happier."

The farm is manicured — all eight acres of strawberries (pick your own in June and July) separated by lanes of lawn; six acres of vegetables; beef cattle in the summer, and farm stand that is really a year-round store now.

The farmer is a low-key, easy-to-be-with person who will gladly take you on a tour, show you the machinery, and explain planting and nurturing. If it's harvest time, maybe the kids could pick an ear of corn. The farmhouse, constructed in 1794 with additions made in the 1880s, is freshly decorated. The living room is made for lounging with big comfortable sofas and a sizable hearth. In every sense of the word, it's a neat place.

Restrictions: No smoking.
Bed: Four rooms. One with one double bed, two with two double beds, one with one double and a twin. Cot available. One shared guest bath.
Breakfast: Continental only in summer, when it is self-serve. Full available in other seasons for an additional $2.
Rates: $30 single, $35 for two, $5 for additional guest in room.

LANESBOROUGH

Berkshire Bed & Breakfast Connection Host #1

Location: At the base of Mt. Greylock, highest point in Massachusetts.
Reservations: Available year round through Berkshire Bed & Breakfast Connection, page 278.

One family owned this 1750 farmhouse until 12 years ago, when the present owners switched from the women's-apparel business to a working farm that now has added a baking business. Here they have a commercial sheep flock and raise Labrador retrievers and registered Morgan pleasure horses. For some diversion they enjoy classical music and dance skating.

The children are grown and gone; their rooms are redecorated for guests. The wonderful old floorboards are still 18 inches wide. After a few years of hosting the couple concludes, "Everyone wants to move to the Berkshires and live our lifestyle."

Restrictions: No guests' pets.
Foreign language spoken: Some French.
Bed: One room with a double bed, one with twin beds, and one with a double bed and a single plus an adjoining sun porch with twin beds (available in warmer months).
Breakfast: It's work time on the farm. The dining-room table is set with lace tablecloth and fine china and a self-serve continental breakfast with hostess's own breads — blueberry crunch or cranberry, peach, maybe Irish soda.
Plus: A tour of the farm. In June you can watch the shearing of the 90 sheep.
Rates: $16 single, $20 for two, $25 for three.

Super hosts. Their home is delightful and the cooking is sinfully good. Need a restaurant? Lots of suggestions. Need a haircut? That can be found too. Want the sheep to pose for pix? That can be arranged. Need I say more?   Nancy Cheney Low, Visalia, California

LEE

1777 Greylock House

58 Greylock Street, Lee, MA 01238
Phone: 413/243-1717
Location: Two miles to town. Three miles to Tanglewood.
Hosts: Terry and Walt Parry
Open: Year round.

Terry and Walt Perry are not innkeepers as such; they are hosts who have invited people to be their guests in their charming, comfortable home. We love them.   Rose and Lester Roseman, Pompano Beach, Florida

The Parrys are an energetic, flexible "retired" couple who exclaimed that "you have to do something!" So when they sold their 10-year-old restaurant business to their son, they bought this 18th-century colonial house, one that had remained in the same family from 1777 until 1955. They started restoration in March of 1981 and together did everything, including a new kitchen, in time to receive their first guests three months later. It has antiques, stenciled walls, and the original wide floorboards.

Restoration is a bit of an avocation at this point. All the Parry children, including the one who lives across the street, have older homes that they are restoring. And then there's always furniture refinishing to be done.

Previous careers include operating a snowmobile resort and growing potatoes (for potato chips) in seven states. Retirement does provide a little more time for cross-country skiing. Terry and Walt enjoy it together, with guests, and with their grandchildren too.

Restrictions: No pets. Children should be at least five.
Foreign language spoken: Some French.
Bed: Four rooms. On the air-conditioned second floor there are two rooms with double beds and one with twin beds. Shared baths. On first floor: two-room suite with twin beds in bedroom, living room with fireplace, TV, and pull-out couch for additional bed.
Breakfast: Continental, 8–10. Served in the dining room, but guests often move into the inviting homey kitchen. "Our guests seem to be sharers, and the kitchen is the focal point of activity in the house."
Plus: Grounds, beautifully maintained by Walt, of course. Porches. Place to store skis.

Rates: Summer: $45 per night for two people in one room. $12 for extra person in room. Suite is $65 for two, $12 for each additional person. Rates are lower off-season.

LEE

Berkshire Bed & Breakfast Connection Host #13

Location: Five minutes from the Turnpike entrance and within walking distance of town center.

Reservations: Available June through August, preferably for three- or four-day weekends, and some of September and October. Book through Berkshire Bed & Breakfast Connection, page 278.

The hosts have seen lots of changes in the Berkshires. He has lived in this 1843 house all his life. It has been home for his wife for 35 years. Both have full-time jobs. Sometimes their grandchildren, ages 2 to 11, are visiting. "The guests, especially those who swim, love them."

In residence: One son in his 20s. And they have a poodle. No one smokes, but smoking is allowed.

Restrictions: No guests' pets. Children should be at least five.

Foreign language spoken: Some Italian.

Bed: Guest rooms, both with television, are in a separate wing. One double-bedded room. And one with a queen-sized bed that has an adjoining room with single bed. One shared guest bath.

Breakfast: Continental. Serve yourself and eat on patio.

Plus: Use of in-ground swimming pool and patio. Window fans in bedrooms.

Rates: $30 for two people. Adjoining room $10.

Very enjoyable and informal. Good location on a quiet street. Hostess made us feel very much at home. We have since recommended it to friends.   Gordon White, Cornwall-on-Hudson, New York

LENOX

Cornell House

197 Pittsfield Road, Lenox, MA 01240
Phone: 413/637-0562
Location: On a main road, just up the hill from center of town. Near bus stop from New York City and Boston.
Host: Charles Bowers
Open: Year round. "Reservations essential July, August, October, January, February." Three-night minimum stay on weekends in July and August.

An industrial-exhibit designer (Allan) and a banker (Chuck) changed careers when they changed Cornell House. In five months of 1980 they personally renovated and redecorated the entire guest house; hung the portrait of Charity Cornell (Allan's great-great-grandmother) in the front hall; named the B&B establishment after her; and then in May hung the sign on the front elm tree.

The 1888 Queen Anne Victorian feels like a big private home furnished with antiques. The smaller rooms of Hill House, the converted carriage-house barn, are furnished with oak and painted pieces.

In residence: Ludwig, "the PR man in our business" — part shepherd and part brindle Great Dane.
Restrictions: No guests' pets. No cigars. Children should be at least teenagers.
Bed: Sixteen rooms. Five single, 11 double. Cot available in main house.
Breakfast: Buffet style, 8–10. Continental with bakery and Cornell House jams that could include zucchini and lime, pumpkin, banana pineapple, or spiced grape. Guests walk through kitchen (where biscuits and muffins are made daily) on way to dining room.
Plus: Sherry after dinner in front of living-room fireplace. (Sheet music from '30s and '40s framed on wall.) Impromptu concerts at baby grand piano. Library. Four hundred acres of marked cross-country ski trails in wooded Kennedy Park, just in back of house.
Rates: Vary according to location, day of week, and season. $40–$55 July and August. $30–$45 September and October. $25–$40 November–June. $10 for additional cot. Group and weekly rates available. Master-Card and VISA accepted.

LENOX

Walker House

74 Walker Street, Lenox, MA 01240
Phone: 413/637-1271
Location: On one of the main streets into Lenox, but set on three acres. Within walking distance of shops and restaurants. Buses from New York and Boston stop a block away.
Hosts: Richard and Peggy Houdek
Open: Year round. Three-night minimum stay on July and August weekends and all holiday weekends. Two nights for fireplace room on all weekends.

They were a successful arts-oriented couple living in a Spanish-style house on a southern California hill and looking for adventure. Once the Houdeks decided on the Berkshires, they set out to establish a B&B that would give them the feeling of having some friends visit for a few days. And that's exactly what has happened since 1980. It is an ongoing open house, and it is quite a commitment; but still their new lifestyle affords the sought-after change from the consuming pace of their professional lives back in Los Angeles. Peggy was managing editor of *Performing Arts Magazine*; Dick was director of public affairs at California Institute of the Arts, a contributing critic for the *Los Angeles Times*, and a consultant for Long Beach Grand Opera. And he found time to serve as president of Guild Opera of Los Angeles, a group that staged full productions for children.

The Houdeks have revitalized, with the help of some local handy-people, the vintage 1804 Walker House, one of the last remaining examples of Federal architecture in Lenox. It has eight fireplaces and is furnished with antiques. In true Houdek style the guest rooms are named after composers. Appropriate decor and furnishings can be found behind the doors designated as Beethoven, Mozart, Handel, Chopin, Tchaikovsky, and Verdi. Being people-oriented as well, Dick and Peggy have also collected much oral history — just about every local person has a tale about something that happened in the house. Guests, upon inquiring, may hear about structural changes and the five previous owners. At one point it was a headmaster's house for the private Lenox School, disbanded in the early 1970s.

In residence: Five cats but only Elizabeth, a bobtailed cat, is allowed in the inn.

Restrictions: Guests' pets permitted by approval. And children should be at least eight.

Foreign languages spoken: French and Spanish.

Bed: Six rooms, all with private baths. One with two double beds, two with twin beds in each, one with a double, and two with queens.

Breakfast: Continental, sort of. Includes fresh fruit (baked in winter), several kinds of muffins and croissants, freshly ground coffee. Served in dining rooms around large oak tables, or on the plant-filled veranda. Not before 8, but it can go beyond 10.

Plus: Lots of music around. "Morning Pro Musica" radio program in the morning or samplings from a large collection of recordings. The grand piano in the parlor is often the scene of a recital, either by a professional artist or in an impromptu performance by a guest. Occasionally, Peggy, a trained singer, is persuaded to join a pianist for a Mozart aria or Broadway hit song.

Tours of unoccupied rooms given to guests and nonguests. Also for guests: chess, checkers, and puzzles; refrigerator; large lawn for picnics; and a fleet of 10 bicycles.

Rates: $50–$90 for two/per night, depending upon season and day of week. Weekly rates available. Single rate is 10 percent less except July, August, and October.

Peggy and Dick are charming and gracious hosts and provide their guests with an elegant but informal home-away-from-home. The rooms are spacious and comfortable, and offer privacy if desired. But we found it equally enjoyable to mingle with the other guests over breakfast, tea, or wine, in the dining room, the parlor, or on the porch which is a virtual forest of flowers. What a delightful spot — one which also offers the proximity to wonderful cultural events!

Mr. and Mrs. Steinberg, West Hartford, Connecticut

PITTSFIELD

Berkshire Bed & Breakfast Connection Host #3

Location: In historic district of Pittsfield, 12 miles from Tanglewood, 20 from Jacob's Pillow.
Reservations: Available spring through fall through Berkshire Bed & Breakfast Connection, page 278. Two-night minimum stay preferred.

The spacious Georgian residence, built in 1912, has been home to this family of eight for five years. They have restored and redecorated. The dining room now has a Waterford chandelier and the oak flooring has been refinished. The oversized living room features mahogany woodwork and beamed ceiling.

"We have met the world in our dining room." And that world continues to be filled with happy connections. A recent guest, an artist born in China who is living in New Jersey, was en route to a show in upstate New York. Subsequently the hosts talked about the artist when another guest, a woman from New Jersey, spoke about an exhibit she was assembling. Yes, it has happened. The woman followed up. Via Pittsfield and these B&B hosts the artist will be represented at the woman's upcoming New Jersey show.

The host is a manager in information processing and the whole family is sports-oriented.

In residence: Six children, ages 7 to 14. One parakeet, one gerbil.
Restrictions: No pets. Nonsmokers preferred.
Foreign language spoken: Host speaks some French.
Bed: Two rooms on third floor. One single and one double-bedded room share one guest bath. Another room has two double beds and a double sleeper couch, private bath. With advance arrangements, a crib is available.
Breakfast: Continental. Pastries or fresh fruit with yogurt served in formal dining room. Leisurely.
Rates: $18 single, $32–$40 for two, $10 extra person.

I'm working for airline business, so I'm very interested in service. The host has everything needed for it. Not only comfortable bed and excellent breakfast served in the gracious dining room, but the warm family atmosphere which their children help to make greatly welcome all of guest. . . . Delightful memories.   Kunio and Mayumi Hirata, Fukui City, Japan

PITTSFIELD

Berkshire Bed & Breakfast Connection Host #8

Location: Three miles from downtown Pittsfield, six miles to Tanglewood. Overlooks Onota Lake and is next to the Pittsfield State Forest.
Reservations: Available year round through Berkshire Bed & Breakfast Connection, page 278.

If you're up early you can watch the sun coming up over the lake. The atmosphere here is conducive to complete relaxation or maybe hiking or cross-country skiing in the Berkshires. The scene includes three horses grazing nearby.

The host, a realtor, lives in a stately colonial on five acres with the illusion that you are miles from anyone.

In residence: Three daughters, ages 9–14. Two dogs. Three cats.
Bed: Two huge rooms in winter. One with queen-sized bed and private bath. One with king-sized bed, marble fireplace, and private half bath. In July, two additional rooms — one with twin beds and one with a double bed — share a bath. Crib and cot available.
Breakfast: Continental. Available 6–10. Served in formal dining room with lake view or outside.
Plus: Coffee or tea available anytime.
Rates: $45 for two. July rooms are $35 for two people. Cot $7. Crib $3.

RICHMOND

Berkshire Bed & Breakfast Connection Host #5

Location: On the top of a hill, not on a main road, but easy to reach. About 10 miles north of West Stockbridge and Lenox. Near Bousquet and Butternut ski areas.
Reservations: Available year round through Berkshire Bed & Breakfast Connection, page 278. Minimum reservation on summer weekends. Two days.

"After people get a bit settled they get the courage to ask what that is in the front hall. They wonder what they've come to! Five-gallon carboys filled with wine in process — that's what they are. My son often says that the name of this place should be 'Top of the Hill Still.' "

The host is of Scottish background and explains that "to be wasteful is sinful" and she just had to do something with 147 acres. Since the Agriculture Department told her that she had champagne taste on beer soil, she acquires grapes from a Pennsylvania vineyard that custom presses them for her. For other details you'll just have to meet this energetic, cheerful host who "just got promoted" on her nursing job. Oh yes, she also makes her own cheese and jams.

Some day the winery will move out to the barn that is being constructed. Meanwhile, I wondered what she does with the final product. "I sell a bag for $4 and if it's filled, you're in luck."

All this is a bonus to what you expected to come to: fantastic views of rolling hills and mountains from a magnificent site off the main road. The family purchased the farm 20 years ago and at first used it just summers and weekends. In 1980 the host sold her Albany home; moved here; designed and added a 36-foot living room on the south side of the house, a new kitchen, two baths, and three bedrooms; and refurbished the former carriage house/home with "simple elegance and elegance in its simplicity."

In residence: Two Irish setters and one cat.
Restrictions: No pets. Sorry, no children.
Bed: Three double rooms with individual electric-heat controls. Shared guest bath.
Breakfast: Continental includes those homemade jams. Served in formal dining room with English bone china, crystal, and silver service.
Plus: Complimentary carafe. Two of the rooms are air conditioned. Use of picnic tables, lawn chairs, gas barbecue. Laundry possibilities.
Rates: $40 per room Memorial Day–Labor Day. $20 rest of year. MasterCard and VISA accepted.

SOUTH LEE

Merrell Tavern Inn

Route 102, Main Street, South Lee, MA 01260
Phone: 413/243-1794
Location: Main street in small village, a mile from Stockbridge.
Hosts: Charles and Faith Reynolds

Open: Year round. Two-night minimum reservation on July and August weekends.

The only surviving circular colonial bar in America is now the official sign-in desk.

For their work over a one-year period, the innkeepers, two former teachers, received the 1982 restoration award from the Massachusetts Historical Society. The authentic color combinations in the rooms are a result of color research. Remnants of the mid-19th-century exterior colors can be seen behind plastic protectors. Chuck, a high-school history teacher and cabinetmaker, and Faith, an elementary-school teacher and weaver, were living in the Rochester, New York, area when they learned about the inn through their membership in the National Trust for Historic Preservation. They came here two years ago and brought their period furniture (Hepplewhite and Sheraton, 1790–1820) collected over 25 years.

In running the inn, the Reynoldses do almost all the work themselves. It is Faith's mother, now age 86, who makes all the beds "with the diligence and pride of an artist."

Some guests wrote pages of praise. Excerpts from a few letters are below.

Restrictions: No guests' pets.
Bed: Seven rooms. All air conditioned and with private baths. Two with twin beds in each. Five with doubles. Six rooms have canopy beds, one has a four-poster. All have down quilts in winter. Crib and cots available.
Breakfast: Continental. Available 8–10 in old tavern room with fireplace. Atmosphere invites a leisurely meal.
Plus: Tea and coffee available at any time. Path to river behind the inn. Baby-sitting possibilities.
Rates: All double occupancy. July 1–October 31, weekdays $45, weekends $70–$85. November 1–June 30, weekdays $35–$45, weekends $45–$55, highest rates for room with fireplace. Cot $15. MasterCard and VISA accepted.

. . . Captures the feeling of the 19th century most successfully, while more than satisfying the expectations of 20th-century travelers by anticipating all of their needs.   David Dunton, Woodbury, Connecticut

Innkeepers extraordinaire — friendly, knowledgeable, and eager to please.   Al and Becky Harmon, Clearwater, Florida

. . . Lends itself to all seasons. We have usually decided long before we reach home when we can return.   Barbara Mancktelow, Toronto, Canada

WILLIAMSTOWN

Berkshire Bed & Breakfast Connection Host #9

Location: Two miles from the village on a hillside with spectacular mountain views in all seasons.

Reservations: Available year round through Berkshire Bed & Breakfast Connection, page 278.

"It's just a simple, comfortable, welcoming place in the country with books all over and anthropological artifacts from my work in different parts of the world — a haven of peace. I deeply want my guests to love the Berkshire countryside as I do."

The contemporary flat-roofed building is the home of a dual-careered grandparent — a cultural anthropologist (in South America and the Caribbean) and psychotherapist (locally). The setup provides a great deal of privacy for guests and for the warm host. "Generally B&Bers are active during the day because I'm not around to help out."

In residence: An enormous black seven-year-old Newfoundland.

Restriction: No guests' pets, please.

Foreign languages spoken: French, Spanish, Portuguese.

Bed: Suite with private entrance sleeps a family (or friends) totaling five. Large living-room area with twin beds and two private rooms, one with twin beds (or king) and the other with a single. Private bath.

Breakfast: Continental with fresh fruit, "special" bakery, freshly ground coffee, herb teas, hot chocolate. Served in living room with picture window and crackling fire on the hearth.

Plus: Wood stove, library, piano. Lawns, gardens, sun deck, woodland trails, cross-country ski trail, and small pond.

Rates: $40 for two (minimum occupancy), $12 each additional adult. $5 for each child under 12.

How delighted our two children, ages 4½ and 1½, were after a long ride to be greeted by "that nice lady," a refrigerator in our room stocked with healthful snacks, and the warmth of our own woodburning stove! We joined our hostess at her church service Sunday morning and participated in "Souper Sunday," a special after-church function with soups and muffins and with the people who live in Williamstown. How else but through this B&B experience would we ever have been able to be so totally immersed in Old New England?

M.C.A., Springfield, Massachusetts

WILLIAMSTOWN

Berkshire Bed & Breakfast Connection Host #6

Location: Three miles from the center of town, high on a hill with panoramic views that take in New York, Vermont, and Massachusetts.
Reservations: Available year round through Berkshire Bed & Breakfast Connection, page 278.

"We both have summers off. Our six children have grown. We're not ready to put our feet up yet. It was time for a whole new regime."

So two years ago they sold the summer camp where their kids were first campers and then staff, and bought this 52-acre site with house, three barns, 1-acre pond, and apple, cherry, and nut trees. The family never had animals before but they are learning everything as they go along. When you take a tour you will see a couple of oxen, cows, calves, sheep, pigs, some turkeys, capons, geese, 40 chickens — all signs of energetic people who are interested in self-sufficient farming.

The host is a teacher, the hostess a nurse. Only one child, their oldest son, is home; he's the one who generally keeps things going. They have stocked the pond with trout. By reading books they have learned to shear sheep. (The hostess knits.) The honey you eat at breakfast comes from their bees. There are more customers for fresh eggs than there are eggs. The garden is so successful in summer that the hosts participate in the local farmers' market one morning a week. And yes, B&B "just fits because we have the room and have found that every guest has been wonderful."

In residence: Two dogs.
Restrictions: No smoking. No guests' pets.
Bed: Two rooms with antique oak beds and marble-topped bureaus. One single and one room with a double bed. One shared guest bath.
Breakfast: Continental with fresh milk, cream, butter ("put the plug in and the churn makes it in 20 minutes"), homemade breads, jams, and jellies. Eat in dining room in winter, or in screened porch with tri-state view in summer.
Plus: Watch maple sugaring (they tap 85 trees) in the shed, if you're there at the right time. Rowboat, canoes, and raft with diving board on the pond. Five kilometers of hiking and cross-country ski trails.
Rates: $20 single, $32 double.

WILLIAMSTOWN

Berkshire Bed & Breakfast Connection Host #15

Location: Not far from Williamstown Theater, 45 minutes to Tanglewood. An hour to Saratoga Springs.
Reservations: Available year round through Berkshire Bed & Breakfast Connection, page 278.

Tourists aren't the only ones who appreciate this location. About eight years ago the neighbors decided that it was important to preserve this small portion — almost two miles — of the old Boston-to-Albany stagecoach road. Consequently it will not be paved without the consent of the neighbors, who like the idea that the views are similar to those of over a century ago. From the B&B you can see only three houses and it is another mile down the road to the next.

The restored colonial farmhouse, built in 1820, is surrounded by 160 acres of rolling meadows and woodland. One family spotted the "just right" cattails by the pond and were thrilled to cut some for their city home decor. Explore here or drive short distances for Berkshire doings and flavor.

The host, a former teacher who now works at the college, gets a thrill from sharing region's resources with visitors who in turn are excited about all there is to do and see.

In residence: A 10-year-old son, a good helper. A lovable airedale, a stray calico cat.
Restrictions: No smoking. No guests' pets.
Bed: Two rooms. One with double bed, one with twins. Portacrib available.
Breakfast: Includes homemade bread and muffins, granola, oatmeal cooked on wood stove (winter only).
Plus: Large pond for skating in winter, fishing, and swimming. Walking, skiing, hiking in surrounding acreage.
Rates: $25 single, $35 for two. One bath shared with host. Crib $5.

RHODE ISLAND

RHODE ISLAND

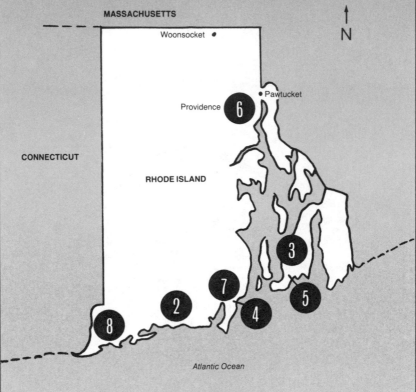

MASSACHUSETTS

N

Woonsocket

Pawtucket

Providence

6

CONNECTICUT

RHODE ISLAND

3

7

2

4

5

8

Atlantic Ocean

1

The numbers on this map indicate the locations of B&Bs described in detail in this chapter.

RHODE ISLAND

RHODE ISLAND

Reservation Services

Castle Keep

This service places guests in Newport homes. Please see page 315.

Pineapple Hospitality

This service matches guests with hosts all over New England. Their Rhode Island listings are on Block Island and in Hopkinton, Jamestown, Middletown, Newport, Providence, Saunderstown, Tiverton, and Wakefield. Please see page 170.

Bed & Breakfast of Rhode Island Inc.

P.O. Box 312, Barrington, RI 02806
Phone: 401/246-0142
Open: Year round.
Listings: About 40 homes. Many are near the Ocean State's 400 miles of shoreline. Several are in or within minutes of Newport. Directory describing listings: $1.
Reservations: At least two weeks notice preferred. Phone reservations accepted.

Joy Meiser and Ken Mendis share their interest in local history by sending a brief history of "your" area with each reservation confirmation. If the host home is of historic significance, you will know something about that ahead of time, too.
Rates: Singles $25–$40, doubles $35–55. Rates may be higher in heavy demand areas. MasterCard and VISA accepted on deposits.

Narragansett hosts are listed for direct booking. See page 308.

*

Some services that are based outside of the Northeast have hosts in many states including Rhode Island. See pages 26-29.

B&Bs

BLOCK ISLAND

Old Town Inn

Old Town Road, Block Island, RI 02807
Phone: 401/466-5958; off-season, 617/237-6751
Location: In a quiet country setting on a paved road one mile from town center. Block Island is reached by ferry from Point Judith, R.I. (1¼ hours); New London, Conn. (2 hours); Newport; and Providence too. Check schedule with Interstate Navigation Company, 401/783-4613.
Hosts: Monica and Ralph Gunter, David Gunter
Open: Last week in May through September. Minimum reservation: three nights June through Labor Day, two nights other times. Reservations strongly recommended.

"Why can't we stay longer?" the Gunter children used to ask when they were visiting relatives on Block Island. One way to have their own place was to have paying guests. Dad, an architectural engineer, and Mother, a legal secretary, thought of that old empty inn that was for sale for five or six years; and in 1968 they took the plunge. The grown family still loves Block Island and they all come — even from California — at some point during the summer. The youngest, David, is full-time manager. Now grandchildren, too, love the fog, the beaches, the coves — the whole island, a place that reminds Mrs. Gunter, cook and hostess, of her native England. By now the enthusiastic Gunters are well versed in and quite willing to share some of the island's history.

The old section of the house was built around 1832. A wing at least as big as the original inn was added in 1981 by demand of repeat visitors, many of whom are now good family friends.

In residence: Fred, the cat.

Restrictions: Children should be at least five. No pets allowed. Smoking is permitted but not encouraged.

Bed: Twelve rooms. One single, four rooms with twin beds, seven with doubles. The six rooms in new wing and two in old have private baths. Cots available.

Breakfast: Full; includes hot blueberry muffins. Served in small quaint breakfast rooms.

Plus: Afternoon tea served by Mrs. Gunter from the tea wagon with her own English tarts, scones, or cake: a great time to meet other guests and the family. Big traditionally furnished lounge in new wing. Maid service. Lawns and patios with lounge chairs and picnic tables. Three-speed bicycles for rent from the Inn.

Rates: $28 single. $40 double with shared bath, $50 with private bath in old house, $60 with private bath in new wing. Extra cot $10. Weekly rates available.

GREEN HILL

Fairfield-by-the-Sea

861 Green Hill Beach Road, Green Hill, RI 02879
Phone: 401/789-4717
Location: Between Westerly and Wakefield in a secluded country setting, ¾ mile from ocean beach, 40 miles from Providence, 30 miles from New London, 10 miles from University of Rhode Island. Host will meet train at Kingston station.
Host: Jeanne Lewis
Open: Year round.

"Last year, my first as a host, was just a whole summer of laughs. When I think of the different people, each one lovely, and the blend of interesting conversations around the table, I look forward to my retirement (in a few months) from teaching (grades 5–8) when I can be here year round to share this special home with more guests."

The contemporary country home on 3½ acres was what Jeanne's husband always wanted to design and build. And that's what he did. It is a lovely place filled with art and a relaxing atmosphere, but the total picture includes a creative home economist, one who has had a multifaceted career. She has been a consumer consultant all over the country and has edited national publications. A poet, she is also an avid gardener, and a grandmother. Her newest role brings back memories of "all the grand folks we met through B&B" in her childhood days on the Vermont family farm.

Carless guests find that Fairfield-by-the-Sea is a good place to unwind. They read, bird-watch, and walk on the beach. Equipment is provided for catching blue crabs or harvesting mussels. For day-trippers the possibilities are endless — Block Island, Mystic, Newport, Plymouth, and even factory stores. Jeanne's collection — "a mountain" — of information includes restaurants that she has tried out first.

In residence: Snofi, a Maine coon cat, "aloof and yet ever present."
Restrictions: No pets. Well-behaved children are welcome. Smokers should be thoughtful of other guests.
Bed: Two rooms. One with twin beds, one with double. Shared guest bath. Cot available.
Breakfast: Available generally 8–10, but can be flexible. Continental with fresh fruit and homemade breads. Eat in dining room or on screened balcony.
Plus: The balcony, living room with fireplace, lovely picnic area. Sometimes Jeanne gives tours of Galilee, Watch Hill, and surrounding areas. Baby-sitting available. Option of seafood feasts if it's a cooperative venture. "Mine is an equal opportunity kitchen."
Rates: $39 per room. Cot $6 under age six, $10 over age six.

MIDDLETOWN

Bed & Breakfast Registry Host #02840

Location: Two and a half miles from downtown Newport. Within walking distance of Second Beach.
Reservations: Available year round through Bed & Breakfast Registry, page 27. Minimum reservation of two nights July–September.

Away from the hubbub is this split-level house hosted by a couple who find that guests have a wide variety of interests. Some eat and run but others enjoy breakfast as the calm before a busy day. Conversation runs the gamut — from family to Newport attractions, from hints about bargain hours at good restaurants to stained-glass making, from gardening to shell collecting.

The host traveled the world over in his days with the Navy food services. He and his wife have seven grown children and eleven grandchildren.

In residence: People who smoke.
Bed: Three rooms. One double with private bath. Two rooms with twin beds share family bath. Cot and crib available.
Breakfast: Continental, usually with homemade muffins or preserves. Option of full breakfast for extra charge.
Plus: Yard, off-street parking.
Rates: $28 twin bedded rooms, $33 double. Cot or crib $5.

NARRAGANSETT

A Book-Your-Own Arrangement

In 1981 the Narragansett Chamber of Commerce, beset with the problem of limited accommodations for unlimited visitors to the seaside, actively sought out families for participation in a bed-and-breakfast program. The names and addresses (only) of the current hosts are on a list that can be obtained by writing or calling the Narragansett Chamber of Commerce, The Towers, Narragansett, RI 02882, 401/783-7121.

Guests may book their own arrangements directly. Because hosts stay in touch with one another, they know — and often recommend — others who have openings. In addition, the Chamber of Commerce acts as a reservation service without charge to the guests; if you call the Chamber (open seven days a week in summer, five days a week the rest of the year), staff members will either suggest three places or put you "on hold" and actually make the booking for you on the phone.

The beaches are the main attraction. There are, as one host said, "people beaches, radio beaches, quiet beaches, surfing beaches"; and hosts can direct you accordingly. Newport is only a 20-minute drive away. Watch Hill is a half hour. The fishing village of Galilee is just down the road. Block Island, reached by the ferry that leaves from Point Judith, is a popular day trip. Musical theater and restaurants make the list too. Cycling in this pocket of Rhode Island is scenic and pretty flat.

NARRAGANSETT

The Phoenix

29 Gibson Avenue, Narragansett, RI 02882
Phone: 401/783-1918
Location: In a very quiet residential area. Ten minutes' walk to beaches.
Hosts: Joyce and Dave Peterson
Open: Year round.

It was a rare 70-degree November weekend when we made last-minute reservations at The Phoenix. After our stay we knew why, although this B&B has been in operation just two years, it wouldn't be so easy to find an opening in season.

The front porch note written in Joyce's calligraphy read "Welcome to the Petersons. The bell doesn't work. Please knock." The bell, we learned, is just one of the many projects on the "to do" list, but the guests reap the rewards of the efforts to date. The ambiance is just fine for relaxation surrounded by space and comfort. Some guests sit by the fire in winter (for fun or, as one did, to work on a thesis); in summer the porch can be the focal point for greeting and meeting. Our evening tea arrived on a tray with a Russian doll-cozy "brought back by my sister."

Joyce obviously enjoys decorating, plants — and people. The Phoenix is a brightened-up, impeccably maintained Victorian with shades of soft yellow in the north living room, some refinished floors, and fresh flowers in all the rooms. One guest room has an antique lace tablecloth used as a bedspread over a blue blanket, and one bath has a wonderful high long old tub on a marble stand.

The rambling house was built in 1889, kitchenless, as part of a compound by restaurateur Louis Sherry. It burned soon after; it was rebuilt in 1912; and when the Petersons first saw it about 10 years ago, it was ready to fall down. They have done all the work — real work — themselves, with the aid of a do-it-yourself guidebook. They have learned far more than they ever expected to. The refinished cherry banister is obvious. But the more hidden achievements have sagas that are related with a smile by a cheerful hostess. (Ask about the dramatic first — and extremely cold — winter when they realized they were *not* connected to a sewer line.)

Joyce rises at 5:30 and fits more than a day into her waking hours — sports, photography, some real-estate work, Sunday school teaching, and The Phoenix. When Dave is home from his job as marketing manager for General Electric, he is evening and weekend host, fire tender, chef's helper, builder, electrician, and local guide. Daughter Kim is a big help too.

Because the Petersons have lived in five other states where long driving distances were more common than the five-minutes-from-everything concept, they have explored resources in a wide area. Their home is filled with zest and contagious joy.

In residence: Teenage daughter Kim.
Restrictions: No pets. Smoking only in living room and on porch.
Bed: Five rooms. Three with double beds, two with two twin beds in each. Three shared baths. Cots available.
Breakfast: Brunch. As Joyce's mother used to say, "Eat breakfast like a king, lunch like a prince, supper like a pauper." Maybe broiled grapefruit and homemade muffins and blueberry pancakes, eggs Benedict, or omelets filled with avocado and shrimp. Cooked, served, and planned by Joyce with timing that allows her to enjoy it with you.
Plus: Half-price tokens for Newport Bridge, good collection of menus from restaurants hosts have tried, large lawn for sunbathing, croquet, living room with fireplace, clothesline for wet bathing suits.
Rates: $40 single, $50 for two. Cots $10.

NARRAGANSETT

Mon Rêve

41 Gibson Avenue, Narragansett, RI 02882
Phone: 401/783-2846
Location: One mile to town beach. Ocean is three blocks away.
Host: Eva Doran
Open: Year round.

A perfect blend at the right time. When the Narragansett Chamber of Commerce encouraged local homes to host B&Bs, they must have been thinking about places like this — a private home built for a New York financier in the 1890s and later owned by sculptress and artist Florence Kane. It's now on the National Register of Historic Places, and for most of Eva Doran's 25 years here, there has been an ongoing open-house style. She has taught French at four Rhode Island colleges and universities, is a lecturer and writer, and now finds time for jogging and baking too.

Victorian furnishings are everywhere. And so is attention to detail

— fresh flowers, mints at bedside, turned-down beds, pretty table settings. How far can consideration go? "I just want to point out that it is important for couples with wee babies to notify me well in advance so that I can reserve the room that is located where a crying baby won't disturb guests. (It also has a convenient rocking chair.)"

In residence: Shannon, a good-natured red Irish setter. One daughter in winter and another home from college in summer. Nonsmokers live here, but smoking is allowed, except in bedrooms.
Foreign languages spoken: French and Italian. College daughter speaks Chinese.
Bed: Four rooms. One single, one with twin beds, two with double beds. Two shared guest bathrooms.
Breakfast: Continental and leisurely. Served on enclosed sun porch. Could include blueberries from nearby woods, raspberries from Mon Rêve's patch, and basket of homemade breads.
Plus: Picnic table and grille. No additional charge for use of (four) bicycles. Half-price tokens for Newport Bridge.
Rates: $22–$25 single, $28 for two.

What a delight to find the traditional down-home "southern comfort" in a dear New England town!   Rosaline R. McClanahan, Little Rock, Arkansas

NARRAGANSETT

The Four Gables

12 South Pier Road, Narragansett, RI 02882
Phone: 401/789-6948
Location: One block off Route 1A, a major scenic route. On a main town road.
Hosts: Joyce and Peter Turco
Open: Year round.

"We just started B&B hosting in 1982. The first guest liked the place so much that follow-up bookings were made for every weekend thereafter!"

"The place" was built in 1898 by Willard Kent (an architect and the designer of all the water lines in South Kingston and Narragansett, R.I.) as a summer home with wonderful woodwork, four fireplaces, and interesting nooks and crannies. The Turcos, owners for 13 years, have furnished it with antiques and traditional pieces. In one room there's a huge counter-march loom. Just say the word and Joyce will give you a demonstration and, if you'd like, an opportunity to try it.

Peter is around at the ends of the day because his shopkeeping, especially in summer, is time-consuming. Joyce is a former airline stewardess. "It gives me great pleasure to provide the added touches such as fruit in the room or fresh flowers from my garden in season. One does these things naturally anyway and to get paid for it is an added bonus."

The family enjoys the area. In addition to the beaches, there's fishing right off the nearby dock. Their jogging route is along the seawall that borders the ocean. And they are familiar with a wide variety of restaurants — from seafood to Chinese to Italian.

In residence: David and Matthew, two teenage sons. One family member smokes. And there is Reuben, "a very affectionate lovable dachshund."

Bed: Two rooms, one with double and one with queen-sized bed. One room has a handmade quilt and stenciled walls. Cot available. One guest bath.

Breakfast: Continental. Fresh fruit in season; usually blueberry muffins. Available whenever you'd like. Eat at round mahogany dining-room table with view of ocean or on balcony beyond sliding doors.

Plus: Patio. Backyard for badminton or croquet. Beach passes. Bicycles.

Rates: $20 single, $25–$30 for two. Cot $5.

A delightful Newport weekend highlighted by our stay at The Four Gables, a charming and most interesting home as were our hosts, the Turcos.   Charmian and Ivars Zvirbulis, Ivyland, Pennsylvania

My stay will be a long-remembered experience. Their lovely home and warm hospitality kept me coming back. I met many interesting people that summer. In fact I will be marrying a gentleman they introduced me to. That kind of thing would not have happened if I had chosen to stay in a motel. My life turned around the day I found out about bed and breakfast at The Four Gables.   Joyce G. Marks, Rocky Hill, Connecticut

NARRAGANSETT

Steven and Nancy Richards

104 Robinson Street, Narragansett, RI 02882
Phone: 401/789-7746
Open: Year round.

The family lives in a 10-room "ever growing Cape" that was originally built 50 years ago by a professional landscaper. The home borders a wooded area and is at the end of a quiet dead-end street in the center of town. A profusion of flowers adds to the charm outside and inviting country decor is inside. Nancy paints, enjoys tennis, and creates a relaxing B&B atmosphere with fresh flowers in guest rooms, thick towels, and breakfast as a high point. Steven, cochef on weekends, is a director of a program run through the state legislature.

Although the beaches, Newport, and Block Island are the destinations of most guests, you could walk to riding stables from here.

In residence: Two daughters, Victoria, 11, and Kristina, 10. Roscoe and Otis are their cats.
Restrictions: No guests' pets. No smoking.
Bed: Three rooms. One with twin beds and one with a double bed share a guest bath. One double-bedded room has a private bath and entrance. Cots available.
Breakfast: Full. Served at 8:30. Homemade muffins or bread. And sausages, bacon or ham, eggs Florentine, baked apple pancakes, or scrambled eggs.
Plus: Deck, patio, badminton, croquet, half-price tokens for Newport Bridge. Guests may leave their things at "home" for the day, then shower and change before departing.
Rates: $22–$28 single, $30–$35 for two. Cots $5 for children, $10 adults.

Steven and Nancy, personable hosts, went out of their way to make our stay enjoyable. They even made a special wheat-free, nonallergenic breakfast for us and it was delicious!

R.K.W. & M.E.D., Jamaica Plain, Massachusetts

Gracious hosts . . . feeling of spending a weekend with friends . . . thinking of your every comfort. . . . Delightful breakfast with family . . . remember the hot cranberry muffins . . . everything so good!

Mrs. Arthur F. Daniel, Fair Haven, New Jersey

NARRAGANSETT

Maus Cottage

46 Rockland Street, Narragansett, RI 02882
Phone: 401/783-8732
Location: Quiet village setting, half mile from public beach.
Hosts: Roberta and Ralph Tutt
Open: Memorial Day–Labor Day. Other times by special request. Reservations strongly advised for weekends and August.

"We don't smother our guests with attentiveness, but there's always someone here to find a safety pin or bring a bucket of ice."

Roberta and Ralph, both English professors — Roberta is also a designer of hand-knits — have lived in this shore shingled house for 10 years. It was built in 1889, is on the National Register of Historic Places, and is comfortable "though not quaint," furnished in a style that is "eclectic and colorful but not eccentric."

Friends who are local hosts suggested that the Tutts would be a good B&B. The enthusiastic guests of their first (1982) season are glad that the family made a positive decision. You can count on a supply of books and magazines — and information too. And still the Tutts find that guests sometimes add to the list of interesting places by sharing some discoveries.

In residence: People who smoke. Oliver, a teenage son. Two cats — Jake, a tabby, and Nelson, a friendly marmalade tiger.
Restrictions: No pets allowed. Children (usually) should be at least seven. Infants okay if parents arrive with "necessary gear."
Foreign language spoken: Some Spanish.
Bed: One single with shared bath. One double with shared or private bath. Cots available.
Breakfast: Full. Menu includes fresh fruit by the bowl, maybe pancakes or crepes, beverage by the pot. Served in formal dining room with bay window overlooking lawn or on screened veranda, weather permitting.
Plus: Spacious living room with color TV, veranda, large lawn with croquet. Half-price tokens for Newport Bridge.
Rates: $20 single. $30 double with shared bath, $40 with private. Ten percent surcharge for one-night stay; 5 percent discount for six nights or more. Cots $8.
You feel like a welcomed and invited guest rather than a business patron.   Carol Agneta, Peabody, Massachusetts

NEWPORT

Castle Keep (Reservation Service)

44 Everett Street, Newport, RI 02840
Phone: 401/846-0362
Established April 1982.
Listings: About 25 or 30 residences that vary from modest to elegant, with a total of 50 rooms. Included are restored colonials, sumptuous Victorians, and some modern houses too — located throughout Newport. Dorothy Ranhofer and Audrey Grimes take last-minute reservations and place visitors in a particular area in a specified price range. "We usually do not get involved in matching interest or nonsmoking requirements." All listings have a host in residence.
Rates: Singles $25–$40, double $45–$70. MasterCard and VISA accepted for phone deposits.

NEWPORT

The Brinley Victorian Guest House

23 Brinley Street, Newport, RI 02840
Phone: 401/849-7645
Location: Centrally located one block from Bellevue Avenue and within walking distance of wharves and most historic homes.
Hosts: Amy Weintraub, Edwina Sebest, Susan Jenkins
Open: Year round. Minimum reservation is two nights from Memorial Day until October 15, three nights on holiday weekends.

The restored Victorian inn has been under new ownership since October 1982.
Amy, an award-winning television writer and executive producer, and Edwina, a psychologist with a private practice and weekly television segment, decided to change careers, move from Pittsburgh, and open an inn in Newport. The one they found in the spring of 1981 was a nursing home. So they decided to move in and learn the nursing-home business! Because they still had the unfulfilled desire to be innkeepers, they bought The Brinley, three blocks away, when it came on the market. Susan, a life-long resident of Newport, lives in The Brinley and is manager and baker; but from their own B&B stays, Amy and Edwina

feel strongly about the hosting role. They enjoy being with guests at breakfast and in the afternoons, when the questions about local places and evening plans usually arise. And it seems that there are a number of guests who are thinking of changing careers or opening an inn.

The Brinley was originally built as two single-family homes with clapboard siding and mansard roof lines. After a checkered history and after the addition of the breezeway (1965) that joins the buildings, the whole establishment was restored in 1981 and 1982 with modern-day bed and bath furnishings before being sold to the current owners. Guests now experience Victorian ambiance, with an antique miniature kerosene lamp and candlestick (from Edwina's collection) and fresh flowers in each room. Let the hosts know in advance about special occasions and they'll provide wine, champagne, maybe candlelight — some nice touch.

In residence: Susan's school-age daughter.
Restrictions: Children should be at least 12. No pets allowed.
Bed: Sixteen rooms, each with at least one double bed. Some have two doubles and others have an added twin bed. Suites, private baths, and shared baths available.
Breakfast: Continental. Homemade bakery. Served buffet style, eaten in parlor.
Plus: Off-street parking. Small library, two parlors, two porches. Safe storage for bicycles.
Rates: Per room: Memorial Day–October 15, $55 shared bath, $60 private. January and February, $35 shared bath, $40 private. Other months, $40 shared, $45 private. $10 for extra person in room beyond two.

Excellent accommodations, very friendly and helpful hostesses, arranged dinner reservations, provided a great breakfast in a family-type atmosphere where we met other travelers and talked about sightseeing experiences. Highly recommended!

P. Deland and E. Weston, Staten Island, New York

NEWPORT

Cliffside

2 Seaview Avenue, Newport, RI 02840
Phone: 401/847-1811
Location: Near Cliff Walk. Five minutes to First Beach.
Host: Kathleen Russell
Open: Mid-April until mid-October. Minimum stay on weekends: two nights.

Because Newport is so popular, I tried to find several B&Bs in town that were hosted and personalized. Because everyone mentioned Kay Russell, I was surprised to learn that she is a newcomer, having started in business just two years ago.

Cliffside has had her full attention; and evidently guests sense that she finds it satisfying, challenging, and exciting. She is aware of guests' needs and enjoys seeing those who have been in town for a couple of days become guides for new guests. And there are many opportunities to exchange opinions about the mansions and the restaurants too.

Kay knew that this business was the right thing at the right time for her. And she knew that much was to be done to the large rooms in the inn, which was built in 1880 as a summer cottage by the governor of Maryland. When we spoke she was between strips of wallpaper. By now the whole place has been repapered and redecorated. Almost all the furnishings are older pieces. There were seven rooms and now there are ten. Five baths have been added. In redoing the kitchen Kay discovered not one but three chimneys, and that room has been rebuilt with fireplace. Give Kay time and she'll do some research about Newport natives and use their names for various rooms.

In residence: Two cats.
Restrictions: No pets. Children should be at least 12.
Bed: Ten rooms, all with private baths. Two have two twin beds, five have doubles, one has antique queen-sized bed, two have two doubles, one has a double and a twin.
Breakfast: Continental. Homemade rolls or popovers. Special diets can be taken care of.
Plus: Sitting room on third floor with television and a pump organ that works.
Rates: $40–$65 double. $35 single in twin-bedded room.

NEWPORT

Ellery Park House

44 Farwell Street, Newport, RI 02840
Phone: 401/847-6320
Location: About four blocks from waterfront in quiet historic Point section.
Hosts: Margo and Michael Waite
Open: Year round.

Volunteer hosts were needed for participants in a sailboat race from England to Newport. In 1979 the Waites signed up and hosted a wonderful French family for ten days, and the idea of B&B was launched. Since then they have visited many of their guests from Australia, France, and England; and those guests are all booked for return visits to Ellery Park House in the next two years!

Many Americans, too, appreciate the hospitality in the 1889 Victorian cottage, one that was originally built to fit the lot so all four walls are different lengths.

Michael runs a restaurant in town; the home kitchen is equipped with a restaurant stove and extensive cookbook collection. Margo is associate publisher of a sailing magazine.

In residence: Raspberry, "an extremely gentle Doberman," and Hari, "our 16-year-old feisty cat."
Restrictions: Smoking allowed, but not in bedrooms. Children? Prefer under age two or over eight.
Foreign languages spoken: None (a very little French) but "we had visitors who didn't speak English and it was fine."
Bed: Two rooms. One with twin beds, one with double. Shared guest bath.
Breakfast: Continental with homemade muffins and jam. Could be quite social or self-serve, depending on everyone's schedules.
Plus: Many books available. Patio. Box lunch or dinner is an option.
Rate: $40 per room.

NEWPORT

Moulton-Weaver House

4 Training Station Road, Newport, RI 02840
Phone: 401/847-0133
Location: Near Naval Base Gate 1.
Host: Patricia Collins Sherman

Mrs. Sherman, an interior designer — a busy one — has made this 1905 house into a bright cheerful home. Since taking a neighbor's overflow guests almost as a favor, she has become a successful B&B host with many repeat guests.

The antique furnishings include Victorian in the living room, a spinning wheel by the fireplace in the dining room, four-poster beds in two of the bedrooms, and old bureaus and washstands. The dining-room fireplace has a bread oven; and that paneling in the library came from a captain's cabin on a sailing ship. The moldings are unusual and the newel-posted staircase has three different styles of spindles.

Because the Sherman household has always been the setting for entertaining, the hosting style is thoughtful. Spring water in carafes will be found in the bedrooms. The color-coordinated decor is detailed down to the hangers in the closets. You can count on recommendations for restaurants and on pleasant conversation. After three years of dovetailing appointments, Mrs. Sherman suggests that it would be helpful if guests could be specific about arrival time.

In residence: Howard, a 15-year-old cat. The English setter puppy is confined and infrequently escapes to visit with guests.
Bed: Three rooms. One with a pair of twin beds, two others each have a double. One shared guest bath.
Breakfast: Continental. In dining room with table set with china and cloth napkins.
Plus: Guest living room with television.
Rate: $45 per room.

NEWPORT

Queen Anne Inn

16 Clarke Street, Newport, RI 02840
Phone: 401/846-5676
Location: In Historic District, two blocks from waterfront.
Host: Peg McCabe
Open: At least March through mid-November. Minimum reservation: two nights weekdays in summer, two nights weekends all year, and three nights on holiday weekends.

"Have you contacted Queen Anne Inn? Now that's the place for charm and location." Some of Peg McCabe's competitors are fans, quick to recognize what she offers.

Anyone who has walked among the blocks of restored colonials in Newport remembers this striking Queen Anne Revival, painted a tasteful pink/rose on the outside. With the open-door policy, guests take their own inside tour of the Victorian elegance without clutter to admire the fresh floral arrangements, period papers, a four-poster bed here, an armoire there — all in rooms with refinished hardwood floors. Changes that will greet this season's guests include a refurbished reception room, renovated baths, and another guest room.

And all this from a woman who until five years ago was "a New York suburban housewife and mom to four." Along came "a series of fortunate accidents" and a multifaceted career. "Sometimes I think I'm a mini–Chamber of Commerce!"

Restrictions: No pets please. No incoming or outgoing phone service is available between 11 p.m. and 8 a.m.
Foreign language spoken: The most rudimentary French.
Bed: Twelve rooms. One single, four rooms with twin beds, seven with double beds. Seven shared baths.
Breakfast: Continental in the garden or reception room.
Plus: Parking provided. Use of garden.
Rates: $30–$55. No credit cards accepted.

A lovely, comfortable, conveniently located inn with an exceptional owner to add charm and humor to the glorious surroundings of Newport.   Dr. and Mrs. Sylvester J. Ryan, Middlebury, Connecticut

NEWPORT

The Yellow Cottage

82 Gibbs Avenue, Newport, RI 02840
Phone: 401/847-6568
Location: Five-minute ride to town or beaches.
Host: Nancy A. Rubeck
Open: Year round.

The Yellow Cottage, built as a summer home about 1900, has been the Rubeck residence for 12 years. Nancy comes from a big family and is used to having numbers of people around. For many years, as a military wife, she lived in several states, Hawaii, Barbados, and Panama. So it was natural for her to turn to B&B as a way to work and stay home with her children. After two years of hosting "in my grandmother's style of 'clean, courteous, and kind,'" she finds that her two teenagers and even the preschooler participate. "I could run a B&B training course for children!"

Flexibility can be a serious word here. When one family had plans to leave for a long drive at 3 a.m., Nancy insisted on rising to serve them a full breakfast.

In residence: One who smokes. Two cats. Trina, age 15; James, age 13; and Amy, age 4.
Bed: Three rooms. One single, one double, and one queen. Shared guest bath.
Breakfast: Full with fresh juice, fruit, and homemade bread.
Plus: Fresh flowers and candy in rooms, turned-down beds at night, postcards with stamps. Half-price token for Newport Bridge sent if time permits. And if you're unhappy with a local restaurant, Nancy follows up!
Rates: $30 single, $50 double in summer; $25 and $35 other months.

PROVIDENCE

Pineapple Hospitality Host #RI 205

Location: In a lovely residential area that is a 20-minute walk to universities and the historic preservation district. Bus stop is one block away.

Reservations: Available mid-September through mid-June through Pineapple Hospitality, page 170.

"My husband is an architect and I am a lapsed interior designer who now loves the part-time bookkeeping I sometimes do. Both of us are natives of Providence and know the city well. Ours is a case of the shoemaker's children (and six grown children at that). Although I am an interior designer, this is not a decorator's showroom. It is a pleasing and comfortable home that was built around 1895. I call the architecture Late Unremarkable Victorian. Our accommodations are on the third floor under the eaves where it behooves very tall people to proceed with care. One such who stayed with us said it reminded him of the kinds of places he stayed in when he was in France."

Guests report that the hosts really love their city and are extremely helpful. The attention to detail — flowers and fruit in the room — is appreciated.

In residence: One who smokes if she hasn't managed to stop. A Doberman and a cat.
Restrictions: No guests' pets.
Bed: Two rooms each with a double bed. Shared guest bath.
Breakfast: Continental. Homemade breads, fresh bagels, freshly ground coffee or properly made tea.
Plus: Living room with fireplace.
Rates: $28 single, $40 for two.

WAKEFIELD

Blueberry Bush

679 South Road, Wakefield, RI 02879
Phone: 401/783-0907
Location: Suburban/rural and quiet. Fifteen minutes from Interstate 95; 10 minutes to beaches, 25 minutes to Newport, 5 minutes to Wakefield shops, 25 minutes to Mystic, Connecticut.
Hosts: June and Pete Nielsen
Open: Year round.

June and Pete Nielsen have a lovely home, ideally set up for bed and breakfast. They are excellent hosts — friendly, open but never intrusive, knowledgeable about the area, and helpful to travelers. And June makes a great breakfast. We like to consider Nielsens' our home away from home in southern Rhode Island.

G. and D. Pedersen, Wakefield, Massachusetts

June teaches Oriental-rug making and knitting. Pete, an executive with a textile company, enjoys woodworking. Their inviting Cape Cod–style home is traditionally furnished and has some lovely antiques and refinished pieces. Friends suggested hosting, so in 1980 the Nielsens thought they would try it. Three years later they can say, "Our guests have been interesting, informative, and fun! And they frequently mention that their children behave better in a B&B home atmosphere than they do in a hotel or motel."

In residence: Smudge, the cat. People who smoke.
Restrictions: No guests' pets.
Bed: Two rooms. One with twin beds, plus accommodations for two more if needed. One double-bedded room with rollaway. Crib available.
Breakfast: Special. Available 7–9:30. Homemade bread or muffins, jams and jellies, their own blueberries or peaches, at least three choices on main course. Menu changes daily.
Plus: Use of yard, cookout facilities, outdoor table and chairs. Laundry facilities available if stay is three days or longer. High chair available.
Rates: $25 single, $35 for two. Extra cots $5 child, $7.50 over age 14.

WESTERLY

Woody Hill Guest House

RR 3, Box 676E, Westerly, RI 02891
Phone: 401/322-0452
Location: Just off busy Route 1, but really in the country.
Host: Ellen L. Madison
Open: Year round.

I've traveled the world, but one of the luckiest things I've ever done is to stop at the Woody Hill Guest House. It's a wonderful house, set atop a hill, off the main road, and near some of the very best beaches anywhere. Ellen Madison is such a delightful and resourceful person that I've been coming back for eight years. It's my favorite retreat. So far I've only introduced my best friends to Woody Hill. Now that the secret

*is out, I guess I'm glad that other folks will get a chance to enjoy this
great little place too.*   Dr. Robert Wyman, New Haven, Connecticut

Ellen Madison's family has lived within a two-mile radius of her
home since 1636. She designed and did much of the finishing work on
the gambrel-roofed colonial reproduction that was built on the "family
farm." It has wide floorboards; weathered shingles; and large, airy, welcoming rooms filled with inherited furniture, crafts, and some wonderful handmade (by Ellen) quilts.

Her inspiration for hosting is deep-rooted too. "My parents took
tourists in their home while I was growing up and I saw what treasured
friendships they made." The assortment of her own guests is broad —
old guests who have become friends, old friends who have become
guests, an older couple who returned several times in one season, a
couple with a child, professional innkeepers, off-season visitors, and
some who prefer the midweek segment. One wrote, "Cheers to your
sanctuary of the past."

Guests can tell that cooking and gardening are interests. "What I'm
supposed to be interested in right now is finishing my doctoral disserta-
tion on Harriet Beecher Stowe's *Uncle Tom's Cabin*." And what else? "I
have taught at the university and junior-high level but am now teaching
English on the high-school level."

In residence: Two cats. "Lady — aloof, skittish, picky yellow cat as
becomes her name, and Treasure, a fat happy lazy black cat who cozies
up to anyone and molds himself to that person."
Restrictions: Nonsmokers preferred. No guests' pets.
Bed: Two rooms. One with double bed, one with double and a ¾ bed.
Shared guest bath. Cot available.
Breakfast: Homegrown raspberries year round. Homegrown pork
products, homemade muffins, fruit of the season. In winter you'll
probably be served warm applesauce and waffles. Served 8–9:30
in cozy dining room with harvest table, Windsor chairs, braided rug,
wainscoting.
Plus: Extensive library. Use of yard with gardens and privacy, "and
sometimes mosquitoes. Once in a while we take a tour of the next-door
farm that has pigs and chickens."
Rates: $38 for two, $42 for three, $46 for four. Winter rates are lower.
Cot $5.

*The house's warm ambiance is only outdone by the hospitality of Ellen
Madison. One visit is never enough!*
                              Nancy Halyburton, Old Lyme, Connecticut

CONNECTICUT

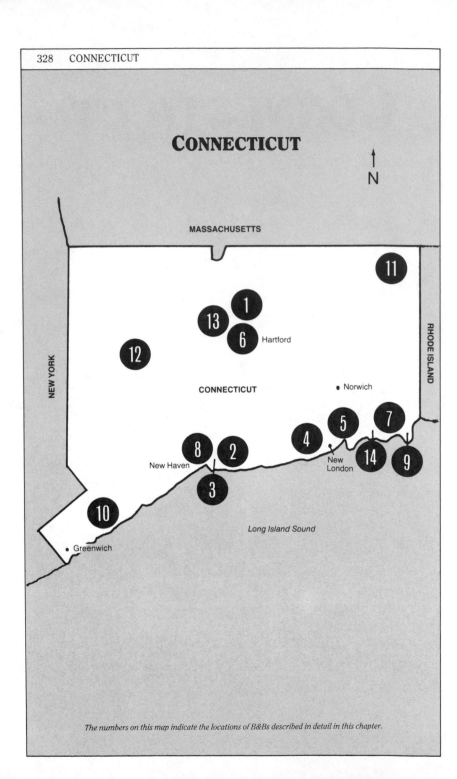

The numbers on this map indicate the locations of B&Bs described in detail in this chapter.

CONNECTICUT

CONNECTICUT

Reservation Services

Hosts represented by Connecticut services live in restored farmhouses, ranch homes, beachfront locations, elegant properties, and historic homesteads. All five services below are constantly adding hosts.

Bed and Breakfast, Ltd.

P.O. Box 216, New Haven, CT 06513
Phone: 203/469-3260 weekends and between 5 and 7 weekdays.
Established August 1982.
Listings: Jack Argenio's hosts were originally concentrated in the New Haven area. Recent expansion has added B&Bs in the communities of Bethany, East Haven, Killingworth, North Haven, Northford, Woodbridge, and through southern Connecticut into Guilford.
Rates: Singles $20–$25, doubles $30–$40. A few higher. Weekly and monthly rates available.

Covered Bridge Bed and Breakfast

West Cornwall, CT 06796
Phone: 203/672-6052
Established March 1983.
Listings: A growing list that began with about 12. Antique-filled old New England homes are Rae Eastman's specialty. Her territory encompasses the northwest part of Connecticut — with current listings in Canaan, Cornwall, Kent, Lime Rock, Sharon, and Watertown, the southern Berkshires in the Tanglewood area, and in neighboring New York communities including Copake.
Rates: $35–$80.

Nutmeg Bed & Breakfast

222 Girard Avenue, Hartford, CT 06105
Phone: 203/236-6698
Established March 1982.
Listings: Approximately 100 all over the state.

Maxine Kates and Phyllis Nova, two former teachers, thought this would be a part-time business. It is full-time-plus for them now. Their directory ($2 and business-sized SASE) has general characteristics of each area as well as house descriptions. Selected hosts are in lovely and interesting homes and a few inns. *Hartford area:* Cromwell, Hartford, Old Wethersfield, West End, West Hartford. *Bloomfield area:* Avon, Bloomfield, Farmington. *East of Hartford:* Columbia Lake, Enfield, Glastonbury, Manchester, Mansfield, Somers, Suffield, Tolland. *Shoreline:* Clinton, East Haddam, East Lyme, Essex, Guilford, Moodus, Mystic, New London, North Stonington, Old Lyme, Old Saybrook. *New Haven:* Cheshire, Hamden, Milford, New Haven, West Haven. *Fairfield County:* Darien, Fairfield, Greenwich, Norwalk, Rowayton, Silvermine, Stratford, Trumbull, Weston, Westport. *Litchfield County:* Falls Village, Kent, Lakeville, Lake Waramaug, Lime Rock, Sharon, Washington, Woodbury.
Rates: $25–$65 for two. Ten percent less for singles. Higher rates on holidays. Weekly and monthly rates available.

Pineapple Hospitality

This service matches guests with hosts all over New England. Their Connecticut listings are in Danbury, Fairfield, Groton Long Point, Mystic, New Haven, Simsbury, and Westport. Please see page 170.

*

Some of the reservation and referral services with listings in many states throughout the country, pages 26-29, have a few hosts in Connecticut.

B&Bs

BLOOMFIELD

Nutmeg Bed & Breakfast Host #14

Location: Five miles northwest of Hartford on a quiet road but a couple of miles to everything.
Reservations: Available year round through Nutmeg Bed & Breakfast, page 331.

"I love to have this wonderful house filled with happy people. I'm not much of a letter writer, so if everyone starts corresponding the way my early guests do, I don't know what I'll do."

A student of Frank Lloyd Wright designed the addition to this reproduction Federal residence. The glass walls bring the outside in. In the spring more than 200 varieties of daffodils bloom with 20,000 blossoms. The magnificent tulip tree is alleged to be the oldest and largest in the state. Pastures, two barns, and 11 pet goats (each will answer to its name) on over five magnificent acres make for a memorable setting.

The host is a crewel-embroidery designer who usually shows interested visitors the processes including silk screening and cutting. What an array of bird, flower, animal, and hobby designs on linen, cotton, and rayon ready to become finished pillows, hangings, pocketbooks, or ties.

Who comes here? A young couple with two children walked in the extensive woodlands, picnicked, fed the goats, and generally relaxed. A group of women, conventiongoers, found time to "kibitz in the kitchen" while food was being prepared for a big party; they also enjoyed singing around the piano. The sharing possibilities go beyond bed and breakfast.

In residence: Two cats.
Bed: Four rooms. Two with two twin beds and private bath; one room with king-sized bed, fireplace, private bath, and private balcony; one with ¾ bed and shared bath.
Breakfast: Full breakfast.

Plus: TV in smaller living room, piano in larger living room, swimming pool.
Rates: $35–$65.

. . . Like coming back home to a rediscovered relative. The beautiful house, the setting, the forest nearby — all in fall color — reflected the peace and elegance of the New England countryside which we hoped we would find, and did.   E.G.S., Hong Kong

BRANFORD

Bed & Breakfast, Ltd. Host #2

Location: Eight miles east of New Haven. Close to I-95.
Reservations: Available year round through Bed and Breakfast, Ltd.,
page 330.

"I've met some lovely people. My last guest stayed until noon and worked out with me to Jane Fonda's cassette!" The hostess, a keen runner (two times in the Boston Marathon), is a professional art salesperson. An atmosphere of creative casualness prevails in the large contemporary condominium.

In residence: Two children, ages three and six.
Restrictions: No pets please. And nonsmokers are preferred.
Foreign language spoken: French.
Bed: One double room with private bath.
Breakfast: Whatever, whenever.
Plus: Air conditioning. Use of swimming pool in season.
Rate: $35.

EAST HAVEN

Bed and Breakfast, Ltd. Host #3

Location: About 15 minutes from New Haven. On Long Island Sound.
Reservations: Available year round through Bed and Breakfast, Ltd., page 330.

You're right on the water with magnificent views, a private beach for swimming, and miles of sand for walking nearby. The two-story house, brick with a tile roof, was built in 1952 as a summer home and later converted to a year-round residence. Conversations with this creative, community-oriented couple are most likely to take place evenings and weekends, over sherry or tea, by the fire or on the terrace.

Restrictions: No pets and no smoking.
Foreign languages spoken: Some French and Italian.
Bed: Two rooms. One single and one with twin beds. Private baths.
Breakfast: Full. Eat with water views from inside or on breakfast terrace in warm weather.
Rates: $35 single, $45 double.

ESSEX

Bed & Breakfast Registry Host #06426

Location: A country setting 1½ miles from Essex village, in an area known for boating, yachting, antique shops, art galleries, and restaurants; 35 minutes to Yale, 15 minutes to public beaches.
Reservations: Available year round, except late December, through Bed & Breakfast Registry, page 27.

This two-year-old passive solar contemporary home, a semifinalist in a contest sponsored by *Metropolitan Home*, was designed and decorated by the host, who is an artist, gardener, and gourmet cook. Comfortable furniture and antiques, a wood stove, walls of books, flowers, and lots of windows create a delightful setting.

"I like my guests to treat this house as an intimate inn, spending as much or as little time in it as they wish. I love fixing tea trays and using my pretty things. Pillowcases are often embroidered antique linen ones."

Because she just started B&B last fall by taking overflow guests from a local inn, she could be considered a "lucky find." Everyone leaves saying they want to return.

In residence: One cat and occasionally one dog. Sometimes there are one, two, or three teenage children; other times guests have entire house to themselves.

Restrictions: No guests' pets. No smoking inside.

Bed: Three rooms, all with view of pond. One single with large comfortable window seat that could accommodate a child. One double with brass bed and loveseat. One double with antique four-poster, sofa, and deck.

Breakfast: Available 7–9:30, later on Sunday. Continental, extra charge for full.

Plus: Pond bank for picnics. Yard for sunning and reading. Option of dinner by request. Ice bucket and tea tray in afternoon or evening.

Rates: $40 single, $50 for two.

GROTON LONG POINT

Shore Inne

54 East Shore Road, Groton Long Point, CT 06340
Phone: 203/536-1180
Location: Overlooking tranquil harbor 3½ miles from Mystic Seaport.
Host: Helen Ellison
Open: Mid-March until mid-November.

Guests feel like residents rather than tourists in this quiet community of large older homes. Of the three clear-water ocean beaches within walking distance, one has a diving dock and separate fishing pier. The roads are flat (good for cycling). Area conservation lands are used for walks and bird-watching. Major attractions are a short drive away. Whenever (frequently) guests ask about establishing a B&B, they hear about Shore Inne's origin: just before 1920 — and before current zoning laws — vaudeville performers, owners of the summer home next door, had so many guests that they built this as an inn.

After just four seasons of being the proprietor, Mrs. Ellison has a long list of happy guests who appreciate her freshly made bran muffins, the hand-stenciled walls in the library/sunroom, the white wicker furniture, and the fireplace made of beach stones in the living room, and bedrooms that all have quilts made by grandmother Helen Ellison herself.

Restrictions: No smoking in the dining room. No guests' pets.
Bed: Seven rooms. Three have private baths. Four share two baths.
Breakfast: Continental with homemade bakery. Leisurely; served 8–10 in dining room that faces the water.
Plus: Use of refrigerator, picnic table, lawn chairs, and lawn games.
Rates: $32–$42 in summer. Other months, slightly lower. VISA and MasterCard accepted.

The gracious host, cheery atmosphere, and ideal location make our stay here a treasure. 　　　　　Don and Barbara Brown, Media Pennsylvania

HARTFORD

Nutmeg Bed & Breakfast Host #1

Location: Downtown.
Reservations: Available year round through Nutmeg Bed & Breakfast, page 331.

Long-time Hartford residents moved into the 1862 historic-district brownstone five years ago when the interior was rebuilt. The central open stairwell now gets sun from a cupola skylight and the color-coordinated interior has authentic lighting fixtures and family antiques. Your hosts are very involved in the arts and appreciate being able to walk to almost everything in the city.

In residence: Nonsmokers. Two cats.
Restrictions: No children. No pets. Cigarette smoking only. Parking available on the street.
Bed: One double room. Three flights of stairs up to a four-poster in room with fireplace and window seat.
Breakfast: Continental. In large open kitchen with fireplace and city view.
Plus: Air conditioning.
Rate: $50.

MYSTIC

1833 House

33 Greenmanville Avenue, Mystic, CT 06355
Phone: 203/572-0633
Location: Next door to Mystic Seaport, on Route 27, one mile from I-95.
Host: Joan Brownell Smith
Open: Year round.

"As a volunteer at the Tourist Information Center I found that many people asked for a place not a plastic palace." Four years ago, at the "right time" this "small, unassuming but comfortable home just 100 yards from Mystic Seaport" became available and Joan Smith started her venture. And now that she's a volunteer lecturer for the nearby Aquarium, she's still an information bureau of sorts. You can tell that she enjoys travel and photography, but you have to delve a bit to find that scuba diving is also an interest of this grandmother (of grown-up grandchildren) who worked for the telephone company for 30 years.

In residence: House cats Thumper and Po' Baby, and two outdoor cats.
Restrictions: Smoking reluctantly allowed.
Bed: Five rooms. One single and one with twin beds share one bath. One with twin beds and private bath. One family two-room unit with private bath. Cots and crib available.
Breakfast: Continental and leisurely in a large sunny kitchen 8–9:30.
Plus: Parking. Pet-sitting. Pickup service from Amtrak station half a mile away, living room with color TV, backyard, window fan in each room. Slide show of Smith travels by guests' request only.
Rates: $22 single. $42 for two with private bath, $38 shared. Family unit $52 for four people. Cot $5. Slightly less in winter. No credit cards accepted.

Going to 1833 House each summer is like coming home.
Russel and Nancy Kuelz, Wauwatosa, Wisconsin

Anyone visiting the area should not miss the opportunity to enjoy the comfort of the pleasant home, clean accommodations and the warmth and hospitality of Mrs. Smith.   Mr. and Mrs. F. Schott, Woodside, New York

NEW HAVEN

Bed and Breakfast, Ltd. Host #1

Location: On a main road, convenient to I-95 and I-91. Five minutes to Yale.
Reservations: Available year round through Bed and Breakfast, Ltd., page 330.

Guests quickly sense that the host is well traveled and an antique collector. And the host is quick to sense whether guests prefer to socialize or be alone.

For two years his Italian villa–style house with river view was on the New Haven historic house tour. It is furnished eclectically, mostly with antiques from various periods, but with some modern pieces. The grandfather's clock, the paintings, the tall candlesticks, the samovar, and the chandelier in the dining room all contribute to an interesting setting.

Restrictions: No children and no pets.
Foreign languages spoken: French and Spanish.
Bed: A suite with double bedroom and a sitting room. Shared bath.
Breakfast: Guests' choice. From simple to candlelit. (Host is a superb cook.)
Plus: Air conditioning. Fresh fruit, chocolates, a cocktail, sherry, or coffee.
Rate: $40 double occupancy.

NORTH STONINGTON

Nutmeg Bed & Breakfast Host #39

Location: Ten minutes from Stonington village, 20 minutes to Mystic, 30 minutes to Rhode Island beaches.
Reservations: Available year round through Nutmeg Bed & Breakfast, page 331.

"We try to ignore clocks and let nature dictate needs." In the spring of 1982 the carpenter and his wife and daughter moved to this hilltop location to plant a garden. Before that he was a teacher in New York

City, Denver, and rural West Virginia. They delight in sharing their new homestead. It was built in 1742 and added onto in 1859, and again in 1939. From the big kitchen used as a common room you view cows and sheep in pastures, rolling hills, and Massachusetts 50 miles away. In the morning gather your own eggs from the dozen hens; enjoy fresh milk and join in "philosophizing" at breakfast or at tea time, "natural coming-together times."

In residence: Four-year-old daughter, two dogs, five cats.
Restrictions: No cigars.
Bed: One room with double bed and private half-bath.
Breakfast: Often leisurely. Bountiful. Could include pancakes, home-made bread, bacon and eggs. Usually cooked by Dad.
Plus: Screened porch.
Rate: $40.

NORWALK

Nutmeg Bed & Breakfast Host #56

Location: On a quiet lane, 10-minute drive to train station or beach, 50 minutes to Manhattan.
Reservations: Available year round through Nutmeg Bed & Breakfast, page 331.

The touch of the English can be seen in the antiques inside and the flowers outside. And then it is heard in the welcome given by the hosts who regularly traveled to B&Bs in their native England. There she owned an exclusive dress shop. Here he is a computer consultant.

Because the Cape house they found here had been abandoned for 15 years, what you see is a full restoration, completed just three years ago. Being new to the area, the hostess could see the need to assist other newcomers; and now she has her own very personalized business to do just that.

They accept long-term as well as overnight guests. All can expect "a dry British humor."

In residence: People who smoke. A Pembroke corgi who is really not good with children.
Restrictions: Children should be at least eight. Only small dogs allowed. No smoking in bedrooms.

Bed: Two rooms. One with twin beds, one with double bed. Private bath for one room, shared if both rooms occupied.
Breakfast: Mostly continental. More often quick than leisurely.
Rates: $40.

PUTNAM

Bed and Breakfast Associates
Bay Colony Host #801

Location: In rural country. On route 21, 3½ miles from Putnam, 1½ miles from Route 52, 2 miles from Route 44, 30 miles from Sturbridge, 50 miles from Mystic, 65 miles from Boston.
Reservations: Available year round through Bed and Breakfast Associates Bay Colony, page 220.

"In November of 1979, after 30 years in Los Angeles, we fled east to escape the smog of a city that had grown too big too fast." There he was a "professional rescuer of homes" and she wrote advertising copy.

Here they found a center-chimney colonial gem, one with five working fireplaces, which had been built in 1742 as a tavern and converted to a private home in the 19th century. The classic red barn is actually 30 years older than the house. The Keeping Room with beehive oven was where Revolutionary militia relaxed, drank ale, and smoked their pipes.

The host has restored the home to its 18th-century beauty. He made the handsome mahogany-paneled front door. A porch has become a charming room. His craftsmanship extends to furniture making; it's hard for the untrained eye to tell that his slant-front mahogany desk or the black walnut lowboy are reproductions. The English-oak-paneled study, just completed for guests, is another one of his projects carried out with love. Guests have a chance to see everything — from the basement to the attic.

The hosts discovered the joys of B&B in England on seven trips there, and they are delighted with their new home and with a new lifestyle that is ideal for the arrangement. And what a setting for writing copy for classical record liner notes (the hostess's present occupation)!

There is a great area for walking. Canoeing, sailing on a lake, and horseback riding are nearby, but most guests seem to be sightseers who dine, then come "home" to relax and maybe to enjoy wine and cheese with the gracious hosts.

Restrictions: No smoking in bedrooms; nonsmokers preferred. No pets. No children preferably.

Bed: Two huge rooms, each with a fireplace and furnished with antiques. Each has a queen-sized four-poster bed, a sitting area, and a private bath.

Breakfast: Really full. Could include eggs scrambled with cheese, beef sausage, homemade muffins. Served at guests' convenience in charming dining room with fireplace, fresh flowers, and music.

Rates: $40 single, $50 per couple.

We were entranced at the strong feeling of historic mystique and antiquity we experienced. The warm reception, delightful meal, and expert directions and advice regarding points of local interest were outstanding. We left with great reluctance, feeling like one of the family and with a strong desire to return.

Col. and Mrs. R. Neal, Redondo Beach, California

WASHINGTON

Nutmeg Bed & Breakfast Host #41

Location: In a historic district. Right in the village, on the green.
Reservations: Available year round through Nutmeg Bed & Breakfast, page 331.

"We chose Washington because it's at the corner of Currier & Ives." And that's just what they were looking for. In 1981 (while still in their early thirties) they left his native city of Kansas City when he, an interior designer with a passion for what he does, gave himself a sabbatical and attended the Parsons School of Design in New York. The move inspired his wife to begin a career in banking. One year later they decided not to return to the Midwest but instead to search for a new address in "real" New England. And here it is — with the Green, the library, a museum, white houses and picket fences, and the church with a carillon that rings every hour. When they moved in last December, neighbors arrived with welcoming cakes and cookies.

After a conversation with the host I am still reeling from the idea of living in, restoring, and decorating seven houses in 11 years. But this is home. If you are interested in what it took to create a whole new lifestyle and "a more balanced life," or in house restoration or decor, plan on some fascinating conversations (evenings and weekends). And your hosts can direct you to walks, private-school campuses with ivy-covered walls, antique shops, and art galleries.

Furnishings are a collection — family pieces, reproductions, some antiques, Oriental, French, and English. Altogether there is a country feeling. The house itself is a mixture too, having been started in 1850 and added to umpteen times in different periods. This is not the residence of a purist and there's no intention of making everything authentic. The decor is really finished, but dreaming up projects is not hard for this family.

And the grounds? The hosts love gardening. Entertaining? They love that too, and feel that preparing for guests provides the impetus to get things done. Their two young boys round out the picture of a lively growing family.

In residence: Two sons, ages two and seven. A houseman. One dog and one cat.
Restrictions: No smoking. No pets. No guests' children.
Bed: Three rooms. Two with twin beds, one with a brass double bed. Shared guest bath.
Breakfast: Continental with homemade biscuits, muffins, or sourdough bread. Eat in large formal dining room or by the fire in the parlor.
Plus: Library, "sittin' & sippin' front porch." Option of dinner on request.
Rates: $50 per room per night. Ten percent less for singles.

WASHINGTON

Nutmeg Bed & Breakfast Host #47

Location: One mile from Washington Depot.
Reservations: Available year round through Nutmeg Bed & Breakfast, page 331.

The family is all grown, and now B&B guests receive a warm welcome in this cozy house on a winding road. It has been "home" for 23 years, so guests can be prepared for information about what-to-see-and-where-to-go-and-where-to-eat.

The up-to-date clippings are likely to include the schedules of local digs, exhibits, and special events of the American Indian Archaeological Institute, just a half mile away. Or maybe a vineyard tour would interest you.

Some recent guests were walking parts of the Appalachian Trail (about 10 miles from here) and the host found that a source of good conversation because a grandson had just completed the Trail. But if you are interested in a shorter walk, a huge wildlife reservation is right next door.

In residence: One who smokes.
Restrictions: No children.
Bed: One room with twin beds. Private bath.
Breakfast: Continental with homemade coffee cake.
Rates: $35 for two, 10 percent less for one.

WEST HARTFORD

Nutmeg Bed & Breakfast Host #6

Location: On a main road. Local bus (20 minutes to downtown Hartford) stops at the door.
Reservations: Available year round through Nutmeg Bed & Breakfast, page 331.

The university professor and her husband, a realtor, welcome you to their lovely Tudor home situated on 1½ acres. They have accommodated business people on a tight schedule, parents of university students, guests who don't really want to socialize very much, and others who are very chatty or want recommendations and directions (six restaurants are one mile away). There is a flexible style of hosting here.

In residence: One dog who spends his days outside and nights in the kitchen.
Restrictions: No guests' pets. Infants or teenagers, but not toddlers. No smoking in bedrooms.
Foreign languages spoken: French, Spanish, Hungarian.
Bed: Two rooms. One with a double and a twin bed. One with queen-sized bed and sitting area. Private baths. Portacrib available.
Breakfast: Continental. Self-serve weekdays. Host is more available on weekends.
Plus: Off-street parking.
Rates: $35 single, $45 for two.

WEST MYSTIC

Leventhal B&B

40 West Mystic Avenue, West Mystic, CT 06388
Phone: 203/536-1341
Location: In a historic district, 10-minute ride to Mystic Seaport, 15 minute walk to village.
Hosts: Bob and Natalie Leventhal
Open: Year round.

"The house was built by a boat builder, George Owen Lamb, direct descendant of Elder Brewster of Mayflower fame. When we bought the house 22 years ago it hadn't been lived in for 10 years and had to be completely refurbished."

Bob and Nat, both former schoolteachers, are experienced travelers who sometimes take guests on a local tour. Their own street, "one of the prettiest in town," has many old captains' houses. The boat-oriented couple has been hosting for two years.

In residence: People who smoke.
Restrictions: No pets allowed.
Foreign language spoken: French.
Bed: Three rooms. One single, one with twin beds, one double. One shared guest bath. Cot available.
Breakfast: Hosts usually join you for continental fare in family room, or when weather permits, on the sun porch with view of Mystic River.
Plus: Air conditioning. Free pickup service at train in Mystic; or at Groton or New London airports.
Rates: $25 single, $30 double. Cot $5.

Good accommodations. The Leventhals treated me like a long-lost relative. The location is at the top of a hill, close to the water and about a one-mile (scenic) walk to the main part of town.

Bob Kunkel, Chicago, Illinois

NEW YORK

NEW YORK STATE

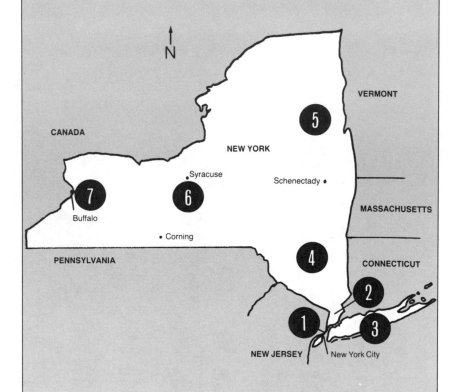

The numbers on this map indicate the locations for which there are detailed maps in this chapter.

NEW YORK STATE

Page numbers refer to pages on which regional maps appear.

NEW YORK

Reservation Services

NEW YORK CITY

The B&B Group (New Yorkers at Home). Please see page 352.

Urban Ventures. Please see page 353.

WESTCHESTER COUNTY

Bed & Breakfast, U.S.A. Please see page 357.

LONG ISLAND

A Reasonable Alternative. Please see page 360.

Alternate Lodgings. Please see page 361.

Bed and Breakfast of Long Island. Please see page 361.

Hampton Bed & Breakfast Registry. Please see page 362.

Hampton Hosts. Please see page 362.

UPSTATE NEW YORK

Bed & Breakfast Referral of the Greater Syracuse area. Please see page 392.

Cherry Valley Ventures. Please see page 393.

B & B Rochester. Please see page 393.

MANHATTAN, WESTCHESTER COUNTY, LONG ISLAND, AND SOUTHERN NEW YORK

MASSACHUSETTS

CONNECTICUT

N

NEW YORK

Long Island Sound

NEW JERSEY

Suffolk County

Nassau County

Atlantic Ocean

The numbers on this map indicate the locations of B&Bs described in detail in this chapter.

MANHATTAN

WESTCHESTER COUNTY

LONG ISLAND

SOUTHERN NEW YORK

NEW YORK CITY AREA

Reservation Services

There are two major reservation services in Manhattan. Both are well patronized and growing at a rate that beginning services would like to duplicate. Both find that guests frequently have strong preferences for specific locations. Breakfast at New York B&Bs is usually continental. It could be eat-and-run or help-yourself-and-lounge. The two services:

Urban Ventures

P.O. Box 426, New York, NY 10024
Phone: 212/594-5650
Established June 1979.
Open: Year round 9–5, six days a week. Closed Sundays and holidays. Minimum reservation: two nights.
Listings: About 400 in the city.

Frances Tesser and Mary McAulay run this service. For an idea of "what attractions are where" in Manhattan, request a copy of their brochure.
Rates: Singles $23–$62, doubles $32–$70. Some have monthly and three-week rates. MasterCard, VISA, and American Express accepted.

The B&B Group
(New Yorkers at Home) Inc.

301 East 60th Street, New York, NY 10022
Phone: 212/838-7015
Established April 1981.
Listings: About 100.

Most of these B&Bs are in the city. A few are in other areas such as Westchester or Queens. About half are described on sampler sent when you send a SASE to the director, Farla Zammit. Minimum reservation: two nights.
Rates: Singles $30–$40, doubles $45–$55.

*

Westchester County reservation service information is on page 357.

Several national reservation services (pp. 26-29) have a few listings in New York City. In particular, the Bed & Breakfast League, page 27, usually has some.

New York City B&Bs

The more than 500 B&Bs available in New York are located just about everywhere, near any place you want to be. They're in town houses, brownstones, apartments, penthouses, lofts, and other possible city spaces. Among the hosts are legal secretaries, lawyers, interior decorators, social workers, executives, craftspeople, actors, teachers, writers, caterers, antique shop owners, and scientists. And some places are hostless, entirely private for you. Here, as in all major cities, depending on the location, parking can be an added expense.

B&B in New York City may be different from any other large city in the country. It's a place where guests may be looking for a particular location at a particular rate and personal interaction may not be the top priority. Some hosts arrange for you to have the key, your own access to continental breakfast and very little face-to-face exchange. But among the hundreds of Manhattan hosts there are many interesting, busy, and caring people who have comfortable to luxurious residences that they are happy to share. B&B in New York can be a home-away-from-home arrangement; and when the chemistry is right, some find that they have made new friendships and/or become repeat guests.

While preparing this book I have had occasion to think that, at least for bed and breakfast and probably for many other reasons that we can all think of, New York City is a world apart. Communication with hosts for this first edition has been somewhat limited. So the following will give you just a glimpse of some Manhattan hosts.

MANHATTAN

Urban Ventures Host #2137

Location: On the Upper East Side in the low 70s between First and Second Avenues.
Reservations: Available year round through Urban Ventures, page 352.

Recently, after two years of hosting, this dancer was delighted to find a better, quieter apartment that could accommodate her "diverse and wonderful guests." She's a native New Yorker who knows the city well and feels that her new neighborhood is "almost villagey." When we spoke she was looking forward to cultivating her postage-stamp-sized yard. Her professional schedule, always a busy one, differs according to her performance commitments. Her concentration, both as a teacher and student, is ballet; but "you have to know how to do everything in theater." And so she does!

Restrictions: No pets. No smoking.
Bed: One double-bedded room with private bath.
Breakfast: Although food is not important to her ("dancers are always on a diet") croissants are usual guest breakfast fare.
Rates: $34 single, $44 for two.

MANHATTAN

Urban Ventures Host #422

Location: East 30s. Residential midtown area. Five blocks from East Side Air Terminal, three blocks from Empire State Building, near all public transportation. "In an area heavily occupied by medical people, UN people, and a variety of others including ordinary New Yorkers like me."

Reservations: Available year round through Urban Ventures, page 352.

"I love my apartment, the neighborhood, and New York City and hope that my enthusiasm inspires my guests." Maybe she's New York's original B&B hostess. Or unofficial ambassador. She used to keep a correspondence going when some guests started the practice. But after four years, with hundreds of "only good experiences, each one different, and many repeaters" she's not able to. But she's quite capable of knowing when to keep a distance and when to extend herself. In addition to her full-time position as a vocational counselor with special populations, at home she's a tutor in English as a second language. The week we spoke she was assisting one student from Japan and another from Russia. The apartment offers a beautiful view of the city skyline and is decorated with rugs, weavings, paintings, and crafts collected from the hostess's own travels.

In residence: A nonsmoker. (Smoking by guests is permitted.)
Restrictions: Children should be school age. No pets allowed.
Foreign languages spoken: A little French and Spanish.
Bed: One large room with high-riser that opens to two twin beds that can be put together as a double.
Breakfast: Continental. Help yourself if after 7 a.m. weekdays. Hostess frequently joins weekend guests.
Plus: Air conditioning (entire apartment). Accessible to handicapped.
Rates: $44 single, $52 for two.

. . . Conveniently located close to transport and centers of interest. Our stay was not just a bed-and-breakfast experience. Our host's warm welcome, continuing kindness, and concern for our comfort made our New York stopover a joy which we still recall with the greatest pleasure.
Alice and Gordon Campbell, Hawks Nest, N.S.W. Australia

MANHATTAN

Urban Ventures Host #1004

Location: Upper West Side between Broadway and West End Avenue.
Reservations: Available year round through Urban Ventures, page 352.

Both husband and wife have at-home businesses as portrait and commercial artists. They like to feel that their 16-year residence is a friendly place. As frequent hosts they find that generally the guests are busy and tend to spend little time at "home."

In residence: One teenage daughter.
Restrictions: No pets. No smoking.
Foreign languages spoken: A little French and Spanish.
Bed: One room with twin beds. Private bath.
Breakfast: Fresh fruit and homemade pastries available at any time.
Plus: Air conditioning. Children are allowed and because of the many teenagers in the building, baby-sitting could probably be arranged.
Rates: $26 single, $32 for two.

WESTCHESTER COUNTY

Reservation Service

Bed & Breakfast, U.S.A. Ltd.

P.O. Box 528, Croton-on-Hudson, NY 10521-0528
Phone: 914/271-6228 or 737-7863
Established January 1982.
Open: Year round.
Listings: A growing list of about 20 homes in suburban and rural communities in Westchester County, all accessible by train (one-half to one hour's ride) to New York City, including the communities of Cortland, Croton-on-Hudson, Eastchester, Hartsdale, Harrison, Irvington, New Rochelle, Ossining, Tarrytown, and Yorktown. Expanded service has added listings in Rockland with historic homes in Newburgh, in Delaware County three hours north of New York City; and just recently a representative has been appointed in Ithaca (upstate).

Ann Dantzig and Barbara Nortarius provide a range of settings including a 200-year-old farmhouse on eight acres near a nature reservation, new and old suburban homes, a stone mansion, and Victorian residences. Arrangements can sometimes be made to meet guests at the train station. Many young families are involved with this program and baby-sitting, too, can be arranged. Many hosts have traveled by B&B abroad. One of the original host families speaks Japanese and now the service fills the need for interpreters/guides by the hour or day.

Rates: Singles $30, doubles $40. A few are higher for use of pools available at some homes in summer months. Weekly rates are $10 less per day.

B&Bs

CROTON-ON-HUDSON

River View

Location: In a friendly neighborhood. It's a ten-minute walk to the center of town and a 50-minute train ride from New York City.
Reservations: Available year round through Bed & Breakfast, U.S.A., page 357.

English B&B experiences were the inspiration for this family's host activities. The psychologist wife and computer consultant husband enjoy sharing their family life with visitors. Guests take walks in nearby woodlands and bird sanctuaries; bicycle (it's hilly); attend town meetings; shop with the family; visit an historical restoration (Van Cortlandt Manor); swim; and sometimes use the home as a base for touring New York City. The large Victorian residence, situated on a cliff with a view of the Hudson River, is furnished with oriental rugs and antiques.

In residence: Three-year-old daughter. Two French bulldogs.
Foreign languages spoken: French and Russian.
Bed: One room with double bed and one with two twin beds. Shared bath. Cots available.
Breakfast: Full. Could include raspberries from hosts' garden or apples from their orchard. In summer may be served on patio near gardens and pool overlooking river.
Plus: Air conditioning. Pool arrangements can be made in summer.
Rates: $30 single, $40 for two. $10 cots. Weekly rates available.

Tremendous fun.   Bill Warby, Yeronga, Queensland, Australia

YONKERS

Gloria and Norman Bantz

82 Vermont Terrace, Yonkers, NY 10707
Phone: 914/779-6411

Location: On a residential street, one block from train station (half-hour ride to Manhattan), 10-minute drive to White Plains.
Open: Year round.

The big brick Federal-style house is no longer home for the six Bantz children; but it is a home-away-from-home for conventiongoers, visiting parents (Sarah Lawrence is one of many nearby colleges), and tourists too. The friendly hosts (now grandparents to nine) are a good source for sightseeing and travel information. Gloria was a commercial artist and now works in oils and water colors. Norman, a Master Bee-keeper, has 65 hives in various Westchester County locations; 8 are here in Yonkers. One couple from upstate New York came for B&B and went away with the inspiration to become beekeepers — and they've gone and done it.

If you have time to explore the immediate neighborhood, there are bicycles for rent one block away and you are three minutes from a path that runs for miles in a parkway along the Bronx River. (Norman jogs five miles a day there.)

In residence: Nonsmokers.
Restrictions: No pets allowed. Smokers are tolerated. Children should be at least seven.
Foreign language spoken: Some Spanish.
Bed: Five rooms. Four with double beds and one shared bath. One large room with private bath and both a queen-sized and a single bed.
Breakfast: Considered a party. Norman loves to cook. Menu could include fresh fruit; traditional foods (waffles or sausage); and maybe even broiled fish. Always there's honey from their own hives, served as comb honey, in cakes or breads. Guests choose the time and length of meal.
Plus: Air conditioning. Use of large screened porch, TV. And the Bantzes serve their own homemade mead to guests. Free off-street parking. Baby-sitting possibilities.
Rates: $32 single, $40–$44 double. Weekly rates $160 single, $200–$220 double.

Being a very private person I reluctantly agreed to spend two nights at a B&B on our trip to New England. No need to worry! Our hosts greeted us with such warmth that I immediately felt as though I was one of the family. Our room was spacious, clean, and most of all, quiet. Breakfast with them and another traveling couple was homey and fun.

R.G.G., Bainbridge, Georgia

We enjoyed complete hospitality and appreciated the convenience of taking the train into New York City.   Anabel Carlson, Amenia, New York

LONG ISLAND

Reservation Services

Long Island reservation services are filling the needs that services everywhere fill: less expensive housing, more available facilities where few (or none) exist — and always, that personal touch and human contact that more conventional lodging can't provide. The selected hosts appreciate the screening of guests and the advance notice. A Reasonable Alternative started in March 1981 and other services quickly followed. There are signs of still more to come. All together they list close to 300 hosts. And when the weather is just plain hot, the homes that are near beaches, like their more expensive competitors — the hotels and motels — tend to fill early.

All services say that they have marvelous anecdotes about their efforts to match guest and host. Considering the layers of wishes, that *is* a task. One service director mentioned that in the summer everyone wants to be both in the town and on the beach, but that the mile in between makes that an impossibility.

If you *call* for information, there's usually a real person on the other end of the phone in the warmer months. But during the rest of the year, you're more likely to be greeted by an answering service or machine.

For printed material, it's a good idea to send a self-addressed, stamped envelope. Some Long Island services respond with a sampler. Only one sends information about all current listings.

A Reasonable Alternative

117 Spring Street, Suite E, Port Jefferson, NY 11777
Phone: 516/928-4034
Open: Year round.
Listings: Throughout Nassau and Suffolk Counties in private homes, apartments, a carriage house, a corn crib, and on a yacht.

Reservations: At least 72 hours' notice required. Some hosts, not all, require a two-night minimum stay in summer. No pets please.

Kathleen Dexter sketches some highlights from her listings: "Swim at a private beach. Outgoing host. . . . Book-lined sitting room overlooking charming garden. . . . Small apartment that has a private deck with view of water. . . . Boat hooked up to full dockside facilities. Host will transport you to Hamptons, Fire Island, the North or South Fork. . . . New England style homes, some with original 'cooking' fireplaces."

Rates: Singles $20–$60, doubles $24–$125, $4–$8 extra per child where accepted. Lower rates in winter. Weekly and monthly rates available. MasterCard and VISA accepted.

Alternate Lodgings

P.O. Box 1782, East Hampton, NY 11937
Phone: 516/324-9449
Open: Year round.
Listings: In just a year Francine and Robert Hauxwell have established one of the larger services for the Hamptons. Their B&Bs include the communities of Remsenburg (near Westhampton), East Moriches, Westhampton, Westhampton Beach, Quogue, Hampton Bays, Southampton, Watermill, Bridgehampton, Wainscott and Sagatonack, Shelter Island, Sag Harbor, East Hampton, Amagansett, and Montauk Point.
Reservations: Minimum of two nights in season and three nights for July 4th and Labor Day weekends.
Rates: Singles $40–$65, doubles $55–$80, Memorial Day through Labor Day. A few deluxe accommodations are higher. Off-season rates: singles $26–$45, doubles $45–$65. Monthly rates available. MasterCard and VISA accepted.

Bed and Breakfast of Long Island

P.O. Box 312, Old Westbury, NY 11568
Phone: 516/334-6231
Open: Year round. Closed weekends November–March. Many accommodations available through the winter.
Listings: Charlotte Friedman and Naomi Kavee have hosts in all the Hamptons as well as other areas of Long Island. Settings include a

charming Victorian home with swimming pool within walking distance of village . . . a rambling ranch where children are warmly welcomed . . . a large contemporary home with sun deck overlooking the dunes . . . a lovely cottage with wooded backyard, walk to beach . . . a beautiful old home on tree-lined street . . . a pre–Civil War farmhouse on several acres . . . a comfortable apartment in the village.

Rates: May 15–September 15, $35 up for singles, $45 up for doubles. Extra deluxe $85. Off-season rates apply other times except holiday weekends.

Hampton Bed & Breakfast Registry

Box 378, East Moriches, NY 11940
Phone: 516/878-8197
Open: Year round. A few hosts will accept same-day reservations.
Listings: Initially in just the Hamptons but now in private homes and apartments all over the island — in 26 communities at last count. Karin Storer and Nancy Cuthbert offer some listings in western Long Island near Adelphi and Hofstra; and in Bayport, Babylon, and Syosset there are charming houses that can accommodate two couples. ". . . A unique country home on the North Shore . . . a newer home on a beautiful beach . . . arrive by boat or car to lovely home in Huntington or quaint Cold Spring Harbor."
Rates: Singles $24 up, doubles $32 up. Weekly rates available. A small fee charged for MasterCard or VISA.

Hampton Hosts

P.O. Box 507, East Hampton, NY 11937
Phone: 516/324-9351 or 212/696-1938
Open: Year round.
Listings: Private homes and apartments in all the Hamptons, Montauk, and Sag Harbor are selected by Renee Fisher and Goldie Scher.

Some hosts provide beach permits, bicycles, baby-sitting services. A packet of information about events and attractions is given to each guest.
Rates: Singles $45–$55, doubles $55–$65. Summer rates prevail from June 15 until weekend after Labor Day. $10 per night less during spring and fall season. Weekly and monthly rates available.

Long Island B&Bs

In addition to the ocean and bay beaches, the long list of area attractions includes boating, fishing, golf, horseback riding, tennis, cycling, shopping, antiques, theatres, museums, farms, concerts, and zillions of restaurants.

Everywhere hosts report that they do B&B partly because they appreciate the supplemental income, but that they also like having the company and meeting new people. A few Long Island hosts have surprised themselves and found that although they went into it primarily for economic reasons, they learned that they also liked being hosts. And some have even gone into business independently after having tried it through a service. Some summer hosts decide on an annual basis whether they will do B&B, rent out their entire house, or not have any paying guests. Although a few insist on offering a big American breakfast, continental breakfast is more common here.

There are shared bath situations, but private baths predominate. What you can count on is a variety of homes in rural, suburban, town, and beachfront locations. Of course, the more in advance your arrangements, the wider your choice.

The following are descriptions of a few experienced and enthusiastic hosts who have agreed to have some details published in this book. For more, for the moment, consult the friendly services listed on the preceding pages.

AMAGANSETT

Hampton Hosts "Host A"

Location: Near Long Island Railroad and jitney service from city. Not on a main road. Ranch house ¼ mile from village, two blocks from ocean beach.
Reservations: Available April–November through Hampton Hosts, page 362.

At heart the host feels that he's a frustrated innkeeper. Guests are welcome to use his bicycle, accompany him on a sightseeing tour, or share conversation over a drink. Now retired from public relations work in New York City (and before that in England), he has time for local politics, music, and literature.

In residence: One dog.
Restrictions: No guests' pets please.
Bed: Two rooms, each with twin beds. Shared bath.
Breakfast: Hours and menu are flexible.
Plus: Patio and grounds. Parking available.
Rates: $50 single, $65 for two in summer; $10 less spring and fall.

EAST HAMPTON

Alternate Lodgings Host #12

Location: On two acres surrounded by oak and pine trees — and blueberry bushes. "Not a house in sight!" Two and a half miles to village "voted the prettiest in the country"; three miles to ocean, two miles to bay.
Reservations: Available year round through Alternate Lodgings, page 361. Minimum reservation: two nights; three nights on holiday weekends.

Long Island natives built this contemporary home in 1982 and immediately welcomed B&Bers. "Most of our guests are so content with our place that they only leave to eat."

The living and dining rooms have sliding glass doors that lead out onto a deck which completely surrounds the pool and overlooks the tennis court. A large woodburning fireplace and four skylights are in the cathedral ceilinged living room.

The hostess is a homemaker. Her husband will be retiring soon from his airline position.

In residence: One teenage son.
Restrictions: Some pets allowed; make arrangements. Children are welcome.
Foreign language spoken: German.
Bed: Four rooms. Three with twin beds; one with private bath, two with a shared guest bath. One with double bed and private bath.
Breakfast: Served 8–10. Juice, muffins (usually homemade), coffee. Served in kitchen or on deck.
Plus: Air conditioning. Use of refrigerator, tennis court, 20-by-40-foot swimming pool, ping-pong table, bicycles.
Rates: In season for two nights: $170 per couple for shared bath, $190 for private; off-season $130 shared, $150 private.

EAST HAMPTON

Hampton Hosts "Host B"

Location: One block from the village and a half mile from ocean beach.
Reservations: Available year round through Hampton Hosts, page 362.

The enthusiastic host couple, music teachers and long-time residents in this ranch house, find B&B work interesting and exciting because of the people they meet.

Restrictions: No children. No pets. Nonsmokers preferred.
Bed: One room with two twin beds with private bath.
Breakfast: Continental.
Plus: Guests are welcome to use their in-ground swimming pool and deck. Parking available.
Rates: $50 single, $65 for two; $10 less out of season.

HEMPSTEAD

Hampton Bed & Breakfast Registry Host #17

Location: Within walking distance of Long Island Railroad (40-minute ride to Manhattan); a short drive from airport or to beach.
Reservations: Available year round through Hampton Bed & Breakfast Registry, page 362.

"Signing up for B&B is the best thing I ever did. It's fun and rewarding in all ways. We are just very open and friendly. Our home is our guests' home and we like a family atmosphere. If they'd rather be alone, that is respected also. My husband is in textiles — printing and export/import. I teach makeup, skin care, and hair care to teenagers and at adult education. Our home was built for a doctor, his wife, and housekeeper over 50 years ago. They lived here 25 years and sold it to another doctor and his wife (who had no maid). They lived here 25 years and sold it to us. I'm the maid! We hope to be here 25 years too." The charming Dutch colonial home has been on a house tour and is filled with personal touches. The hosts, grandparents who have enjoyed all ages, were surprised to see how attached they became to a young English couple who stayed 18 days.

We have always been under the impression that the Europeans have been the masters at Bed & Breakfast, but after visiting here we just can't imagine ever thinking that again. It was our first visit to the States . . . warmth, friendliness and generosity . . . Thank you America!
Peter and Wendy Girtley, Sheffield, England

Restrictions: No smoking or dogs in the house.
Foreign languages spoken: German and Spanish.
Bed: One double room with twin beds or together as a king-sized bed. Private bath.
Breakfast: Full. Could include broiled grapefruit, homemade breads, yogurt. Served in plant-filled breakfast room.
Plus: Patio, secluded backyard, kitchen privileges, pool membership. Baby-sitting ("I love it!") too. The hosts have driven some guests to their destinations.
Rates: $35 single, $48 for two.

. . . Found a delightfully furnished bedroom, old-fashioned, very comfortable high beds, our own large bathroom . . . shared fond memories of the area with pleasant and gracious hosts. Max K. Stein, Atlanta, Georgia

WESTHAMPTON

Hampton Hosts "Host D"

Location: Near Long Island Railroad and jitney service from city. Not on main road, but on one that leads to beach one mile away.

Reservations: Available April–November through Hampton Hosts, page 362. Minimum reservation: Two nights on weekends, three nights on holiday weekends.

Southern hospitality is the byword for this hostess, a resident of New York City before moving to this ranch house 10 years ago. Guests appreciate the yard and lovely lawn, the proximity to the beach and good restaurants.

In residence: One cat and one dog.
Restrictions: Smokers are reluctantly allowed and the minimum age for children is nine.
Bed: One room with twin beds. Private bath.
Breakfast: Continental. Available at your chosen hour.
Plus: Parking available.
Rates: $50 single; $65 for two in summer, $55 in spring and fall.

WESTHAMPTON BEACH

Hampton Bed & Breakfast Registry Host #29

Reservations: Available September 15–May 15 through Hampton Bed & Breakfast Registry, page 362.

Although she's only been hosting since March 1982, this former teacher has established a definite style. In her century-old antique-filled home on a quiet lane she has a hideaway that's intended to be a getaway. You wake up to the aroma of bakery in the oven and freshly brewed coffee. Most guests walk the beach (five blocks away), play tennis, shop, go out to eat, and sit by the fire. You're likely to leave with a jar of homemade jam — and fond memories.

In residence: One who sometimes smokes.
Restrictions: No children. No pets.
Bed: Two double-bedded rooms, plus one single adjoining one of the rooms. Both doubles have brass beds and private baths.
Breakfast: Available 8–11. Continental includes fresh juice. Served in dining room with pot-bellied stove. A leisurely time.
Rates: $52 for two in each of the rooms, $26 for the single.

SOUTHERN NEW YORK

B&Bs

ACCORD

Rose Hill B&B

Box 176, Accord, NY 12404
Phone: 914/687-9880
Location: Rural. Set on 44 acres. About 10 minutes from High Falls, 40 miles from Woodstock. In antiquing country.
Hosts: Karin and Timothy Tetlow
Open: Year round. Advance reservations required.

Karin and Timothy, originally from England, have been in this 1820 stone-and-frame farmhouse since 1971. "Our friends have always enjoyed visiting, so we thought we'd open it to others."

B&B vacationers started coming in the fall of 1982. Most seem to be city people who seek the quiet, the rural winding roads, and the glow of a wood stove. The Tetlows find that their guests tend to spend their days exploring the area — "where there's much to discover."

It's an informal country home — with some antiques, some sheepskins on the beds, and comfort. Karin is an environmental psychologist focusing on home as the workplace and Timothy is a fine-arts appraiser. Their two children assist with B&B hosting.

In residence: Georgia, age 10, and Sam, age 12. Nonsmokers live here but smoking is allowed. Four cats. The homestead has sheep and horses on the property.
Restrictions: No guests' pets. Children are particularly welcome here.

Bed: Two rooms, each with a double bed. Cot available. One shared guest bath.

Breakfast: Available until 9:30. Fresh fruits, breads, eggs, mushroom omelets cooked by Georgia. Served in country kitchen.

Plus: Two porches in summer, family living room with wood stove in winter. Hiking trails and cross-country skiing nearby.

Rates: $42 per room. Cot $5.

HIGH FALLS

A 1½-hour drive from Manhattan. Or Trailways bus stops in Rosendale; arrange for pickup with hosts. Antique emporiums abound within a 10-mile radius. Wonderful hiking opportunities. Visitors take time to enjoy waterfalls, views of rock formations, and the old Delaware and Hudson Canal locks in the village. Fine restaurants (two are famous) here. This Hudson Valley area seems to attract real-estate hunters. The nearby communities of Accord, Hyde Park, New Paltz, and Stone Ridge (see map, page 350) also have B&Bs.

HIGH FALLS
Captain Schoonmakers B&B

RD 2, Box 37, High Falls, NY 12440

Phone: 914/687-7946

Location: On Route 213, a state highway but a country-style road. Half a mile from High Falls Village and 1½ miles from Rosendale Village.

Hosts: Sam and Julia Krieg

"Perhaps because we have vivid pictures of before, during, and after restoration, many of our guests appreciate the work and creativity involved in our home. Truly a labor of love. Not our first but surely our finest. We've been in the area for 16 years. When, in May 1981, we purchased this charming cottage-type 1760 stone house with an 1800 eyebrow colonial Greek Revival addition, it was without plumbing, electricity, water, heat, or cosmetics. Together and with the assistance of only our three college-student children we completed enough by November to move in. By February we were ready to hang out the B&B sign for a new experience inspired by an extended European trip. The house is decorated with authentic antiques, reproductions and early family." All this and they manage their "other professional lives" too. Julia teaches elementary school and Sam is a biology professor.

In residence: Kat, their black cat, and Schooner, a golden retriever.
Restrictions: No pets, please.
Foreign language spoken: A little Spanish.
Bed: Seven rooms. Some are cozily tucked into eaves. One with twin beds and six with double. Four rooms share two baths in house. Three rooms in restored 1800 barn each have a woodburning stove; one shared bath. Cots available. And so is a cradle!
Breakfast: Very full. Guests staying for several days see a changed menu daily. Might include fresh fruit compote, homemade breads, jams, eggs done in various ways, cheese souffle, crepes, pancakes, bacon or sausage. Served in front of original working fireplace with candlelight, fine china, crystal, and fresh flowers on an antique cherry table. Available at 8 or 9 or earlier on request.
Plus: Time with the Kriegs with before-dinner sherry, wine, or tea and jam pastries in room with candle chandelier. Solarium with Victorian wicker furniture. Hudson River sailing as an option on their 1939 30-foot Hinckley sailboat.
Rates: $45 per room. $10 for additional cots. No charge for cradle.

A warm and homelike atmosphere.   C. F. Matthews, Bradford, Pennsylvania

The Krieg family made us feel special.
Tom and Gale Kochan, Greenwich, Connecticut

HIGH FALLS

House on the Hill

P.O. Box 86, High Falls, NY 12440
Phone: 914/687-9627
Location: On a hill just off country Route 213. Minutes' walk from the village of High Falls.
Hosts: Shelly and Sharon Glassman
Open: Year round for Thursday–Sunday.

Shelly was a business executive in New York City and Sharon was a teacher before they moved to this charming big old house and the worlds of real estate and professional flower arranging. Their happy B&B traveling experiences in England and Pennsylvania made them think that it would be fun to host "and have more sharing parenthood." Now hundreds of guests, dating back to 1981, can testify that the Glassmans know how to cook and serve and when to be available for conversation, suggestions, and information. And the Glassmans have quickly learned some generalities that experienced hosts and owners of old homes know as part of the fun. "Be prepared! Have matches, toothpicks, ice, disinfectant, bandaids, and backup heaters. Know how to catch bats in the belfry and how to deal with skunk odor. Know emergency numbers. Above all, smile and be calm."

The 1825 eyebrow colonial house with graceful stone and hand-forged iron fence (1856) across the front was in the same family until the Glassmans bought it. A strong personal touch in the decor is a collection of quilts made by Southern Illinois women (mostly Sharon's family members) and displayed at the huge landing at the top of the center hall and on every bed in the house.

In residence: Five-year-old son, Gregory. A dog named Bill and cats named Kiddo, Oddik, and Panda Cat. Ducks Wynken, Blynken and Nod-plus-two reside in the barn and on the pond.
Restrictions: Smoking allowed in keeping room and dining room. Pets allowed in barn.
Bed: Five rooms. One with twin beds, four with doubles. One double-bedded room has a private bath. Family suites and cots available.
Breakfast: Special. Fresh fruit dishes, home-baked pastries, bread, omelets, crêpes, country meats — served in the keeping room in front of original fireplace in winter; or on glassed-in porch or eat-in kitchen with view of pond, woods, and old pink brick smokehouse. Served 8:30–10.
Plus: Wine, cheese and crackers, or chowder at just the right moment. In every room a bowl of fruit, fresh flowers, candies, nuts, and even a bottle of seltzer. Lawn games, barbecue facilities, rubber raft for use on pond in summer. Skating in winter. One-and-a-half-mile canal walk runs along the property. Beach and waterfalls a five-minute walk away.
Rates: $38 single, $45–$55 for two. Cots $12.

HYDE PARK

Fala

East Market Street, Hyde Park, NY 12538
Phone: 914/229-5937
Location: Minutes off Route 9 north. One mile from Franklin Delano Roosevelt's home and library and Vanderbilt Mansion. Close to shops, restaurants, many antique shops, golf courses, and even public roller skating.
Hosts: Ish and Maryann Martinez
Open: Mid-April through October. Advance reservations preferred.

Previous owners had converted the small building into a bed-and-bath guest house for visiting family. Ish and Maryann find it a perfect arrangement for sightseeing B&B guests. Maryann has had several years of public relations work and thinks — in European fashion — that hosting is a way to exchange ideas with other adults (and help them enjoy the area) while being a full-time mother. Ish is a computer software programmer. They enjoy refinishing antiques and gardening — "especially herbs."

In residence: Adam, age four, and Ryan, age one. Dolly is their dog.
Restrictions: No smoking.
Foreign language spoken: Spanish.
Bed: One room with double bed and private bath in cottage about 100 feet from main house. Carpeted. Wicker furniture. Cot available.
Breakfast: Served 7:30–9:30. Homemade breads and waffles or pancakes with bacon or sausage or omelets. Served in enclosed glass solarium in Martinez's contemporary home, overlooking pool.
Plus: Fan and heat unit built into wall. In-ground pool. Baby-sitting possibilities.
Rates: $26 per night for the cottage. Cot is $5 under age 18, $10 age 18 and over.

JOHNSON

Elaine's Guest House

P.O. Box 27, Johnson, NY 10933
Phone: 914/355-8811
Location: On Route 284, near Middletown. Ten miles off I-84.
Host: Elaine Scott
Open: Year round. Reservation only.

"You ought to stop in and see my mom when you get to the States."
Elaine's son has said that to so many of his friends in Europe that she
decided to "keep it going" because "people should have a reasonably
priced, clean, comfortable place to stay when they come through this
area." And so it is that she meets people en route — going north to
Canada or south to wherever. The 100-year-old house is one of those big
country places that has had an addition with each new owner. Elaine has
not put an addition on since she came here about eight years ago from
California, and has not filled the chicken coop. She has filled the yard
with a beautiful flower garden though. And the octagonally shaped
building on her rural property houses her antique business.

In residence: Maurice, Alvin, Freddy — three cats.
Restrictions: No smoking. Pets? Maybe.
Bed: Two rooms, one with double, and one with twin beds. Shared bath.
Breakfast: Full. Traditional. Guests' choice for menu and time. Served
in dining room with china, silver, and cloth napkins.
Plus: Great country view from screened front porch.
Rates: $10 per person per night.

NEW PALTZ

Ujjala's Bed & Breakfast

2 Forest Glen, New Paltz, NY 12561
Phone: 914/255-6360
Location: Ten minutes from the New York State Thruway. On a corner
lot, set back from the main road, among apple, pear, and quince trees.
Three and a half miles from village. Antiquing country. Minutes from

cross-country skiing in Shawangunk Mountains.
Host: Ujjala Schwartz
Open: Year round. Advance reservations required.

"Some people use my place as a retreat." Ujjala likes to think of her 1910 Victorian country-style home as one with "Old World flavor that is relaxing and comfortable — an extension of my work in the holistic field."

Her interests in food and people were combined into B&B hosting as of June 1982. She has taught cooking and is now a health counselor and body therapist who works in the field of stress management.

In residence: Two sons, ages 10 and 15.
Restrictions: Nonsmokers preferred. Children should be at least seven.
Bed: Three double rooms. One has an additional single bed. One has a working fireplace and Murphy bed and can double as a sitting room. One shared guest bath.
Breakfast: Generally 8:30–9:30, Sunday until 10. Fresh fruits, eggs, homemade breads, freshly ground coffee, and teas. No meat. No sugars. Food garnished with flowers. Special diets catered to. Served in country kitchen surrounded by large windows overlooking the orchard.
Plus: Living room, outside deck, and surrounding land. Wine, fruit, and cheese on arrival in rooms. Afternoon tea. Sherry in winter. Menus from area restaurants. Dinner here with advance arrangements. Kitchen privileges may be arranged. Laundry privileges for stays over one week.
Rates: Depend on length of stay and day of week. $25–$35 single, $35–$50 for two. Ages 7–12 $5, 13–17 $8. Weekly rates available.

RED HOOK (RHINEBECK AREA)

Carol and Gary Paschal

RD 2, Box 417, Red Hook, NY 12571
Phone: 914/758-5452
Location: Two miles from Taconic State Parkway in the town of Milan. Seven miles from Rhinebeck and Red Hook center.
Open: May through October.

Since the Paschals built this colonial brick-faced house themselves, they have established a self-sufficient lifestyle with an extensive garden, lambs, pigs, geese, and a solar hot-water system. Most guests appreciate the quiet and the magnificent view of Catskill Mountains: "Last year we had one couple who came for one night and stayed for four." Harvest-time visitors may leave with picnic tomatoes.

In residence: Eleven-year-old son (four grown children are married).
Restrictions: Nonsmokers preferred. No pets inside.
Bed: Five rooms. One with twin beds, private entrance, and half-bath. Two other twin-bedded rooms and two double-bedded ones. Cot available. Several rooms open onto decks.
Breakfast: Continental. Fresh fruit in season.
Rates: $18 single, $25 for two. Cot $5.

STONE RIDGE

Baker's Bed & Breakfast

RD 2, Box 80, Stone Ridge, NY 12484
Phone: 914/687-9795
Location: Country road without traffic. Two miles from small towns with shops, antiques, museums, and restaurants.
Hosts: Fran Sutherland and Doug Baker
Open: Year round. Minimum reservation: Two nights on weekends (single nights by chance).

Fantasize about the ideal B&B — everything from the comfort of the beds and the quality of the breakfasts to the personalities of the host and hostess and the beauty of the surroundings. You've just pictured Fran and Doug's place. Now forget it. We want to keep it to ourselves.
                              Fred and Martha Zimmerman, Hoboken, New Jersey

He's a biology professor. She's an art teacher and works in oil and watercolor. They've been in the area for over twenty years and in this home for four. Their children are grown and the couple is enthusiastically doing B&B to share — lots. The old stone house with hand-hewn beams, Rumford fireplace, and 18th-century furnishings is on 16 acres in an area that is much as it was in the 1700s. Fran is currently working toward a state Cultural Historical Landscape designation. Who comes here? Recently they have had soap-opera actors getting a divorce on the air but getting married in real life; a couple given the weekend as a gift;

artists who exchange opinions and ideas; friends from Boston and New York weekending together here; outdoor types who cross-country ski, bird-watch, or rock-climb; and some who purposely time their visit to see a particular farm activity.

In residence: Two cats and two dogs, outside dwellers.
Restrictions: Nonsmokers preferred. No pets allowed. Children should be at least 15.
Bed: One room with twin beds and four with double beds. Shared baths.
Breakfast: An event. Menu determined by Fran after she has an idea from previous night's discussion about guests' likes. Possibilities: frittata made in iron skillet; corn muffins made with Doug's maple syrup and served with maple butter; cheddar-cheese sauce on shirred farm-fresh eggs; homemade orange rye bread; garden asparagus, rhubarb, or snow peas in spring; home-cured meats including venison upon request; herbal tea made with Fran's own spearmint. Available from crack of dawn until 9:30. Served in solarium with view or in dining room with fireplace.
Plus: Air conditioning. Hot tub in greenhouse with view of fields, woods, pond, and mountains. Music room with hi-fi. Flower and vegetable gardens, chickens, geese, pigs, ducks, spring-fed pond. Grist mill in working condition within short walking distance. In season: See maple sugaring process — done in an outdoor pan here.
Rates: $38 single, $48 doubles. Cots $15.

NORTHEASTERN NEW YORK

CANADA

N

NEW YORK

VERMONT

Lake George

Wells 8

5   3

4

Schenectady 7

1

6

Hudson River

MASSACHUSETTS

NORTHEASTERN NEW YORK

NORTHEASTERN NEW YORK

Reservation Services

Bed & Breakfast, U.S.A.

This service considers that Delaware County is undiscovered. Hosts are in the beautiful rural communities of Delhi, Oneonta, Stamford, and Watertown. One property has a tree farm, maple sugaring, an 18-foot pond, and a dock and canoe. "Guests will find some antiquing, cross-country skiing, few tourists, and reasonable rates."

Bed & Breakfast, U.S.A. also has hosts in Ostego County's popular Cooperstown. Please see page 357.

Cherry Valley Ventures

This service covers some communities in this area. Please see page 393.

B&Bs

ALTAMONT

Appel Inn

Route 146, Box 18, RD 3, Altamont, NY 12009
Phone: 518/861-8344
Location: Twelve miles from Albany and Schenectady, 45 miles from Saratoga, one hour from Lake George. Near SUNY and Union College, ½ mile from golf course, 2 miles from Altamont and local performing-arts center with free summer Thursday evening presentations.
Hosts: Laurie and Gerd Beckmann
Open: At least June through September.

The pillars give it the feeling of a southern mansion. And the experience of the innkeepers gives the impression of middle age. Wrong on both counts!

Hendrick Appel — hence the name — originally built the generously-sized rooms for a tavern in 1765. The site of the first (1803) town meeting of Guilderland, the house is now on both the State and National Registers of Historic Places. Those six pillars, the solarium, and the third floor were added in 1890. A restaurant in the 1930s, it was a private home when the young couple, not yet 25, bought it in 1981. "Ruffled curtains, dust ruffles, and big thick towels" are just about in place for the first season (1983) as a B&B run by Laurie and Gerd.

The Beckmanns have known each other since they were 12. While in college — she majored in psychology, he studied metallurgy — they collected antique pocket watches and silver. At the end of her first year at Carnegie Mellon she spent time as a cook and steward on charter boats along the Riviera — followed by a total of eight months of B&B travel in Europe. After coming to the Albany area five years ago, she was manager of the restaurant at the Empire State Plaza that catered the governor's wedding. Her small home antique shop, "mostly oak and Victorian as well as more interesting period pieces," is being expanded so that the bed you sleep in — and many other pieces — are for sale. (Some are on consignment from other dealers.)

Gerd, a metallurgist who is "heavily into computers," is studying for a Ph.D. at RPI. He is comfortable around the kitchen and lots of people.

In residence: Gerd David, born January 1983. Many pets — two Great Danes, Blitz and Dana, and two cats, Huey and Pumpkin. Three goats. One very friendly chicken who hops in cars and loves people.
Restrictions: No guests' pets. Nonsmokers preferred.
Foreign language spoken: German.
Bed: Four rooms, each about 25 by 15. One with twin beds, three doubles. Two shared guest baths. Two of the rooms have porches and fireplaces. Crib available.
Breakfast: Generally 7:30–9. Fresh fruit; home-baked sweet breads; homemade jams, yogurts, and cereals; coffee and assorted teas. Served in an oval solarium with wraparound windows overlooking grounds and flowing stream, swimming pool, and wishing well.
Plus: Almost the entire house including the living room with a great big wonderful fireplace. Games and TV. Guest refrigerator. Swimming pool (as of 1984). Tennis court. Volleyball, croquet, badminton. Beverages in evening. And just across the street in the old cemetery (oldest stone is 1811) is the burial place of Hendrick Appel.
Rates: $27–$30 single, $35 for two. Less for stays of five nights or more.

CHAZY LAKE

Lakeside

Mailing address: Box 417, Dannemora, NY 12929
Phone: 518/492-2322
Location: On a back road that ends one mile from the house and 20 feet from the lake. Two and a half miles from main road. Five miles from the village of Dannemora, 20 miles west of Plattsburgh, 30 miles from Ausable Chasm, 60 miles from Montreal; 75 minutes from Lake Placid, 40 minutes from Lake Champlain.
Hosts: Maurice and Marion Young
Reservations: Available year round. An American Bed & Breakfast (page 132) host. Book directly.

Informality is the keynote in this wood frame house located near a huge stone dwelling. Both places were built by an opera singer in the late 1920s. Many of his visitors were proteges being tutored. The Youngs, owners of the frame house since 1971, have been hosting at their still-being-remodeled place since the summer of 1982. Most guests comment on the large stone fireplace, cedar-paneled interior, and lake view. One of their first guests fell so much in love with the region that he has purchased a nearby lot with cabin. Maurice is a retired naval officer; Marion has taught high-school and college English, and most recently has been literacy volunteer supervisor at Dannemora Prison.

In residence: Irma the dog, part German shepherd, and two cats: Renee and Minoye. Sometimes there are visiting grandchildren. (They have eight, ages 1–12.) And there is one pipe smoker, Maurice.
Restrictions: No pets, please.
Foreign languages spoken: A little French and Spanish.
Bed: Three rooms. Two with double beds. One with a pair of bunk beds. Crib available.
Breakfast: Whatever you want when you want. Full American menu with homemade bakery. Eat in the kitchen, dining room, at picnic table, or in enclosed porch overlooking lake.
Plus: "Pot luck dinner at guests' request" because of the isolated location. Piano, TV, bridge playing, croquet, rowboat, canoe, snowshoes. Bring your own skis for cross-country skiing on their road.
Rates: $18 single, $25 for two.

Tops! Charming and intelligent hosts, good food and accommodations, beautiful location and ambiance — all at very modest prices.
Mr. and Mrs. Allen Landowne, Southbury, Connecticut

GRANVILLE

Jim and Jo Keats

RFD 1, Box 40, Granville, NY 12832
Phone: 518/642-2079
Location: On Willow Glen Hill on Route 22, just 1500 feet from the Vermont border, not far from Manchester, Vermont.
Open: Year round.

When Jim retired from the Garden City, Long Island, police force in 1979 they bought this century-old farmhouse located near the place where they had spent many summers. He's now a car salesman and she has continued her work in a bank. Their "nothing fancy, but clean and homey" residence is surrounded by farmland and views of the neighbors' cows, corn, and grain fields. They are close to every possible vacation activity. The nearest is in Granville, two miles away, where there are tours of quarries that produce 75 percent of all this country's colored slate. It's 15 minutes to Dorset Theatre, a half hour to Lake George, and one hour to Saratoga.

In residence: Nineteen-year-old John, youngest of four sons. People who smoke. Paddy, Newfoundland dog, mostly outside in pen; Fanny, calico cat, indoors and out; Ici Pie, lovable indoor Siamese cat.
Bed: Four rooms. One single, one with twin beds, two with double beds. One crib and one cot available.
Breakfast: Continental, available 7–9.
Plus: Volleyball; walking or jogging path to river.
Rates: $12 single, $18 doubles. Cot or crib $4.

Home away from home. A permanent part of my vacation plans.
Angel Capodagli, West Orange, New Jersey

GREENFIELD

Bed & Breakfast League Host #268

Location: Five minutes from Saratoga, 20 minutes from ski resorts and Lake George.
Reservations: Book through membership in the Bed & Breakfast League Ltd., page 14. Maximum stay is one week.

"We truly enjoy sharing our home that we have built and are still working on. It is an English Tudor that we've been in for four years. Much of the inside work, such as the refinished 100-year-old railings and balusters, has been done by hand and with tender loving care. We have a corral and shed where we can provide a place for show or race horses."

In residence: Three daughters, ages 9–18.
Restrictions: No smoking, no pets, usually no children.
Bed: One room with twin beds. Shared bath.
Breakfast: As full as you'd like. Available till noon. Served in dining room overlooking woods.
Rates: $30 single, $38 for two. In August, $45 single, $50 for two.

Spotless house, delightful family, delicious breakfast . . . treated me like a relative. Amelia Ceballos, New York, New York

LAKE GEORGE

Corner Birches Guest House

86 Montcalm Street, Lake George, NY 12845
Phone: 518/668-2837
Location: Right in the middle of everything. It's the only bed-and-breakfast guesthouse in the village.
Hosts: Ray and Janice Dunklee
Open: Year round.

"We like children, senior citizens, and everyone in between. People often ask about getting into the business. You have to have faith in humanity and know how to smile and laugh and be very understanding. Promote a family atmosphere! Years ago I was an information aide for the New York State Department of Commerce and I'm still trying to help people have an enjoyable vacation. When we had young children this seemed like a good home industry — and still does. The house was built as a guest house. It's a good basic house with dark natural woodwork, very homey. The boys, now in their 20s, used the living room as a playroom. When the doorbell rang I would kick toys under couches that had skirts. Now Ray, one of the few true natives in town, has retired after 32 years as a school custodian and he's a terrific help in all phases of the business."

In residence: People who smoke.
Restrictions: Pets should be well behaved.
Bed: Four rooms, all with cross-ventilation and window fans. One with double bed, one with two twin beds, one with double and single, one with double and rollaway.
Breakfast: Juice, toast, and coffee in sunny dining room.
Plus: Living room with TV. Rockers on front porch for sitting and watching the world go by. Parking in side yard.
Rates: $17 double room, $20.50 twin, $24.50 double and single.

I don't think we ever expected such a warm welcome in such a cozy setting.   S. Katzman, Closter, New Jersey

LAKE GEORGE

East Lake George House

c/o 492 Glen Street, Glens Falls, NY 12801
Phone: 518/656-9452 summer, 792-9296 winter.
Location: Quiet pocket in big vacation country. Convenient to Lake George Opera Festival; 15 minutes from Lake George Village with amusement places, boat cruises, and rentals; 30 minutes from Saratoga Performing Arts Center and Race Track. Hiking, shopping, museums here, too.
Hosts: Joyce and Harold Kirkpatrick
Open: Late June–Labor Day.

When the Kirkpatricks bought this century-old summer inn in 1976, they were looking for a summer business that could also be their summer residence, just ten miles from home. They found a location that was once all farmland and still has the 1820 farmhouse and ice house. It is off the beaten path, with clean clear water and a view of the mountains across the lake. The family accepted the challenge of rewiring, installing new baths, and redecorating. Now they all (Mom, doctor Dad, and five children, ages 3–19) live in an adjacent but connected building. "We're not elegant, but not rustic either. All mattresses are new and other furnishings are a combination of old and new. Families and couples seem to fit right in, become part of a larger family, and enjoy swimming at the private beach, sailing (one boat provided) and canoeing (two available)." Rockers are on the screened-in porch and wooden furniture is on the 150-foot expanse of lawn that separates the house from the water.

In residence: One cat.
Restrictions: No pets. Smoking allowed everywhere but dining room.
Foreign language spoken: One daughter speaks French.
Bed: Seven double-bedded rooms. Some are in suites of two rooms and a bath. Semiprivate and private baths. Crib and cots available.
Breakfast: Full and hearty. Served by family members in dining room or on porch. Available 8:30–10; linger as long as you want.
Plus: Boats, shuffleboard, ping-pong, volleyball, badminton, TV. Babysitting possibilities.
Rates: $50 single, $80 for two; weekly $325, $500. VISA and Master-Card accepted.

RENSSELAER

Tibbitts Guest House

100 Columbia Turnpike, Rensselaer, NY 12144
Phone: 518/472-1348
Location: On Routes 9 & 20, opposite the gates of Sterling-Winthrop Research Company, two miles from Albany.
Hosts: Herb and Claire Rufleth
Open: Year round.

"We are old-fashioned homespun extroverts. The house is cozy. Our floors are highly polished. The beds are comfortable." Fifty-seven years ago Claire's grandfather Tibbitts converted the old farmhouse (now 135 years old) into a tourist house. Claire bought it from her widowed grandmother 40 years ago. "We changed it to B&B in 1978 after many guests requested breakfast as they had enjoyed it in Europe." Herb is a retired postal employee and Claire works in the medical records department of a hospital. Together they love to greet guests (at their car); and through the years, with visitors from all over the country and the world, they "have discovered the universality of man." They enjoy suggesting places and directing guests to shopping; historical sites; the 45-mile jogging, cycling, and hiking path starting in downtown Albany; Saratoga attractions; and restaurants, from gourmet to fast-food.

In residence: Welcome and Spooky, two cats.
Restrictions: No pets please. Minimum age for children: two years.
Bed: Five rooms. Two singles and three doubles.
Breakfast: Continental or full. Eat in dining room or on 84-foot porch overlooking shaded lawn.
Rates: $17.50–$19.50 singles, $23 doubles including continental breakfast. Full country breakfast $1.50 more per person.

. . . A unique interesting couple who make you feel right at home . . . their proximity to the Empire Plaza in Albany and easy access makes it a desirable place to stay.

Mr. and Mrs. Loren E. Skinner, Niagara Falls, New York

SCHENECTADY

Bed & Breakfast Registry Host #12309

Reservations: Available year round through Bed & Breakfast Registry, page 27.

The cheerful hostess is knowledgeable about cultural events including folk, popular, and classical music, theater, and dance in Albany, Saratoga, and Schenectady. Her residence for 20 years, a comfortable Dutch colonial house with a peaceful backyard, reflects her travels in Europe and Japan. Now that the family has grown, this teacher has concluded that it's a good time to emulate the hospitable people she has met elsewhere.

Restrictions: No smoking. Pets allowed. "Dogs by all means, but snakes, never!"
Bed: Four rooms: Two singles, one with twin beds, one double-bedded. Shared bath.
Breakfast: Full. "Whatever fits my fancy." Served from 8 on. By the fireplace in winter, on the patio in summer.
Plus: Use of bicycles.
Rates: $30 singles, $40 doubles.

WELLS

Bed & Breakfast Registry Host #12190

Location: One mile from village on road that encircles lake, at foot of mountains, 50 miles northwest of Saratoga in the Adirondacks.
Reservations: Accepted May through October through Bed & Breakfast Registry, page 27.

Maybe you're just looking for bed and breakfast — literally — but this grandmother, a former school secretary, loves to have guests who enjoy being pampered in her comfortable two-year-old ranch house that has electric and wood-stove heat, an open deck, and an enclosed porch. The view from those rockers is wonderful, but she finds time for hiking, antiquing, refinishing, organization work — and all those water activities that are right there for guests too.

Restrictions: No pets please.
Bed: Two double-bedded rooms. Shared bath.
Breakfast: Available 7–10. Full and varied. Wild strawberries, huckleberries, raspberries, or blackberries in season, served as is or in muffins. Pancakes with locally produced syrup.
Plus: Rowboat, canoe, and swimming.
Rates: $22 single, $28 for two. Extra cot $5. One-night surcharge: $6.

FINGER LAKES

N

CANADA

Watertown

Lake Ontario

Rochester

NEW YORK

Finger Lakes

Syracuse

Corning   Elmira   Binghamton

PENNSYLVANIA

The numbers on this map indicate the locations of B&Bs described in detail in this chapter.

FINGER LAKES

THE FINGER LAKES

Reservation Services

Bed & Breakfast, U.S.A.

This service has hosts in Ithaca. Please see page 357.

Bed & Breakfast Referral of the Greater Syracuse Area

143 Didama Street, Syracuse, NY 13224
Phone: 315/446-4199
Listings: About 12 in the city of Syracuse and within a 25-mile radius. Elaine Samuel's growing list includes one on Oneida Lake.
Rates: Singles $25–$30, doubles $35–$40.

Cherry Valley Ventures, a Bed and Breakfast System, Inc.

6119 Cherry Valley Turnpike, LaFayette, NY 13084
Phone: 315/677-9723
Established June 1982.
Listings: At least 50 B&Bs including private homes, apartments, condominiums, inns, and guest houses. The wide area covered includes all of the state north of New York City, in urban, suburban, and rural settings.
Reservations: Most hosts require advance notice, but a few will accept last-minute guests. Full payment required before the stay.

This service, run by Gloria Pallone, is experiencing a growth spurt just as we go to press, so several hosts are anticipating their first guests.
Rates: Singles $20–$30, doubles $28–$38.

B & B Rochester

Box 444, Fairport, NY 14450
Phone: 716/223-8510 or 223-8877
Listings: A starter group of five within ten miles of downtown Rochester. Bess Kinsman has one listing on Keuka Lake available only during the summer.
Rates: Singles $25–$30, doubles $30–$35.

B&Bs

CHITTENANGO

Cherry Valley Ventures Host #3008

Location: Fifteen miles east of Syracuse in country setting, three or four miles to nearest village, near Green Lakes and Chittenango Falls.
Reservations: Available year round through Cherry Valley Ventures, page 393.

There's a family atmosphere in this large, spacious colonial home. Dad works for a local company and she manages to find time for crafts, sewing, canning, baking, and candy making too.

In residence: One dog. Four children, ages 12–22.
Restrictions: No pets. No smoking.
Bed: One room with double bed and private bath. Private entrance. Cot and crib available.
Breakfast: Available until 11:30. All homemade including breads, pastries, and jellies.
Rate: $30 single, $38 for two. Cot or crib, $4.

CORNING

Small city (population 12,000). Third largest tourist area in New York state. Downtown area is restored with Victorian facades, trees, and brick sidewalks. In town or nearby: Corning Museum of Glass, Rockwell Museum of Western Art, National Soaring Museum, Mark Twain study, Watkins Glen, country road, summer theater, wineries, restaurants.

CORNING

Laurel Hill

2670 Powderhouse Road, Corning, NY 14830
Phone: 607/936-3215
Location: On a quiet country road one mile from downtown attractions.
Hosts: Marge and Dick Woodbury
Open: Year round.

It was 1982 and the Woodburys knew the time and place were right. They had experienced B&Bs in England. Two of their daughters had just been married. Marge, a former teacher, was ready for a new focus. Inspiration and encouragement came from the proprietors of an established personalized Corning guest house. And so their 14-year-old Cape Cod home, furnished with many antiques, welcomed its first guests. The name? "Before we bought our acreage, we would bring the children here every year to ramble through the woods and gather laurel (which grows in profusion) for our Christmas wreath." Their hallmark now is careful attention — to detail and to people.

In residence: Two cats — Snooky, age 13, and Gabardine, age 14. Dick smokes a pipe.
Restrictions: Well-behaved pets are welcome.
Foreign language spoken: A little Spanish.
Bed: Two large rooms, each with two twin beds. Shared bath. Crib and cots available.
Breakfast: Continental, but not traditional. Tends to be leisurely. Fresh fruit and homemade muffins accompanied by Laurel Hill's own whipped sweet butter with Cointreau, Marge's special blend of coffee, and a selection of herb teas. Served 8–9 at a big round table next to sliding doors with view of woods and bird feeders. Fire usually burning in huge kitchen fireplace in winter.
Plus: Music room with parlor organ, grand piano, stereo, eclectic record collection. Screened porch. Hammock. The grounds. Baby-sitting possibilities.
Rates: $25 single, $29 for two if one night. A little less for two nights or more. Cots: age 16 and up $10, under 16 $5.

Everything ample, tasteful, good in quality, full of evidence of thoughtfulness. Nadine, age 16, remembers the good books. Amy, age 12, liked the bowl of fresh fruit in our large pleasant room. My husband liked being invited to sit on the screened porch. I was impressed by the Woodburys themselves who combined efficiency and generosity.

Bette and Burton Weidman, Nadine & Amy, Long Island, New York

CORNING

Rosewood Inn

134 East First Street, Corning, NY 14830
Phone: 607/962-3253
Hosts: Dick and Winnie Peer
Open: Year round.

"When we decided to sell our house outside the city, buy the old 14-room house and open an inn, our neighbors thought we were crazy. 'They'll ruin and steal your beautiful antiques and damage everything!' they said. Do you know, Bernice, that in three seasons we haven't lost anything, not even a towel, haven't had a burn in a rug or any damage. In fact we get much in return — best of all, return visits."

The Peers, the editor of Corning's daily newspaper and a first-grade teacher, waited until their children were grown before experiencing their first English B&Bs. Now the grandparents of two preschoolers have (or make) time to share with travelers who comment that it's just like visiting grandmother's; the floors do creak and slant. Or sometimes the Peers hear that it's like sleeping in a museum. Their home, built in 1853 as Greek Revival, renovated in 1922 to English Tudor, has each guest room decorated in a different theme such as the sea, glass, or Jenny Lind.

Bed: Five rooms. Two doubles with semiprivate bath. One double with private bath and solarium. One room with twin beds and private bath. One air-conditioned studio apartment. Rollaway beds available.
Breakfast: "We're in no hurry." Served by candlelight in wood-paneled fireplaced dining room at a communal table that can seat 16. Fruit in season, hot cereal, homemade sweet breads, homemade muffins, special Rosewood brandy butter. Starts 8:30–9:30.
Plus: Sitting room. Tours of the house. Off-street parking.
Rates: $34–$39.

PENFIELD

The Bed & Breakfast League Ltd.
Host #254

Location: Twenty minutes from Rochester on a quiet street near a main road.
Reservations: Available year round through membership in The Bed & Breakfast League Ltd., page 27.

After her five children were grown, the hostess returned to school for a degree in speech correction. And now she finds time to teach reading through Literacy Volunteers, to garden, and to study piano. You might have a discussion with her about the "Planetary Initiative for the World We Choose."

"My area is rural. There's a big apple orchard where pick-your-own arrangements are possible in the fall. In Rochester the Eastman House and Eastman Theatre are my special places. The Finger Lakes are 45 minutes away and Niagara Falls is a two-hour drive."

Restrictions: No pets and no smoking.
Bed: One room with twin beds. One room with studio bed and trundle. Shared bath and powder room.
Breakfast: Available 7–9:30. Continental with homemade bread and muffins. Cooked breakfast $2.50 extra.
Plus: Three bicycles for country rides. Vegetarian dinner on request.
Rates: $30 single, $38 for two.

SKANEATELES

Cherry Valley Ventures Host #3005

Location: On a quiet road in a community that is considered the eastern gateway to the Finger Lakes, ¾ mile from the village and 17 miles west of Syracuse.
Reservations: Available year round through Cherry Valley Ventures, page 393.

The hosts, both teachers, let guests determine how much time to spend socializing in this "newer" two-story colonial home. Their location is particularly good for water activities — sailing, powerboating, swimming, and wind-surfing — on the nearby "crystal-clear lake." Some guests come for events at Syracuse University's Dome and to eat at the famous restaurant (The Krebs) in town.

In residence: Teenage son. One quiet old cat. One springer spaniel.
Restrictions: No smoking. No pets.
Bed: One room with twin beds. One double. Private baths. Cots available.
Breakfast: Full American style with homemade muffins served in formal dining room or on the deck in summer. Available 7–10.
Plus: Cross-country skiing right at the door or downhill not far away.
Rates: $30 single, $38 for two. Cot $4.

SYRACUSE

Cherry Valley Ventures Host #3003

Location: In the heart of the city in a lovely residential area close to downtown, arterial highways, and universities and colleges.
Reservations: Available year round through Cherry Valley Ventures, page 393. Holidays may be excepted.

Among their first guests have been college-visiting parents who appreciated both the location and the personalized atmosphere. Perhaps the most memorable to date was the nurse who transferred to Syracuse and spent five days with them while apartment hunting. In that time they became friends — and neighbors, with the nurse enjoying their firsthand knowledge of the locale. He's an administrator in education and she's a retired teacher who enjoys having the time for B&B.

In residence: One adult daughter. One small dog.
Foreign language spoken: Italian.
Bed: One double room and one suite with private entrance that can sleep up to four. Private baths. Portacrib and cot available.
Breakfast: Continental. Usually includes homemade bakery. Available 7:30–9. Served in formal dining room.
Plus: Kitchen privileges in suite ($5 extra). Double room is air conditioned.
Rates: $30 single, $38 for two.

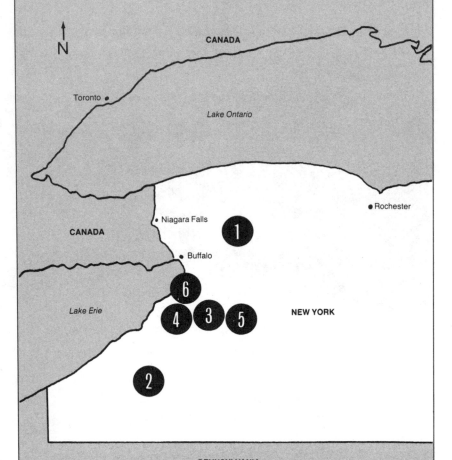

BUFFALO AREA

The numbers on this map indicate the locations of B&Bs described in detail in this chapter.

BUFFALO AREA

BUFFALO AREA

B&Bs

AKRON

Cherry Valley Ventures Host #1005

Location: In the village within walking distance of everything. About 20 miles east of Buffalo.

Reservations: Available year round through Cherry Valley Ventures, page 393.

The house, originally built by the town mayor 100 years ago, has been a doctor's office and a church. It has been the hosts' residence for a couple of decades. They are grandparents to a six-year-old, juggle several careers, and have just begun to host.

In residence: One cat and one dog. No smokers, but smoking is allowed.

Bed: One room with twin beds and one with a double. Cot available. Shared family bath.

Breakfast: At least continental.

Plus: Use of pool depending on timing. Laundry facilities.

Rates: $20 single, $28 for two. Cot $4.

CHERRY CREEK

Cherry Valley Ventures Host #2001

Location: Fifty miles south of Buffalo. Rural country, 1½ miles from the village, not far from winery, ski area, and Chautauqua.
Reservations: Available year round through Cherry Valley Ventures, page 393.

Wildflowers in season are an attraction on the property of this century-old house, the very home that the host was born in. She was a schoolteacher, he drove a school bus, and together they ran a 400-acre dairy farm. Now that all their own children are grown and gone, the hosts find time for plenty of gardening, canning, woodcutting, and B&B guests who like informality.

In residence: One dog, big and very friendly, loves children.
Restrictions: No smoking. Pets allowed if on leash.
Bed: Two single rooms with ¾-size beds. One double room. One room with two bunk beds and one single. Crib, cot, and cradle available. One shared guest bath.
Breakfast: Choice of continental or full that could include waffles with homemade maple syrup or blueberry muffins and scrambled eggs. Served 6–10:30.
Rates: $30 single, $38 double. Cot, crib, or cradle $4.

COLDEN

Cherry Valley Ventures Host #1004

Location: Twenty-five miles south of Buffalo, 35 miles from Niagara Falls. Within half an hour of five downhill ski areas. On side road off Route 391/219.
Reservations: Available September–April through Cherry Valley Ventures, page 393.

"Simplicity is our style but we entertain frequently. I am a good cook of the start-from-scratch ilk. We both have motorcycles and enjoy touring. Cyclists are welcome; we can lead them to many interesting byways." They have both been teachers, have changed careers, and are artists. He carves wood, bone, and stone, and she does much hand work including stitchery.

In residence: One dog. People who smoke.
Foreign languages spoken: Some rusty Spanish and a little German.
Bed: Two double rooms with private baths.
Breakfast: At least continental, sometimes full.
Plus: Television, library, space for ski equipment, and use of beamed-ceilinged living room that has a walk-in fireplace. Hiking and cross-country skiing possibilities in their woods. Dinner option by arrangement with reservation service.
Rates: $30 single, $38 for two.

EDEN

Cherry Valley Ventures Host #1001

Location: Twenty miles south of Buffalo on a main country road, a half hour from major shopping areas and ski resorts. Five miles from the New York Thruway.
Reservations: Available year round through Cherry Valley Ventures, page 393.

What was a real barn is, five years of work later, a large, spacious, comfortable home for a couple who enjoy casual country living. He's an insurance agent and she, a retired nurse, is involved in quiltmaking and physical fitness.

Restrictions: No pets. Nonsmokers preferred.
Bed: Three double rooms with private baths. Cot available.
Breakfast: Continental. Available 6–9.
Plus: Large whirlpool spa with view of the woods, exercise equipment, cross-country skiing from the door.
Rates: $30 single, $38 for two. Cot $4.

HOLLAND

Cherry Valley Ventures Host #1003

Location: Twenty-seven miles from downtown Buffalo in a country setting. Very close to several ski areas.
Reservations: Available year round through Cherry Valley Ventures, page 393.

A windmill produces part of the electricity for this refurbished farmhouse, situated in 50 acres with rolling hills, streams, woods, and abundant wildlife. Architectural details include paneling from a Buffalo mansion, leaded windows, church doors, and a marble-floored dining room. Antiques are everywhere. Each room is decorated in a different period. The hostess, retired from 17 years as a secretary, has "turned to B&B as a way to share a more relaxed lifestyle." Her husband is still working and between the two of them there's time for their interests in antiques, refinishing, real estate, cooking, and gardening.

In residence: One dog, a rare Japanese breed.
Restrictions: No guests' pets. No smoking.
Bed: One room with twin beds in a private wing. Private bath.
Breakfast: Continental. Served in front of roaring fire in dining area overlooking rural landscape; or, weather permitting, on patio.
Plus: Private lounge with television. Marked trails for hiking or cross-country skiing.
Rates: $30 single, $38 for two.

LAKE VIEW

Cherry Valley Ventures Host #1002

Location: On Lake Erie. Half an hour from Niagara Falls, 10 miles south of Buffalo.
Reservations: Available year round through Cherry Valley Ventures, page 393.

"Let's go up to Jean's Place," everyone is always saying. So although there's no sign out, that's the name. Jean and her husband have traveled through Europe staying at B&B places and have had many years of doing "B&B without pay." So they feel that they are quite experienced and "the time has come" now that she has retired.

It's a great place for fishermen and sightseers.

In residence: One cat and one golden retriever.
Restrictions: No pets please.
Foreign language spoken: German.
Bed: Two single rooms each with private bath. One room with twin beds and private half baths. Crib and cot available.
Breakfast: Continental with quiche. Available until 11.
Plus: Air conditioning. Private beach for boat launching. Beach for swimming in summer. Yard, picnic table, barbecue.
Rates: $30 single, $38 double. Crib or cot, $4.

NEW JERSEY

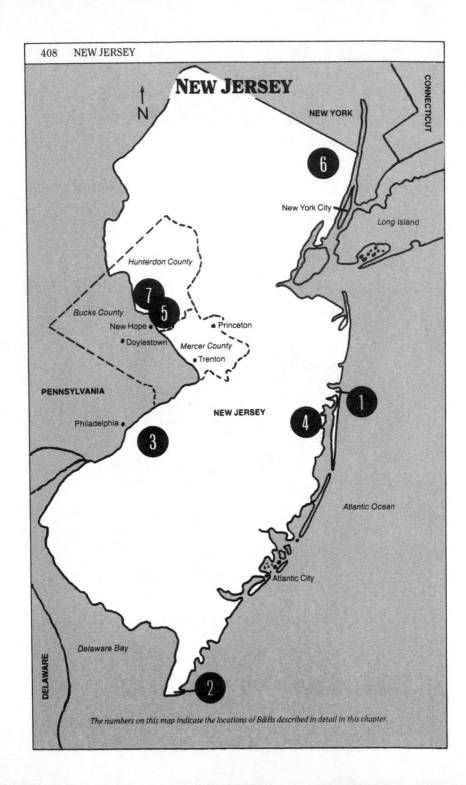

The numbers on this map indicate the locations of B&Bs described in detail in this chapter.

NEW JERSEY

NEW JERSEY

Reservation Services

Bed and Breakfast of New Jersey

Suite 132, 103 Godwin Avenue, Midland Park, NJ 07432
Phone: 201/444-7409
Established June 1982.
Open: Year round. (Answering machine. Same-day call-back.)
Listings: About 50 hosts in the northern part of the state and in the seashore area.

Communities include Allendale, Asbury Park, Chester, Fort Lee, Hackensack, Hasbrouck Heights, Hawthorne, Island Heights, Leonia, Long Valley, Madison, Midland Park, Norristown, Northvale, Norwood, Oakland, Port Republic, Ramsey, Red Bank, Ridgewood, Rutherford, Somers Point, Wayne, Woodcliff Lake, and Wyckoff.

Private homes, apartments, condominiums, villas, and one refurbished mansion are among the residences represented. A few of the listings could be considered student specials. Overnight and long-term stays can be arranged. Much information on area resources and attractions provided by Aster Mould, who runs this service.
Rates: Singles $20, doubles $30. Atlantic City rates 10–25 percent higher in high season.

Town and Country Bed and Breakfast

P.O. Box 301, Lambertville, NJ 08530
Phone: 609/397-8399
Established January 1983.
Open: Year round. (Answering machine. Same-day call-back except Sundays.)
Listings: Elegant to modest lodgings in private homes, apartments,

town houses, and commerical inns. In Hunterdon County — Milford, Clinton, Frenchtown, Flemington, Stockton, Lambertville. In Mercer County — Titusville, Hopewell, Princeton. In neighboring Bucks County in Pennsylvania (see map, page 436).

Service is run by Anita Impellizeri, an experienced innkeeper in the area. Last-minute reservations (if available) will be booked with credit-card deposit.

Rates: $30–$100. Special rates for business travelers. Weekly and monthly rates available. MasterCard and VISA accepted for deposit ($30 per reservation).

*

For Hunterdon and Mercer Counties (see map, page 408):

*

Other services with New Jersey listings:

Bed & Breakfast of Philadelphia

This service includes the communities of Cherry Hill, Haddonfield, Medford, Moorestown, and Riverton. Please see page 438.

The Bed & Breakfast League Ltd.

This service has hosts in Princeton; near Drew University in Chatham and Madison; in Passaic Park, Scotch Plains, and Tenafly; and on the south coast in Strathmere. Please see page 27.

*

Some of the reservation and referral services with listings in many states throughout the country, pages 26-29, have a few hosts in New Jersey.

B&Bs

BAY HEAD

Conover's Bay Head Inn

646 Main Avenue, Bay Head, NJ 08742
Phone: 201/892-4664
Location: One block from the beach. Fifty miles from New York City, 65 miles east of Philadelphia, an hour from Atlantic City.
Hosts: Beverly and Carl Conover
Open: February 15–December 15. "Reservations always recommended. In off-season we enjoy our area; please call to make sure we are here." Minimum reservation on weekends: two nights.

Because the Conovers had spent their childhood summers in Bay Head, they were well acquainted with the peaceful one-square-mile town. Still without parking meters and billboards, it is a place that was almost completely developed a hundred years ago as a summer retreat for wealthy Princeton residents. Strict zoning laws have retained the flavor and appearance.

Only when Beverly, the full-time hostess, and Carl, a structural steel erector, were looking (14 years ago) for their very own home and were shown this 1912 residence that had a still-valid 1916 hotel license did they think of becoming innkeepers. "We had no experience but quickly learned." They furnished with turn-of-the-century pieces. Plants, ruffles, needlework, and pillows add to the charm.

Beverly "did everything" at first. She and Carl still set the style and enjoy their roles, but the inn has become a real family business with the personal touches constantly being renewed and embellished. Those framed original house blueprints in the hallways were found just two years ago when Carl took a ceiling down. The gauges in one room are Carl's; he has rebuilt two steam engines and used to own one. There are plenty of crocheted bureau scarves and doilies in evidence. And every single washcloth has a crocheted edge. Beverly's mother has made an afghan for every one of the color-coordinated flower-inspired bedrooms. There is help from college-age sons Timmy and Christopher, and in July and August you will meet Beverly's parents as well as an aunt and uncle.

Antiquing and shopping and (most years) golf are year-round activities. Guests play tennis and go swimming, fishing, and crabbing. In the summer a local shop rents one-speed bicycles. It's easy to tour Bay Head and find that you have actually pedaled into Mantoloking, a duplicate town in appearance.

Restrictions: No pets allowed. Children at least age 12 are welcome in the summer months.

Bed: Twelve rooms in summer. (Six rooms heated in winter.) Four with two twin beds, three with doubles, two with queens, three with a double and a twin. Four rooms have private baths. Eight rooms share four baths.

Breakfast: Continental. Beverly bakes and serves muffins every day. Full breakfast (fancier in winter) $1.75 extra.

Plus: Popular garden sitting area and porches for rocking in summer, fireplace in winter.

Rates: Private bath $60–$65. Shared bath $43–$46. Single occupancy $5 less than double rate. Extra person in room $20 daily. Sunday to Sunday, one night free.

CAPE MAY

Known as the oldest seaside resort in America, Cape May might well be called the largest B&B community of today. Homes, guesthouses, and hotels too, all with Victorian architectural detail, were built by the hundreds in the 19th century. Other resorts closer to home by way of "the machine" became more fashionable after the turn of the century. About a decade ago Cape May, now a National Historic Landmark city, began to experience a renaissance.

The profiles of B&B owners on the following pages indicate how one has inspired another. Several hosts don appropriate hats and conduct walking tours of the historic district or of their own restored and refurbished B&B. There are trolley tours in town, a boardwalk, and the main summer attraction, the beach. Some B&Bs provide bicycles, direct you to the restored Physick Estate, and tout their proximity to the Washington Street Mall with its many art galleries, craft shops, and antique emporiums. Hiking and bird-watching opportunities are here too.

B&B proprietors are small entrepreneurs. As Cape May becomes even more popular — but still is quieter than other shore areas — it is often difficult to make last-minute reservations in season; the friendly and enthusiastic hosts operate their own informal referral network. If you experience a B&B that isn't in this book, perhaps you will let me know if you feel it is among the missing.

CAPE MAY

Albert G. Stevens Inn

127 Myrtle Avenue, Cape May, NJ 08204
Phone: 609/884-4717
Location: Across the street from Wilbraham Park, within three blocks of the "better" beach, and at a trolley stop if you want to leave your car and take public transportation around the town.
Hosts: Dick Flynn and Dean Krumrine
Open: April–October. Minimum reservation two nights on weekends.

Because Dick and Dean, 12-year Cape May residents, have so many friends who are B&B hosts, it was natural for them to think of B&B when the house next door to theirs came on the market in 1981. Originally built in 1900 by Dr. Albert G. Stevens for his bride, the house was (mostly) restored by August 1982 when the first guests arrived. (There's no end to work on old houses; Dick and Dean are usually around — inside or out.) In their first season of operation, they also learned that "hosting is fun and that B&Bers are among the really nice people in the world." Stevens's touches remaining are the oak mantel above a gas fireplace that is on spring and fall, and the mother-of-pearl inlay parlor suite that Dr. Stevens gave to his wife. And you're allowed up to the "lookout," the Tower Room, reached by an unusual staircase.

Wilbraham Mansion, the hosts' own private 20-room residence, is furnished with antiques and open to the public daily for tours. There's no charge for Stevens Inn guests to go through what was a simple farmhouse in 1840 but was enlarged with wing, bay windows, and a tower too, by a wealthy industrialist in 1900.

Restrictions: No children. No pets. Smoking is not encouraged.
Bed: One room with twin beds, two rooms with double beds. Three suites with double beds. One suite has a private entrance. Private baths for all.
Breakfast: Full. Served between 9 and 10 in a double dining room with six guests seated in each section.

Plus: Full bath available to guests on day of departure after a day on beach. Beach passes. Free parking.
Rates: $45–$65 double occupancy.

CAPE MAY

Barnard Good House

238 Perry Street, Cape May, NJ 08204
Location: Two blocks from main beach.
Hosts: Tom and Nan Hawkins
Open: April 1–November 1. Minimum reservation on weekends: three nights June 15–September 15, two nights other weekends.

About the time of their 30th wedding anniversary, a purchasing director for a plastics manufacturing firm and a marketing director for a shopping center were searching for new careers. When Nan and Tom fell in love with a vacant 1869 Second Empire mansard-roofed house in Cape May, they made many changes. The early American decor of their previous home (in a central New Jersey seashore resort) was exchanged for 19th-century Victorian elegance. The actual move was made in February, just five months before the arrival of their first guest in July 1980.

Now, as hosts to "many who are the ages of our children (25–35) and to others who seem to be young at heart," they find that there is often conversation about restoration and decorating. The dining room has a gasolier made of iron, pewter, and brass. Their Turkish Corner with draped ceiling is complete with Barney the Buddha, often rubbed by guests for good luck. And the 100-year-old organ in the living room really works if you pump hard. All the bedrooms are true to the period. The Leggatt Room (named, as the house is, after ancestors) features a four-poster canopy bed. The flamboyant pink, white, and green Hawkins Suite, with enormous birds on the wallpaper, is popular with honeymooners. Restored wainscoting, a copper tub and pull-chain john can be found in one of the bathrooms.

Restrictions: Children should be over 12. No pets allowed.
Bed: One room with twin beds and shared bath. One with double bed and private bath. Four doubles with shared bath. One suite with bedroom, sitting room, private bath.
Breakfast: Their hallmark. Elaborate setting in dining room with lace tablecloth. Menu never repeated regardless of your length of stay. And

they cater to allergies. Continental is served June 15–September 15. Juices are freshly extracted or squeezed and blended. Muffins, crepes, or even chocolate-chip banana cake. Full gourmet breakfast other months might include soup; corn casserole; cheese puffs with ham-Mornay sauce, the house specialty; apple cake. Meal can last two or three hours "depending on how much fun we're having." Officially starts 8:30–9:30.
Plus: Pick-up service at ferry if you want to leave your car at Lewes, Delaware. Picnic tables with umbrella, rockers on wraparound veranda where beverage is sometimes served. Bicycles provided at no extra charge. Off-street parking. No television.
Rates: For two people — $50 for twin room, $50–$55 for doubles, $70 for suite. Single rate is $5 less per room.

One week wasn't nearly long enough!
Jennifer and Thom Brewster, Slippery Rock, Pennsylvania

You can taste the care that goes into all delicious homemade meals.
The Cardonis, Ellicott City, Maryland

Nan and Tom treat all their guests like adopted children.
Sharon and Terry, Summit, New Jersey

CAPE MAY

The Brass Bed Victorian Guest House

719 Columbia Avenue, Cape May, NJ 08204
Phone: 609/884-8075
Location: In historic district, 2 blocks to ocean.
Hosts: John and Donna Dunwoody
Open: Year round.
Reservations: Three-day minimum May 15–September 15.

We feel like we've been in another era for a couple of days and it was truly delightful and relaxing. What makes the stay really enjoyable is the personal touch so willingly given by Donna and John.
Mr. and Mrs. Robert J. Tobin, Ivyland, Pennsylvania

This 1980 addition to the local B&B scene has personal touches everywhere — the hosts' presence at breakfast or in late afternoon, the family heirlooms, the 1895 upright piano that may be a gathering spot for singing, the restored photos of relatives, and daughter Mary's dollhouse in the parlor.

The Dunwoody's came for a retreat, "fell in love with Cape May, sold everything, borrowed as much as we could and jumped in." It's a new lifestyle that the family feels was worth the interim stage. Until they bought the 1872 Carpenter Gothic house, it had been occupied only in the summer months. They moved from Voorhees, New Jersey, in the month of January and John continued all that winter to commute at dawn to Philadelphia for his graphic design position. Dishes, now used for breakfast, were "discovered" in cartons and many of the furnishings were found to have been the original pieces delivered to the first owner.

Some of the brass beds are reproductions, but all the old ones have been Dunwoody-restored. John also restored the 19th-century rosewood Graphonola, an 1962 purchase, and frequently winds it up so that some of his many early recordings can be heard. And family and friends helped with the restoration of armoires, marble-topped tables, washstands, and dressers.

"Our motto is 'Like visiting grandma's house.' Everything is touchable and guests are treated like family."

In residence: Twelve-year-old Mary and 18-year-old Mike; Poocher the dog and Clousea the cat.
Restrictions: Children should be at least 12. No guests' pets allowed. Smoking only in public rooms.
Foreign languages spoken: Some French and Spanish.
Bed: Eight rooms. Two private baths, three shared. Cots available.
Breakfast: Fresh fruit, cereal, homemade bakery, beverage. Served at dining-room table under brass chandelier. A leisurely time.
Plus: Hot-and-cold outside shower and dressing room, bicycle rack, beach tags, front porch with rockers. Tours of first-floor rooms and selected bedrooms.
Rates: Three different double rate schedules depending on season. Shared bath $35–$40 winter, $40–$45 spring and fall, $45–$50 May 15–September 15. Private baths $45–$60. Cots $10. Weekly discount of 10 percent.

CAPE MAY

Captain Mey's Inn

202 Ocean Street, Cape May, NJ 08204
Phone: 609/884-7793 or 884-9637
Location: Historic district, around corner from Victorian Mall 1½ blocks to beach and walking distance to all restaurants.
Hosts: Carin Fedderman and Milly LaCanfora
Open: Year round.

Milly and Carin, both originally from Holland, have been in the area for the last twenty years, but it is only in the last four that they have exchanged the hats of computer programmer and travel coordinator for those of innkeepers, an idea that came to them because they had good friends in the business.

Some of their restoration efforts include the dining-room wainscoting and a fireplace with oak carvings and mantel that have been closed off for 50 years. Other features include Tiffany stained glass, Victorian furniture, and a Delft Blue collection. Milly's 75-year-old mother made all the afghans and quilts on the guest beds. Fresh flowers, mostly from the garden, are in the rooms.

At one time Ocean Street was known as Doctor's Row. This particular residence became a tea room and later a rooming house before the hosts converted it to Captain Mey's, naming it after the Dutch founder of Cape May. An exterior paint analysis followed by custom mixing resulted in the current authentic shades of beige and brown with accents of plum.

Carin was born and grew up in Holland. Milly is of Dutch ancestry. Together they orginated Cape May's spring Tulip Fest. Their own grounds have a show of 400 bulbs as well as an herb garden with 15 varieties.

In residence: One basset hound named Sobat (which means friend in Indonesian), and Co-Co and Wetzel, two cats.
Restrictions: No pets allowed. Smoking in bedrooms only. Children should be over 12.
Foreign languages spoken: Dutch, Italian.
Bed: Nine double rooms, three with private bath.
Breakfast: Fresh fruit in season, homemade breads and cakes, yogurt and assorted Dutch cheeses. Set in buffet style in dramatic foyer. Enjoyed in dining room or on veranda.
Plus: Garden area for picnic lunch. Iced tea (with mint from the gar-

den) on the veranda in summer, sherry by the fire in winter. Off-street parking, no charge.

Rates: All double occupancy. $65–$70 private bath, $45–$60 shared. Rates differ according to floor and season. Cots $15 for extra person. VISA and MasterCard accepted.

We've visited Cape May many times and have always stayed at Captain Mey's because of its excellent location, its exceptional cleanliness, the comfortably furnished rooms, home-baked breakfast breads, the friendly gatherings on the wraparound porch, the reasonable prices, and the warm hospitality of the innkeepers.

Phil and Toetie Welch, Berkely Heights, New Jersey

CAPE MAY

The Duke of Windsor Inn

817 Washington Street, Cape May, NJ 08204
Phone: 609/884-1355
Location: Four blocks from beach, "close enough, but quiet too."
Hosts: Bruce and Fran Prichard
Open: All weekends mid-April until Thanksgiving. Open daily mid-June until mid-September and Christmas week. Minimum reservation is two days on weekends, three on holiday weekends.

The first (1982) season extended itself "by demand" and summer bookings of returnees had already started when I spoke with Fran in March.

Although the Prichards love Cape May and its pace ("People greet strangers in a friendly way on the street") they are newcomers and B&B hosts almost by chance. "We were a little horrified at what the Dunwoodys, our good friends from home [Voorhees, New Jersey], had taken on but we came many times to help them prepare to open The Brass Bed, found it neat to see the changes, and 'got into it and Cape May.' Now here we are with this grand (in every way) 1896 house, a private home until we bought it, extending our entertaining style to new friends. We find that people appreciate the romance of the Victorian era."

The classic Queen Anne detailing includes Tiffany stained glass, plaster ceiling medallions, and three-story cantilevered stairway. Furnishings are antiques and period pieces. Restoration work is ongoing.

After the first season the Prichards attended to removing the varnish from the oak woodwork and researching wallpapers to make decor historically accurate. There are plans for restoring the exterior too.

At the moment Fran and Bruce still live in Voorhees and they both juggle hosting with teaching. (His subjects are chemistry and physics and she teaches special-needs classes.) Daughter Barbara, a college student, helps with the hosting. Son Bruce, at age 17, is becoming known around town for his talents in restoration, a new application for someone who is "good with his hands."

In residence: Barbara and Bruce. Duchess, a black-and-white cat, is not allowed in guests' rooms.
Restrictions: No guests' pets. No cigar smoking inside. Children should be at least 12.
Bed: Nine rooms. One has twin beds. The others are double or king. Private and shared baths are available. One tower room has a private bath and one has shared.
Breakfast: Served 9–10:30 but late sleepers won't go hungry. In summer there's a home-baked specialty of the day. Off-season, bacon or sausage and eggs are added.
Plus: At 4 p.m., tea and crumpets; or lemonade, hot mulled cider, cookies. Bicycles for guests' use; beach tags; hot-and-cold outside shower; game room (first floor tower room) for cards, chess, checkers.
Rates: Per room. Shared baths are $40 in season, $35 off. Private baths are $50–$55 in season, $45 off.

Warm and interested people . . . ambiance they create is one of comfort and informality . . . we were nurtured, attended to, and left alone just enough. We went home as calm and relaxed as if we had been on vacation for a month instead of only four days. What a way to go!

Rob Pearlman and Barbara Gline, Silver Spring, Maryland

CAPE MAY

Gingerbread House

28 Gurney Street, Cape May, NJ 08204
Phone: 609/884-0211
Location: Half a block from the beach.
Hosts: Fred and Joan Echevarria

Open: Year round. Minimum reservation is three nights on summer weekends, two nights other weekends.

Visitors first notice the gingerbread on the outside of the 1869 house that is listed on the National Register of Historic Places. Then they are given a warm welcome by Fred, a clinical psychologist turned B&B manager, photographer, and woodworker. On weekends and in the evenings, Joan, a daily commuter to her Philadelphia job, is hostess at home for the new way of life that began when they bought the house in 1979. With help from family members they have done a great deal of restoration and created a bright, warm, and airy feeling. Walnut, wicker, and oak furnishings; fresh flowers and plants; and displays of Fred's photography are the backdrop for interesting conversations.

Restrictions: No pets. Children should be "at least five and well behaved."
Bed: Six double rooms. One with its own private porch has two double beds and a private bath with footed tub and pedestal sink. Two other rooms have private baths and three share one bath.
Breakfast: At 8–10 a.m. Continental with homemade coffee cake or muffins. Help yourself.
Plus: Outside enclosed shower. Front porch.
Rates: $48–$70 June–September, $42–$65 May and October, $38–$62 November–April.

With numerous return visits we have stayed in every room. Our favorite is the room with the private second-floor porch.

Mr. and Mrs. Smith B. Coleman, Ambler, Pennsylvania

CAPE MAY

The Mainstay Inn

635 Columbia Avenue, Cape May, NJ 08204
Phone: 609/884-8690
Location: On a side street in town, within walking distance of everything.
Hosts: Tom and Sue Carroll
Open: April through October. Three-day minimum reservation from mid-June to mid-September. Advance reservations strongly recom-

mended. First-time guests, in particular, should call so that the rooms and amenities can be described.

Elegance, yes. Attention to detail, yes. And in many ways this is considered a model of the evolution of a B&B business, all the way from the hosts' struggles to overcome opposition (to making a big old once-magnificent place into a form of lodging business) to their joy in hosting ("I wouldn't last a week without spending time with the guests — at breakfast, check-in and at tea") that remains even after 12 years.

But a hidden treasure? No! There's hardly a national publication that hasn't photographed at least the long walnut dining-room table, gas chandeliers, and ceiling-high mirrors along with the beautiful exterior of what was built in 1872 as an exclusive clubhouse for gamblers. It's all a visual feast that is enjoyed both "by those who want to be alone and others who seek friendship and community."

How did a couple still in their thirties have such foresight in their youth? They came to know Cape May when Tom was in the Coast Guard. Even then they loved the big old houses. And so they stayed for post-service living. Sue taught, Tom worked with the planning board, and in 1970 they bought a house, one that provided supplemental income through summer guests. As Tom says, "I wanted to own and live in a mansion." In 1977 they acquired their new Mainstay (they moved the name), which had many of the original furnishings and fixtures, and the possibility for a variety of accommodations.

Victoriana is so "in" now that it's hard to imagine the ingenuity they had to use less than a decade ago. Sue experimented with swag patterns for her window treatments and used vertical strips of wallpapers for borders. Some of the answers to the usual questions can be heard along with oohs and aahs during the regular (five times a week) public half-hours tours of the main parlors and dining room. The business, one run with style, is a lot of work, but you can tell that Sue means it when she says, "We love what we do."

In residence: Othello the cat, "very important and he'll let you know it."

Restrictions: Children should be over 12. "Young children generally find us tiresome." No pets allowed. "We tolerate light smoking."

Bed: Eight rooms with private bath, four with shared. All furnished with antiques.

Breakfast: Available 8:15–9:45 on veranda or in dining room. Light meal with homemade breads in season. Full meal off-season could include corn quiche, chicken pie, or bacon and fish rolls.

Plus: Afternoon tea. Tour of house. Drawing room with coal stove (and baseboard heating), two parlors, rockers and swing on veranda. Garden.

Ladder climb to cupola for ocean view. Outside shower.
Rates: For singles $40–$54 in season, $30–$50 other times. For doubles $40–$60 shared bath, $50–$72 private bath.

My summers are not complete without time spent at the Mainstay Inn. The highlights for me: comfortable large rooms authentically furnished, a wide veranda with rocking chairs and hammock guaranteed to put you to sleep, breakfast and afternoon tea served on the veranda, and all this only a short walk from the beach. Mainstay's innkeepers enjoy their guests, making them feel welcome and "at home." It's a wonderful place.

Jessie C. Daniels, Arlington, Virginia

CAPE MAY

The Queen Victoria

102 Ocean Street, Cape May, NJ 08204
Phone: 609/884-8702
Location: In historic district, one block from beach; 1½ blocks from mall.
Hosts: Dane and Joan Wells
Open: Year round. Reservations, preferably by phone, recommended. Holidays and weekends may require much advance notice. Minimum reservation: two nights on weekends, three or four nights June through September. Family-style Thanksgiving. In December ("Christmas is fast becoming our favorite season") there are a decorations workshop weekend, a caroling weekend, and a Dickens weekend.

What can it take to restore completely a century-old summer cottage? The picture book in the library documents the before-and-after of the two-year project completed in 1982. The Wellses did all of the research and most of the work themselves. They did have professional help for technical work and exterior painting; and friends and neighbors helped with demolition, caning chairs, woodwork, and locating antiques. Just to give you an idea of quantity, imagine 240 yards of lace for the window curtains; 1½ miles of copper pipe; 300 rolls of wallpaper (some hand-printed); and 372 pounds of spackle. The result is an elegant and comfortable country inn at the seashore. All guest rooms have antique beds — brass, iron, walnut, and there's a four-poster too — with handmade quilts. Fresh flowers or flowering plants are in the rooms year round. "And guests are encouraged to pull up a stool and chat with us while we cook in the country kitchen. The coffeepot is always on and the cookie jar full."

"House restoration and people" are on the list of interests for all Cape May B&B hosts, but here there are a few twists. Joan was executive director of The Victorian Society of America, and before that she was curator of the "Unsinkable" Molly Brown House Museum in Denver where she was responsible for the beginning of its restoration (which is still continuing). Dane was in neighborhood commercial revitalization and economic development in Philadelphia, "but most important, as a boy he worked in a hardware store!"

The hosts are active members of the community and provide guests with plenty of organized, helpful information on sights and schedules.

Current projects include Joan's role as gardener in restoring the Victorian flower beds; and the newest member of the family, Elizabeth, a January 1983 arrival.

In residence: Four cats — Mumbles and Sketty, named for Welsh towns; Shoes (short for Snowshoes, because of his extra thumbs); and Scamper.

Restrictions: Smoking allowed in parlor and library only. "We're not keen on heavy smoking guests." Children aged two to five are discouraged. No guests' pets, please. Charge ($2) for parking on property in summer; or free parking in lot four blocks away.

Foreign languages spoken: Dane is fluent in French. Joan struggles with some Spanish.

Bed: Twelve rooms, all with at least a private sink. Four rooms each have a private bath and small refrigerator. Eight have shared baths and share a small refrigerator. Crib available.

Breakfast: Available 8–10. Buffet style. Could include homemade granola, breads, baked apple. A different egg dish prepared each day. Eat at dining-room table (seats 12); in bay window of parlor; or on side porch if warm enough. Leisurely time. Hosts enjoy it too.

Plus: Eight rooms have ceiling fans. Others have a minimum of six windows. Porches. Fireplace in winter. Bicycles provided for guests. Beach tags. Bathhouse with changing room and showers. Late-afternoon tea with homemade cookies, pâtés, and cheese spreads. Shared recipes. Turned-down beds at night with a nugget of fudge on each pillow.

Rates: $40–$85 for double occupancy. Vary according to season. Single occupancy discount $5. Crib, $10. Fifty percent deposit required with reservation. MasterCharge, VISA, and American Express cards accepted.

CAPE MAY

The Victorian Rose

715 Columbia Avenue, Cape May, NJ 08204
Phone: 609/884-2497
Location: In historic district, 2½ blocks from ocean.
Hosts: Bob and Linda Mullock
Open: March–January 1. Three-day minimum reservation June–September.

It was a private home, a tea room, a school for girls, and an inn. For the last three years The Victorian Rose has been a bed-and-breakfast establishment owned and run by a young couple who feel they got into the business "by luck." Bob's insurance office is just three blocks away. And now he wears a straw hat on Saturday mornings when he leads walking tours in the historic district. Their "before" life was in Philadelphia where he was in marketing and she was a realtor and nursery-school teacher.

The Mullocks have done most of their own restoration work. The 1930s, with music and candlelight, is the parlor theme. Bedrooms and dining room are Victorian. And outside they have planted more than 200 rose bushes.

In residence: Daughter Cynthia, age six.
Restrictions: No pets allowed. B&B children should be over 10. (All ages allowed in cottage.)
Bed: Eight rooms. Two singles, four doubles, two with king-size beds. Three private baths, two shared, and two half-baths. Cots available. (Downstairs suite and cottage have their own kitchens.)
Breakfast: At 9. Fruit, quiche, or homemade sweet rolls. Served at one long table that seats 18. Linda cooks, serves, and joins guests. "It's my favorite part of the day." Can last up to three hours.
Plus: Front porch with highback rockers.
Rates: Summer $35–$50 single, $45–$60 double, $60–$70 king. In winter most rooms are $10 less.

No better place to relax and enjoy life. . . . Terrific hosts make you feel right at home. We like it in the winter months as well as the summer.
Judy and Jerry Miller, Cockeysville, Maryland

CHERRY HILL

The Balabans

6 Willow Court, Cherry Hill, NJ 08003
Phone: 609/428-6206
Location: Lovely suburban area. Twenty-five minutes to Philadelphia, 10 minutes to New Jersey Turnpike and Route 295, and one hour to Atlantic City.
Hosts: Rae and Harold Balaban
Open: Year round except November 15–January 15.
Reservations: Required.

Oriental rugs, art, sculpture, music, and books contribute to a relaxing atmosphere among friendly people. Rae, a professional investigator for the federal government, finds gardening rewarding and enjoys sharing the array with travelers. Harold, a professional kitchen designer, saw to it that they had the ultimate when they had their colonial-style home custom-built 13 years ago.

In residence: One grown son.
Restrictions: Children should be at least 10. No smoking in bedrooms. No pets please.
Bed: Two rooms with twin beds. One guest bath.
Breakfast: Continental on weekdays. House specialty of pancakes (extra charge) on weekends.
Plus: Billiard room. Central air conditioning. Terrace.
Rates: $20 single for one night, $18 if staying two nights. $30 for two for one night, $28 for two nights. Family rate for four in the two rooms is $54 per night.

ISLAND HEIGHTS

The Studio of John F. Peto

102 Cedar Avenue
Mailing Address: P.O. Box 306, Island Heights, NJ 08732
Phone: 201/270-6058
Location: Three miles from Toms River, one hour from Philadelphia,

two hours from New York City, one hour from Atlantic City.
Hosts: Joy M. Smiley and Blossom Smiley Bejarano
Open: Year round.

"We thought we would have 'arty' guests who know about our grandfather. So far no one who has come here knew about him. They come to be in a quiet historic village!" So if you haven't seen John Frederick Peto's paintings in the 1983 one-man show at the National Gallery in Washington, D.C., or at the Amon Carter Museum in Fort Worth, Texas, you can still enjoy his recently restored Victorian home that was opened as a B&B in the summer of 1982 by his two granddaughters. The still-life artist designed his studio with its large fireplace first, then in 1889 had the rest of the house built around it. Guests seem to congregate either around that fireplace in the charming studio with memorabilia and paintings, or in the cheery large renovated country kitchen.

Joy and her sister Bee's extensive travels gave them the idea of making The Studio a bed-and-breakfast establishment. Because Island Heights is on the National Register of Historic Places, guests frequently take walking tours to see some of the 375 houses. (The town is also dry and without commercial traffic.) Ocean sailing, swimming, and fishing are main summer attractions here where the river meets the bay.

In residence: Mostly Joy (who also gives lectures about her grandfather and museum tours of the studio). "The official greeter is Smirnoff, a blue-and-brown-eyed lovable Siberian husky."
Restrictions: No guests' pets allowed. Children should be at least four.
Foreign languages spoken: Spanish, Portuguese, and Italian.
Bed: Seven rooms with original furniture. Two have double beds, three have two twin beds, and two have single beds. Two shared guests baths. and there is one suite with double bed, living room, and private bath. Cots are available.
Breakfast: Menus vary. May be hot popovers and jam, eggs Benedict, homemade biscuits, waffles for children. Two-hour session not unusual.
Plus: Refreshments at other times. Bicycles for rent. Motorboat rides (extra charge) in their boat on the river.
Rates: $35–$40 singles, $45–$50 doubles. Suite $60, $75 if couch is also used. Cots are $10. American Express, MasterCard, and VISA accepted.

LAMBERTVILLE

York Street House

42 York Street, Lambertville, NJ 08530
Phone: 609/397-3007
Location: Two blocks from the center of town in an area listed on the National Register of Historic Places. Lambertville is just across the Delaware River from New Hope, Pennsylvania, and 30 minutes from Princeton.
Host: Cornelius (John) Peck
Open: March 1–mid-January. Minimum stay: two days on weekends.

A *House & Garden* home in 1911 and a Designer's Showhouse in the spring of 1983, this magnificent Georgian house has become a B&B under the first owners outside the coal-magnate family who built the high-style brick mansion in 1909.

The newest house in the neighborhood (the others are Victorian dating from the railroad boom), it is situated on an acre of land fronted with a beautiful wrought-iron fence; it is surrounded by huge old trees and has its own formal flower garden.

The host is an antique dealer and interior designer; he and his partner, James Bulger, the person responsible for the restored Swan Hotel & Coryell Gallery in Lambertville, are filling a need in a community that has a strong tradition of art and artisans. They are in a location where you can walk to art galleries, at least a dozen antique shops, and nine gourmet restaurants. Within a five-mile radius there are more than 50 restaurants. There are delightful surprises all over town with shops (*not* the souvenir type) here and interesting alleyways there.

Restrictions: No pets please. And sorry, no children.
Bed: Seven large rooms. Four with queen-sized beds and one shared bath on second floor. Three with double beds and two shared baths on third floor.
Breakfast: Juice, homemade bakery, coffee served in a marvelous breakfast room with stained-glass door leading onto screened porch overlooking gardens.
Plus: A large lounge comfortably furnished with the feeling of a stately English country house and the original Waterford chandelier. Of three Mercer tile fireplaces, one is in the paneled library filled with memorabilia and with the ambiance of a London club.
Rates: $50 single, $60 for two. MasterCard and VISA accepted.

RIDGEWOOD

Bed and Breakfast of New Jersey
Host #1

Location: On a through street in village, but in a quiet neighborhood. Walking distance to bus and train (about a 45-minute ride to New York City). Forty-minute drive to Manhattan and Atlantic Ocean beaches.
Reservations: Available year round through Bed and Breakfast of New Jersey, page 410.

"When we moved here 10 years ago from a very different life style, I found this area at times very frightening, especially because of the fast New York Metro area pace. That was one of the reasons why I eventually started a business to assist transferees in their move to New Jersey. And after running the community orientation service for three years, I have accumulated a great deal of information and a completely different feeling about New Jersey. It's really not the 'great refinery-lined turnpike between New York and Philadelphia' but a wonderful place to live, offering every type of community, so many things to do and see and warm, friendly people. You can do anything and everything here or you can do nothing! This is the New Jersey feeling I want my guests to remember.

"My home is the stopover for friends and relatives from around the country on their way to New York City or the Jersey shore, but because I love to entertain, I started B&B to be able to do it more often."

The hostess now works with a travel agency and her husband is associated with a large chemical company. Their two-story colonial home is within either a half hour or one hour of a very long list of attractions and possibilities.

In residence: A lovable and gentle six-year-old collie, loves children.
Restrictions: No guests' pets please.
Bed: Two rooms. One single and one double. And a hide-a-bed for extras.
Breakfast: Continental on weekdays with du jour goodies (homemade bakery). Option of joining hosts on weekends when a full breakfast is served either in the dining room or in the attractive kitchen that is filled with plants and copper pots.
Plus: Beverage and munchies in late afternoon or evening. Free off-street parking. Screened-in porch or den with music, wine, and TV. Air conditioning. Kitchen privileges and laundry facilities available. Baby-sitting possibilities.
Rates: $20 single, $30 double, hide-a-bed $5.

STOCKTON

The Woolverton Inn

RD 3, Stockton, NJ 08559
Phone: 609/397-0802
Location: On outskirts of village of Stockton, on the Delaware River. Thirty minutes to Princeton, 15 minutes to Flemington and bus to New York City.
Host: Deborah Clark
Open: Year round.

. . . Hospitality, relaxation, and delicious country breakfasts. We have enjoyed fresh croissants in our lovely room, in the large colonial kitchen, and outside on the patio. The inn is surrounded by beautiful gardens, sheep grazing in the back field, and lovely old trees. A great getaway!　Bob and Kathy Litzinger, Glassboro, New Jersey

The innkeeper has raised Siberian tigers and published a museum newsletter. Her interests range from art collecting to camping. Since the inn opened in 1980 she has been at the helm and seen how "the special magic of this place touches and transforms almost all who visit." Although she is not the owner, the style of the Woolverton is very much her creation, something most guests are aware of and appreciate.

Debo, an area resident since 1960, has known proprietors George and Ann Hackl, for a long time. After the Hackls bought the property in 1972 they lived in it until 1980 when they turned it into an inn, one furnished with their family antiques.

The house is now in the process of applying to the National Register of Historic Places. It was built as a manor house in 1793 and remodeled in 1876; and its blend of 18th- and 19th-century architecture was carefully kept when Whitney North Seymour restored it in 1939.

Guests take advantage of canoeing, tubing, jogging, and horseback riding on and along the Delaware River. Special towpath trail rides are arranged by the inn. And the area has many antique shops, crafts studios, and fine restaurants.

Restrictions: No guests' pets.
Bed: Eight double rooms, and one suite with two bedrooms. Five shared baths.
Breakfast: Time arranged on weekdays. Weekends 8–11. Continental with home-baked (by local housewives) bread, croissants, fresh orange juice and fruit.

Plus: Air conditioning. Parlor with fireplace. "The entire inn is for the guests." Afternoon tea. Croquet, bocce, formal gardens, extensive lawns, tree swing, large patio. Turned-down beds. Mints on pillows.
Rates: $45–$60 doubles, $65 suite. American Express card accepted.

Friendly warm innkeeper helped me bring about a surprise celebration for my husband's birthday — a real personal touch.

Sally Fish, Chicago, Illinois

PENNSYLVANIA

PENNSYLVANIA

Reservation Services

CENTRE COUNTY (PENN STATE AREA)

Rest & Repast. Please see page 472.

PHILADELPHIA AREA

Bed & Breakfast of Philadelphia. Please see page 438.

PENNSYLVANIA DUTCH COUNTRY

Bed & Breakfast of Lancaster Co. Please see page 460.

POCONOS

Bed and Breakfast Pocono Northeast. Please see page 465.

SOUTHEAST PENNSYLVANIA

Bed & Breakfast of Southeast Pennsylvania. Please see page 456.

*

Some of the reservation services with listings in many states throughout the country, pages 26-29, have a few hosts in Pennsylvania.

PENNSYLVANIA

N

Lake Erie

NEW YORK

OHIO

PENNSYLVANIA

Scranton ⑦ ⑥

NEW JERSEY

⑧

Allentown ④

New Hope

③

⑨ Pittsburgh

Lancaster

⑤ ② ①

Philadelphia

WEST VIRGINIA   MARYLAND   DELAWARE

The numbers on this map indicate the locations for which there are detailed maps in this chapter.

PENNSYLVANIA

EASTERN PENNSYLVANIA

NEW YORK

N

NEW YORK

22

• Scranton

19

21

20

PENNSYLVANIA

NEW JERSEY

Allentown

12

14

15

New Hope

13

11

9

10

8

18

6

2

• Lancaster

7

5

1

Philadelphia

4

3

17

16

MARYLAND

DELAWARE

The numbers on this map indicate the locations of B&Bs described in detail in this chapter.

PHILADELPHIA

NEAR PHILADELPHIA

BUCKS COUNTY

SOUTHEAST PENNSYLVANIA

PENNSYLVANIA DUTCH COUNTRY

THE POCONOS

SCRANTON AREA

PHILADELPHIA

Reservation Service

Bed & Breakfast of Philadelphia

P.O. Box 680, Devon, PA 19333–0680
Phone: 215/688-1633
Established January 1981.
Open: Year round. Closed Sundays in winter.
Listings: About 100 hosts. Private homes, apartments, and a few B&B inns, all within a 25-mile radius of city limits.

Sandra Fullerton, Joanne Goins, and Carol Yarrow list B&Bs of great variety. The range includes small town houses with simple furniture and steep stairs, apartments in buildings with elevators, luxurious homes filled with antiques, farmhouses, and some students' specials. General inquiries are answered with a descriptive folder and reservation form. A directory that describes listings is $3, refundable with three-day reservation.

Breakfast: Some serve elaborately. Others allow guests to sleep until after host leaves for work and to help themselves.

Rates: $18–$35 singles, $35–$50 doubles. A few with special facilities run higher. Some hosts insist on keeping lower rates so that they can enjoy the company of interesting foreigners; some just believe in providing an economical way to travel. VISA and MasterCard accepted.

B&Bs

PHILADELPHIA

Italian Market House

Reservations: Available all months except August. Book through Bed & Breakfast of Philadelphia, page 438.

You'll probably be greeted by more than the hosts of this South Philadelphia three-storied town house. Because the street has interesting and interested neighbors, there's usually a full exchange of opinions and lifestyles. The hosts are opera lovers. (Neither are Italian. She visits Italy annually; he was brought up in Japan.) Ask them about their experiences with the Pavarotti competition. Or about the young Swiss couple who returned with their parents. Or the music lover who taped from their record collection. They've been known to take visitors folk dancing or to a local ethnic festival. It's a lively, spontaneous, warm household where entertaining is a way of life.

They know that their first B&B guests (from Wisconsin), upon seeing the questionable aspects of the neighborhoods en route to their home, reassured each other that they would switch to a hotel if necessary; but once they caught sight of the "dear little street" they changed their minds. (As with many large cities, neighborhoods here change from block to block.) A constant stream of guests has concurred.

Restrictions: Smoking only in specified rooms. Children should be at least 12.
Foreign languages spoken: Fluent Italian and Spanish and very little Japanese.
Bed: The whole third floor. Two twin beds in one room, a sitting room with a sofa that converts to two single beds, television, stereo, and a private bath.
Breakfast: Available 8:30–10. He or she cooks a (very) full breakfast, often a leisurely meal. In summer it's served in walled patio beneath fig tree.
Plus: Air conditioning. Free parking two blocks away.

440 PHILADELPHIA, PENNSYLVANIA

Rates: $30 single, $35 for two. $5 surcharge for one-night stay.

*You were the extra special ingredient that made our stay so enjoyable
. . . a wonderful job of opening your home and your hearts to us.*
                                        Nancy Collett Morrison, Phoenix, Arizona

PHILADELPHIA

Rittenhouse Square High Rise

Reservations: Available year round through Bed & Breakfast of Philadelphia, page 438.

Almost every attraction is near this high-rise built in the 1920s.
One host is a banker and part-time church organist and the other is an
art educator who grew up in old China. Both enjoy seeing visitors discover that city living can be relaxing as well as exciting. Often there's
time for a cup or glass of something and by special arrangement they
will prepare (for additional cost) lunch or dinner. Both are semiprofes-
sional genealogists and history buffs, and they have an interesting library. Their apartment, part of a house tour for two years, is furnished
in Oriental and American antiques.

In residence: A white Persian cat who has the run of the apartment
and an inordinate affection for your black clothes.
Restrictions: Minimum age for youngsters is usually 16 with parents.
No pets, please.
Bed: One room overlooking city lights has twin beds and private bath.
Other room with double sofa-bed also has a private bath.
Breakfast: Everything is available for do-it-yourself on weekdays. If
your tastes lean to the unusual, you are welcome to store foods in the
kitchen during your visit. On weekends hosts prepare a full breakfast of
just about anything and serve it in the formal dining room; or it may be
taken in the gold guest room when it is not occupied.
Plus: Air conditioners cool the apartment, but neither bedroom is sep-
arately air-conditioned. Laundry facilities available.
Rates: $35 single, $45 for two. $5 surcharge for one-night stay.

*We almost hate to recommend them too highly because we're not sure
we want to share them with the whole world. They're too special!*
                                        R.E.R. and C.H.R., Edina, Minnesota

PHILADELPHIA

Society Hill Courtyard

Reservations: Available year round through Bed & Breakfast of Philadelphia, page 438.

When a Swedish couple stayed here for a month, they became a part of the neighborhood, a quiet cul-de-sac in the midst of city bustle. The host, a special-education teacher who has lived in many states and traveled worldwide, has a casual lifestyle. Her home for the past four years has been in this new brick town house built at the far end of a courtyard in an old section of the city. Guests walk to most places. Public transportation is a half block away.

In residence: One cat.
Restrictions: No smoking, guests' pets, or children.
Bed: One room with queen-sized bed and private bath, on top of penthouse-like floor.
Breakfast: Full. Do-it-yourself. Eat in dining room.
Plus: Separate air conditioner. Living room. Skylight in bedroom, TV, roof deck.
Rates: $30 single, $40 for two. $5 surcharge for single night.

Excellent location. . . . Privacy of guest room is unique. . . . Most appealing advantage is your hostess . . . charming personality, thorough knowledge of Philadelphia. Getting to know her and staying in her house was one of the highlights of our trip out East.
Beth Teasdale, Grandville, Michigan

PHILADELPHIA

University City International

Location: Next to the University of Pennsylvania campus.
Reservations: Available year round through Bed & Breakfast of Philadelphia, page 438.

"There have been times that we have felt our home had become living history." That's not hard to believe when you hear about the discussions with and among guests: an Israeli couple, each with a different viewpoint, during the massacre in Lebanon; or the French PhDs who spoke umpteen languages ("some we have never even heard of"); or the economists from Beirut meeting with Palestinian and Israeli representatives. (After eating they mentioned that their meeting would probably benefit from the breakfast.) Or the Harrier jet pilot returning from the Falklands and his wife who flew over from England for a reunion; the man for Lima, Peru; the girl from Sidney, Australia; another from Capetown, South Africa. "We have had a number of Americans and students too."

One host teaches remedial English and computer courses to handicapped people. The other manages a dining service at the University. Together they have brought up their children in this brick Victorian located in a delightful residential pocket on a small historical block where all the houses have dark green porches and window trim. Their refurbished home never gets boring. Although all major work has been done, there's constant redoing, rearranging, and lots of work — all appreciated by guests. The eclectic furnishings include Orientals, brass, and "reclaimed junk lovingly refinished."

In residence: People who smoke. Two Siamese cats, very popular with guests.
Restrictions: No pets allowed.
Foreign language spoken: French.
Bed: Two singles, one with a brass bed, one with bamboo. Two double rooms. Shared bath.
Breakfast: Fruit, hot croissants, coffee or tea, on trays, sometimes brought to your room. Available 6:30–8:30.
Plus: Use of telescope with five-foot cylinder and six-inch mirror. (Mounted on roof. Discovered by one host in a thrift shop, brought home by her sons, and together they made it work.) Double rooms have air conditioning. Laundry facilities. Kitchen privileges for those with extended stays.
Rates: $25 singles, $30 doubles, $15 student. Added cot in room, $8. $5 surcharge for single-night stay.

NEAR PHILADELPHIA

Reservation Service

Bed & Breakfast of Philadelphia

This service has hosts in communities served by bus and commuter railroad including Lansdowne, Havertown, Upper Darby, and Media; and in the "Main Line" locations of Ardmore, Gladwyne; Rosemont, Merion, Radnor, Wayne, Devon, Berwyn, and Malvern. To the west toward Pennsylvania Dutch country and near Brandywine Battlefield, Winterthur, and Longwood Gardens there are hosts in Chadds Ford, Wilmington (Delaware), and West Chester. Please see page 438. To the north, hosts are in Pottstown, Phoenixville, and Valley Forge. To the northwest, Jarrettown and Flourtown are Montgomery County representatives. For Bucks County, see page 450.

B&Bs

CHESTNUT HILL

Chestnut Hill Serenity

Location: A quiet residential neighborhood northwest of city, near shops and restaurants. Half a block to commuter railroad (30-minute ride to center city).

Reservations: Accepted year round except July and most holidays. Book through Bed & Breakfast of Philadelphia, page 438.

"Our house was bought by a girl's private school in 1950 and converted to classrooms for 20 years. We bought it in 1970 and converted it back to a house. My husband did some of the work. I painted the entire house. We both love remodeling and have done three houses so far. We enjoyed traveling on B&B in England and love meeting new people. Now that our four children are grown we like making good use of a house that is too big for us." And so it is that they are now sharing their colonial-style home of Chestnut Hill fieldstone, with its spacious center hall, winding spindled staircase, and traditional furnishings.

Restrictions: No pets please. Nonsmokers preferred.
Bed: Two rooms, each with two twin beds. Shared guest bath.
Breakfast: A full meal served, usually between 8 and 9:30, in the dining room.
Plus: Possible use of patio in summer, study in winter.
Rates: $30 single, $40 for two. $5 surcharge for single night.

A haven after a long day of shopping and sightseeing.
K. Westmoreland, Anaheim, California

Gracious home . . . warm hospitality . . . beyond expectation.
M. J. Breedlove, Schenectady, New York

DEVON

Devon Manor House

Location: Three blocks from 35-minute train ride to city. Three blocks from Devon Horse Show.
Reservations: Available year round through Bed & Breakfast of Philadelphia, page 438.

Now it's a busy household where everyone or no one may be around. But a Philadelphia family used to come here in a horse and buggy each summer to play lawn tennis, walk through the formal gardens, and sip tea on the veranda.

In the four years since the hosts became the third owners of the 1890 Greek Revival house, there have been enough changes to fascinate many house-tour-goers and now B&B guests. The huge fireplaced center hall, for instance, has been made into a formal dining room.

The host has been with the same company, in various locations, for 25 years. The hostess, a former airline stewardess, restored their previous seven-year residence, a historic house in Chicago. She is a sportswoman, does all kinds of stitchery (needlepoint is in the guest rooms), is involved in community activities, and has plenty of printed and first-hand information on the area.

In residence: People who smoke. Two teenage sons and a seven-year-old daughter. Golden retriever and Siamese cat are both confined to kitchen area of house. Fifty goldfish live in an outside fountain and survive under the ice in winter.
Restrictions: No pets please.
Bed: On the third floor away from family living area. One large room with three spool beds: double, youth, and crib, all with handmade coverlets. The other room has two twin beds with white wicker furniture and flower-sprigged fabric on walls and beds. Private bath on the same floor.
Breakfast: Really a brunch. Served at guests' convenience by roaring fireplace in dining room in winter, on the wraparound veranda under century trumpetvine in summer. Hosts often join guests.
Plus: Jacuzzi and swimming pool. Kitchen privileges. Laundry facilities.
Rates: $35 single, $45 for two, youth bed $10, crib $5. $4 surcharge for one-night stay.

A pure delight . . . enjoyed the home, the antiques, the interesting and accomplished host and hostess . . . a professional decorator and she might well be a professional gourmet chef.

Mrs. Donald R. (Sally) Turley, Clearfield, Pennsylvania

KENNETT SQUARE

Mrs. K's B&B

404 Ridge Avenue, Kennett Square, PA 19348
Phone: 215/444-5559
Location: Three miles from Longwood Gardens, six miles from Winterthur, eight miles from Brandywine River Museum, 30 from Philadel-

phia, 30 from Lancaster, 15 from Wilmington, Delaware.
Open: Year round.

"My home is on a quiet residential street and is surrounded by trees and shrubbery. The only antique is me!"

Mrs. K. has worn the hats of a secretary, wife, mother, and now word-processor operator. Her home has accommodated students, boarders, and travelers through the years, and she is now in her third year of B&B hosting.

Restrictions: Nonsmokers preferred "but will gladly accept those who have this bad habit." No pets please. Children out of diapers are welcome.
Bed: Three rooms. One room with two twin beds, one with a double. One sleep sofa also available. Shared bath.
Breakfast: Served by 7:30 weekdays; help yourself if later. Traditional foods. Available anytime on weekends; extras such as muffins then.
Plus: Air conditioning. Two screened porches. Large backyard.
Rates: $20 single, $35 for two twin beds, $30 for double.

It's not the Ritz, but it's pleasant, homey, and pin-clean. What makes Mrs. K's worth the visit is Mrs. K herself. She is quite a character — welcoming, warm-hearted, chatty, cheerful — the perfect hostess when you are feeling a bit frazzled after a day of driving. After five minutes you feel more like an old friend than a paying guest.

Sean and Susan Morrison, Hingham, Massachusetts

LANSDOWNE

Lansdowne International

Location: A mile and a half west of city limits. Within 1½ blocks of 45-minute public transportation ride to center city. Five miles to University of Pennsylvania, 7½ miles from City Hall.
Reservations: Accepted year round through Bed & Breakfast of Philadelphia, page 438.

When the family moved to this area five years ago, they took up residence in this 1922 stone house, built as a copy of an 18th-century colonial home. It has 18th- and 19th-century English furnishings, Oriental rugs, a grand piano, a library, and a flexible host family that enjoys sharing both their home and their love of their adopted city. The constant stream of guests rave about the hospitality, helpfulness, and suggestions and directions for sightseeing and restaurants. "It seems to take people about 10 minutes and they are at home. Sometimes their kids sleep up with our kids, play ball, go to the pool — as if they have always known each other."

In residence: One who smokes. Three sons, ages 11–15. One Persian cat.
Restrictions: No smoking in bedroom.
Foreign language spoken: German.
Bed: One double tester bed with private bath. Children's room with twin beds on third floor. Crib available.
Breakfast: Whatever, whenever, cooked by whomever. Full range of possibilities including bacon and eggs, hot or cold cereal, scrapple. Served in breakfast area of kitchen.
Plus: Possible evening tours of historic sites. Babysitting. Free parking.
Rates: $18 single, $25 for two, $8 for cots. Family rates available. $5 surcharge for one-night stay.

We wished we had known about this place sooner.

G.B., Brooklyn, New York

We were met at the station and found the hospitality first class.

The Gray family, York, England

RADNOR

Radnor Charm

Location: WNW suburb. Ten-minute walk to RR station, 25-minute commuter ride to city. Forty minutes from airport.
Reservations: Available year round except August and early fall weekends through Bed & Breakfast of Philadelphia, page 438.

They really care about making people feel comfortable and at home in this stately 111-year-old Victorian, originally a frame house, now stucco. They've been here eight years and in the last five have restored it. Their children are grown; at times they've offered emergency shelter to foster children; and now B&B guests — conventiongoers, house-hunters, and tourists — fill part of the "rattling empty" house that is furnished with American primitive antiques. The warmhearted hosts lead busy lives (he is an investment counselor and she's a nursery-school teacher and singer) but they find that getting to know people is a big part of the B&B fun.

Recent guests wrote that they were treated "like royalty."

In residence: One "cockapoo" dog.
Restrictions: No smoking or drinking in the house. No guests' pets.
Bed: Two beautiful double-bedded rooms "up in the trees" with fire-places and private baths. Third floor has two rooms, one with twin beds, one with single. Shared bath. Portacrib available.
Breakfast: Available at guests' convenience (promptly!) at arranged time. Bountiful and made on old-time commercial cast-iron stove. Pennsylvania Dutch crumb cake featured. Served in breakfast room just off the kitchen, by window in living room, or on screened porch.
Plus: Private TV and second-floor screened porch. Even though house is on a rather busy road, it's surrounded by woods on three sides and there are some country roads to walk on.
Rates: $25 single, $30 doubles. $5 surcharge for one-night stay.

WEST CHESTER

West Chester, Circa 1840

Location: One and one-half miles from Philadelphia limits near Long-wood Gardens, Winterthur, Brandywine River Museum (Wyeths), and Brandywine Battlefield.
Reservations: Available year round through Bed & Breakfast of Phila-delphia, page 438.

This retired host (40 years with the same corporation) says that he tries to fill the shoes of a European concierge in his beautiful home surrounded by lovely grounds with big old trees. He's a flower and vege-table gardener, and a golfer, and collects "old anything." Some time during a visit guests' curiosity is satisfied with a walk through the mansard-roofed Victorian that is furnished with collectibles and some antiques.

In residence: One who smokes.
Restrictions: No pets please. Children, any age, welcome.

Bed: Three rooms. Two with double beds and one with two twin beds. All share one bath. Crib available.

Breakfast: Likely to be juice, grapefruit, bacon and eggs, scrapple — cooked by host or by guests who wish to. Served anytime in dining room furnished with early American collectibles.

Plus: Swimming pool and patio in country setting. Fireplace in winter. Kitchen and laundry privileges. Baby-sitting, if prearranged. Free parking. Public transportation nearby.

Rates: $25 single, $35 for two. $5 surcharge for one-night stay.

The consummate host.   D.B., New York, New York

BUCKS COUNTY

Reservation Services

Bed & Breakfast of Philadelphia

This service has hosts in Collegeville, Warrington, Doylestown, New Hope, Churchville, and Huntingdon Valley. Please see page 438.

Town and Country Bed and Breakfast

This service has hosts in Doylestown, Lahaska, New Hope, Upper Black Eddy, and Washington Crossings. Please see page 410.

B&Bs

COLLEGEVILLE

Collegeville Digs

Location: Twenty minutes NW of Philadelphia near college town, historic spots, country auction; 20 minutes to Spring Mountain, one hour to Poconos.

Reservations: Available year round through Bed & Breakfast of Philadelphia, page 438.

The hostess and her husband, a building contractor, came to the

United States from England in 1958. As B&B hosts here they have the reputation of outdoing the English. You may be offered tea or wine upon arrival or in the evening, and in the morning hot tea is at your door. Their stone ranch-style home, built by them 20 years ago, has exotic indoor and outdoor plants that illustrate her interest and success in gardening.

In residence: One who smokes. Two dogs.
Restrictions: No guests' pets. Smoking only in living and dining rooms. Children are welcome.
Bed: One double-bedded room, private bath, private entrance.
Breakfast: Different English breakfasts. The first morning's may be sausage, poached eggs, tomato, and English muffins with homemade marmalade. Served in dining room filled with greenery overlooking garden pool.
Plus: Use of lovely patio and pool in summer.
Rates: $18 single, $25 for two. $5 surcharge for single night.

DOYLESTOWN

Bucks County Farmhouse

Location: Seven miles from Doylestown.
Reservations: Available all months except fall. Book through Bed & Breakfast of Philadelphia, page 438.

Hosting — mostly for international visitors — has been their tradition for years, so for this family, B&B is a natural. The setting for their warm reception is on a rolling country road; an 1819 white stone farmhouse that has beamed ceilings, antique furnishings, and five fireplaces. Because this has been their residence for 22 years and his family has been in the area since 1723, they are well familiar with the local history, culture, and crafts and can suggest almost anything including historic sites, museums, restaurants, and even places to go canoeing and tubing on the Delaware River. When he's not teaching industrial arts or sculpting wood, and when she's not substitute-teaching or sewing or reading or gardening, they frequently spend time (together with their son) buying, refinishing, and selling primitive furniture.

In residence: People who smoke. Teenage son. Himalayan grey cat.
Restrictions: A cat or small dog would be allowed.

Foreign languages spoken: Some German, Spanish, and French.
Bed: One double room. Hide-a-bed for children in adjacent room. Shared family bath.
Breakfast: Full. Available between 7 and 9:30. Menu may include homemade scrapple, shoofly pie, or waffles from a 50-year-old waffle iron. Guests sit in the old Windsor chairs at the trestle table set with lovely silver and china.
Plus: Cozy living room, five acres for walking or cross-country skiing, badminton, croquet.
Rates: $23 single, $32 for two. $8 per child. $5 surcharge for single night.

Cozy, warm, full of life. They even helped us purchase our first auction pieces.   Tom and Patti Townsend, Collingswood, New Jersey

HOLICONG

Barley Sheaf Farm

Route 202, Holicong, PA 18928
Phone: 215/794-5104
Location: About an hour out of Philadelphia; ten minutes from New Hope.
Hosts: Ann and Don Mills
Open: March until the week before Christmas. Two-night minimum reservation on weekends; three nights on holiday weekends.

The family had three teenagers when they first moved into the former home of noted playwright and drama critic George S. Kaufman. In 1979, after traveling the B&B way in England, the Millses opened their own farm to travelers. Don is still president of a New Jersey-based perfume company. The children, all in their early 20s, are now home only in the summer.

The gracious 1740 stone house, a designated national historic site, offers a peaceful, elegant, warm ambiance. Throughout, antiques are accompanied by personal touches. There is some help to keep things going, but it's definitely the personalized home-turned-inn. Ann and Don try out new recipes before introducing them to guests. Ann is responsible for the decor, the homemade jams and bakery, and the sumptuous breakfasts. Don cohosts on weekends, is justly proud of his herb garden, and enjoys many tasks, including furniture refinishing.

The sheep, about 30 at last count, announce their presence, and early spring guests are around to see the lambs. You're welcome to watch the sheep-shearing if you happen to be there when the busy itinerant shearer arrives. Pigs, chickens, and (boarded) horses add to the pastoral scene.

In residence: In addition to the farm animals, they have friendly outside dogs, Ricky and Rusty. Missy is their indoor dog, and the cat is Winston.

Restrictions: No pets please. Minimum age for children is eight.

Foreign language spoken: Ann speaks French.

Bed: Six rooms in main house. Private baths for one double-bedded room, one fireplaced double-bedded suite overlooking the pool, and one room with queen-size bed. Shared bath for room with ¾-size bed, room with mahogany double sleigh bed, and one room with twin beds. Cottage has three double rooms with private baths.

Breakfast: Full farm breakfast possibilities include apple crêpes, "Barley Sheaf Soufflé," sausage, honey, breads, and the freshest of eggs. Served on sun porch (wood stove used in winter) overlooking lawns and animals.

Plus: Pool. It's okay just to stay and relax right here.

Rates: The single rate, 20 percent less than double rate, is unavailable on weekends and holidays. Doubles $35–$55. Suite is $70. Additional cots in room $15.

NEW HOPE

Pineapple Hill

River Road, RD 2, New Hope, PA 18938
Phone: 215/862-9608
Hosts: Mary and Stephen Darlington
Open: Year round.

Teenage antique collectors grew up to be a banker (because there weren't any jobs in archaeology) and a personnel director (Stephen still is). Along the way they restored an old house and had the idea that they'd like someday to have a bigger one for bed and breakfast. So here are the Darlingtons, in their early thirties, with two-year-old son Jesse, in a farmhouse that is filled with their treasures. They opened it as a B&B in 1981. Originally built in 1800 with 18-inch stone walls, the house has had numerous additions that ramble all the way up to the Victorian attic. Restored floors and decorated rooms add to the charm. Guests appreciate the antique quilts, Pennsylvania primitives, Victoriana, early colonial architecture — and the hosts. And in her new career Mary enjoys her guests, motherhood, and working hard for herself. ("This is the best life to live!") In the relaxed environment Mary has been known to give impromptu lessons in stenciling, a recently acquired technique that she used to decorate walls, a quilt, and chests.

In residence: Tokay, "Hungarian sheepdog who loves having the attention she deserves."
Restrictions: No guests' pets. Smoking allowed, but please ask how others feel about it.
Foreign language spoken: A little German.
Bed: Four double-bedded rooms. One with a spool bed and one with a brass bed on the second floor. Shared bath. Two cozy rooms with Victorian and country furnishings on third; shared bath. Trundle bed. Crib.
Breakfast: Continental with homemade breads, available 8:30–10.
Plus: Five acres. Swimming pool surrounded by stone walls of the former barn. Late-afternoon tea with goodies around the fireplace in dining-room/parlor. Sherry and chocolates at turn-in time.
Rates: $45 per room. $6 for trundle or crib.

NEW HOPE

Wedgwood Inn

111 West Bridge Street, New Hope, PA 18938
Phone: 215/862-2570
Location: Two blocks from the heart of New Hope (sometimes called a tourist mecca).
Hosts: Nadine Silnutzer and Carl Glassman
Open: Year round.

Dinie and Carl have lived in the area for seven years, but now at the age of 30 they are living their "dream come true." He's a researcher at a social-policy think tank, and (until Wedgwood became their home in 1982) she worked in gerontology. Hosting allows them to combine some of their current interests: travel, historic preservation, antique collecting, and people.

They can direct you to the wide variety of cultural and recreational opportunities of Bucks County. An interesting touch is the guests' comments that accompany the collection of sample menus of nearby restaurants.

The 1870 house, eligible for entry on the National Register of Historic Places, has been a guest house for 30 years. The Glassmans have renovated it from top to bottom. Period furnishings, original cubist and abstract art work by Dinie's great aunt, and fresh flowers are in each room. Craftspeople and other artists are represented in rotating exhibits. On display in the sitting room is a still-growing collection of Wedgwood pottery. Outside there's a wraparound porch and a gazebo.

Bed: Eight rooms. One single and one triple with shared bath. Six doubles, three with private bath. There are several antique brass beds and one lace-canopied four-poster.
Breakfast: Contintental includes freshly squeezed juice, fresh fruit salad, and home-baked goods. Available 8–10 in breakfast room, or in bay window of the parlor.
Plus: Homemade amaretto, chocolate mints, and turned-down beds in the evening.
Rates: $40 single, $45–$60 doubles, $60 triple. Ten percent discount weekdays. Cots $10. Weekly rates available.

SOUTHEAST PENNSYLVANIA

Reservation Service

Bed & Breakfast of Southeast Pennsylvania

Box 278, RD1, Barto, PA 19504
Phone: 215/845-3526.
Established October 1982
Open: Year round.
Listings: About 25 places in the region between Easton and Reading, including homes, apartments, and a small country inn. Directory: $1. Includes urban and rural sites and the communities of Bethlehem, Allentown, Quakertown, and Boyertown.
Reservations: Some hosts have a two-day minimum.
Breakfast: May be continental or full depending on host.

Joyce Stevenson's service offers hosts in what is considered a relatively unexplored area. Attractions include historic sites, auctions, antiques, flea markets, summer ethnic festivals, and winter skiing. Not far from Pennsylvania Dutch country, Winterthur, Longwood Gardens, and Brandywine River Museum. Near Hawk Mountain.
Rates: Singles $18–$20, doubles $35–$60. Cots for children $5.

B&Bs

ALLENTOWN

Large Tudor

Location: Two miles from center city. One block from parks with walking, jogging, and duck-feeding possibilities.
Reservations: Available year round through Bed & Breakfast of Southeast Pennyslvania, page 456. Please check in by 10 p.m. and out by 11 a.m.

The home reflects the extensive traveling experiences of this English couple. Their interests run from tennis to refurbishing grand pianos, from the arts to macrobiotics. In the seven years that they've been in their large stone English-country-style residence, they've added their own decorating touches including stained glass windows done by the hostess in all the bathrooms.

In residence: One small very friendly long-haired Tibetan terrier.
Restrictions: No pets. No smoking. Children should be school age.
Bed: Three twin-bedded rooms. Two share a guest bath. One on ground floor with private bath has a resident Paddington Bear and large picture window.
Breakfast: Full. Cooked. Regular or macrobiotic menu available 7–9:30. Announced with sounding of 1840 Indian gong. Served in dining room or by poolside.
Plus: Recreation room with table tennis, pool table. Patio and swimming pool. Laundry facilities.
Rates: $25 single, $40 for two. $65 for family of four. Cots $10.

BERNVILLE

Sunday's Mill Farm

Location: On Tulpehocken Creek, 15 minutes from Appalachian Trail, about ten miles to Reading Outlet Center, an hour to Amish country. Four miles from Bernville and Womelsdorf.
Reservations: Available year round through Bed & Breakfast of Southeast Pennsylvania, page 456.

When it came time to "retire" from California city (Los Angeles) life, this realtor and interior decorator found "the house of their dreams," this 1850s brick farmhouse. The couple had been B&B guests on both coasts and knew they wanted to become hosts.

The hostess makes new quilts and restores old ones. She is compiling information for state records about all the old homes in the county. Her husband runs a small cattle operation and farm. They are both very enthusiastic about all the area has to offer.

In residence: Black Labrador named Seren, short for Serendipity.
Restrictions: Children should be at least ten. No pets, please.
Bed: Two guest rooms. One with queen-sized bed and private half bath. One with double bed. Full bath shared by guests and hosts; "no problem."
Breakfast: Served at pre-set time with guests "as we do enjoy auctions on Saturdays" in dining room, or in winter by kitchen fireplace. Juice, bacon or sausage, and scrambled eggs.
Plus: Air conditioning. Creek for canoeing (rentals five miles away). Pond fishing. "Now and then" scrapbook about mill and farm. Tour of mill that still has most parts intact.
Rates: $32 or $35 single. $40 for two in double room, $45 in queen.

BETHLEHEM

The Gaslamp Gasthaus

Location: On main street in historic section. Near shops, restaurants, museums — everything!
Reservations: Available year round through Bed & Breakfast of Southeast Pennsylvania, page 456.

The name refers to the ever-burning gaslamp outside the front door and also reflects the Pennsylvania Dutch heritage of this area. The hosts, a university professor and his wife, a health care consultant, came here from Ontario two years ago. When they bought this high-ceilinged 1851 town house a year ago, they felt it "just said B&B, a place to share our enthusiasm for this city."

Foreign language spoken: Some French.
Bed: One main guest room with double bed and private bath. First floor room with private bath has a double sofa bed. Extra cots available.
Breakfast: 7–9. Full English meal including homemade muffins.
Plus: Air conditioning. Garden. Laundry facilities.
Rates: $35 single, $35 double.

FLEETWOOD

The Old Forge

Reservations: Available year round through Bed & Breakfast of Southeast Pennsylvania, page 456. Minimum stay is two consecutive days. Please check in by 8 p.m. and out by 11 a.m.

The hostess, an artist originally from Holland, has had several interesting careers. Now she's a watercolorist, works in art therapy, and is a gracious B&B hostess. For a while she designed chocolates for one of the finer manufacturers. Since coming from Michigan eight years ago and discovering the attributes of this area, she enjoys sharing what she considers the best-kept (views and shopping) secrets of Pennsylvania. Home is a converted stone forge with addition, small but cozy. Other old farm buildings that guests sometimes explore are the barn and her art studio. Across the road is the 1795 manor house and a big pond.

In residence: One college-age daughter. One magnificent cat. A medium-sized sheepdog-terrier. One rooster who lives outdoors.
Restrictions: No children, pets, smoking.
Foreign languages spoken: Dutch, some French and German.
Bed: One double-bedded room with private balcony and bath.
Breakfast: Full. Specialty is cream-cheese-with-chives omelet. Available 8–9 and served in front of picture window with a view.
Plus: Ten acres with hiking possibilities.
Rates: $27 single, $30 for two.

PENNSYLVANIA DUTCH COUNTRY

Reservation Service

Bed & Breakfast of Lancaster Co.

Box 215, Elm, PA 17521
Phone: 717/627-1890
Listings: Twenty. Most are within 15 miles of Lancaster city. Others are in York county and include Gettysburg, and in Dauphin county, including Hershey.

Carol Ann Patton lists hosts who live on Mennonite farms in old stone houses with Indian doors and in quaint inns too. Some homes are luxurious, and many are historic.
Rates: Singles $20–$38, doubles $30–$89.

B&Bs

AIRVILLE

Spring House

Muddy Creek Forks, Airville, PA 17302
Phone: 717/927-6906
Location: Over a running spring in a tiny (population: 17) pre-Revolutionary village, very rural and scenic, off the beaten track (detailed directions are useful), five miles from shops, 30 minutes from York, 45 minutes from Lancaster.
Open: March–December. Two-night minimum stay for weekends. Check in after 5 p.m. and by 9 p.m.; check out by 11 a.m.

Ray Constance Hearne has observed that "sometimes guests are startled by the life so different from their city lives, and are quiet; suddenly a connection is made with their own past and they feel at home." Ray, a dairy-farm girl who became a York County historic preservationist, turned B&B host after a 3½-month backpacking trip in England. B&B experiences there introduced a way to be home more, something she was ready for after ten years of singlehandedly restoring every inch of this 18th-century stone house to its "simple strong character." Since the spring of 1981 visitors have asked lots of questions about the plastered, whitewashed and stenciled walls, floor cloth, country antiques, oriental rugs, pottery (some done by hostess and fired in a kiln she made while a student at Antioch College), paintings (some her own) of local scenes, and herb garden too. She lives here "in the way I grew up — with wood heat, coal stoves, unheated bedrooms, and good pure food and water."

In residence: Hadrian, a setter-like dog that gives tours. Siamese cats are Chirk, Rutabaga, and Tachyon.
Restrictions: No smoking and no pets in the house. Children of any age welcome.
Foreign language spoken: Spanish.
Bed: Three double bedrooms, one with stove, with shared bath. One room has an adjoining room for a child (or, if unoccupied, for one of the

house cats). Electric blankets, down puffs, and flannel sheets in use in winter.

Breakfast: Varies with season and mood. All made with locally produced ingredients. Whole wheat flour organically grown and ground in wonderful-smelling stone and brick mill that has been in the same family for three generations. Jams and jellies (Ray makes her own pectin from green apples), and syrups from strawberries, raspberries, Concord grapes, and beach plums she picked and preserved. Maybe wineberries on buttered pancakes with honey from her own bees or Pennsylvania maple syrup. Or a frittata with sauteed zucchini and cheese; scrapple; or sausage or home-cured ham. Everyone eats together some time before 9 at an hour arranged the evening before. Served on porch, weather permitting, or in dining room.

Plus: Porch swing, piano, bicycle, popcorn at just the right time, fresh flowers in the rooms, wine from a local (three miles away) winery, trout-stocked Muddy Creek, swimming and canoeing possibilities, unused Ma and Pa Railroad beds for hiking, unpaved road in town along creek through farmlands and orchards.

Rates: $35 for one, $50 for two. Extra room is $6 for under age 12, $10 over.

Luxury lovers stay away. This is "country" as it has always been. May Spring House long prosper.   A. W. Leech, Chapel Hill, North Carolina

ATGLEN

The Farmhouse

Location: One mile off Route 372 on a farm with woods and stream. Ten miles from Intercourse.

Reservations: Available year round through New Age Travel's "International Spareroom," page 36.

Here's an opportunity to stay on a Mennonite farm, to learn firsthand about local customs and the language, and to be away from some of the touristy sections of Pennsylvania Dutch country. You are given a hearty welcome by the couple who have gradually — over 45 years — renovated their 1878 farmhouse. The bunkhouse, originally a woodshed and garage, has been paneled and insulated.

The host, semiretired now, "just" does crop farming — corn, hay, wheat, and vegetables; but guests may watch cow milking and see the animals on a neighboring farm. The exuberant hostess loves to cook. "And we have a grand time sitting around in the evening with people who come from all over. Quite a few are from Germany. Returnees seem to be families with young children and older people. Teenagers find it a little too quiet here." Their own grandchildren range in age from 4 to 20; three live just a mile up the road.

In residence: Two dogs. One person who smokes.
Foreign language spoken: Pennsylvania Dutch.
Bed: Two rooms in farmhouse, one with twin beds, one with a double. Shared bath. Bunkhouse, available for one party, has a living room, a room with two double beds, and a bath.
Breakfast: Full. Could include French toast, hot cakes, bacon and eggs. Available 7–10:30.
Plus: Berry picking in season. Snacks, maybe chocolate cake, a specialty at bedtime. Laundry facilities available. B&B guests have the option of country-style cooked dinner, $10.50 per person.
Rate: $22 per person.

WILLOW STREET VILLAGE

Pennsylvania Dutch Bed & Breakfast Host #1

Location: Four houses from the main road down a wide lane. Ten minutes from downtown Lancaster.
Reservations: Available year round through Pennsylvania Dutch Bed & Breakfast, page 460. Maximum stay: three days.

Are you interested in history, scenery, culture, or just "something to do?" Enthusiasm reigns here. The hosts love the area and will tell you about the importance of Lancaster in the early move westward; great local theater; Mennonite or Amish practices; farmers' markets; and good reasonably priced restaurants too. Their interests range from alternative energy methods to ham radio. Until a few months ago the family lived in a century-old house in the historic district of Lancaster. Now they are in a modern ranch with an in-ground pool. Art objects from the Near East, Africa, Japan, and the Caribbean remind them of previous homes. The hostess was an early education teacher in Saudi Arabia, in Kenya, and in her native Lancaster, Pennsylvania. He was a manufacturer in Puerto Rico and now specializes in health insurance for the aging.

In residence: Two boys, ages four and seven. And "the brightest, muttiest poodle Dad has ever seen."
Restrictions: No smoking allowed. No pets in the house. ("Children? We love them!")
Foreign languages spoken: Fluent Spanish, a little French, some Swahili and Arabic.
Bed: Four rooms. One single, one with twin beds, one with double bed, and one huge family room. Shared bath. Cots available.
Breakfast: Usually continental. Served near the sliding doors that lead to the pool and pine grove beyond.
Plus: Air conditioning. Use of pool (fenced with oaken boards from one-family sawmill located nearby). Family room has a private entrance. Kitchen privileges. Laundry facilities. Excellent baby-sitters.
Rates: $22–$34 single, $32–$44 for two, $44 for family room.

THE POCONOS

Reservation Service

Bed & Breakfast Pocono Northeast

P.O. Box 115, Bear Creek, PA 18602
Phone: 717/472-3145 (live at least 9 a.m.–12 noon. Closed Tuesdays)
Established January 1983.
Open: Year round.
Listings: About 25 hosts are located in the Poconos. The area covered is essentially a square that starts west on the New York state border in Sayre, goes east and south along New York state to Port Jervis, south to Bangor — just below Stroudsburg, east to Sunbury, and north to Sayre.

Patricia Mack and Ann Magagna, long-time residents here, thought they were going to open an antique business: one of them traveled to Philadelphia on B&B and returned with the notion that her home region needed a B&B service. The antique business never opened, but their B&B reservation service is very active in both the academic communities and the vacation areas.
Rates: Single $12–$25, doubles $22–$45. $5 surcharge for one-night stay.

B&Bs

BENTON

The Mill House

Location: On a paved country road in a valley surrounded by hills. On wooded property, but the house is on the edge of a field. Close to state park; 26 miles from Eagles Mere, a Swiss-like resort town — with tobogganing — in the mountains; an hour southwest of Wilkes-Barre; an hour northeast of Bucknell University.
Reservations: Available year round through Bed and Breakfast Pocono Northeast, page 465. On alternate weekends April through October.

A getaway — in a unique home fashioned from an honest-to-goodness pigsty by an artist who fled the city for suburbia before living and working in a town hall before coming to this rural area about 15 years ago. His works — pastels, oils, and watercolors — are in galleries and in this country home, his own conversion. He installed a skylight; used boxcar siding — 2½ inches thick — as flooring; and made trim, closet doors, and kitchen cabinets from barnwood. A seven-foot piano is in the dining/living area. His (private) studio is located in a grist mill. For a living he draws cartoons.

His wife is now in the antique business, specializing in primitives and jewelry, but her career experiences are diverse. She grew up in several large cities throughout the country, attended art schools, has owned and managed an art gallery, and was an arts and crafts instructor in an occupational-therapy program at a psychiatric hospital. She has also been a food consultant and stylist in New York, and a caterer. Benton has been her home for 10 years except for a sabbatical spent in the Peace Corps in the Caribbean, where she managed an arts and crafts coop until Hurricane David destroyed the coop and much of the island of Dominica.

A corncrib on the property serves as new living-quarters-in-process, their residence when B&B guests take over the finished home.

Foreign language spoken: Some Spanish.
Bed: One double bed in a loft. Private bath. Double hide-a-bed also available in living room.

Breakfast: At least continental. Announced on menu done in calligraphy. Cooked and served by hostess.
Plus: Use of entire cottage. Patio. Living where blinds are not necessary, except to reduce heat in summer. Creek with trout right here. Thirteen acres for hiking, berry picking. Cross-country skiing and snowmobiling. Advice on area activities that include dogsled races (in February), fairs, flea markets, and antiquing.
Rates: $35 per night for loft. $5 surcharge for one-night stay.

CANADENSIS

Nearbrook

RD 1, Box 630, Canadensis, PA 18325
Phone: 717/595-3152
Location: Heart of the Poconos. On a state road between Interstates 80 and 84.
Hosts: Barbie and Dick Robinson
Open: Year round. Minimum stay: two nights preferred.

The property has woods, a stream, and several lovely rock gardens. Some guests relax in the tranquil atmosphere here; others sightsee, hike, golf, canoe, ski, go to theater — and more.

"Our boys are all grown, leaving time for crafts, rock gardens, and teaching art classes." The Robinsons, former Philadelphia teachers, have been hosting for ten years. They have a homemade map that, according to interests, is custom marked for each guest.

Restrictions: No smokers please.
Bed: Five rooms. Two singles, two doubles, one large room with twin beds; shared baths. Small sink in every room. (In the 1930s and '40s when the house was used as the overflow for a well-known Pocono resort, The Pinehurst, it was nicknamed "Seven Sinks.")
Breakfast: Full and hearty. Menu decided night before. Dick cooks and Barbie serves and frequently "sooner or later" they join guests who are not in a hurry. Dining room used in winter. In summer you eat on a long porch that is on treetop level and overlooks one of the rock gardens.
Plus: Croquet, toboggan, trunk full of games.
Rates: $15 single, $25 double, $30 twin beds. Weekly rates available.

Fond memories of the simplicity, homey atmosphere, the friendliness and charming ways of the hosts.   Ann Berman, Englewood, Florida

LaAnna

LaAnna Guest House

RD 2, Box 1051, Cresco, PA 18326
Phone: 717/676-4225
Location: In the town of LaAnna between Cresco and Newfoundland on Route 191, a two-lane road that runs through the Poconos.
Hosts: Kay and Julie Swingle
Open: Year round.

Kay Swingle acquired the family homestead in 1974, just a hundred years after her grandfather built it as a wedding gift for his bride. It had left the family and remained a private home until real-estate salesperson Kay, having traveled B&B in Europe, decided to welcome guests in the rural setting. On a paved road in a wooded area off the beaten path is this informally run place that repeaters treat like home. The trout-stocked pond is used for skating; cross-country skiers track down a country road; downhill skiers go to Camelback or Buck Hill. Summer visitors swim (a short drive), hike, and visit in the Poconos.

Bed: Two twins and a single in the Blue Room. One double and one twin in the Green Room. The Red Room and Gold Room each have a double bed. All are very large rooms furnished with Empire and Victorian antiques. Two shared baths. Crib available.
Breakfast: Continental available 8–12 a.m. served in dining room by Kay or daughter Julie.
Plus: Wonderful mountain views at top of hill about 500 yards behind the house. Waterfalls on the property of Holley Ross Pottery, just across the road. Near shops and restaurants. Television lounge available in guest house.
Rate: $10 per person.

SCRANTON AREA

B&Bs

TUNKHANNOCK

Anderson Acres

RD 1, Box 206-4, Tunkhannock, PA 18657
Phone: 717/836-5228
Location: Twenty-five miles from Scranton, half hour from Route 81, four miles from Tunkhannock center.
Hosts: John and Doris Anderson
Open: March–November.

Most guests during the first year of B&B at this modernized farmhouse seemed to be "just passing through," but you are welcome to tour the huge old barn built in the 1850s and to see the herd of Herefords, the pigs and geese, and the chicken house too. Or how about paddling a canoe on a lake with mountain vistas?

Since the family moved here from Long Island seven years ago, John, a building contractor, has specialized in renovating old barns. Even with the farm and gardening, the Andersons find time for nearby archery, hunting, fishing, and skiing.

In residence: People who smoke. Two cats.
Restrictions: No pets allowed. Children should be at least five.
Bed: Two rooms, one double and one with two twin beds. Shared bath.
Breakfast: Continental. There's an extra charge for full American fare. Doris is cook, waitress, and company for you.
Plus: Use of canoe and 50 acres of fields and woods for hiking.
Rates: $20 single, $25 for two. No credit cards accepted.

CENTRAL AND
WESTERN PENNSYLVANIA

Lake Erie

N

NEW YORK

4

OHIO

PENNSYLVANIA

Centre County

1 **3**

State College

2

● Pittsburgh

WEST VIRGINIA   **MARYLAND**

The numbers on this map indicate the locations of B&Bs described in detail in this chapter.

CENTRE COUNTY (PENN STATE AREA)

WESTERN PENNSYLVANIA

CENTRE COUNTY
(PENN STATE AREA)

Reservation Service

Rest & Repast Bed & Breakfast Service

P.O. Box 126, Pine Grove Mills, PA 16868
Phone: 814/238-1484
Established: August 1982.
Listings: About 15 homes and a few inns.
Reservations: Most hosts require advance arrangements. Minimum stay: two nights for Homecoming Weekend in fall and Arts Festival in July.
Breakfast: About two-thirds serve continental; others serve full.

Although Linda C. Feltman and Brent R. Peters welcome hosts with contemporary homes, they are actively recruiting those that are historic and in beautiful neighborhoods. Because of the Alleghenies, many homes have mountain views. Rural communities with hosts include Howard, Old Fort, Potters Mills, Spring Mills, and Tusseyville. Suburban communities include Bellefonte, Boalsburg, Centre Hall, Houserville, Lemont, and State College.

Rates: Singles $20–$27, doubles $28–$37. $40 for football weekends.

B&Bs

CENTRE HALL

Thunder Hill

Location: Fifteen miles from State College, 4½ miles from a major road, nestled on side of mountain, alone in the woods with a man-made lake at the foot of the driveway.
Reservations: Accepted year round through Rest & Repast, page 472.

A map is a definite must, but the isolated site is worth the hunt. This house with a wraparound stone veranda and stone terracing was originally built in the 1930s as a vacation retreat. The host is a pharmacist. His wife is an exercise teacher, bookkeeper, and secretary. Together they share interests in art, music, photography, travel, cooking, and this unique house, their home for the last seven years. Deer graze in the front field; turkeys can be seen in the fall; wildlife abounds; there are spectacular views of mountains and valleys, and fresh mountain spring water too.

In residence: People who smoke. One 10-year-old long-haired grey cat. One five-year-old short-haired calico cat. One big red dog.
Bed: One double-bedded room with shared bath.
Breakfast: Delicious. You won't be hungry. Served 8–12, usually around 9, in spacious windowed kitchen.
Plus: Sleep-tight tea or wine before bed.
Rates: $25 single, $30 for two. $40 on football weekends.

A pleasure for all the senses.

Marguerite and John Celani, Willowboro, New Jersey

CENTRE HALL

Tusseyville Trading Post & Herb Farm

Location: On a main road 13 miles east of Penn State University, set back from the highway with trees, cows, and old bridge — just plain pretty.
Reservations: Accepted year round through Rest & Repast, page 472. Minimum reservation: two days.

Flowers and fragrances are part of the hospitality at this lovely Victorian home and herb farm. Herbal wreaths are in the guest rooms. Potpourri may be in bowls and under your pillow. Fresh blooms in season are arranged attractively. Guests, treated like family, are delighted to have the invitation to tour the house and gardens. The house was built by the hostess's great-grandfather and it came back into the family when she bought it 14 years ago. The furnishings, antique and comfortable, include some items (such as a cherry bedroom suite) that belonged to her great-grandmother.

In residence: One 12-year-old son. One adult who smokes ("but hopefully not for long"). Four cats, one German shepherd, 30 ducks, and one goose — all with names.
Restrictions: Smoking allowed but not encouraged. Children are welcome.
Bed: One double room with shared bath.
Breakfast: Served in country kitchen or summer kitchen. Home-baked bread, rose-petal or violet jams, eggs and herbs.
Plus: Pond and stream for swimming, fishing, and fun.
Rates: $37 single, $40 for two. $40 football weekends.

POTTERS MILLS

General Potter Farm

Location: Near Amish country, Penn State University, caves, museums, state recreational areas, summer playhouses, fairs, outlets.
Reservations: Accepted March–December through Rest & Repast, page 472.

The hosts are the big plus here. They are delightful; welcome you with an immediate feeling of friendship, and spoil you with great food and conversation. . . . After visiting once a year for two years it is fun to see the changes that are taking place. It is a beautiful old property being cared for lovingly. Grace and George Groves, Dauphin, Pennsylvania

After coming to the area for college in 1960, the hosts became permanent residents. In 1979, when the "for sale" sign appeared before the home and on the farmland of the first judge in the county, the couple, a chemist and a teacher of English as a second language, were inspired to take on additional responsibilities and become owners of this 17-room Georgian period house. It's on the National Register of Historic Places and has 12 outbuildings, reminders of the variety of activities that were part of farm life here for over a century. Guests often help feed the ducks, chickens, geese, pigs, horses, calves, and bunnies. And all ages are welcome to (learn to) harvest herbs; garden (crops include wheat, corn, alfalfa, asparagus, red raspberries, and black-eyed peas); collect eggs; make flower arrangements; and even "shovel" for creatures. Much of the renovation work on the main house (a continuous process) has been completed. Some of the furnishings are antiques. And if you ask you'll find that the new farmers have become pretty knowledgeable about the history of the property.

In residence: A Brittany spaniel, one Persian cat, a calico cat, and a miniature goat are among their pets.
Restrictions: No smoking in public rooms, dining room, or barn. No guests' pets. Children are welcome.
Bed: Late spring through fall, eight or nine double rooms, in clusters of two or three with a shared bath. In winter months, four double rooms. Cots available.
Breakfast: At an hour arranged with guests, usually 7:30–9. Full farm breakfast with farm meats, produce, and eggs. In summer the hostess's mother, a retired professional nutritionist, cooks with her.
Plus: Use of "all of downstairs" with its formal parlor furnished with period pieces, judge's parlor, formal dining room, library, and keeping room. Dinner by arrangement summers and weekends. Nightly campfires in summer. They also have a picnic area, hiking and nature paths, and streams for fishing. They are sometimes dubbed the Chamber of Commerce because of their accumulation of available pamphlets and clippings.
Rates: $25 single, $30 for two. Cots $12. $40 per room in football season.

A city girl's dream come true. I chose a farm vacation for the pigs and

"fell in love" with Pierre, the baby goat. Guests not only enjoy gracious hospitality in restored elegance that includes "scratch" pancakes, but also the warm feeling of being part of an extended family.

Lucy Sidney Morris, Coral Gables, Florida

SPRING MILLS

Major Jarad B. Fisher Home

Location: In a rural area, 17 miles from State College and Penn State University.
Reservations: Available year round through Rest & Repast, page 472.

They've lived in several foreign countries. The youngest of their six children is a teenager. He's a retired professor and she's an administrator at a day-care center for infants and toddlers. They live in a lovely 19-room red brick residence listed on the National Register of Historic Places. If you're interested and when time allows, the hostess will show you through many of the rooms. Then you're likely to hear about some of the treasures collected in their travels.

In residence: One son in his 20s, one in his teens.
Restrictions: No children. No pets. And no smoking. (Well, maybe a good-smelling pipe.) Please check in by 9 p.m. and out before noon.
Foreign language spoken: French.
Bed: One double-bedded room with shared bath on second floor. Double-bedded room in a complete guest apartment on third floor.
Breakfast: Continental. Available 8–10.
Plus: Swimming pool in season.
Rates: Second floor room $30, $40 on football weekends. Third floor is $37, $47 on football weekends.

Great!   S. Boyles, Levittown, Pennsylvania

WESTERN PENNSYLVANIA

B&Bs

JAMESTOWN

Das Tannen-Lied

Route 1, East Lake Road, Jamestown, PA 16134
Phone: 412/932-5029
Location: Halfway (85 miles) between Pittsburgh and Cleveland, in a country setting overlooking the largest man-made lake in Pennsylvania.
Host: Marian Duecker
Open: April 1–November 1.

A cupola tops this century-old Victorian/colonial farmhouse, and many a guest's curiosity is satisfied by a climb that is rewarded with a great view of the countryside. Hardly a puddle, Lake Pymatuning, just across the street, is 70 miles around and has about 1500 acres of bordering parkland and recreational facilities. And this area abounds with antique shops.

Eat and run? Fine! But most guests must be on vacation. "This is a learning experience for me. People say they want to be on the road at 9 a.m. and many are still here at noon!" In her first year of hosting, Mrs. Duecker has extended her family in many ways. Visitors from Missouri later wrote for a recipe. Folks from Ohio stopped in to say hello on a winter Sunday afternoon. And two New Yorkers expanded her coffee inventory with a gift of a new kind.

Professionally she has been a home-economics (food) teacher and dietitian. After her family was grown she went back to college for another degree and trained mentally retarded young people for work in food services. Since coming to Jamestown in 1975, she has established a raspberry patch, a large vegetable garden, and a new vineyard.

In residence: Duke, a Norwegian elkhound who spends the days outside and the nights in. No smokers live here, but smoking is allowed.
Restrictions: No pets please. Children should be at least 12.
Bed: Two large newly redecorated rooms, one with twin beds, one with double. Shared guest bath.
Breakfast: Guests' choice. Could be homemade muffins, pancakes, fresh toast, or bacon and eggs. Plenty of freshly ground coffee or herb teas. Served in formal dining room overlooking the lake or in kitchen by picture window and birdfeeders.
Plus: Extensive library, fireplaced living room furnished with antiques, front porch that faces lake and boats, use of private dock and beach. Behind house is a large forest, good for hiking, filled with wildflowers, mushrooms, and wildlife.
Rate: $24 per room.

The house and location are lovely, but the real gem is Marian Duecker with whom we shared three very short hours that Friday night. We think of her often.   Dick and Diane Herman, Kenmore, New York

. . . And we highly recommend Mrs. Duecker's culinary skills. This is certainly a stop we intend to repeat!   R. and T. Cobb, St. Louis, Missouri

WASHINGTON, D.C. BALTIMORE, MARYLAND AREA

WASHINGTON, D.C./
BALTIMORE, MARYLAND AREA

PENNSYLVANIA

N

Baltimore

MARYLAND

Bethesda

2

Washington, D.C.

3

Annapolis

Chesapeake Bay

Alexandria

1

VIRGINIA

Potomac River

The numbers on this map indicate the locations of B&Bs described in detail in this chapter.

WASHINGTON, D.C. AND BALTIMORE

WASHINGTON, D.C. BALTIMORE, MARYLAND AREA

Reservation Services

The Bed & Breakfast League Ltd.

3639 Van Ness Street, N.W., Washington, DC 20008
Phone: 202/363-7767
Established 1979.
Open: Monday–Friday 9–5. Closed Christmas through New Year's.
Listings: About 50 hosts in D.C. (plus hundreds all over the U.S. and in some foreign countries, page 27).

Guest members ($30 per year) may book reservations without additional charges. Non-members pay a $10 booking fee with each reservation.
Rates: Singles $28–$42, doubles $30–$50. MasterCard and VISA accepted.

Bed 'n' Breakfast Ltd. of Washington, D.C.

P.O. Box 12011, Washington, DC 20005
Phone: 202/328-3510
Established December 1981.
Listings: About 30 private residences.

When founder Anna Earle returned to full-time international work, one of her experienced hosts, Jackie Reed, took over. A few students' specials are available. Most B&Bs are in downtown Washington, but nearby Virginia and Maryland are also included. Of those in D.C. many

are in historic districts and have been on one of the area's Historic Homes tours. "All homes provide hairdryers and curling irons, skirt hangers, and complimentary shower caps."
Rates: Singles $18–$40, doubles $35–$65. Slight reduction for weekly or monthly stays. Other rates for unhosted apartments. MasterCard, VISA, and American Express accepted.

Princely/Bed & Breakfast Ltd.

819 Prince Street, Alexandria, VA 22314
Phone: 703/683-2159
Established August 1981 by a retired State Department official.
Listings: Around 25 homes.
Reservations: Advance arrangements are necessary.

Most of E. J. Mansmann's listings are in Old Town and are historically significant (1760-1830), plaqued, and filled with antiques. Others are located in nearby areas toward Mt. Vernon. Public transportation is recommended and used by most guests; the bus runs to National Airport and connects with the subway into Washington. By 1984 the subway will run to Alexandria from Washington.
Rates: Singles $32–$40, doubles $40–$60. Monthly rates available.

Sweet Dreams & Toast, Inc.

P.O. Box 4835-0035, Washington, DC 20008
Phone: 202/483-9191
Established January 1982.
Open: Personally answered phone 11-6 weekdays. Answering service at other times.
Listings: About 100 private residences are part of Ellie Chastain's thriving personalized service. Most hosts are in D.C. Some are in nearby Bethesda, Chevy Chase, and Annapolis, Maryland, and in Arlington, Alexandria, and Vienna, Virginia. Just a couple of the listings are considered students' specials.

Some of the reservation and referral services with listings in many states throughout the country, pages 26-29, have a few hosts in Washington, D.C.

And for neighboring areas:

The Traveller in Maryland

33 West Street, Annapolis, MD 21401
Phone: 301/269-6232 (Annapolis/Baltimore); 301/261-2233 (D.C. Area)
Listings: Over 100, many on the water. Maryland territory covers western and southern areas, Eastern Shore, Baltimore and Annapolis. There are a few hosts in the Washington, D.C. suburbs of Silver Spring, Bethesda, Rockville, Hyattsville, Garrett Park, and Columbia.

The accommodations listed by Cecily Sharp-Whitehill include historic inns, motor and sail yachts, farmhouses, mansions, contemporary and historic houses, a barge, estate and watermen's cottages, and homes with private docks for a guest's arrival by boat. A few unhosted facilities are registered.
Rates: Singles $25–$40, doubles $30–$55. Historic inns are higher. Weekly and monthly rates available. VISA and MasterCard accepted for $25 deposit required with reservation request.

Blue Ridge Bed & Breakfast in Virginia

This service has some homes that are 25 miles from Washington. Please see page 62.

WASHINGTON, D.C.:

Where do you want to be?

The following descriptions of Washington's B&B locations are provided by Bed 'n' Breakfast Ltd.:

Dupont Circle: Located on Connecticut Avenue in the hub of activities. Dupont Circle runs a close second to Georgetown as the city's most popular in-town residential area.

Georgetown: Considered Washington's most prestigious residential and tourist area. Georgetown is a blend of richly restored Georgian and colonial town houses with smart boutiques and restaurants.

Logan Circle: Once home to the gentry. Logan Circle fell into neglect during the 1950s; but renovation of the Victorian town houses is now in full swing, and a renaissance is under way.

Upper Northwest: Lovely homes on broad lawns away from the hustle-bustle of downtown, but still close in.

Nearby Suburbs: Both Virginia and Maryland offer charming accommodations with access to good transportation.

B&Bs

ALEXANDRIA, VIRGINIA

Ann Ianni

8725 Parry Lane, Alexandria, VA 22308
Phone: 703/780-0267
Location: On George Washington's old farm area, five minutes from Mount Vernon, in a quiet neighborhood with a bus at back entrance that leads to Old Town Alexandria, National Airport, Washington, D.C., railroad station, and all subway stops.
Open: Year round.

"Some guests walk along the Potomac hike/bike path to Mount Vernon. Drives west to the mountains are popular in the fall. They go to antique places and tour by beautiful horse farms, and of course there's Old Town and Washington. Valkommen!"

Now that Ann's five children are married or in college there's time and space for B&B guests. She welcomes them in her "homey casual atmosphere" by the fire in winter or on the flower-banked patio in the summer. Because of her own extensive traveling in the United States and Europe, there's usually "a mutual friend, a common place or interest."

In residence: "My 80-year-old Swedish mother and Joshua, a black cat."
Foreign languages spoken: Swedish, German, a little Spanish.
Bed: Three rooms. Two singles share one guest bath. One double with private bath.
Breakfast: Continental includes homemade doughnuts or Swedish coffee bread. Served on the patio in summer, in kitchen or dining room in winter.
Plus: Air conditioning. Laundry facilities ($1 per wash or dry load).
Rates: $20 single, $25 double.

ALEXANDRIA, VIRGINIA

Princely/Bed & Breakfast Host #1

Location: In Old Town, centrally located.
Reservations: Available year round through Princely/Bed & Breakfast, page 483.

"Some of my guests have come for weddings, meetings, or concerts. Some have an early breakfast, spend days 'doing' the sights and fall into bed! They have all been delightful and have seemed pleased. The 1797 Federal three-story red brick home was in a sad state of neglect when we purchased it in 1968. After our restoration it was on a house tour."

One recent guest from upstate New York expressed his delight this way: "I have never had such pleasant hospitality on what I expected would be another impersonal 'hotel' business trip."

In residence: People who smoke.
Foreign language spoken: Some German.

Bed: One room with twin beds. Private bath.
Breakfast: Continental, 7:30–9. Served in the kitchen "where everything takes place in this old house."
Plus: Air conditioning. Parking.
Rate: $55 for one or two in the room.

ALEXANDRIA, VIRGINIA

Princely/Bed & Breakfast Host #2

Location: In Old Town, six blocks from shops, one block to park with view of Potomac, four blocks to D.C. bus.
Reservations: Available year round through Princely/Bed & Breakfast, page 483. Maximum stay: one week.

"We spent a year at Nantucket helping at an inn and most of my breakfast recipes were developed there. Have always stayed at B&Bs in England, loved them, and felt that Old Town Alexandria needed them. We know that some guests do not want an overly solicitous host; others have chosen B&Bs for a chance to meet the hosts and get to know them." He's a business broker and she's a full-time mother who sees B&B as a job that allows her to provide a comfortable inexpensive place, a place with character, antiques, and friendly people.

Their home is a delightful combination. The front half is 1849 with original floors and woodwork. In the rear is a new addition with a hanging staircase under a skylight and sunken living room with Palladian window and French doors.

In residence: A nine-year-old son and a five-year-old daughter. One cat.
Restrictions: No guests' pets please.
Foreign language spoken: French.
Bed: One room with queen-sized bed and private bath.
Breakfast: Might include pineapple creme, sherried grapefruit, or strawberries and champagne garnished with fresh herbs from the garden in summer; and home-baked muffins or coffee cake. Served in formal dining room.
Plus: Air conditioning, garden area, laundry facilities available.
Rate: $45 for one or two in the room.

ALEXANDRIA, VIRGINIA

Princely/Bed & Breakfast Host #3

Location: Two miles from Old Town Alexandria.
Reservations: Available year round through Princely/Bed & Breakfast, page 483.

"Now we're only two people in this big house, so we thought we'd try B&B. All our guests have been not only nice, but very interesting people. We usually have some time with them before they go out to dinner. . . . The house is an old (1820) frame house on three acres of land. Guests love the way it rambles around, very much like an old New England house. They seem to enjoy our artifacts too."

He's in real estate and you can tell that gardening is one of her interests. Tennis is another.

In residence: People who smoke.
Restrictions: No pets please.
Foreign language spoken: A little French.
Bed: Two guest rooms, each with a double tester bed, share one guest bath.
Breakfast: Full. Served at guests' convenience.
Plus: Choice of living rooms. Swimming pool in summer. Parking.
Rate: $60 per room.

A truly unbelievable first B&B experience! The colonial charm of this beautifully appointed home was magnificent. By the end of the weekend the hosts made us feel like one of the family.

Lee and Marion McChesney, Pawlet, Vermont

ALEXANDRIA, VIRGINIA

Princely/Bed & Breakfast Host #4

Location: Suburban, just outside of Alexandria.
Reservations: Available year round through Princely/Bed & Breakfast, page 483.

This host has passed the one-year mark of B&B hosting in her lovely Georgian colonial home. Guests find a relaxed, quiet environment with much land, trees, and flowers. One Seattle couple, among the first to stay here, writes and phones regularly.

In residence: No one who smokes (but smoking is allowed). One cat and one dog.
Restrictions: No guests' pets please.
Bed: One room with twin beds, one with a single. One bath for the two guest rooms.
Breakfast: Full American breakfast served in attractive dining room.
Plus: Air conditioning. Free parking available.
Rate: $40 for single room, $48 for twin-bedded room.

BETHESDA, MARYLAND

Winslow Home

8217 Caraway Street, Cabin John, Maryland 20818
Phone: 301/229-4654 before 8 or after 5:30, anytime on weekends
Location: Twenty minutes to the Kennedy Center, 40 minutes by bus.
Open: Year round.

Two years and dozens of guests later, this busy and enthusiastic B&B host can say that she's enjoyed every guest. Often they "rush out to see as much of the nation's capital as they can while they are here." After dinner (in winter by the fire) is "the best time to exchange ideas with people from all over the world."

The family built this comfortable two-level home in 1964. As long-time residents they have many suggestions and hints to share with tourists.

Bed: Two rooms. One with two twin beds and one with a double bed. One guest bath. Portacrib and cot available.
Breakfast: Continental.
Plus: Air conditioning.
Rates: $25 single, $35 for two. Under age 10, free.

WASHINGTON: CAPITOL HILL

The Bed & Breakfast League Host #8

Reservations: Available year round (not always all summer) through The Bed & Breakfast League, page 482.

"We find that most people are very impressed with the wealth of interesting sights here, and the ease with which they can enjoy them. We hope that our guests have pleasant memories of their visit to Washington, a city of neighborhoods built on a human scale, and will become, in a way, ambassadors of good will from our town to theirs. Within a few blocks we have a wide variety of restaurants. The best that I've been to is about eight blocks away, close enough for us to gaze at the menu more often than we can afford to go there."

The family lives in a three-story 20-year-old brick town house and knows the B&B world both from extensive European traveling and through their hosting here. The host is a nonpracticing physician whose special expertise is in medical technology.

"It's like going home," said my husband, a congressional law researcher, on our second trip to this B&B. The charming hosts make us feel comfortable. And the proximity to the Hill is a primary consideration.   Margaret Stewart, Convent Station, New Jersey

In residence: Nine-year-old son, five-year-old daughter.
Restrictions: No pets. No smoking. Children should be at least two years.
Foreign languages spoken: A little Spanish and French.
Bed: One queen-sized bed on first floor with private ½ bath. Portacrib and foldout bed available.
Breakfast: Available from 7:30 on, earlier by arrangement. Includes homemade breads and muffins.
Plus: Air conditioning. Tennis courts and park with playground are across the street. Free parking in private driveway. Television, radio, and piano in guest room. Plenty of books. Use of living room; and in warm weather, use of patio in garden. Baby-sitting possibilities if advance arrangements made.
Rates: $30 single, $38 double. Cot $3. $5 booking fee for Bed & Breakfast League nonmembers.

Marvelous home. Helpful hosts. Quiet, gracious people. Lovely family. Gourmet breads for breakfast. Ideal location: close to Metro and within

walking distance to Capitol Hill. Especially appreciated the info and suggestions most willingly given us. Would love to stay with them another time.   C.B.B., Burnsville, Minnesota

WASHINGTON: CAPITOL HILL

Sweet Dreams & Toast Host #30

Location: Restored urban area. Tree-lined street.
Reservations: Available year round through Sweet Dreams & Toast, page 483.

Because of the location, many guests here are on government business. And some are sightseers too.

Cordial B&B hosts all over the country frequently invite guests to take part in whatever is happening, but little did this one know that her invitation to two single guests to stay for a birthday party would result in a wedding invitation to Chicago a few months later. It was the reservation service that had placed a sales representative from Milwaukee and a forest ranger from Oregon here. As they have since written, "It was a vacation beyond one's wildest dreams." This is a very sociable home, but a duplicate experience cannot be guaranteed!

Frequently there is an opportunity to have a guided tour through the elegant house, one with curved glass windows, oversized cherry doors, leaded glass in foyer, and cherry banisters and spindles. The host now is in business to renovate, restore, and remodel. This second career follows a couple of decades of being a training director and management consultant all over the country.

In residence: One who smokes. One German shepherd, one Pekingese, three Siamese cats, and one black cat.
Restrictions: No guests' pets, please.
Bed: One single room and one double. Shared bath.
Breakfast: At arranged hour. Fresh fruit (including strawberries in January), croissants, bagels or Danish, beverage. Often a social time.
Plus: Air conditioning. Sitting rooms, library, back patio.
Rates: $35 single, $45 double.

WASHINGTON: DUPONT CIRCLE

Victoria and Maxwell Bed & Breakfast

Location: Dupont Circle, near White House, about a dozen blocks from Georgetown, two blocks from subway.
Reservations: Available year round through Bed 'n' Breakfast Ltd., page 482.

People who stay here never have to wonder what to do. The hostess's activities are all arts-oriented, although catering gets some attention, too. She is a painter, does picture framing, and knows how to organize sizable benefits. And now she finds that through B&B she has pen pals, for the first time in her life, from all over the world. Another resident is an actress and very aware of the Washington theater scene. And there is a direct-mail fund-raiser in the political area who might just as well be a restaurant reviewer.

"And it helps to be an animal lover. My big dog accompanies guests up and down the two flights of steps. If you don't want his official morning greeting in your bedroom, just lock your door."

The row house in a historic district is one of those given to Union generals in lieu of pensions after the Civil War.

In residence: That big dog. And people who smoke.
Restrictions: No guests' pets.
Foreign languages spoken: A little French, less Spanish.
Bed: Two rooms on the third floor. One with twin beds, one with double bed. Shared bath.
Breakfast: Full. Some Southern specialties on occasion. Available 8–9:30 in comfortable country kitchen, the hub of the house. There's usually time for good conversation, but it's often more leisurely on weekends.
Plus: Back garden patio in warm months.
Rates: $30 single, $40 for two.

It's like visiting an old friend — even on the first trip.

K. R. Mitchum, Ledyard, Connecticut

... B&B here is most accurately described as charming — from the historic neighborhood just off Dupont Circle with a little playhouse nearby to the artistically arranged rooms. The two flights of stairs may seem only for the adventurous, but the location is otherwise very con-

venient to the shops, museums, and galleries on Connecticut Avenue and any place near a stop on the Metro. Wanted to stay at least a week and will be going back as soon as I can.   A. L. Moore, Bronxville, New York

WASHINGTON: DUPONT CIRCLE

Bed 'n' Breakfast Ltd. Host #1738

Location: Three very short blocks to Metro and bus.
Reservations: Available through Bed 'n' Breakfast Ltd., page 482. Minimum stay is three nights for single or double, two nights for a party of three or four.

The hosts have lived in Washington for 25 years. He is an administrator in education and she is chairman of a high-school social studies department. Their home hasn't always been its present House Tour self. Early in the 20th century the lot was a tennis court for State Department personnel. In 1919 the handsome Georgian Revival house was built as an investment. By 1976, when the current owners bought it, full restoration was needed. Work has included the removal of seven layers of paint in the butler's pantry. Detailed plaster moldings, self-supporting stairs, ironwork banister, and a marble floor contribute to the ambiance of the elegant entrance hall.

"We have enjoyed, without exception, all of our guests. It's interesting to hear where they are from. Travelers from all over ask about how to get around, what to see, restaurants."

In residence: Nonsmokers, but smoking is allowed.
Bed: Two very private third-floor rooms. Not really suitable for children; steep stairs. One room has two twin beds, one has a double. Shared guest bath.
Breakfast: Continental. Very informal. Usually eat and run.
Plus: Air conditioning. Laundry facilities.
Rate: $30 single, $50 for two.

WASHINGTON: GEORGETOWN

Sweet Dreams & Toast Host #7

Reservations: Available year round through Sweet Dreams & Toast, page 483.

The hosts, professionally involved in real estate and higher-education management consulting, are across the street from a historical house, down the street from one senator, up the street from another, and so it goes in the neighborhood that's not far from the Four Seasons Hotel. They have been in their "typical Georgetown house" for three years, and are casual but gracious hosts.

In residence: One teenage daughter. People who smoke.
Bed: One single with shared bath.
Breakfast: "Minimum to maximum," cooked and served by the husband. Enjoy your start to the day on the patio or in dining room.
Plus: Air conditioning.
Rate: $35.

WASHINGTON: GEORGETOWN

Sweet Dreams & Toast Host #33

Reservations: Available year round through Sweet Dreams & Toast, page 483.

"Anyone who lives in Washington always has someone showing up. It's a surprise to us to find that B&B travelers feel like houseguests." The week we spoke the family had hosted a contractor, a guest not at all upset about, and really rather interested in, the changes going on (from radiators to baseboard heating). That's just one example of happenstances where family and guests are just plain comfortable together here. It's an active household in one of the larger homes in Georgetown. Over the last ten years the patent lawyer and his librarian wife have restored the 1887 house, one with an interesting history. Authentic gas fixtures are on the first two floors and furnishings are mid-Victorian. "We're 'laid back people' who love living in Washington (came from the

Midwest 15 years ago, lived in the house for 10), and sharing our life with guests." The little extras that guests appreciate include change for the bus and — when available — restaurant discount coupons clipped from newspapers.

In residence: Fourteen-year-old daughter, 11-year-old son. One English setter, one black alley cat, and "assorted goldfish too." No smokers in residence, but smoking is allowed.
Restrictions: No guests' pets allowed. Children should be at least 12. There is street parking; "but we need to obtain a guest permit. Advise guests that an automobile is absolutely unnecessary and that they can take cabs throughout the area much cheaper than renting a car. Also, a car is a hassle and cabs or buses usually are not."
Bed: Double bed on third floor with private bath.
Breakfast: Continental with croissants. Served 7–8:30, self-serve after that. Eat in dining room (11-foot ceilings).
Plus: Central air conditioning. Swimming pool in season.
Rates: $35 single, $50 for two.

A wonderful place to visit in an ideal location. . . . Terrific people who abound in warmth and humor. Our experience was an unforgettable one.   Frank and Joana Toller, St. Helena, California

WASHINGTON: LOGAN CIRCLE

Jenny's Place

Location: Ten blocks from the White House. Excellent crosstown and downtown public transportation at the corner.
Reservations: Available year round through Bed 'n' Breakfast Ltd., page 482.

A strong sense of community can be felt in this 100-year-old Victorian hosted by a family that loves living in a neighborhood that is "the last untouched residential circle in Washington." Over a 10-year period the couple has restored "what was left" from rooming-house days of the row house.

Some B&B guests have been known to attend the neighborhood association meeting. But frequently guests have a full schedule and so does the family, so chats occur whenever. "If they want to hear about our restoration trials and tribulations, we sometimes talk about that.

Some are interested in architectural features of the house. There are many times when we learn a lot about and from each other."

The host is an architectural and building consultant; and his wife, in addition to being a full-time mother, has been the Chair of the annual Logan Circle Homes Tour for the past five years. Her degree is in interior design.

In residence: One seven-year-old daughter who has learned about and enjoys hosting. Two Siamese cats, "both curious, and have been found visiting B&B guests."
Restrictions: Sorry, no guests' pets.
Bed: One room on third floor with two twin beds, tiny kitchenette, and private bath (that is occasionally shared with visiting relatives). Cot and crib available.
Breakfast: The kitchenette cupboards are stocked with the makings for breakfast which often include homemade muffins.
Plus: Air conditioning. Light cooking allowed.
Rates: $25 single, $35 for two. Cot or crib $5.

WASHINGTON: LOGAN CIRCLE

The Reeds

Location: About ten blocks from the White House. Busses within one block. Seven blocks from Metro.
Reservations: Available year round through Bed 'n' Breakfast Ltd., page 482.

In the decade that the family has lived in this century-old 18-room town house, it has restored the Victorian house, gardens, terrace, and fountains. The highlight of the extensive woodwork is an oak staircase with interesting floor-to-ceiling spindle arrangements. Several weddings and large cast parties from local theater groups have been held here. Starting in 1984, thanks to a neighbor who was active in the B&B movement, bed and breakfast guests, too, have enjoyed visiting.

The host is a lawyer, formerly with the State Department, now in private practice. He finds time to be a sailor, woodworker, and amateur magician. For several years his wife was in the construction business. She has studied pastry making with the current White House chef, and interior design. This past year she has shown her enthusiasm for B&B hosting by expanding the number of available B&B hosts in the Washington area.

In residence: Eighteen-year-old daughter. Husband occasionally smokes cigars.
Restrictions: No pets, please.
Foreign language spoken: French.
Bed: Six guest rooms share three guest baths. Two single rooms. Four double-bedded rooms; one has a canopied bed. One double has a studio couch that sleeps one. Another double also has a queen-sized sleep sofa. Crib available.
Breakfast: Continental. Served in formal dining room.
Plus: Central air conditioning. Baby-sitting may be possible if requested in advance. Use of latticed porch, garden, and barbecue in summer. Player piano. Help yourself to soft drinks or hot beverage any time. Color television in each bedroom. One off-street parking space available at $3 per day.
Rates: $25–$40 single, $40 double. Additional person in same room, $10 extra.

WASHINGTON: UPPER NORTHWEST

Sweet Dreams & Toast Host #1

Location: Near the National Cathedral. About two miles from Georgetown.
Reservations: Available year round through Sweet Dreams & Toast, page 483.

"Hosting is a passport to the world. In succession I may have one guest from Paris, one from a kibbutz, one from the east coast, then another from the west coast. A typical day for guests? Often they sightsee, eat dinner and collapse. My dual career makes for a busy life, but we usually get a chance to chat at breakfast or in the evening."

B&B here is in a modern condominium furnished with antique accessories.

In residence: A small spoiled dog who is quite personable. The front end is miniature poodle and the back end Lhasa apso.
Foreign language: Understand French.
Bed: One room with twin beds. Private bath.
Breakfast: Fresh orange juice, granola, or omelets, "and preserves from my small jam and jelly business. Most guests are curious and want to try them all."
Plus: Central air conditioning. Free parking.
Rates: $30 single, $45 for two.

WASHINGTON: UPPER NORTHWEST

The Bed & Breakfast League Host #23

Location: Near Chevy Chase Circle. One block to bus stop.
Reservations: Available September–June through The Bed & Breakfast League, page 482.

"I'm a kindergarten teacher in a suburban school system and really enjoy the experience of meeting people from all over the country as well as all types of occupations. . . . My house doesn't have a 'historical story' but it is totally redone in the two years I've owned it."

This native Washingtonian's interests and talents are evident in the stenciling and displays of antique quilts in the bedrooms of the 1947 brick center-hall colonial. The host is also an antique collector.

Restrictions: No smoking.
Bed: Two rooms. One double-bedded room with private bath. One with two twin beds with bath in hall.
Breakfast: Guests' choice. Self-serve after 7:30 on weekdays.
Plus: Free parking. Back porch with stenciled floor looking out on quiet private garden. Kitchen privileges and laundry facilities.
Rates: $30 single, $38 for two. $5 booking fee for Bed & Breakfast League nonmembers.

Comments and suggestions are welcome. They will be considered for the next edition of *Bed and Breakfast in the Northeast*. Please address them to Bernice Chesler, The Globe Pequot Press, Box Q, Old Chester Road, Chester, CT 06412.

INDEX

B&Bs BY STATE

RESERVATION SERVICES BY STATE

ABOUT THE AUTHOR

As a researcher, Bernice Chesler has conducted thousands of interviews throughout the country for documentary films seen on national public television. As Publications Coordinator for *ZOOM*, she edited twelve books that emanated from the Emmy Award-winning television program. She is also the author of the classic guide, *In and Out of Boston with (or without) Children*, and co-author of *The Family Guide to Cape Cod*.

As a traveler, she has enjoyed B&Bs in England and Ireland. For this volume Bernice visited scores of B&Bs and interviewed hundreds of hosts, guests, and reservation service agencies on their experiences with, and insights into, this increasingly popular style of travel in America.

OTHER GLOBE PEQUOT BOOKS
FOR YOUR
FURTHER TRAVELLING PLEASURE

Guidebooks:
A Guide to New England's Landscape
Budget Dining and Lodging in New England
Daytrips and Budget Vacations in New England
Guide to Martha's Vineyard
Guide to Nantucket
Guide to the Recommended Country Inns of New England
Guide to the Recommended Country Inns of New York, New Jersey,
Pennsylvania, Delaware, Maryland, Washington, D.C.,
and West Virginia
Handbook for Beach Strollers
In and Out of Boston with (or without) Children
Special Museums of the Northeast

Short Walk Books:
On Long Island
In Connecticut
On Cape Cod

Short Bike Ride Books:
In Connecticut
On Long Island
In Greater Boston and Central Massachusetts
On Cape Cod, Nantucket and the Vineyard
In the Berkshires
In Rhode Island

Available at your bookstore or direct from the publisher. For a free catalogue of New England books, write: The Globe Pequot Press, Old Chester Road, Chester, Connecticut 06412